ALL OF US

As part of Houghton Mifflin's ongoing
commitment to the environment, this text
has been printed on recycled paper.

ALL OF US

A Multicultural Reading Skills Handbook

Third Edition

Harvey S. Wiener
Marymount Manhattan College, New York

Charles Bazerman
University of California, Santa Barbara

HOUGHTON MIFFLIN COMPANY Boston New York

Senior Sponsoring Editor: Mary Jo Southern
Senior Associate Editor: Ellen Darion
Senior Project Editor: Kathryn Dinovo
Senior Manufacturing Coordinator: Priscilla J. Abreu
Senior Marketing Manager: Nancy Lyman

Cover design: Diana Coe
Cover image: Crowd #11, Diana Ong/Superstock

Acknowledgments begin on page 523.

Printed in the U.S.A.

Library of Congress Catalog Card Number: 98-72093

Student Text ISBN: 0-395-90422-6
Instructor's Annotated Edition ISBN: 0-395-90424-2

89-FFG-09 08 07 06 05

Contents

Preface   xi

HANDBOOK   1

Unit One **Reading Fundamentals**   3

1. Before You Read   5
  1a Prereading   5
    1a(1) Making a List   6
    1a(2) Drawing a Word Map   7
    1a(3) Doing Freewriting   7
    1a(4) Raising Questions   9
    Exercises   10
  1b Skimming   11
    Exercises   11
  1c Previewing   15
    Exercises   16
  1d Previewing Long Material: The Parts of a Book   22
    Exercises   24
  Review Test   36

2. Reading Helpers: Underlining, Taking Notes, and Outlining   38
  2a Underlining   39
    Exercises   41
  2b Taking Notes   41
    Exercises   43
  2c Outlining   45
    Exercises   47
  Review Test   48

3. Building a Strong Vocabulary   51
  3a Context Clues to Word Meanings   52
    Exercises   54
  3b Word Part Clues to Meaning   57

3b(1) Important Prefixes   58
3b(2) Important Roots   59
3b(3) Important Suffixes   60
Exercises   60
3c   Denotation and Connotation   62
Exercises   63
3d   Shades of Meaning   65
Exercises   66
Review Test   84

Unit One Review Test   88

Unit Two   **Basic Comprehension**   95

4. Visual Aids   97
Exercises   99
Review Test   108

5. Reading for the Main Idea   110
5a   Key Ideas in Sentences   110
Exercises   111
5b   Topics and Main Ideas in Paragraphs   113
Exercises   114
5b(1) Stated Main Ideas   117
Exercises   119
5b(2) Implied Main Ideas   123
Exercises   124
Review Test   133

6. Reading for Information   141
6a   Fact-Finding   141
Exercises   143
6b   Major Details, Minor Details   148
Exercises   149
Review Test   154

7. Recognizing Paragraph Patterns   158
7a   Ordering Ideas   159
7a(1) Time Order (Chronology)   159
7a(2) Place Order   159
7a(3) Order of Importance   160
Exercises   161

7b   Listing Details   165
        Exercises   165
7c   Classification   172
        Exercises   173
7d   Comparison and Contrast   175
        Exercises   178
7e   Cause and Effect   182
        Exercises   183
        Review Test   192

Unit Two Review Test   198

Unit Three   **Reading and Critical Thinking**   205

8. Making Inferences   207
        Exercises   213
        Review Test   223

9. Understanding Figurative Language   227
        Exercises   230
        Review Test   234

10. Drawing Conclusions and Predicting Outcomes   236
        Exercises   239
        Review Test   250

11. Generalizing   254
        Exercises   257
        Review Test   265

12. Evaluating Ideas   267
        12a Fact and Opinion   267
               Exercises   271
        12b Evidence   277
               Exercises   278
        12c The Writer's Technique   282
               12c(1) Style   282
               12c(2) Tone   283
               12c(3) Mood   283
               12c(4) Purpose   284
               12c(5) Point of View   284
               Exercises   285

12d Techniques That Twist the Truth   290
    Exercises   292
Review Test   294

13. Making Connections   298
  13a Personalizing   298
    13a(1) Notes in the Margin   298
    13a(2) A Reading Journal   299
    Exercises   300
  13b Connecting Ideas   301
    Exercises   303
  13c Collaboration   305
    Exercises   307
  Review Test   308

Unit Three Review Test   309

READING SELECTIONS   315

Introduction   316

Coming to America   317

A New Dawn / Sam Moses   318
Exercises   322

The Business of Selling Mail-Order Brides /
Venny Villapando   330
Exercises   338

Hearts of Sorrow / James M. Freeman   347
Exercises   352

Immigrants / Aurora Levins Morales   359
Exercises   364

Putting Thoughts Together   370

Education and Learning   371

My Unsentimental Tutee / Laura Billings   372
Exercises   374

Letting in Light / Patricia Raybon   381
Exercises   385

They Treat Girls Differently, Don't They? / Timothy Harper   390
Exercises   396

Model Minority / Felicia R. Lee   405
Exercises   410

Putting Thoughts Together   417

Making Connections   419

My Father's Black Pride / Marcus Bleecker   420
Exercises   423

A Cafe Reopens: Lunch Returns to the Prairie /
William E. Schmidt   431
Exercises   435

Say Something. They're Only Children / Lucie Prinz   442
Exercises   444

Like Mother, Like Daughter / Lloyd Gite   452
Exercises   457

Putting Thoughts Together   465

Identities and Struggles   467

Love Me, Love My (Brown) Mother / Charity Plata   468
Exercises   470

Wilshire Bus / Hisaye Yamamoto   478
Exercises   483

Zoot Suit Riots / Albert Camarillo   490
Exercises   494

Creating Unique Names for Children / Cindy Roberts   500
Exercises   502

Putting Thoughts Together   511

Appendix: Using a Dictionary   513

Answer Key   519

Index   527

Preface

Like its companion texts *Basic Reading Skills Handbook* and *Reading Skills Handbook, All of Us: A Multicultural Reading Skills Handbook* focuses on essential strategies for beginning college readers. These include literal comprehension skills, interpretation, evaluation and other critical thinking skills, and study skills. The text is divided into two main parts. The *Handbook* provides instruction in reading skills, integrated with more than 100 examples as well as practice exercises. The *Reading Selections* includes sixteen longer selections accompanied by exercises that are coordinated with and cross-referenced to the skills taught in the *Handbook*. Throughout the text, students will find questions that guide their understanding and interpretation of specific passages.

A Unique Approach to Reading

What makes *All of Us* stand apart from other reading texts is its devotion to a curriculum of inclusion. Maintaining our attention to selections drawn from typical college reading matter across the curriculum, we tried to compile the richest and most ethnically diverse reading matter available. We wanted this book to reflect the unprecedented diversity of today's college classrooms. We also felt that if we filled our text with writing that trumpeted the voices, concerns, and experiences of an ethnically diverse America, we would strike deeply responsive chords in the lives of today's college reading students.

With these goals in mind, we chose the readings in the examples and exercises from both ethnically diverse materials and challenging, content-rich readings typical of college course assignments. Sometimes these overlap. The material in Richard Schaefer's piece on Native Americans, for example, is essential to any introductory sociology course. Hisaye Yamamoto's story about a young woman's experiences on a Los Angeles bus would suit an introductory literature or fiction writing course.

In other cases the materials stand side by side, complementing each other. In Chapter 1 of the *Handbook,* for example, we call upon these examples to illustrate reading aids to comprehension: a humanities text selection called "A Surging New Spirit: The Hispanic Influence on the American Cultural Mainstream"; textbook excerpts concerning politics during World War II and the success of the Japanese in business; a text chapter called "A Brief Chronology of the Chinese in America"; an excerpt on "Stages of Psychosocial Development" from a developmental psychology textbook and one on "Alcohol and Society" from a health text; the contents page from *Business Enterprise in American History;* the introduction to *Mexican-American Authors* — and many others. Ethnically varied readings by a broad spectrum of writers, wide-ranging topics of interest to a pluralistic audience, challenging college texts — all of these elements fortify both the interest level and instructional potential for *All of Us.*

Focus on Critical Thinking

Critical thinking is a major focus in this textbook. A full unit is devoted to interpretive and evaluative skills, with chapters on inference, figurative language, drawing conclusions and predicting outcomes, making generalizations, and judging writers' ideas. The final chapter in this unit contains special instruction on how to make connections among readings and between readings and other experiences and on how to use collaboration to enhance learning. Because writing is a highly effective tool for expressing and strengthening these cognitive skills, we have included challenging writing exercises throughout the text.

■ "Critical Thinking in Writing" exercises that follow each of the *Reading Selections* as well as many readings in the *Handbook* stimulate interaction between the reader and ideas expressed in the selection.
■ "Connecting Ideas" exercises following each of the *Reading Selections* ask students to make connections among readings in the text and to draw upon their own experiences.

Instructional Features

In this book, students read a careful explanation of a specific skill, followed by an analysis of how that skill applies to a particular passage. They then have a chance to test their mastery of that skill through the many exercises designed for practice and review. This step-by-step approach allows students to progress from simple to more complex skills with confidence.

To address the needs of college reading students, we included a number of other important pedagogical features:

- explanations of basic skills in clear, easy-to-understand language
- more than 120 ethnically diverse and challenging reading selections from many sources, including magazines, how-to books, advertisements, and newspapers, as well as textbooks and other academic material
- comprehensive questions designed to enrich understanding and appreciation of selections while reinforcing key skills
- questions in the *Reading Selections* keyed to appropriate sections in the *Handbook*; if students have difficulty answering a question, they easily can find and review the material that covers that particular skill. For example, an **(8)** after a question means that a review of Chapter 8, "Making Inferences," will help the student recall the techniques readers use to infer important information from the text
- a chapter on how to take tests
- self-tests throughout the book to help students assess their own progress
- collaborative exercises to help students develop and evaluate their ideas and writing
- extensive vocabulary exercises
- engaging photographs, tables, charts, graphs, cartoons, and crossword puzzles to stimulate and maintain student interest in visual aids
- sustained attention to the use of context clues
- chapters on literal comprehension, including reading aids, reading for the main idea, reading for information, and recognizing paragraph patterns
- a chapter on the basic study skills — underlining, note-taking, and outlining
- an appendix on using a dictionary

The organization of the book allows instructors to adapt it to specific courses in several ways. They may choose to teach the *Handbook* units in the early weeks of the term, postponing study of the *Reading Selections* until students master essential reading skills. The brief *Handbook* readings promote reinforcement of newly learned concepts and prepare students for longer *Reading Selections*. Or instructors may choose to reinforce the skills taught in the *Handbook* by immediately assigning appropriate *Reading Selections*, turning to key instructional units in the *Handbook* as specific needs arise in class.

New to This Edition

In this edition, we have added a number of new features:

- self-tests in every chapter that let students check their answers and assess their skill levels
- review tests for each unit in the *Handbook* bring together the material in the unit
- expanded critical thinking activities
- reading selections organized around the following themes:

  Coming to America
  Education and Learning
  Making Connections
  Identities and Struggles

- unit questions that raise thematic issues about groups of readings
- thirty percent new reading selections

Acknowledgments

We have many people to thank for their ideas on the preparations of this text. Colleagues scattered around the country have made thoughtful suggestions and have guided us in writing this book. We are grateful to

Gertrude Robbins Fator, College of Alameda, CA
Carol K. Gregory, Wilberforce University, OH
Karen O'Donnell, Finger Lakes Community College, NY
Michele Peterson, Santa Barbara Community College, CA
Keflyn X. Reed, Bishop State Community College, AL
Nancy J. Rudary, Oakland Community College, MI
Jackie Stahlecker, St. Philip's College, TX

H. S. W.
C. B.

Correlations to Basic Reading Skills Tests

Many states require college students to demonstrate their competence in reading. In the tables below, the reading skills included in three representative state tests are correlated to the sections in *All of Us* in which the specific skills are covered.

Texas Academic Skills Program (TASP)

Determining the Meaning of Words and Phrases
Familiar words	3a, 3b, A-6
Words with multiple meanings	3c, 3d, A-6
Figurative language	9

Understanding the Main Idea and Supporting Details in Written Material
Main ideas in narrative and expository writing	5a, 5b, 5b(1), 5b(2)
Stated vs. implied main idea	5b(1), 5b(2)
Supporting details	6b

Identifying a Writer's Purpose, Point of View, and Intended Meaning
Recognizing writer's intent	12c(4), 12c(5), 12d

Analyzing the Relationship Among Ideas in Written Material
Organizational patterns and relationships in written materials	7a, 7b, 7c, 7d, 7e
Drawing conclusions from written materials	10, 13a, 13b, 13c

Using Critical Reasoning Skills to Evaluate Written Material
Steps in critically evaluating written material	8, 12a, 12b, 12c, 12d

Applying Study Skills to Reading Assignments
Note-taking, outlining, and mapping	2a, 2b, 2c
Interpretation of information in graphic form	4

Georgia Collegiate Placement Examination

Vocabulary
Determining the meaning of a word through context	3a
Determining meaning through word analysis (prefixes, suffixes, and roots)	3b(1), 3b(2), 3b(3)

Referring
Literal comprehension	3a, 5a, 5b, 5b(1), 5b(2)
Determining facts and details	6a, 6b, 7b, 12a, 12b
Recognizing expressed relationships (such as cause and effect)	7a(1), 7a(2), 7a(3), 7d

Reasoning

Making inferences from the text	8
Structural analysis:	
Identifying organizational patterns	7a, 7b, 7c, 7d, 7e
Recognizing point of view	12a, 12c(4), 12c(5), 12d
Identifying mood and tone	12c(2), 12c(3)
Recognizing logical fallacies	12d
Recognizing irrelevant data	6b

Florida College Level Academic Skills Test (CLAST)

Reading with Literal Comprehension

Recognize main ideas	5a, 5b, 5b(1), 5b(2)
Identify supporting details	6b
Determine meaning of words on the basis of context	3a

Reading with Critical Comprehension

Recognize the author's purpose	12c(4)
Identify the author's overall organizational pattern	7a, 7b, 7c, 7d, 7e
Distinguish between statements of fact and statements of opinion	12a
Detect bias	12b, 12c(5), 12d
Recognize the author's tone	12c(2)
Recognize explicit and implicit relationships within sentences	5a, 8
Recognize implicit as well as explicit relationships between sentences	5a, 5b(1), 5b(2), 7b(1), 7b(2), 8, 10
Recognize valid arguments	12a, 12b
Draw logical inferences and conclusions	8, 10, 13a, 13b

ALL OF US

Handbook

Unit One

Reading Fundamentals

1

Before You Read

Most experienced readers use *prereading* and other strategies to make reading easier. You can use these strategies to get a good sense of the material you plan to read. *Skimming* a selection means that before you read closely, you search quickly through the sentences to find facts and answers to questions you may have. *Previewing* a section before you read it gives you a general idea of what you're going to be reading, before you actually begin. Previewing is useful for short selections such as book chapters, stories, articles, or essays as well as for whole books and magazines.

1a Prereading

Reading is not just a matter of recognizing words on a page. It is a matter of what you do with those words in your mind, of connecting what you find on the page with what you know and think. Certainly you learn new information from your reading, but you learn them only by building on ideas you already have. Aware readers always draw on their *prior knowledge,* what they know about a topic before reading a selection.

Prereading — thinking in advance about a topic before you read — helps you prepare for the words on the page. If you consider the topic beforehand, you'll find the writer's ideas a little more familiar than if you jump into the reading without thinking. Your knowledge helps you understand what the writer is saying.

For example, suppose you are ready to read a chapter called "A Surging New Spirit: The Hispanic Influence on the American Cultural Mainstream" in a humanities textbook. Before you read, think about American culture and possible Hispanic influences. What do you know about American culture and its expression? What Hispanic elements can you think of in music? art? film? theater? design? cooking?

As you think about these issues before you read, you remind yourself of what you already know. Also, you stimulate your own interest and curiosity. You get your mind ready to take in new information.

You will find it helpful to write down your prereading efforts. As a warm-up for reading, just let your ideas about the writer's topic flow before you start reading. Make a list. Draw a word map. Use freewriting. Raise questions. Of course you don't have to apply all these strategies for every reading. Choose the prereading activity that works best for you.

1a(1) *Making a List*

One type of warm-up is simply to make a list of everything that comes to mind when you think about the topic of the reading. For example, for a history class one student read an article on world politics during World War II. Before beginning to read, the student wrote the following list of ideas that came to her mind:

```
            Politics during World War II

Who were the political leaders?
Was Franklin Roosevelt president of the U.S.?
Hitler
Nazis--took control of German government
Germany conquered most of Europe--France, Poland
D-Day--America and the Allies start to regain Europe
What to do with Nazis after the war? Political problem
Pearl Harbor, Japanese bombing
Who led Japan? Didn't Japan have an emperor?
Kamikaze fighters, battles in the Pacific
Atom bomb dropped on Japan--Hiroshima
Nuclear weapons became a big political issue in the U.S.
Political alliance between Italy, Germany, and Japan
Allies--U.S., England, France, other countries
Didn't the Soviet Union switch back and forth?
Political results of the war--splitting of Europe be-
   tween East and West
```

Notice how the student just follows her thoughts, with one idea or name leading to another. She mentions many different aspects of politics — leaders, the internal politics of countries, international alliances, the political consequences of the war. Sometimes she is vague on facts and doesn't remember a name. Overall, however, she starts to bring back into her conscious mind much of the information she does know on the subject.

1a(2) *Drawing a Word Map*

Another warm-up, drawing a word map, is like making a list, but it helps you organize your thoughts a bit more. In a word map you try to create some kind of visual relation among the various thoughts you have. There is no single way to do this. Just start putting the ideas down on a piece of paper. Put related words close to each other; draw lines between connected ideas. Use boxes, circles, arrows, or any other visual symbol to show how ideas may be connected. For example, another student, about to read an article on the reasons for the success of the Japanese in business, put her ideas down in the word map on page 8.

1a(3) *Doing Freewriting*

A third way to warm up your thinking on a subject is freewriting. In freewriting you simply start writing about a subject and write whatever comes into your mind. Do not stop. Don't worry about complete sentences. Don't make corrections. Even if you can't think of what to write, just keep producing words. You can even write things such as "I don't know what this topic is all about" or "I've forgotten everything I know about this." Soon one statement will lead to the next, and you will be surprised by how much you do know.

Freewriting also allows you to explore your feelings and interests, so that you can find points of connection between the subject of the reading and those issues you would like or need to know about. You also may find that certain parts of the subject don't interest you. But don't give up. If you look deeply enough, you may be able to find some way of connecting with a subject, no matter how distant it seems from your obvious interests.

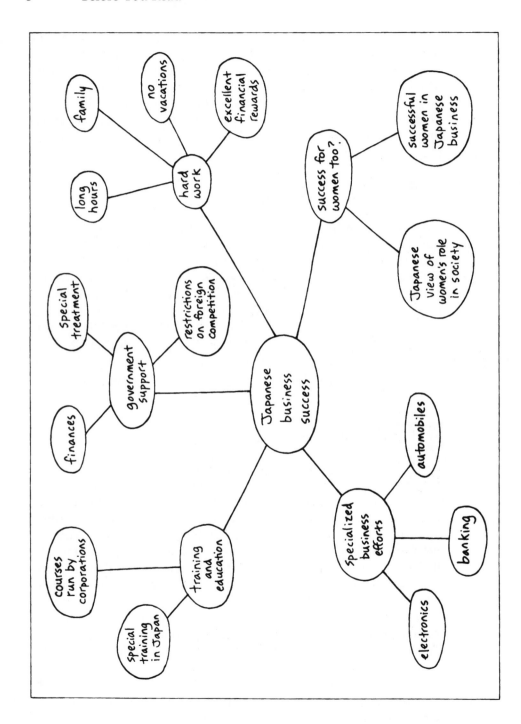

Consider this student's chain of connections, which she wrote before reading an assigned article from *Jet* magazine called "Should Athletes Risk Death for Money?" for her health education course.

Athletes and money. Risk. I'm annoyed that I have to
read this article for this course. Well, money and
sports--at least it might be interesting. But I don't
see how athletes risk death for money. I wonder what the
title means. Maybe kids playing too hard in order to
play professional ball. Lots of my friends thought
they'd go on to be pro. They practiced all the time and
sacrificed their school work. But that's no death risk. I
don't think I get it--risking death for money? Maybe the
dangers of playing ball when your health is bad. Kids
who want to play because of the possibility of future
big money might not listen to their doctors if they hear
that they're physically weak or not able to be athletic
at full steam. I remember some terrific basketball
player had a heart attack and died on the court, and
later they found out he had a heart condition all his
life. Maybe it's the steroid stuff. Athletes take drugs
and injections to build up their bulk so they can compete better. I'm sure there are death risks. Maybe
that's the issue.

1a(4) Raising Questions

Another way to focus in advance on the topic of a reading selection is to write a list of questions that you would like to have answered about the subject. These questions help you identify reading goals. Even if the selection does not answer your questions specifically, you might start making connections between the information in the reading and the information you are looking for. Raising questions helps stimulate your imagination and interest.

Before reading a chapter called "A Brief Chronology of the Chinese in America" for an American history course, one student wrote these questions:

When did the Chinese start arriving in America?
Where did they first live?

What kind of work was open to them?
Under what conditions did they live and work?
What contributions did Chinese Americans make to this
   country? What problems did they face?
Who are the Chinese Americans in my immediate neighbor-
   hood? on campus? in the community?

Notice how, as the list of questions goes on, the student's special concerns appear. He moves from general questions about Chinese Americans to considerations of Chinese Americans in his own world. He no longer sees himself as totally removed from the issue.

EXERCISES

1. Making a List
Your science teacher asks you to read a textbook chapter on ethics in science research. Make a list of your thoughts on the topic in advance.

2. Drawing a Word Map
You have to read an article on starting a small business. Make a word map on the topic.

3. Freewriting
Imagine you have to read a chapter on intelligence (IQ) testing in a psychology textbook. On a separate sheet of paper, freewrite on the topic.

4. Raising Questions
You are about to read a book about slavery in the United States for a history course. On a separate sheet of paper, make a list of questions about the subject that you would be interested in learning the answers to.

5. Prereading on Your Own
For any reading assignment in one of your other courses, explore your own interests in the topic by making a list, drawing a word map, freewriting, or asking questions. Use a separate sheet of paper.

1b Skimming

Rapid reading for facts is called *skimming*. Whenever you have to find *specific* facts in a paragraph, look for sentences that offer the needed information. When you skim a paragraph or a page, you are searching sentences quickly for the answer to questions you have.

Here is how to skim:

- Make sure that you know what information you are looking for. Ask yourself a question. Look for a key word.
- Slowly read the part of the line or sentence that tells you what you want to know.
- Does the information you found answer the question? If not, quickly read the passage again to look for the information you need.
- Jot down the answer to the question.

EXERCISES

1. Skimming

Skim this selection from an education textbook describing the stages of human development proposed by psychologist Erik Erikson. Look for the following information:

- The eight stages of psychosocial development according to Erikson
- How two- to three-year-olds develop autonomy
- At what age and how children develop feelings of inferiority
- What role confusion is
- What generativity is.

Then write the answers to the questions on page 14.

Stages of Psychosocial Development

The following designations, age ranges, and essential characteristics of the stages of personality development are proposed by Erikson in *Childhood and Society* (1963).[1]

---

[1] All quotations under "Stages of Psychosocial Development" are drawn from Chapter 7 of *Childhood and Society*.

Trust vs. Mistrust (Birth to 1 Year)   The basic psychosocial attitude to be learned by infants is that they can trust their world. Trust is fostered by "consistency, continuity, and sameness of experience" in the satisfaction of the infant's basic needs by the parents. If the needs of infants are met and if parents communicate genuine affection, children will think of their world as safe and dependable. Conversely, if care is inadequate, inconsistent, or negative, children will approach their world with fear and suspicion.

Autonomy vs. Shame and Doubt (2 to 3 Years)   Just when children have learned to trust (or mistrust) their parents, they must exert a degree of independence. If toddlers are permitted and encouraged to do what they are capable of doing at their own pace and in their own way — but with judicious supervision by parents and teachers — they will develop a sense of autonomy. But if parents and teachers are impatient and do too many things for young children, two- and three-year-olds may doubt their ability to deal with the environment. Furthermore, adults should avoid shaming young children for unacceptable behavior, since shaming is likely to contribute to feelings of self-doubt.

Initiative vs. Guilt (4 to 5 Years)   The ability to participate in many physical activities and to use language sets the stage for initiative, which "adds to autonomy the quality of undertaking, planning, and 'attacking' a task for the sake of being active and on the move." If four- and five-year-olds are given freedom to explore and experiment, and if parents and teachers take time to answer questions, tendencies toward initiative will be encouraged. Conversely, if children of this age are restricted and made to feel that their activities and questions are pointless or a nuisance, they will feel guilty about doing things on their own.

Industry vs. Inferiority (6 to 11 Years)   A child entering school is at a point in development when behavior is dominated by intellectual curiosity and performance. "He now learns to win recognition by producing things . . . he develops a sense of industry." The danger at this stage is that the child may experience feelings of inadequacy or inferiority. If the child is encouraged to make and do things well, helped to persevere, allowed to finish tasks, and praised for trying, industry results. If the child's efforts are unsuccessful or if they are derided or treated as bothersome, a feeling of inferiority results. Children who feel inferior may never learn to enjoy intellectual work and take pride in doing at least one kind of thing really well. At worst, they may believe they will never excel at anything.

Identity vs. Role Confusion (12 to 18 Years) As young adults approach independence from parents and achieve physical maturity, they are concerned about what kind of persons they are becoming. The goal at this stage is development of ego identity, "the accrued confidence of sameness and continuity." The danger at this stage is role confusion, particularly doubt about sexual and occupational identity. If adolescents succeed (as reflected by the reactions of others) in integrating roles in different situations to the point of experiencing continuity in their perception of self, identity develops. If they are unable to establish a sense of stability in various aspects of their lives, role confusion results.

Intimacy vs. Isolation (Young Adulthood) To experience satisfying development at this stage, the young adult needs to establish a close and committed intimate relationship with another person. Failure to do so will lead to a sense of isolation.

Generativity vs. Stagnation (Middle Age) "Generativity . . . is primarily the concern of establishing and guiding the next generation." Erikson's use of the term *generativity* is purposely broad. It refers, of course, to having children and raising them. In addition, it refers to the productive and creative efforts in which adults take part that have a positive effect on younger generations (for example, teaching, doing medical research, supporting political and social policies that will benefit future generations). Those unable or unwilling to "establish" and "guide" the next generation become victims of stagnation and self-absorption.

Integrity vs. Despair (Old Age) Integrity is "the acceptance of one's one and only life cycle as something that had to be and that, by necessity, permitted of no substitutions. . . . Despair expresses the feeling that the time is now short, too short for the attempt to start another life and to try out alternate roads to integrity."

— *Robert F. Biehler and Jack Snowman*

1. What are the eight stages of psychosocial development according to Erikson?

_____

_____

_____

_____

_____

_____

_____

_____

2. How do two- to three-year-olds develop autonomy?

_____

_____

3. At what age and how do children develop feelings of inferiority?

_____

_____

_____

4. What is role confusion?

_____

_____

5. What is generativity?

_____

_____

Critical Thinking in Writing

Can you identify your current stage of development with any of the stages Erikson describes? If so, write a paragraph about how your current development fits in with one of Erikson's stages. If not, write a paragraph in which you describe your own view of your current stage of development.

1c Previewing

Other steps to take to read for information come *before* you actually begin reading. You can *preview* — that is, look ahead to the content of a passage — in a number of ways.

Here is how to preview a reading selection:

- *Look at introductory information.* Often information about a selection appears before the title in a *headnote.* The headnote may give biographical information about the writer or may suggest the content of the selection. All the readings in the anthology of this text have introductory headnotes.
- *Look at the title.* Does it tell what you will be reading about? If so, you can set a purpose for your reading. Furthermore, titles often suggest the topic or the main idea of a selection. The title of the selection that begins on page 11 is "Stages of Psychosocial Development." How does that help the reader set a purpose? How does it reflect the main idea?
- *Look for headings.* Essays, newspaper articles, and other longer readings sometimes offer help in finding information by printing *headings.* Appearing throughout the text in boldface or italic type, headings suggest the kind of material you will find in a small portion of the reading.
- *Look at the pictures, charts, or drawings.* Often an illustration can help you figure out beforehand what a reading is about.
- *Look at the first paragraph carefully.* The first paragraph usually tells just what a reading will be about. Read it, and then stop to absorb the information it offers before reading on.
- *Look at the first sentence of each paragraph.* This usually gives you a quick idea of what the reading involves before you begin to read carefully.
- *Look at the questions that come after the reading.* If you look at the

questions *before* you read anything, you then have an idea of what's important. Questions tell you what to expect from a passage. When you read with a knowledge of the questions, you know beforehand what kind of information to look for.

■ *Look for key words in different print.* Sometimes bold letters, italics, or even colored ink is used to call the reader's attention to important words or ideas. Titles of books, for example, appear in italics. Noting these in advance can give you important information.

■ *Look for a summary.* At the end of a long factual piece, a writer sometimes summarizes the main points. Looking at the summary before you read can help you grasp more clearly what the selection deals with.

EXERCISES

Previewing

Before you read the following selection from a health education textbook, preview it by answering the questions below.

1. Read the title. What does it tell you about the contents of this selection?

   _____

   _____

2. Read the headings. Judging from these headings, what do you think the selection will discuss?

   _____

   _____

   _____

3. What information appears in the graph?

   _____

   _____

4. Look at the photographs. How do they relate to the topic of the selection?

_____

_____

Alcohol and Society

The 14 million problem drinkers in the United States harm not only themselves but many others as well. Even people who are mildly intoxicated can bring hardship to others on the roads, on the job, at school, or at home. Alcohol abuse causes accidents, increases medical costs, and creates a need for social services to treat alcoholism.

In the Home

One in four families is hurt by alcoholism. Drinking plays a part in 80 percent of deaths by fire, 65 percent of drownings, 70 percent of fatal falls, and 80 percent of suicides. Alcoholism, the "family disease," destroys one of the most important parts of family life — trust. The alcoholic thinks only about the need to drink and cannot be depended on as a parent, husband, or wife. Alcoholics often use money meant for food, rent, clothing, or medical expenses to feed their own habit instead. Family members live in constant fear of the alcoholic's sudden and angry mood changes. Alcohol abuse is also an important cause of spouse beatings.

Alcohol abuse is involved in two thirds of all child abuse cases. Abuse may simply be neglect. The children are not adequately fed or cared for. Children in such a home feel helpless and often have behavior problems in school and in their social life. In some cases the abuse is violent and involves great physical and mental harm to the child.

Family members often feel shame because of the alcoholic's public behavior. This shame can turn into feelings of guilt because the family no longer respects the alcoholic. Separation and divorce are common in families of alcoholics. Many families keep away from their friends and try to hide the problem. Family members begin to lie and make excuses for the alcoholic. But this behavior only makes things worse. Rather than being protected by excuses, alcoholics must see that they are responsible for their own actions.

FIGURE 19-12   Many teenagers underestimate the powerful
effects of alcohol.   © DONALD ROSENFELD

Teenagers

Teenagers use alcohol more than they use any other drug.
About three fourths of all high school students drink alcoholic
drinks once in a while. One third drink them regularly. Almost
one in ten will one day become an alcoholic.

Psychologists believe that teenagers are more likely to develop alcohol problems than adults are. Teenagers have fewer
experiences with alcohol than adults, and they often do not
understand how powerful its effects are. They think they will
be able to handle it but they cannot.

Psychologists believe that the use of alcohol slows social development. Young people are learning about social relations
and emotional control. If they use a drug every time they are
under stress, they may never be able to develop their social
and emotional abilities.

FIGURE 19-13   Alcohol-related automobile accidents kill thousands of people each year.   © 1991 DONALD ROSENFELD

On the Job and in the Classroom

Alcohol use at work or in school leads to days away from work and school, poor work, and accidents. Almost one half of all deaths caused by accidents on the job are connected with alcohol. Whether the drinkers drink before or during school or work, they do less work. Heavy drinkers often lose their jobs. Many companies have faced the problem and now offer their workers treatment programs.

On the Road

In one half of all traffic deaths in the United States, the driver has been drinking. One third of pedestrians struck and killed by cars were drunk. **Driving while intoxicated**, or DWI, is illegal in every state. In most states, it is illegal to drive a car if the BAC [blood alcohol content] is 0.1 percent or greater. In most states, it is illegal to drink alcohol while driving. In some, it is against the law to have an open container of any alcoholic drink in the car.

In truth, anyone planning to drive should not drink at all. Signs of intoxication can appear at a BAC as low as 0.02 or 0.03 percent. Studies show that even one drink harms vision and reactions. A driver with a BAC of 0.05 percent, even though he or she is within the legal limit, is twice as likely to have an

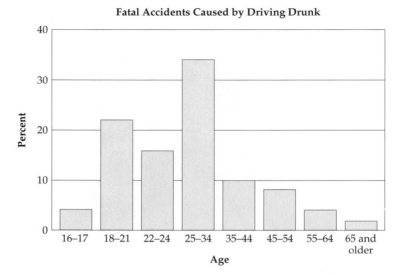

FIGURE 19-14   Most of these fatal accidents are caused by young drivers.

accident as a nondrinking driver. A BAC of 0.1 percent increases the risk of being in an accident by seven times. At BAC 0.15 percent, the risk is ten times greater.

Intoxication can cause accidents in several ways. Intoxicated drivers cannot concentrate on driving as well, and drinking may make them take careless risks. At a BAC of 0.05, reflex time is only three fourths of its normal speed. Visual sharpness is reduced by one third, which is the same as wearing sunglasses at night. The eyes move more slowly and are slow to recover from headlight glare at night. At higher levels of intoxication, the driver may not be able to read signs because of blurred vision.

Drunken driving can be a horrible offense. Thirty thousand people a year are killed and another one half million are hurt. Figure 19-14 shows that drunk drivers aged 18–24 cause more fatal accidents than any other age group. Car accidents in which the drivers have been drinking are also the chief cause of death for teenagers and young adults up to the age of 24.

Drinking and the Law   Due to recent social pressure against drunk driving, new laws now control the sale of alcohol. Many states now outlaw "happy hours," in which bars offer lower prices on drinks to encourage people to drink after work. In many states bartenders are held responsible for damage done by a drunk driver who has been drinking at their bars. People who have parties in their homes are also considered responsible for their guests. The law also forbids bartenders and friends from giving drinks to someone already drunk.

The legal drinking age varies from state to state, ranging from 18 to 21. In several states, any person under the legal drinking age who is caught DWI can have his or her driver's license taken away on the spot. It is illegal in most states for minors, or those under the drinking age, to buy an alcoholic beverage or to pretend they are older than the drinking age. It is also illegal for minors to drink an alcoholic beverage unless they are with an adult. The law also puts part of the burden on the adults. It is illegal for a person to sell an alcoholic drink to a minor.

During the 1970s, many states dropped the drinking age from 21 to 18. It was raised again only after automobile accident deaths among teenagers suddenly increased by a great amount. By 1987, states were required to have a legal drinking age of 21 to receive federal highway funds.

New Drinking Habits

In recent years, drinking has been viewed less favorably than in the past. This is partly due to campaigns against drunk driving. Also, attitudes towards health, fitness, and self-image have changed.

Because of public pressure, prime-time television has cut back on showing alcohol use on the screen. Owners of sports arenas now have family sections where drinking is not allowed. Public tolerance of intoxication is decreasing, so people have cut back on drinking. Sales of alcoholic beverages have gone down slightly. The alcohol industry has brought out new lines of light beers and wines with low alcohol content. Nonalcoholic fruit drinks and carbonated waters now satisfy many people's thirst at parties, lunches, and celebrations.

The Choice Is Yours

Many teenagers and adults choose not to drink. If this is your choice, stick by it. Do not let others decide for you. If you do choose to drink, respect the opinion of others who choose not to drink. More and more, young people are learning to socialize without alcohol. People are also learning to deal with stress through healthy activity or by changing their behavior.

If you must deal with alcoholism in your family, help is available. Al-Anon is an organization that helps the families of alcoholics cope with their situations. It encourages family members to seek help for themselves and not to wait until the alcoholic decides to seek help. Al-Anon reminds the family members not to accept the guilt the alcoholic may try to place on them.

Alateen is an organization of and for teenagers who live with alcoholics. The organization of Alateen is similar to that of Al-Anon. Teenagers come together not to treat family members, but to deal with their own problems. Membership is open to young people who wish to discuss, share, and learn to deal with their own situations.

Lesson Review

The harmful effects of alcohol spread throughout society. People pay a high price for these harmful effects. The high costs are seen in alcohol-related deaths, diseases, and loss of work. Drinkers continue to make life difficult for their workmates and families. Many organizations exist to help family members of alcoholics, particularly teenagers with alcoholic parents. There are other groups that work especially against drunk driving. Tougher laws may help reduce the number of drunk driving accidents.

1. What is DWI?
2. To what age did states have to raise their legal drinking age by 1987 in order to receive federal highway funds?
3. What is the name of an organization of and for teenagers who live with alcoholics?

— *Bud Getchell et al.*

Critical Thinking in Writing

Write a paragraph or two about the kinds of alcohol abuse programs at your school or in your community. How do these programs address the issues described in this selection?

1d Previewing Long Material: The Parts of a Book

Much of what you read appears in long works. Your textbooks in biology, math, or business courses, for example, offer several hundred pages of material. One teacher may require that you read a novel or a play; another may ask you to read an article in a journal; still another may assign a new book that treats the subject of the course in a special way. Before you read a long book for information, you can use several effective previewing techniques in addition to those explained in Section 1c. Here is how to preview a book:

- *Look at the copyright page.* Usually found right after the title page, the copyright page gives the publication date of the book and dates of earlier editions. If you are looking for information about the end of the Cold War between the United States and the Soviet Union (1990), for instance, a book copyrighted in 1984 would not be useful.
- *Look at the table of contents.* Found in the front of the book, the table of contents is a list of the chapters' names and the pages on which they begin. If the book is divided into parts, that information also appears in the table of contents. By studying the chapter titles, you can get an idea of what each section of the book deals with and how the topics relate to one another. Sometimes a table of contents is very detailed, with a listing of the topics treated in each chapter.
- *Look at the preface.* Before the table of contents, the preface (sometimes called the *foreword*) is a brief essay in which the author gives reasons for writing the book. The preface is a personal message to the reader. In the preface you get an idea of the kind of reader the author is writing for; of the aims of the book and just what the author expects you to learn as a result of reading it; and of the topics in the book and the best approaches to those topics. Not all books have a preface, and sometimes a preface deals with matters that interest the author but that do not have much to do with specific ideas in the book. Still, it's good to look the preface over, even if you just skim it, so that you can judge for yourself whether to read it carefully.
- *Look briefly at the index.* At the end of a book you may find an alphabetical listing of the topics, subjects, ideas, and names mentioned in the book. A quick look at the index suggests some of the points the writer deals with and the level of detail in the book.
- *Look at these special features that sometimes appear in books:*

  1. After the chapters in a book a writer sometimes provides a *glossary*, a list of difficult words or terms commonly used in the subject the book deals with. The words are listed in

alphabetical order with their definitions. The fact that a book has a glossary may indicate that the subject is technical but that the author does try to explain difficult terms.

2. An *appendix* (plural *appendixes* or *appendices*) at the end of the book presents additional information that is interesting and useful. An appendix may include charts and graphs, special letters or documents, or facts about the lives of the people mentioned in the book. It just may give information to explain something the author felt needed more attention. A look at the appendix, if the book has one, indicates how the writer deals with special problems.

■ *Read the introduction.* Often the first chapter of a book is an introduction. Like a preface, an introduction gives an overview of the book and states the basic problem the author deals with. It gives background information or discusses the history of the topic. It may summarize what others have said about the subject. It may even explain the method of research the author used. Sometimes — especially in a work of fiction such as a novel, a collection of short stories, or a play — someone other than the author writes the introduction. This kind of introduction usually explains the book to the readers, pointing out key scenes or ideas worth noting.

■ *Look at the bibliography or references.* At the back of the book an author sometimes gives a *bibliography* — a list, in alphabetical order, of some or all of the books that helped the author write this book. The bibliography (sometimes titled *Works Cited*) indicates the author's range of knowledge and basic interests.

■ *Think about the parts the book has and the parts it doesn't have.* A book with a detailed index, a long bibliography, and a number of appendixes may be more appropriate for research than a book with only a short table of contents. Books with glossaries often provide helpful introductions to difficult subjects.

EXERCISES

1. Using a Table of Contents

Look at the table of contents that appears on pages 25–26. It comes from a book titled *Business Enterprise in American History.* Read the table of contents to figure out as much as you can about the book. Then answer the following questions.

CONTENTS

Preface   ix

Introduction   1
Stages and Themes of American Business History   4
Capitalism and American Business   17

Part 1   The Foundations of American Business to 1790   23

1   Business in Colonial America   24
The Growth of Business in Europe   25
Business in Colonial America   36
The Navigation Acts   50
Conclusion   53
Selected Readings   54

2   Business in the Revolutionary Era   56
Business and the American Revolution   57
Adam Smith and the Economics of Freedom   63
Establishing the Tradition of Government-Business Relations   66
The Legacy of the Revolutionary Generation   77
Conclusion   79
Selected Readings   79

Part 2   Business Development in the New Nation, 1790–1850   81

3   The Expansion of American Business: Agriculture, Commerce, and Industry   82
Economic Growth   84
The Transportation Revolution   85
The Agrarian Revolution   94
The Industrial Revolution   98
The Invisible Hand of the Market   106
A Business Ideology   116
Conclusion   120
Selected Readings   120

4   Government and Business   122
Internal Improvements   124
Banking and the Tariff   134
Law and Business Development   142
Conclusion   148
Selected Readings   149

Part 3   The Rise of Big Business, 1850–1920   151

5   The Emergence of Big Business   152
Railroads: Pioneers in Big Business   154
The Spread of Big Business   163
Service Industries   179

The New Conduct of Business   183
The Character of the Businessman   186
Conclusion   193
Selected Readings   194

6   **Government and Business in the Gilded Age**   196
Social Change and Social Thought   198
Politics and Partisanship   201
Government Promotion and Regulation of Business   214
Conclusion   224
Selected Readings   225

7   **Business in a Democratic Society: The Progressive Era**   226
New Ways of Thinking   227
New Institutions   236
Government Regulation of Business   241
Business, Reform, and the Immigrant Labor Force   257
Mobilization for War   260
Conclusion   263

Part 4   The Development of Modern Business,
1920–1945   265

8   **The Diversified, Decentralized Company**   266
Changes in the American Business System   267
Business Diversification and the Spread of Decentralized
   Management   276
The Professionalization of Business   295
Conclusion   300
Selected Readings   300

9   **The American Political Economy in Transition**   302
From War to Peace, 1918–1921   303
Herbert Hoover and the Associative State   309
The Great Depression   313
The New Deal   316
Business and World War II   331
Conclusion   335
Selected Readings   337

Part 5   Recent Trends in American Business,
1946 to the Present   339

10   **The Company in the Postwar World**   340
The Postwar Economy   341
The Conglomerate Commotion   347
Multinationals   359
Small Business   366
The Modern Corporate Business System   367
The Business Executive   372
Conclusion   381
Selected Readings   382

11   **The Political Economy After World War II**   383
The Federal Government and Economic Well-Being   384
Government and the Framework for Business Activity   390

1. What aspect of American history is this book concerned with?

   _____

2. Who might be interested in this book?

   _____

3. In what part of the book would you find out about recent business trends?

   _____

4. In what chapter would you find out about the emergence of big business?

   _____

5. In what chapter would you learn about business in the early years of America?

   _____

6. In what chapters would you find out how modern business developed?

   _____

7. What two elements appear in each chapter from 1 to 11?

   _____

8. Where could you find out about the authors' reasons for writing the book?

   _____

9. What would you learn about in the introduction? How can you tell?

   _____

   _____

   _____

10. In what chapters would you find information on twentieth-century political economy?

_____

2. Using an Index

On page 29 is an excerpt from the index of the book on business enterprise whose table of contents you used in Exercise 1. Use it to answer the following questions.

1. How does the table of contents differ from the index?

_____

2. If you wanted to find information quickly on banking in colonial times, would it be better to look at the table of contents or the index?

_____

3. List the pages on which you will find information about the following:

a. Salvador Allende _____

b. Alcoa _____

c. Black Americans _____

d. Louis Brandeis _____

e. Deregulation of banking _____

f. The growth of the American Federation of Labor _____

g. Antitrust activities after 1945 _____

INDEX

Abraham & Strauss, 167
accounting, innovations on railroads, 160
Adams, John Quincy, 128
administered prices: by railroads, 161;
   spread of, 273–74
advertising, growth of, 274–76
Africa Company, 30
agribusiness, 368
agricultura revolution, 102
Air Quality Act, 409
airline industry, 416–17
Alcoa Aluminum. *See* Aluminum
   Company of America
Aldrich, Nelson W., 248
Alger, Horatio, 187
Allende, Salvador, 363
Aluminum Company of America
   (Alcoa), 289, 334
American Bicycle Company, 177
American Brands Company, 348
American Economic Association, 228
American Federation of Labor: founded,
   210; growth of, 239; and tariff, 252
American Glue Company, 177
American Iron and Steel Institute, 440
American Railway Union, 213
American revolution. *See* revolution
American Smelting and Refining Com-
   pany, 289
American Sugar Refining Company, 224,
   256
American system of manufacturing, 105–06
American Telephone and Telegraph
   (AT&T), 362, 394, 419
American Tobacco Company, 236, 250
Americanization, 259–60
Anaconda, 289
antitrust: and states, 253–54; during
   1900–17, 249–51; in 1930s, 324–25;
   after 1945, 393–94. *See also* Department
   of Justice
Appleton, Nathan, 100, 119
Araskog, Rand, 363–64
Armour, J. Ogden, 277

Articles of Confederation, 67
Astor, John Jacob, 111, 135
Atlanta, Georgia, 132
Atlantic Richfield Company, 357, 380
automobile industry: growth in 1920s,
   271; in 1930s, 293; and Japan, 392; and
   consumers, 406. *See also* company
   name.

Baltimore, Lord, 35
Baltimore and Ohio Railrod: chartered,
   92; and government funds, 132; and
   government survey, 132; and management, 156, 158–59
bank notes, 13
Bank of North America, 62
Bank of the United States: and Hamilton,
   71–72; dispute over, 75; expires, 77; re-
   chartered in 1816, 135; and agrarians,
   136; characterized, 136
banks, state, 135
Banking: in colonial times, 39; expansion
   of, 111–12, 179–80; and industrial revo-
   lution, 103–04; in Gilded Age, 206–09;
   in Progressive era, 247–49; and depres-
   sion, 316, 318; deregulation of, 417–18.
   See also investment banking
bankruptcy laws, 68–69
Baring Brothers and Company, 111
Barton, Bruce, 299
Baruch, Bernard, 261–62
Behn, Sosthenes, 362
Bell Company, formed, 155. *See also*
   AT&T
Bethlehem Steel, 437
Biddle, Nicholas, 136
black Americans, 378–79, 408
Bloomingdales, 167
Board of Engineers for Internal Improve-
   ments, 126
Borden Company, 350
Boston Associates: 100, 103; and factory
   design, 106; and workers, 114–15
Brandeis, Louis D., 244

Blackford and Kerr, *Business Enterprise in American History*, Houghton Mifflin, 1986.

3. Reading an Introduction

Read the introduction from a book about Mexican-American
authors that appears on pages 31–34. Try to determine the special qualities of the book. Then answer the following questions.

1. What makes this book special among books about Mexican
    Americans?

    _____

2. What will you find in the first section of the book?

    _____

    _____

3. Which selections were translated from Spanish?

    _____

4. What kinds of selections other than folklore would you find
    in this book?

    _____

5. Why, according to the introduction, is it important to read
    Mexican-American versions of the Chicano experience?

    _____

    _____

6. What is Aztlán? Why is a map of it included in the intro-
    duction?

    _____

    _____

    _____

Introduction

People like to record their experiences; Mexican-Americans have been no exception. They have had much to write about. Their lives have sometimes been stormy and often tragic, but always vital and intriguing. It is hardly surprising that Mexican-Americans have literary talents, for they are heirs to the European civilization of Spain and the Indian civilizations of Mexico, both of which produced great poets and storytellers. Furthermore, they have also been in contact with the history and the literature of the United States, for Mexican-Americans have played a key role in the cultural development of the American Southwest.

Although their homes are in the United States, much of the literature of Mexican-Americans has been written in their first language, Spanish. Only during the last fifty years or so have they written widely in English. This book deals almost wholly with what Mexican-Americans have written in the English language; that is, it explores only their literature of the past half century. Mexican-Americans have gone through considerable change during this period, and so has their literature. You will note some clear differences between the earlier selections and the later ones in the book.

The earlier selections offer examples of what we call "folklore." Folklore, which may be defined as "the unofficial heritage of a people," is usually passed from one person to another by word of mouth. It includes such things as legends, jokes, songs, stories of adventure, and proverbs. To the Mexican-American his folklore is especially important because he belongs to a bilingual minority: he speaks two languages. His "official" heritage, usually learned in school, is expressed in English, and he shares it with all other Americans. But his folklore is for the most part in Spanish, and it belongs to him alone. The ballad "Corrido de Jacinto Treviño" and the *dichos* (proverbs and other sayings) presented here have been translated from Spanish into English. The Spanish versions of the *dichos* have been included to show how these examples of folklore look in their original language.

Folklore is important in another way: it is the very core of a people's literature, the foundation on which many great literary works are built. Shakespeare, for example, frequently used English folklore in his plays. The great Spanish writer Cervantes used many proverbs and folktales in his novel *Don Quixote*. In the United States Herman Melville, Nathaniel Hawthorne, Mark Twain, and John Steinbeck are some of the many writers who have used folklore in their fiction, Josephina Niggli is a Mexican-American writer who knows her folklore well.

Folklore is significant in still another way. History books are very often the biographies of great men — the Washingtons, the Lincolns, the Miguel Hidalgos and Emiliano Zapatas — but little may be said of what ordinary persons thought and felt. Folklore is the history of the people, not the presidents and generals in Washington, D.C., and Mexico City, but the *campesinos* (country people) in South Texas and Chihuahua.

Besides traditional folklore, this book includes stories, nonfiction, poems, and a play. Some of these selections describe the years preceding World War II, when most Mexican-Americans lived in rural areas; it is natural that literature of this period describes life in villages, haciendas, and farms. Stories of this time are basically "romantic" — that is, they are adventurous and emotional, revealing an optimistic view of people.

The literature of the period after World War II is quite different. The stories are usually set in cities and focus on aspects of urban life. They deal with such problems as education, drugs, juvenile delinquency, and the loss of Mexican culture. Much less optimism is expressed: Amado Muro, for example, in "Cecilia Rosas" describes a Mexican-American girl's lack of pride in her heritage. Some of the writers are clearly angry. Nick Vaca accuses a cruel and tactless Anglo world of mistreating the Chicano, while Richard Olivas bitterly questions the relevance of the American educational system. To many students such problems will seem very familiar.

While the various Mexican-American authors may express different viewpoints and attitudes, they are presenting significant versions of the Chicano experience. And this is very important because many Anglo writers have been less than fair and compassionate in their treatment of Mexican-American character, culture, and history. This book is an attempt to swing the scales back toward a proper balance. Stephen Crane, in his western stories, saw the Mexican-American as cowardly and stupid, but in this volume Josephina Niggli sees the Mexican as daring and resourceful. While John Steinbeck, in *Tortilla Flat*, pictured the Mexican-American as totally incapable of handling his financial affairs, Mario Suarez here presents him as a competent businessman. In this book the Texas Rangers do not always slaughter Mexicans like so many ducks on a pond; the Mexicans, on the contrary, win a few battles themselves.

After all, history is a matter of interpretation. In this book, *barrio* is not necessarily a squalid, filthy slum, but a vital, lively neighborhood

The Aztlán Territory

where people lead a warm, dignified existence, though they may not be reposing in luxury. This is not to say that Mexican-American writers idealize their own people without any awareness of their human faults, for this would be to distort their life styles in another direction. Mexican-American writers do not claim that their people are perfect. They do claim for them a basic equality in virtue (and vice) with all other people.

One last point. Surely a great lesson Mexican-American writers can teach all Americans is the fundamental absurdity of national boundaries. You will notice that the selections which follow are set not only in the southwestern United States but in northern Mexico as well. For the Mexican-American writer — indeed, for the Mexican-American people as a whole — all this vast area is one land. The Mexican-American recognizes the Rio Grande not as a boundary but as a great life-giving artery running through his homeland. The Aztecs had a name for that vast territory — Aztlán. This book is by and about the people of Aztlán.

Critical Thinking in Writing

Write a paragraph or two in which you explain why, according to the writers, folklore is important. Do you agree? What example of folklore can you provide from your own ethnic background?

4. Previewing an Appendix

Preview the appendix of this book (pages 513–517) by following the guidelines in this chapter. Then answer the following questions.

1. What is the appendix about?

   _____

2. What does page 514 show?

   _____

3. On what page of the appendix can you find hints for using

   guide words? _____

4. What do the following sections deal with?

A3 _____

A4 _____

A5 _____

A6 _____

5. Previewing the Parts of a Book

Select a textbook from one of your other courses. Locate the parts
of the book in the following list. In your own words, write what
you can find out about the book from each part. If the book does
not have one of the parts, state what you think that indicates
about the book. Use a separate sheet of paper for your answers.

1. Title and author's name
2. Copyright information
3. Table of contents
4. Introduction or preface
5. Glossary
6. Bibliography
7. Index

CHAPTER **1**   **REVIEW TEST**

Before You Read

In the spaces provided, write answers to the questions. Count 4 points for each correct answer.

1. What is prereading? _____

    _____

2. What four prereading activities can help you improve your reading?

    a. _____   c. _____

    b. _____   d. _____

3. What is freewriting? _____

    _____

4. Define *skimming*. _____

5. What is previewing? _____

    _____

6. What nine features of a selection can help you preview it?

    a. _____   f. _____

    _____   _____

    b. _____   g. _____

    c. _____   _____

    d. _____   h. _____

    _____   _____

    e. _____   i. _____

7. What eight features should you look at to preview the parts of a book?

    a. _____   f. _____

    b. _____   g. _____

    c. _____   _____

    d. _____   h. _____

    e. _____   _____

    _____

    Score: _____ correct × 4 points each = _____

2

Reading Helpers: Underlining, Taking Notes, and Outlining

For your course work you often have to look back at what you've learned from your reading. To study for exams, to refresh your memory for class discussions, and to prepare papers and projects, you need to go over information you've gathered from assigned readings as well as other readings. If you had the time and energy, you could just reread all the material from beginning to end. But reviewing the material is easier and quicker if you identify and mark important information the first time you read it. Then, later, you can go right to the parts you need.

There are several ways to locate and record important information as you read. *Underlining* the material on a page is quickest, but *taking notes* makes you reorganize the reading material into an easy-to-understand form. *Outlining* helps you record the structure of the ideas in your reading. *Summarizing* helps you grasp the meaning of what you read most fully, by restating that meaning in a concise way.

Each of these study techniques does more than create a record of what you think is important in the reading for later review. By making you work actively to get at the important facts or ideas, each of these techniques helps you understand the material better the first time you read it. Because you have to use your mind to identify ideas and facts and your pencil to mark them, you are more likely to remember what you are supposed to learn. The more active a study technique is, the better it helps you understand and remember what you read.

2a   Underlining

If you underline the most important ideas and details in a reading assignment, you can find what you need quickly when you reread the passage. You also can add special marks and comments in the margin about the main ideas and major details you underline. These extra marks and comments help you remember your thoughts and your interpretation of the passage.

A Method for Underlining

- Underline only reading material that belongs to you. Do not mark up library books, borrowed books, or books that belong to your school. Underlining is a personal process. Your underlining can interfere with other readers' use and enjoyment of a book.
- Mark the main ideas and major details differently. Underline the main ideas with a double line and the major details with a single line. Or use a different color highlighter pen for each. Find major details by following the suggestions in Section **6b**.
- Find main idea sentences by following the suggestions in Section **5a**. Underline the sentences or parts of sentences that state the main idea of a paragraph (Section **5b**). If the main ideas are only implied, write your own main idea sentence in the margin.
- Circle key words. Use brackets, asterisks, or any other symbol to mark parts that are especially interesting or important to you.
- Write notes or comments to yourself in the margin. The margins are good places to put down your own thoughts as you read. Marginal notes can help you connect ideas from different parts of the selection. They also can help you connect a passage with other material you have read, with comments your teacher has made, or with your own experience.

Read the following passage from a textbook on business history about the changes that began to take place for women who became business executives during the last decade. Notice how one student used the techniques of underlining and making marginal notes to highlight important points.

Women in Business Management

only one woman!

With the exception only of Katherine Graham of the *Washington Post*, <u>no woman had reached a top managerial position</u> in big business as late as <u>1984</u>, and <u>women remained underrepresented in the management of American business in general</u>. Even though they composed 40 percent of the labor force <u>in 1976, women held only 19 percent of the jobs in management</u> (and of these women managers, 20 percent were either self-employed or unpaid family workers). This situation, in part, reflected the generally low position of women workers in the American economy. <u>In 1975,</u> the <u>median income of working women was only 57 percent of that of men</u>, and the average female college graduate earned less than the average male high school dropout. <u>In 1984,</u> even though women composed 69 percent of the white-collar work force, <u>only 10 percent of all managers were women</u>.

*

some change

educational advance

By the late 1970s and 1980s, however, a <u>growing number of women were obtaining entry-level and middle-management positions</u> in big businesses, heralding their later arrival in the top ranks of business. During this time <u>women</u> also came to <u>compose an ever-larger proportion of the students in graduate business programs at colleges</u> and universities. In the early 1970s, women typically made up about <u>5 percent</u> of the MBA classes at most institutions, but a decade later — by which time the <u>MBA</u> was fast becoming the required degree for entry-level management positions — <u>women</u> composed <u>30 percent</u> of such classes. Not all areas of American business were equally receptive to these women; they had more success in finance and the service industries than in basic manufacturing.

business starts at 2 × men's rate! (70s and 80s)

<u>Women also advanced as entrepreneurs</u> on their own. Women <u>started businesses at twice the rate of men in the late 1970s and early 1980s</u>, so that between 1977 and 1985 the number of businesses owned by women <u>doubled</u>, reaching a total of 3.7

million. Companies owned by women nonetheless generated <u>less than 10 percent of the sales</u> made by U.S. businesses.

an example of women's business
success: J. Moran

<u>Juliette Moran</u> was one of the women who <u>succeeded in business</u>. After receiving a B.S. in chemistry from Columbia in 1939, she went to <u>work in Macy</u>'s book department at <u>$17</u> a week, only to leave that company when turned down for a fifty-cent raise a year later. After a <u>series of research jobs</u> in <u>government</u> and <u>business</u>, Moran accepted a <u>position as a chemist</u> with General Aniline and Film (GAF). From research she moved quickly into the <u>budgeting operations</u> of the company — what she later called "the big change in my business life." Her talents were recognized by one of the company's top executives, <u>Jesse Warner</u>, and Moran became his <u>assistant</u> when Warner assumed the presidency of GAF in 1962. Five years later, she had risen to vice president in charge of <u>marketing, personnel, and public relations</u>; by 19<u>78</u>, she was earning $112,000.

EXERCISES

1. Read the selection on pages 17–22. Use underlining to show important information.
2. Review Chapter 1, "Before You Read" (pages 5–37), by underlining important ideas.
3. Read a chapter in a textbook assigned for another one of your courses. Underline and make other marks to highlight important information.

2b Taking Notes

To take notes on your reading, you must identify the main ideas and major details, and then write them down in an organized list. You can list the information on one line after another down the page. You can number the items. If you decide that some points are more important than others, you can indent the less important ones under the main points.

As you write down the information, you pay active attention to it, making it easier to remember. Also, indenting helps you see how the parts of the reading fit together.

A Method for Taking Notes

- Find the main ideas in paragraphs by following the suggestions in Section **5b**. Write these main ideas down on notebook paper, starting at the left margin of the paper. You can copy the entire main idea sentence as it appears in the reading, shorten it, or put the idea into your own words. You can even jot down just a few key phrases, as long as they capture the main idea.

- Find the major details by following the suggestions in Section **6b**. List them opposite or beneath your notes on the main ideas. Again, you need not copy down whole sentences. Your own wording of the printed text will do, as long as your notes capture the important facts or ideas.

- Use abbreviations, but make sure that you'll be able to understand what they mean when you return to your notes later.

- Add your own comments and thoughts in the margin or in a special section at the bottom of the page. These comments will help you think through the importance of the material or highlight its connections to other reading you have done.

- You can use a similar method for taking notes during course lectures. Make sure you keep up with the lecture. Don't get so caught up in taking notes that you stop listening to the lecture. If you find the lecturer getting too far ahead of you, stop writing and start listening. If you skip a few lines, you can complete your notes later from memory or by referring to a friend's notes. During lectures, avoid fussing over spelling or exact wording. You always can check a dictionary later.

The following notes are based on the passage about women business executives on pages 40–41. You may find it useful to compare these notes with the sample underlining on those pages.

<u>Women</u> <u>Business</u> <u>Leaders</u>
<u>Until</u> 1984 only one woman top executive
In 1976 only 19 percent of management jobs held
   by women
In 1984 only 10 percent of all white-collar managers
   were women.
In 1970s and 1980s women went from 5 percent to 30 per-
   cent of MBA students
Women-owned businesses doubled in 1980s
Women still accounted for less than 10 percent
   of sales.
Juliette Moran succeeds in business from small jobs to
   $112,000 as vice president of GAF in 1978.

EXERCISES

1. Taking Notes from Printed Material

1. Review Chapter 1 of this book by taking notes on a separate
   sheet of paper.
2. Select a newspaper article and take notes on it as you read.
   A few days later, rewrite the article in your own words from
   your notes. Compare your story to the newspaper's version
   to see how accurate your notes were.

2. Taking Notes from Listening

1. Take notes during one of your course lectures. Compare your
   notes with those made by other students. Also, if possible,
   ask your instructor to look over your notes and tell you how
   accurate they are. Did you write down the most important
   facts and ideas?
2. Watch the evening news on television, taking notes on one
   of the major stories. Retell the news story to a friend or family
   member using your notes. How similar were the two versions?

3. Taking Notes for a Reading Assignment

Read the following selection about a sensational shooting and
take notes on a separate sheet of paper.

The Strange, Sad Case of Amy Fisher
as Popular Culture

A Linchpin to Sociology and Cultural Studies

In 1992, a Long Island teenager named Amy Fisher was arrested for allegedly shooting a woman named Mary Jo Buttafuoco, the wife of a man she claimed was her lover. Thus began a sad and violent story that quickly attracted the attention of racy tabloid newspapers and equally exploitative TV programs. The trial was short, since Fisher admitted guilt and plea-bargained a five-to-fifteen-year prison sentence.

The story had many elements of sensationalism, including sex, crime, and a supposed love triangle. In addition, Fisher was an attractive eighteen-year-old. It also left open many questions: Who was telling the truth and who was lying? What was the role of Joseph Buttafuoco, the alleged lover who denied intimate involvement with Fisher? Was the affair the fantasy of a teenager or a real-life drama?

In December 1992 and January 1993, three made-for-television movies aired on CBS, NBC, and ABC networks dramatizing Amy Fisher's story. As a *New York Times* article put it, "Surpassing the expectations of network officials, each of the three made-for-television movies based on the Amy Fisher case . . . was a stunning success, and two of the three are likely to emerge as the most popular television movies of the season."[1] Each movie took sides — one portrayed Amy Fisher sympathetically and blamed Joseph Buttafuoco for her plight, while another took the Buttafuocos' point of view and depicted Fisher as a lying, duplicitous girl with emotional problems.

At the same time, the TV tabloid show "Hard Copy" managed to acquire X-rated videos of Amy and another boyfriend and broadcast them on the air. Before long, popular national talk shows such as "Donahue" and "Geraldo" got involved in the case, inviting the Buttafuocos on the show, where they were heckled and hooted by a studio audience in one case and subjected to a mock trial in another. What began as a serious case of domestic violence involving virtually unknown people in a local community was trumpeted in the print and electronic tabloids and became the subject of hundreds of magazine articles, scores of TV shows, and three network TV movies. In addition, deals for paperback books were quickly in the works.

[1] Bill Carter, "Amy Fisher Story, A Surprise Smash in Three TV Movies," *New York Times*, Jan. 5, 1993, p. C11.

The case and its protagonists were suddenly the "stuff" of popular culture. What had been a matter for the police blotter and the courts became everybody's business as people speculated about the parties in the case, their honesty and ethics. Ruth Slawson, senior vice president for movies at NBC, said that the massive public interest "stunned" her. As she put it, "I don't believe there was anything so unique or gripping to this story to make it that special."[2] On reflection, Slawson thought that Fisher's age might have been a factor in luring young viewers.

From the original facts of the case, about which there is disagreement, came fast and loose TV movies that took considerable license in telling the story. What had been a racy but still fairly factual news story became a quasi-fictional treatment as a TV movie and more fodder for what University of Michigan scholar John D. Stevens calls the "wretched excess" that is so common among the tabloid media.

Though none of the people involved in the case were thought to be particularly attractive by newspeople and commentators, their story had taken off as a popular tale and became an artifact of popular culture. Popular culture portrayals like this can have staying power, but many do not and simply recede from public consciousness as new and more gripping stories emerge.

[2] Ibid., p. C18. Also see "Joey, Mary Jo Rip 'Donahue'," *Newsday,* Jan 6, 1993, p. 1. For a useful discussion of sensationalization and its origins, see John D. Stevens, *Sensationalism in the New York Press* (New York: Columbia University Press, 1990).

— *Melvin L. DeFleur and Everette E. Dennis*

2c   Outlining

Outlining is a more organized form of note-taking. In an outline, a system of numbering and indenting entries helps organize and label ideas according to their level of importance. The main ideas are placed at the left margin and numbered with Roman numerals. Supporting ideas, indented under the main ideas, are marked with capital letters. Less important material is indented further and given Arabic numerals (and then, at the next level, lowercase letters).

An outline of your notes lets you see at a glance how the key ideas relate to one another and how the writer backs up the main points.

A student prepared the following sample outline from the passage about women business executives on pages 40–41. You may find it useful to compare this outline with the sample underlining in the original.

```
I.  Few women in management before the 80s
    A.  Until 1984 only one woman top executive
    B.  In 1976 only 19% of management jobs held by women
II. Recent changes in representation of women in busi-
    ness
    A.  In 1970s and 80s women went from 5% to 30% of MBA
        students
    B.  Women-owned businesses doubled in 80s, but
        still accounted for only 10% of sales
    C.  Juliette Moran one example of successful woman
        in business
        1.  Started at Macy's
        2.  Research jobs led to budgeting operations po-
            sition with GAF
        3.  Became Vice President in 1978
```

Outline Techniques

- List only main ideas as main headings.
- Relate all subheadings to the main heading they follow.
- Make sure all the headings in a series fit together logically.
- Make sure the headings are clearly different, that they don't cover the same material. If there is too much overlap, reorganize the outline.
- When you break down a heading, you must have at least two subheadings.
- Use whole sentences, phrases, or just single words, as long as the entries convey the information and are easy to understand. If you use sentences, however, you should use sentences throughout the outline.
- Indent all items correctly.
- Put a period after each letter or number.

Compare the outline to the notes on page 43 about the same passage. Notice how the outline gives a more complete picture of the organization of the ideas. When you really need to understand and remember the structure of difficult material, outlining is the best study technique. Yet making an outline is time-consuming. Note-taking is a more efficient study method for routine reading assignments.

EXERCISES

1. Outline Chapter 7 as a way of reviewing the sequence of ideas in paragraphs.
2. Using a separate sheet of paper, outline the passage about American Indians on pages 80–81.
3. Imagine that you have been assigned the textbook passage on pages 130–131 for a political science course. To prepare for a quiz on the material and to help you study, make an outline of the selection.

CHAPTER **2**   **REVIEW TEST**

Reading Helpers

In the spaces provided, write answers to the questions. Count 5 points for each correct answer.

1. List five features to help you underline a text for effective study.

  a. _____

  b. _____

  c. _____

  _____

  d. _____

  _____

  e. _____

2. What five elements can help you take notes on your reading?

  a. _____

  b. _____

  _____

  c. _____

  _____

  d. _____

  e. _____

3. List any three techniques that can help you construct effective outlines.

   a. _____

   _____

   _____

   b. _____

   _____

   c. _____

   _____

   _____

4. Read the following selection, a brief explanation of a study system for reading textbooks — SQ3R. Then look at the partial outline based on the reading. Fill in the blanks with complete sentences that will produce an outline that follows the guidelines under "Outline Techniques" on page 46.

Studying for Remembering: SQ3R

When you're reading a textbook, the idea is to think about the material as much as possible, about how it relates to experiences you've had or to things you already know. This concept forms the basis of a study system called *SQ3R* — an acronym that stands for *survey, question, read, recite,* and *review* (Robinson, 1970).

- *Survey* Look at chapter outlines, skim the material, note headings, and read summaries or introductory material for an overview of the material you're going to be studying. You have to know where you're going before you start the trip. This way, when you read something, you'll know the broader context it fits into.
- *Question* Now ask yourself what you should be learning in your reading. Then, as you read, look for answers. Even if your answers are wrong, they can help you recognize what you are actually reading.
- *Read* Go ahead and read. But be aware of the context in which you're reading and the objectives you've set for yourself. Remember, you can think and read at the same time.

- *Recite*   Once you've read a chapter (or, in a book like this one, a section), stop and talk about what you've read (yes, out loud!). If you want to take notes on your reading, this is the time to do it. You may find that details that seemed clear before you tried to put them into words aren't really clear at all. If you have to, go back and reread. This process is very important because it helps you identify what you know and what you don't know.
- *Review*   After you've finished a chapter, review everything you've read, looking at how the parts connect with one another and what the overall message of the material is. This task is the complement of the survey task: now you're looking at the overall organization.

                                    — *James D. Laird and Nicholas S. Thompson*

I.   SQ3R is a study system that stands for *survey, question, read, recite,* and *review.*

    A.   _____

        _____

        1.   Look at chapter outlines.

        2.   _____

        3.   _____

        4.   Read summaries or introductory material.

    B.   Ask questions about what you should be learning as you read.

    C.   _____

    D.   After reading, talk about what you've read.

        1.   Speak aloud.

        2.   _____

        3.   Reread if necessary.

    E.   _____

        1.   See how the parts connect with each other.

        2.   _____

Score: _____ correct × 5 points each = _____

3

Building a Strong Vocabulary

Most of us have vocabularies that allow us to read widely from the everyday sources of information that surround us. These include newspapers, magazines, signs, posters, advertisements, credit card and job applications, instructions, and recipes. The person with a rich vocabulary, however, can easily read more complicated and varied sources of information as well. You may not be as confident about reading a psychology textbook, a history journal, or an encyclopedia entry as you are about reading other materials. But if you add to your usual resources a wide variety of other materials, you can expand your knowledge of words as you improve your reading skills.

The first step to take in improving your vocabulary is to recognize that it is not possible for you to know the meaning of every word you see. Sometimes you may say to yourself, "I sort of know what this means," or "I can get by without figuring this one out." Often, however, you really do need to find out exactly what those words mean. In the short run, not paying attention to words you don't know may save you some work. But in the long run, you just won't know as much as you should.

Here are some ways to find the meanings of difficult words:

- Learn to use the *context* — that is, clues that surrounding sentences often give about the meanings of new words.
- In a word you don't know, look for parts of the word whose meanings you might know.
- Learn the difference between what a word means and what a word suggests or makes you feel.
- Learn the difference between words that mean almost the same thing but have different shades of meaning.
- Learn to use a dictionary so that you can find meanings easily.
- Keep a list of words you want to add to your vocabulary.

51

3a   Context Clues to Word Meanings

Most experienced readers try to guess the meanings of unfamiliar words through context clues. *Context clues* are hints provided by the words and sentences surrounding the unfamiliar word. Because words and sentences are interconnected in any piece of writing, alert readers often can figure out definitions of unfamiliar words from surrounding information. Sometimes, however, surrounding sentences do not provide enough hints, and you have to turn to a dictionary or some other source for the meaning of an unfamiliar word.

How to Use Sentence Hints for Word Meaning

Hint	Example	Explanation
Some sentences set off the definition of a difficult word by means of punctuation.	*Tofu,* a tasty vegetable protein, can take the place of meat or chicken in many recipes.	Commas, dashes, parentheses ( ), brackets [ ]
Sometimes *helping words,* along with punctuation, provide important clues.	David Yip was *ecstatic* — that is, he was wildly happy — when he received his diploma.	Helping words: *that is, meaning, such as, or, is called*
Some sentences tell the opposite of what a new word means. From its opposite, you can figure out the meaning of the word.	His ideas are generally quite mature, but he is very *naive* about politics.	If you are *naive,* you are not mature. *Childish* or *immature* would be good guesses for the meaning of *naive.* Helping words that show opposites: *not, but, yet, although, however, on the other hand*
Sometimes you can use your own	With heavy boots, Reuphehia *trudged*	Heavy boots would make someone *walk*

Hint	Example	Explanation
experience to figure out the definition of a word.	through the densely packed snow.	with great effort or difficulty.
Sentences before or after a sentence containing a familiar word sometimes explain the meaning of the word.	Show business *chroniclers* say that 1944 was Pearl Bailey's first major year. The history writers point to her work in New York's famous nightclubs and theaters.	You can see from the second sentence that a *chronicler* is someone who writes a history.
Some sentences are written just to give the definitions of difficult words — words that readers need to know to understand what they are reading.	The old hotel in Antigua is undergoing a $6 million *refurbishment.* The owners are redecorating the bedrooms, expanding the lobby and restaurants, and adding a huge garden of tropical plants.	The second sentence, which tells you about the various repairs and improvements to fix up the hotel, explains *refurbishment.*
Some sentences give examples for a new word, on which you can build a definition.	Hattie was *agitated*; she couldn't sit still, her hands moved nervously, and she talked rapidly in a high-pitched voice.	The sentence doesn't say that *agitated* means very excited, but you can figure it out from the examples given.
Some sentences use a word you do know to help explain a word you do not know.	A *nutritious* lunch gives you the essential food elements your body needs.	From clues in the sentence, you can figure out that *nutritious* means providing food substances that are needed for life.

EXERCISES

1. Choosing Definitions from Context

Using the clues you learned about in the chart and the surrounding words and sentences, determine what the word in italics in each sentence below means. Then, from the choices that
follow, select the word that comes closest to the meaning you've
decided on. Write the letter of the correct answer in the space
provided.

_____ 1. Anyone working with the highly *toxic* chemical had to wear
a full protective suit.
a. new
b. unusual
c. heavy
d. poisonous

_____ 2. After the large meal, the *satiated* guests could not even look
at the dessert, a rich triple-chocolate pie.
a. badly confused
b. fully satisfied
c. truthful
d. invited

_____ 3. He tried hard not to love her, but his *ardor* grew stronger
every day.
a. lack of love
b. annoyance
c. very strong love
d. unloving feeling

_____ 4. In very high places, such as mountaintops or high floors of
tall buildings, she felt that she was going to fall off and die.
Her doctor said she had *acrophobia.*
a. depression
b. anxiety
c. fear of high places
d. hatred of nature

_____ 5. *Vagabonds* (people without permanent homes who travel from place to place) are a problem for many cities.
a. city workers
b. homeless drifters
c. city problems
d. uncertain times

_____ 6. Juanita always told the truth, but her boyfriend, Ivan, *prevaricated.*
a. told lies
b. told the truth
c. told secrets
d. was old-fashioned

_____ 7. The *cacophonous* music made José cover his ears.
a. soft and pleasant
b. jarring and unpleasant
c. modern
d. old-fashioned

_____ 8. As a result of the *coup* — the forced takeover of the government — many people were killed and wounded.
a. war
b. disagreement
c. army
d. government overthrow

_____ 9. The doctor's *prognosis* was that she would have no lasting effects from her short illness.
a. fee
b. opinion about the cause of a disease
c. medical prediction
d. guess

_____ 10. The actors were dressed in the *livery* originally designed to clothe the servants of an Indonesian prince.
a. uniform
b. hat
c. shoes
d. orders

2. Context Clues for Your Own Definitions

Use clues in the sentences to write definitions for the words in italics. Do not use a dictionary.

1. Our manager showed respect for all his *subordinates,* bringing out the best work from each of us.

    Subordinates means _____

    _____.

2. May Loong showed the *dexterity* of an acrobat as she climbed the rock wall.

    Dexterity means _____

    _____.

3. Calvin is more interested in himself than in others; Tanya, on the other hand, is an *extrovert.*

    Extrovert means _____

    _____.

4. Her mother gave her the valuable object passed down through the family over many years, but Regina immediately sold the *heirloom.*

    Heirloom means _____

    _____.

5. Carlotta thought she was *prescient;* but every time she tried to tell my future, she failed badly.

    Prescient means _____

    _____.

6. She cursed and called him terrible names, leaving out no *epithets* in her anger.

    Epithets means _____

    _____.

7. The rock *fissures* — narrow cracks in the surface — filled with water and expanded when the water froze.

   Fissures means _____

   _____.

8. Comedies, Westerns, horror movies, and mysteries are some of the *genres* we study in film class.

   Genres means _____

   _____.

9. Instead of forming a single waterfall over the cliff, the water tumbled down the other side of the hill in a *cascade* over the rocks.

   Cascade means _____

   _____.

10. I do not understand how you could be so *crass* as to insult our guest by asking him to pay for his dinner.

    Crass means _____

   _____.

3b   Word Part Clues to Meaning

Occasionally two words are put together to form a new word that is not familiar to you. If you look at each word part, though, you sometimes can recognize their meanings. Then you can try to understand the meaning of the new word. For example, look at these words:

stonewall	(stone + wall)
heartwarming	(heart + warming)
lunchroom	(lunch + room)
flagpole	(flag + pole)
wildlife	(wild + life)

Often words that are new to you contain certain groups of letters that have meanings you can learn. If you don't know what the word itself means, these groups of letters may help you reach a definition.

When a group of letters with a special meaning appears in front of a word, it is called a *prefix*. When a group of letters with a special meaning appears at the end of a word, it is called a *suffix*. The *root* (or *stem*) is the basic part of a word. We add prefixes or suffixes to roots to create new words.

Look at the word *introspective*:

■ The root *spect* means "look."
■ The prefix *intro* means "within" or "inward."
■ The suffix *ive* means "to tend to" or "to lean toward."

If you knew the meanings of these word parts, you would know that *introspective* means, in a very exact sense, "to tend to look inward." You would not need a dictionary to discover that definition. When we say people are introspective, we mean that they look into and examine their own thoughts and feelings. Maybe you wouldn't be able to figure out all that from the prefix, root, and suffix, but at least you would have some idea of what the word means.

If you learn certain key prefixes, roots, and suffixes, you will have some idea of the meanings of many words without looking them up in a dictionary.

3b(1) *Important Prefixes*

The following prefixes all mean, in some way, "no" or "not":

Prefix	Meaning	Example
a	not, without	amoral
in	not	insensitive
im	not	immobile
non	not	nonreturnable
mis	wrongly	misdirected
mal	badly	malformed
anti	against	antisocial
ir	not	irresponsible
un	not	unattractive
il	not	illegal

These prefixes all deal with time:

Prefix	Meaning	Example
pre	before	prerequisite
post	after	postoperative
ante	before	antedated

These prefixes all deal with numbers:

Prefix	Meaning	Example
uni	one	unicycle
mono	one	monologue
auto	self	autograph
bi	two	bifocal
tri	three	tripod
poly	many	polygon
multi	many	multicolored

These prefixes all deal with placement:

Prefix	Meaning	Example
ab	away from	abnormal
circum	around	circumspect
com	with, together	committee
de	down from	deceit
dis	away	discharge
ex	out of	expel
inter	among	intertwine
per	through	perceive
re	again	return
sub	under	submarine
super	above	superior
trans	across	transition

3b(2) *Important Roots*

Root	Meaning	Example
cred	believe	credible
equ	equal	equate
fac, fact	do, make	factory
graph	written	monograph
mis, mit	send	missile

Root	Meaning	Example
mor, mort	die	mortify
nomen	name	nominal
port	carry	portable
pos	place	position
spec, spic	look	spectator
tang	touch	tangible
vert	turn	subvert
vid, vis	see	vision
voc	call	evoke

3b(3) *Important Suffixes*

Suffix	Meaning	Example
able ible	able to be	manageable defensible
al ance ence ic	relating to	regal resistance independence heroic
ion ism hood ity ness ment	state of, quality of	union patriotism brotherhood legality weakness puzzlement
er or ite	one who	writer advisor Mennonite
y ful	full of	soapy wishful

EXERCISES

1. Word Part Clues

Each word in the following list is made up of smaller parts. In some, two words are put together to make a new word. In others, prefixes, suffixes, and roots help make up the word. Without turning to a dictionary, use your knowledge of word part clues to write your definitions on the blank lines.

1. spaceport _____

2. teetotaler _____

3. subterranean _____

4. multidimensional _____

5. overachiever _____

6. unspeakable _____

7. equidistant _____

8. badmouth _____

9. interposed _____

10. unreachable _____

2. Word Part Clues

1. Look at the examples in **3b** on page 57. Write definitions for the words listed there, using your knowledge of the words that make up the new one. Use a separate sheet of paper. After you write your definitions, check them by looking up the words in a dictionary.
2. Look at the examples of words in the right-hand columns next to the prefixes, roots, and suffixes on pages 58–60. Using your understanding of word parts, write definitions for the words. Use a separate sheet of paper. Don't check a dictionary until you are completely finished.

3. Word Parts in Words You Know

Using separate paper, make a list of words you already know, including

1. three that begin with the prefix *in*
2. three that begin with *ex*

3. two that begin with *anti*
4. two that begin with *pre*
5. three that begin with *re*
6. two that end with *ible* or *able*
7. two that end with *hood*
8. two that end with *ism*
9. two that end in *y*
10. two that end with *ment*

4. Combining Word Parts

By combining prefixes, suffixes, and roots, make a word that means

1. state of being carried across: _____

2. not able to be believed: _____

3. not able to be touched: _____

4. send under: _____

5. not subject to death: _____

3c Denotation and Connotation

What we have been studying is the *denotation* of words — that is, what the words literally mean. *Bicycle,* for instance, means "a two-wheeled vehicle." *Addax* is "an animal that is like an antelope and that has two spiral horns."

But many words have other kinds of meaning beyond their surface meanings. The word *blue,* for example, denotes "the color of a clear sky." Beyond the denotation of the word, however, we can find many other meanings in the name of the color. We usually do not like feeling *blue,* but we may enjoy hearing a great *blues* singer. We would like to have friends who are *true blue,* to win a *blue ribbon,* and to own *blue-chip* stocks. But we might not like being called a *bluenose.* As you can see, even a simple word naming a color can have a wide range of possible meanings, depending on how we use it. This is what is meant by *connotation,* the implied (suggested) meaning of a word.

Often words with similar denotations have very different connotations. All the words in the left column below denote a person who is not a male. Yet in each case the connotation is different.

female	a member of the sex that produces eggs or bears young
woman	an adult female human being
girl	a human female who has not matured into womanhood
lady	a woman with refined habits and gentle manners
chick	a slang word for a young woman

Knowing connotations of words helps you understand language more fully than you might otherwise. You can see from the list above, for example, that *female, woman, girl, lady,* and *chick* should not be used interchangeably, even though the words share similar denotations and even though many people ignore the differences among them. Unless you are commenting on her social behavior, you'd be inaccurate if you referred to a physician who was not a man as a "lady" doctor. (If you *have* to signify the doctor's gender, *woman* would be much more accurate.) And most young women dislike being called *chicks,* although young men talking among themselves might not think twice about using the word.

A writer has many options in choosing words to make a point. Be aware that the writer's choice of one word over a similar one can influence you when you read. In fact, writers can make you feel the way *they* want you to feel about ideas and people through connotations. Dictionaries do not usually include in their definitions all the connotations of a word. That's where your own thinking comes in. You need to be able to recognize that writers who use the word *lady* where they could have used the word *woman* may be offending some members of their audience — deliberately or not.

The more you develop a sense of connotation, the better you will understand how a writer can influence your emotional reactions to words.

EXERCISES

1. Denotation and Connotation

In the following groups of sentences, the denotations of the words in italics are very similar. However, because the connotations are different, each sentence says something slightly (or not so slightly) different. Explain the meaning of each sentence by indicating the connotations and denotations of the words in italics. Use a dictionary if necessary.

1. Tammy *met* the new student.

_____

   Tammy *befriended* the new student.

_____

   Tammy *confided in* the new student.

_____

2. Cleon is *polite*.

_____

   Cleon is *urbane*.

_____

   Cleon is *slick*.

_____

3. Juana picked up her boyfriend in a *sports car*.

_____

   Juana picked up her boyfriend in a *jalopy*.

_____

   Juana picked up her boyfriend in a *limousine*.

_____

4. Michael Jiminski is a *teacher*.

_____

   Michael Jiminski is a *professor*.

_____

Michael Jiminski is a *tutor*.

_____

5. The preacher's wife *died*.

_____

The preacher's wife *passed on*.

_____

The preacher *lost* his wife.

_____

2. Denotation and Connotation

All of the words below have reasonably clear denotations, but each has a number of connotations as well. Write the denotation of the word and at least one connotation. If necessary, use a dictionary.

1. capitalism _____

_____

2. government _____

_____

3. welfare _____

_____

4. taxes _____

5. immigrant _____

_____

3d Shades of Meaning

Some words, although they seem to mean nearly the same thing, actually mean different things. If you recognize the small differences between the meanings of such words, you can understand precisely what the writer intended. For example, a writer who says *corpse* instead of *carcass* is referring to the body of a human being. Even though both words refer to dead bodies, *carcass* usually means a dead animal. The word *carcass* is used for a living or dead person only as a joke or to make fun of the person.

All of the following words indicate fear, but notice how different each is:

fright	agitated fear, suddenly brought about and lasting for a short time
dread	an uncontrollable, strong fear of something coming
terror	a violent, paralyzing fear in a dangerous situation
horror	a combination of fear and strong dislike
panic	a strong, sudden fear, often without cause and often producing thoughtless action
alarm	fright at the first sign of danger
dismay	a strong fear that robs one of the power to take effective action
consternation	a state of being helpless as a result of fear
trepidation	a great fear marked by trembling or hesitation

Use a dictionary to find the shades of meaning of a word. (Review the use of a dictionary in the Appendix.)

EXERCISES

1. Shades of Meaning in Related Words

Each word below means "to disturb or upset a person," usually "to make a person angry." Explain the shades of meaning of each word. Use a dictionary if necessary.

1. annoy _____

    _____

2. irritate _____

    _____

3. bother _____

_____

4. irk _____

_____

5. vex _____

_____

6. provoke _____

_____

7. peeve _____

_____

8. rile _____

_____

2.   Meanings of New Words: A Review

Using the vocabulary skills explained in this chapter, determine the meanings of the words in italics in the following sentences. Write the letter of the correct choice in the space provided. Do not use a dictionary.

_____ 1. Calling the city "confusing" was a *misnomer* because once you were there for a while, it was easy to find your way around.
a. a lucky guess
b. an error in naming something
c. a convenient way of talking
d. an inconvenience

_____ 2. My teacher dismissed the point as unimportant and without much content, but I thought it was *substantial.*
a. made of a foreign substance
b. having substance
c. without content
d. foolish

_____ 3. The language she suggests to alter the law changes only its surface meaning, not anything of real importance. These were only *cosmetic* changes.
a. relating to the face
b. makeup
c. relating to the cosmos
d. relating to the surface only

_____ 4. Aspirin is still very valuable in treating *maladies* such as cold, flu, virus, sinus attacks, and the ordinary headache.
a. people
b. drugs
c. situations
d. illnesses

_____ 5. Stomatis liked to *reminisce* about his early, happy life in Crete before he came to America.
a. write letters home about
b. bore everyone
c. forget
d. recall and tell past experiences

3. Finding Word Meanings in Textbooks

Each selection below comes from a textbook. As you read each piece carefully, determine the definitions of all the words in italics by using whatever clues you can. In your own words, write definitions in the spaces provided. You may not be able to get every meaning from context clues, but use a dictionary only as a last resort.

1. *Business*

A *cycle* is a repeating period of time. The term we use to describe how the economy moves from good times to bad times and back again is *business cycle*. The four stages of the business cycle are prosperity, recession, depression, and recovery. Sometimes this series of stages is like a roller coaster. For a while, everything seems to be going very well. Jobs are *plentiful*, and anyone who wants to work can find a job. People feel good about the economy and are willing to spend their money. Because people are buying, business is good. And when business is good, we say we are enjoying prosperity. *Prosperity* is the high point of a business cycle. Sometimes it's called a *boom*.

Employment is way up, the demand for goods and services is high, and businesses are turning out goods and services as fast as they can.

— Betty J. Brown and John E. Clow

a. *Cycle* means _____

_____.

b. *Business cycle* means _____

_____.

c. *Plentiful* means _____

_____.

d. *Prosperity* means _____

_____.

e. *Boom* means _____

_____.

2. *Health Education*

Stress is as much a part of life as eating or sleeping. *Stress* is the body's response to a physical or mental demand or pressure. The physical and mental demands are called *stressors.* Physical stressors might be hunger, thirst, or cold. Feeling tired, maybe from *overwork,* can be a physical stressor. Certain drugs, such as tobacco or caffeine, cause physical stress, too. Mental or emotional stressors can *trigger* the same *responses* in the body that physical stressors do. Such stressors include worry about work or school and problems in relationships. Worry about money or poor health are other causes. Even happy events may be stressful.

— Bud Getchell et al.

a. *Stress* means _____.

b. *Stressors* mean _____.

c. *Overwork* means _____.

d. *Trigger* means _____.

e. *Responses* means _____.

3. *Biology*

The smallest *structural units* of matter, living matter included, are *subatomic particles* — mainly electrons, protons, and neutrons. The next larger units are *atoms,* each of which consists of subatomic particles. Atoms in turn form still more *complex combinations* called *chemical compounds*; and these are *variously* joined together as even more *elaborate* units, or *complexes of compounds.*

These units can be regarded as representing *successively* higher levels of organization of matter. They form a pyramid, or *hierarchy,* in which any given level contains all lower levels as *components* and is itself a component of all higher levels. For example, atoms contain subatomic particles as components, and atoms are themselves components of chemical compounds.

— *Paul B. Weisz and Richard N. Keogh*

a. *Structural* means _____

_____.

b. *Unit* means _____

_____.

c. *Subatomic particles* means _____

_____.

d. *Atoms* means _____

_____.

e. *Complex* means _____

_____.

f. *Combinations* means _____

_____.

g. *Chemical compounds* means _____

_____ .

h. *Variously* means _____

_____ .

i. *Elaborate* means _____

_____ .

j. *Complexes of compounds* means _____

_____ .

k. *Successively* means _____

_____ .

l. *Hierarchy* means _____

_____ .

m. *Components* means _____

_____ .

4. *Sociology*

False definitions of individuals and groups are *perpetuated* by prejudice. *Prejudice* is a negative attitude toward an entire *category* of people, often an ethnic or racial minority. If you *resent* your roommate because he or she is sloppy, you are not necessarily guilty or prejudice. However, if you immediately *stereotype* your roommate on the basis of such characteristics as race, *ethnicity*, or religion, that is a form of prejudice.

In recent years, college campuses across the United States have been the scene of *bias-related* incidents. Student-run newspapers and radio stations have ridiculed racial and ethnic minorities; threatening literature has been stuffed under the doors of minority students; *graffiti* endorsing the views of White *supremacist* organizations such as the Ku Klux Klan have been scrawled on university walls. In some cases, there have even been violent clashes between groups of White and Black students. These *distressing* incidents serve as a reminder that prejudice is evident among both educated and uneducated members of our society (Bunzel, 1992; Hively, 1990).

Prejudice can result from *ethnocentrism* — the tendency to assume that one's culture and way of life are *superior* to all others. Ethnocentric people judge other cultures by the standards of their own group, which leads quite easily to prejudice against cultures viewed as inferior.

One important and widespread form of prejudice is *racism,* the belief that one race is *supreme* and all others are *innately inferior.* When racism *prevails* in a society, members of *subordinate* groups generally experience prejudice, discrimination, and exploitation.

— *Richard T. Schaefer**

a. *Perpetuated* means ————————————————

————————————————————————————

————————————————————————————.

b. *Prejudice* means ————————————————

————————————————————————————

————————————————————————————.

c. *Category* means ————————————————

————————————————————————————

————————————————————————————.

d. *Resent* means ————————————————

————————————————————————————

————————————————————————————.

* From *Sociology,* 5/e, by Richard T. Schaefer, copyright 1995 McGraw-Hill, Inc. Reproduced by permission of McGraw-Hill, Inc.

e. *Stereotype* means _____

_____

_____

_____.

f. *Ethnicity* means _____

_____

_____.

g. *Bias-related* means _____

_____

_____.

h. *Graffiti* means _____

_____

_____.

i. *Supremacist* means _____

_____

_____.

j. *Distressing* means _____

_____

_____.

k. *Ethnocentrism* means _____

_____

_____.

l. *Superior* means _____

_____

_____.

m. *Racism* means _____

_____

_____.

n. *Supreme* means _____

_____

_____.

o. *Innately* means _____

_____

_____.

p. *Inferior* means _____

_____

_____.

q. *Prevails* means _____

_____

_____.

r. *Subordinate* means _____

_____

_____.

> **Critical Thinking in Writing**
> Write a paragraph or two to share your thoughts and feelings about a moment in your life when you observed or experienced prejudice, ethnocentrism, or racism. First describe what happened; then write about your response to it.

5. *Psychology*

   Two reasons young children may seek the mother rather than the father when *distressed* are *familiarity* and *availability*. In most homes, even those where the father may share infant-care responsibilities, the mother has more frequent and *sustained* contact with the child. Consequently, the mother is more likely to be present to supply comfort and sympathy when they are needed in everyday "emergencies" and the child thus learns to turn to her more or less *habitually* when distressed. In a review of studies on father–infant *interaction,* Campos and others concluded that fathers can be as responsive as mothers to an infant's needs, but it is not clear that they are as responsive. One reason may be that just mentioned: they have not had as many opportunities as mothers to be responsive. Other reasons may *stem* from findings that fathers tend to respond to infants in different ways than mothers. Campos and his colleagues note the following ways that fathers and mothers differ in interacting with infants: fathers provide *bursts* of *stimulation,* mothers are more *rhythmic*; fathers respond to motor cues, mothers to social cues; fathers *engage* in more stimulating and *unpredictable* play; fathers respond more to boys, mothers to girls.

   — *Robert F. Biehler and Lynne M. Hudson*

   a. *Distressed* means _____

   _____.

   b. *Familiarity* means _____

   _____.

   c. *Availability* means _____

   _____.

d. *Sustained* means _____

_____.

e. *Habitually* means _____

_____.

f. *Interaction* means _____

_____.

g. *Stem* means _____

_____.

h. *Bursts* means _____

_____.

i. *Stimulation* means _____

_____.

j. *Rhythmic* means _____

_____.

k. *Engage* means _____

_____.

l. *Unpredictable* means _____

_____.

Critical Thinking in Writing

Write a letter to a father in which you give advice on how to improve his interactions with his child and how to be more responsive than he is now.

4. Recognizing Meanings: More Review

Using the vocabulary skills explained in **3a** through **3d**, determine the meanings of the words in italics in the following sentences. Write the definitions in your own words in the spaces provided. Do not use a dictionary.

1. I thought Van was *gullible,* but I could not get him to believe any of my stories.

   Gullible means _____

   _____.

2. David Chan's *emotionalism* makes it difficult to talk to him because every subject seems to attack his feelings.

   Emotionalism means _____

   _____.

3. My teammates insisted that my dropping the fly ball led to the most *infamous* loss of the season, but I didn't see why they thought it was so important.

   Infamous means _____

   _____.

4. When two kinds of music — for example, classical and rock — are combined to make a new style, it is known as *fusion.*

   Fusion means _____

   _____.

5. Over time, his plan for a neighborhood peace corps *evolved* from a simple idea to a fully developed program.

   Evolved means _____

   _____.

6. The past is *irretrievable*; look ahead to what you can have in the future, not back to what you would like to have from years gone by.

   Irretrievable means ————————————————————————

   ————————————————————————————.

7. The principal bears some *culpability*, or blame, for the poor behavior of the children during the visit of the official from the state education department.

   Culpability means ————————————————————————

   ————————————————————————————.

8. Should we continue the *dichotomy* between arts and science in American education, or should we try to bring the two together in new ways?

   Dichotomy means ————————————————————————

   ————————————————————————————.

9. The ideas of the great philosopher Sartre *permeate* Professor Ciapetta's own and give them substance.

   Permeate means ————————————————————————

   ————————————————————————————.

10. Some chemical compounds show *deliquescence*. Deliquescence is the act of becoming a liquid by absorbing moisture from the air.

    Deliquescence means ————————————————————————

    ————————————————————————————.

11. Robbing freely on the open road, the *highwayman* was a serious threat to travelers in England during the sixteenth century.

    Highwayman means ————————————————————————

    ————————————————————————————.

12. Ideas in philosophy are often hard to understand because illustrations of those ideas are *intangible*.

    Intangible means _____

    _____.

13. Every life has a series of high points and successes, but Ivan Karinsky insists that his has only *nadirs*.

    Nadirs means _____

    _____.

14. It is very simple to face the high costs of going to college if a rich uncle or aunt serves as your *benefactor*.

    Benefactor means _____

    _____.

15. The counselor spoke at length to the young man. She tried to reason earnestly with him about the importance of remaining in school. But clearly the *expostulation* had no effect: By the end of the week, the student had dropped out of college.

    Expostulation means _____

    _____.

16. Before its decision to stop using foam packages that people tossed as litter on our streets and highways, McDonald's was a symbol of our *throwaway* society.

    Throwaway means _____

    _____.

17. *Sycophants* (flatterers who seek their own gain) always have surrounded people in power.

    Sycophants means _____

    _____.

18. The use of the words "pass away" for "die," of "ladies' lounge" for "toilet," and of "funeral director" for "undertaker" are all examples of *euphemisms.*

   Euphemisms means _____

   _____.

19. In her chemistry class, the professor insisted that all answers be *quantitative;* no word descriptions were allowed.

   Quantitative means _____

   _____.

20. After the Montez family had faithfully paid the mortgage on their house for many years, the house was almost fully *amortized;* they owed less than $1,000.

   Amortized means _____

   _____.

5. Word Meanings from a Longer Textbook Selection

This selection from a sociology textbook deals with Native Americans. It contains a number of words in italics. Using any of the vocabulary skills explained in this chapter, determine the meanings of the words and write definitions in the spaces provided. Use a dictionary only as a last resort.

American Indians: The Native Americans

1   There are *approximately* 2 million Native Americans (or American Indians). They represent a *diverse array* of cultures *distinguishable* by language, family organization, religion, and *livelihood.* To the *outsiders* who came to the United States — European settlers and their *descendants* — the native people came to be known as "American Indians." By the time that the Bureau of Indian Affairs (BIA) was organized as part of the War Department in 1824, Indian-white relations had already included three centuries of *mutual misunderstanding* (Berg, 1975). As we saw earlier, many bloody wars took place during

the nineteenth century in which a significant part of the nation's Indian population was wiped out. By the end of the nineteenth century, schools for Indians operated by the BIA or church missions, often *segregated, prohibited* the practice of Indian cultures. Yet such schools did little to make the children effective *competitors* in white society.

2   Today, American Indians are an *impoverished* people; life is difficult whether they live in cities or on the reservation. For example, the death rate of Navajo babies over 18 weeks old is 2½ times that of the *overall* population of the United States. One Native American teenager in six has attempted suicide — a rate four times higher than the rate for other teenagers. In 1987 the National Urban Indian Council *estimated* that 60 to 80 percent of Native Americans living in cities were *unemployed.*

3   In 1972 a regional director of the Commission on Civil Rights *characterized* government policy toward Indians as "assimilate — or starve!" Indians who chose to *abandon* all *vestiges* of their tribal cultures may escape certain forms of prejudice. Those Indians who remain on the reservation and *cherish* their cultural *heritage* will suffer the *consequences* of their choice.

— Richard T. Schaefer*

Paragraph 1

1. approximately _____

    _____

2. diverse _____

    _____

3. array _____

    _____

4. distinguishable _____

    _____

---

*From *Sociology*, 5/e, by Richard T. Schaefer, copyright 1995 McGraw-Hill, Inc. Reproduced by permission of McGraw-Hill, Inc.

5. livelihood _____

_____

6. outsiders _____

_____

7. descendants _____

_____

8. mutual _____

_____

9. misunderstanding _____

_____

10. segregated _____

_____

11. prohibited _____

_____

12. competitors _____

_____

Paragraph 2

1. impoverished _____

2. overall _____

3. estimated _____

4. unemployed _____

Paragraph 3

1. characterized _____

   _____

2. assimilate _____

   _____

3. abandon _____

   _____

4. vestiges _____

   _____

5. cherish _____

   _____

6. heritage _____

   _____

7. consequences _____

   _____

Critical Thinking in Writing

How have the movies portrayed Native Americans? Write a page describing the view of Native Americans taken in *one* film (or television program) that you have seen. Does the film support any of the points in this selection?

Building a Strong Vocabulary

A. In the space provided to the left of each numbered item, write the letter of the sentence that, through context clues, best helps you arrive at the meaning of the word. Then, write a definition of the word in the space at the right of each word. Count 5 points for each correct answer.

_____ 1. averted _____

   a. She averted her eyes as her grandmother began to cry.
   b. Because of mounting debts, the firm averted disaster by declaring bankruptcy. Some believe that the bankruptcy strategy is the best way to deal with financial issues.
   c. As the car ahead came to a sudden stop, Tom averted an accident by swerving into a ditch.
   d. New taxes averted the school crisis until next year's vote.

_____ 2. chaos _____

   a. I can find items in the chaos of this cabinet.
   b. After the earthquake, the town was in a state of chaos — that is, total disorder.
   c. Many people were surprised by the chaos at the rock concert.
   d. There is chaos on my desk but my brother's desk is the same.

_____ 3. imagery _____

   a. English teachers encourage their students to use imagery in their writing.
   b. People often buy new products because of the imagery in the ads.
   c. The speaker's imagery helped us appreciate the beauty of the Swiss Alps. Descriptions that produce mental pictures always stimulate an audience.

d. A poet's use of imagery brings poetry alive for the reader.

_____ 4. convivial _____

a. The picnickers became convivial as they shared their food, their cooking utensils, and their experiences on the mountain.
b. Last July 4, the convivial atmosphere at the parade prevailed throughout the day.
c. A square dance usually puts people in a convivial — festive and merry — mood.
d. You seem to be feeling very convivial today.

_____ 5. transcend _____

a. A person's ability to transcend (rise above) the cares of this world is both a philosophical and a religious belief.
b. Helen Keller was able to transcend her physical state.
c. We must transcend our limits.
d. His genius was that he forced himself to transcend bodily concerns.

B. A prefix, suffix, or root is underlined in each item below. In the space provided, write the letter of the word or words that best define the underlined word part.

_____ 1. <u>in</u>distinct
a. badly
b. wrongly
c. not
d. easily

_____ 2. companion<u>ship</u>
a. one who
b. full of
c. state of being
d. without

_____ 3. <u>tri</u>o
a. three
b. two

c. outside of
d. inside of

_____ 4. inspection

a. name
b. write
c. speak
d. look

_____ 5. sensible

a. in favor of
b. able to be
c. full of
d. quality of

C. Select the correct word, based on its denotation and connotation. Write the letter of the correct word in the space provided.

1. Our mother's good food made us content, _____ children.

a. obese
b. brawny
c. husky
d. swollen

2. Into the opposition's line of defense charged the_____ quarterback.

a. obese
b. brawny
c. plump
d. husky

3. On short, unsteady legs, the _____ puppies frolicked with the children.

a. obese
b. plump
c. husky
d. swollen

4. He became _____ after years of using food as a comfort for his problems.

   a. obese
   b. brawny
   c. plump
   d. husky

5. The large eyes and _____ bellies of half-starved Third World children waiting for rice and milk from volunteers made us grateful for what we have.

   a. plump
   b. husky
   c. swollen
   d. brawny

D. Each word below describes a quiet, undisturbed state, but there are differences in shades of meaning among the words. Select the letter of the word being defined in items 1–5 and write the letter in the space provided.

a. serene   _____ 1. motionless; not able to move

b. lethargic   _____ 2. unconscious

c. immobile   _____ 3. peaceful; tranquil

d. placid   _____ 4. sluggish; dull

e. comatose   _____ 5. calm and unemotional

Score: _____ correct × 5 points each = _____

UNIT **1**   REVIEW TEST

Read the following selection, "Pavlov's Discovery," about a famous experiment to find out why dogs salivated when no food was present. This experiment gave rise to an important theory in psychology. Follow instructions, as indicated, before and after you read.

A.   Before You Read

1.   On a separate page, do prereading of your choice.

2.   Preview the selection on pages 89–91 and write answers to the questions below.

a.   What do the introductory information (above under "Review Test") and title tell you about the

reading? _____

_____

_____.

b.   What does the caption for Figure 1.1 tell you?

_____

_____.

c.   What does the caption for Figure 1.2 tell you?

_____

_____.

d.   What does each phase refer to?

1.   Phase 1 _____

2.   Phase 2 _____

3.   Phase 3 _____

88

e. What key words in the five paragraphs do the writ-

ers place in italics or boldface? _____

_____

_____

_____

_____.

Pavlov's Discovery

1   Pavlov is one of the best-known figures in psychology, but he was not a psychologist. A Russian physiologist, Pavlov won a Nobel Prize in 1904 for his work on the physiology of dogs' digestive systems. During his research, Pavlov noticed a strange phenomenon: his dogs sometimes salivated when no food was present — for example, when they saw the assistant who normally brought their food.

2   Pavlov devised a simple experiment to determine how salivation could occur in the absence of an obvious physical cause. First he performed an operation to divert a dog's saliva into a container, so that the amount secreted could be measured precisely. He then confined the dog in the apparatus shown in Figure 1.1. The experiment had three phases.

3   In the first phase of the experiment, Pavlov and his associates (Anrep, 1920) confirmed that when meat powder was placed on the dog's tongue, the dog salivated, but that it did not salivate in response to a neutral stimulus — a white lab coat or a musical tone, for example. Thus, the researchers established the existence of the two basic components for Pavlov's experiment: a natural reflex (the dog's salivation when food was placed on its tongue) and a neutral stimulus (the sound of the tone). A *reflex* is the swift, automatic response to a stimulus, such as shivering in the cold or jumping when you are jabbed with a needle. A *neutral stimulus* is one that initially does not elicit the reflex being studied, although it may elicit other responses. For example, when the tone is first sounded, the dog pricks up its ears, turns toward the sound, and sniffs around; but it does not salivate.

4   It was the second and third phases of the experiment that

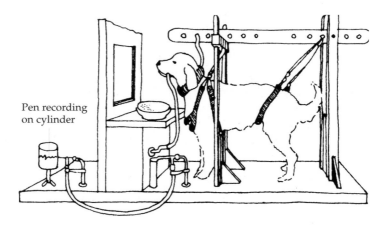

FIGURE 1.1
Apparatus Used in Pavlov's Experiments
Dogs were surgically prepared and then placed in a harness. Saliva flowed
into a tube inserted in the dog's cheek. The amount of saliva secreted was then
recorded by a pen attached to a slowly moving drum of paper.

Phase I: Before conditioning has occurred

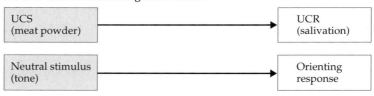

Phase II: The process of conditioning

Phase III: After conditioning has occurred

FIGURE 1.2
Classical Conditioning
Before classical conditioning has occurred, meat powder on a dog's tongue
produces salivation, but the sound of a musical tone — a neutral stimulus —
does not. During the process of conditioning, the tone is paired on numerous
trials with the meat powder. After classical conditioning has taken place, the
sound of the tone alone acts as a conditioned stimulus, producing salivation.

showed how one type of learning can occur. In the second phase, the tone was sounded and then meat powder was quickly placed in the dog's mouth. The dog salivated. This *pairing* — the tone followed immediately by meat powder — was repeated several times. In the third phase of the experiment the tone was sounded alone, and the dog again salivated, even though no meat powder was presented. In other words, the tone by itself now elicited salivation, as if the tone predicted the presentation of the meat powder.

5   Pavlov's experiment was the first demonstration of what today is called **classical conditioning** — a procedure in which a neutral stimulus is paired with a stimulus that already triggers a reflexive response until the previously neutral stimulus alone provokes a similar response. Figure 1.2 shows the basic elements of classical conditioning. The stimulus that elicits a response without conditioning, like the meat powder in Pavlov's experiment, is called the **unconditioned stimulus (UCS).** The automatic, unlearned reaction to this stimulus is called the **unconditioned response (UCR).** The new stimulus after being paired with the unconditioned stimulus is called the **conditioned stimulus (CS),** and the response it comes to elicit is a **conditioned response (CR).**

— *Douglas A. Bernstein et al.*

B. Reading Helpers

Fill in the blanks with sentences that will produce an outline of the selection.

I.   Pavlov, a Russian physiologist, noted that dogs sometimes salivated when no food was present.

II. He performed a simple experiment.

    A. _____

    _____

    B. _____

III. In the first phase of the experiment, dogs salivated but not in response to a neutral stimulus.

    A. The researchers identified two components for Pavlov's experiment.

1. _____

_____

2. _____

_____

B. A reflex is the swift automatic response to a stimulus.

C. _____

_____

IV. Phases II and III showed how a type of learning occurs.

A. In Phase II meat was put on the tongue after the tone sounded.

1. _____

2. Researchers repeated the pairing of tone and meat powder many times.

B. _____

V. Pavlov's experiment was the first to show classical conditioning, which is a procedure in which a neutral stimulus, paired with a reflexive response stimulus, ultimately produces a similar response to the neutral stimulus.

C. Context Clues

Using context clues, determine the definitions of the words in italics below and write the letter of the correct choice in the space provided.

_____ 1. A strange *phenomenon* (par. 1)
a. psychologist
b. occurrence
c. digestion
d. assistant

_____ 2. Dogs sometimes *salivated* (par. 1)
    a. barked at the assistants
    b. jumped up and down
    c. produced saliva
    d. reduced the amount of saliva production

_____ 3. *Divert* a dog's saliva (par. 2)
    a. collect
    b. measure
    c. reroute
    d. deodorize

_____ 4. The amount *secreted* (par. 2)
    a. given off as fluid
    b. told in secret
    c. collected
    d. determined

_____ 5. Measured *precisely* (par. 2)
    a. quickly
    b. thoughtfully
    c. with a ruler
    d. exactly

_____ 6. Pavlov and his associates *confirmed* (par. 3)
    a. discovered
    b. made certain
    c. experimented
    d. made appropriate

_____ 7. Two basic *components* (par. 3)
    a. parts
    b. composers
    c. scientists
    d. experiments

_____ 8. A *reflex* (par. 3)
    a. a white lab coat
    b. the sound of the tone
    c. an established research program
    d. swift response to a stimulus

_____ 9. *Elicited* salivation (par. 4)
      a. prevented
      b. brought about
      c. illustrated
      d. threatened

_____ 10. *Provokes* a similar response (par. 5)
      a. puzzles
      b. predicts
      c. causes
      d. withdraws

Using context clues, write in the space provided definitions for the words below.

12. neutral stimulus _____

_____

13. classical conditioning _____

_____

_____

14. unconditioned stimulus (UCS) _____

_____

15. unconditioned response (UCR) _____

_____

16. conditioned stimulus (CS) _____

_____

17. conditioned response (CR) _____

_____

Score: _____ correct × 3⅓ points each = _____

Unit Two

Basic
Comprehension

4

Visual Aids

Readings can contain more than just words arranged in sentences and paragraphs. Pictures, graphs, tables, charts, maps, and diagrams often add to the meaning of the main text. Often, a caption — a brief explanation in words — accompanies the visual aid and highlights its most important elements. Knowing how to read visual aids and how to relate them to the ideas of the selection can help you get more from your reading.

Each visual aid carries a message in itself, but the message also connects with the ideas and information in the main text in some way. Sometimes a picture or diagram simply illustrates or reinforces a point made in the text. A newspaper article describing a meeting between the leaders of two Latin American countries, for example, may be accompanied by a picture of them shaking hands and smiling.

In other cases, visual aids add new but related information that helps enrich your understanding of the points made by the main text. This is true of the photographs and graph that accompany the selection from a health education textbook on pages 17–22.

Sometimes an essential part of the reading is visual in nature. In this case an illustration may best represent the point. In cartoons and advertisements, for example, illustrations work hand in hand with words.

Finally, the visual aid may be the most important part of the selection — the words only help explain the picture. This is the case, for example, in instructions for putting together a stereo set or a child's toy. In such instances, the words only explain what the illustration shows.

Visual Aids: A Review Chart

Type	Purpose	How to Use
Photograph	To show people, places, or events that support written information	Ask questions: Who are the people? What are they doing? What are their moods? Why is the photograph included? What does the caption say?
Diagram	To present a visual with labeled parts that explain how something works	Study labels and captions. Figure out how parts of the object relate to one another and to the whole.
Word chart	To present information in summary form, to make material easy to find	Examine title of chart carefully. Study column headings. Fill in necessary or omitted words to make sense of the points.
Statistical table	To present numbers in chart form	Examine title and column headings carefully. Study captions. Create sentences to explain numbers to yourself. Compare numbers in the various columns and state how they are related. Which are bigger? Which are smaller?

Type	Purpose	How to Use
Graph	To present statistics visually — with lines, bars, or circles — so that number relations are clear	Study labels and captions carefully. Determine why certain visuals are smaller or larger than others. For example, why is one bar smaller than another? Why is one piece of a circle (or pie) larger than another?

EXERCISES

1. Reading a Word Chart

Examine the word chart on pages 98–99. Then answer the questions below.

1. What does the word chart attempt to show?

_____

2. What are the three columns in the chart?

_____

3. What are the five different kinds of visual aids listed?

_____

_____

4. What, according to the chart, is the purpose of a word chart?

_____

_____

5. In your opinion, does the chart fit the purpose you described in answer 4 above? Explain your answer.

_____

_____

2. Visual Aids in Textbooks

Read this selection from an economics book. Look carefully at the graph and table. Then answer the questions that follow.

The Definition of Poverty

If income or per capita income is to be used as a measure of poverty, then the proper definition of *income* must be used. Economists can measure income before any government intervention affecting the distribution of income, after accounting for government cash transfers, or after accounting for government cash transfers and assistance like food or shelter.

The first of these measurements indicates what people would earn from the market system in the absence of government intervention. To obtain a good measure of this income figure is virtually impossible because the government is such an important part of the economic system in almost all countries, including the United States. The U.S. government transfers over $400 billion annually from taxpayers to various groups.

Poverty statistics published by the federal government are based on incomes that include earnings from cash transfers but often not in-kind transfers. **Cash transfers** are unearned funds given to certain sectors of the population. They include social security retirement benefits, disability pensions, and unemployment compensation to those who are temporarily out of work. **In-kind transfers,** or noncash transfers, are services or products provided to certain sectors of society. They include food purchased with food stamps and medical services provided under Medicaid. Although economists agree that these in-kind transfers increase the economic well-being of those who receive them, there is much debate over how they should be accounted for and the extent to which they should be added to money income for the purpose of defining *poverty*. For example, the official poverty rate measure does not account for in-kind transfers. If it did, the 1990 rate of 13.5 percent of the U.S. population who are in poverty would have been 11.0 percent.[1]

The U.S. government uses after-transfers income to measure poverty, but does not include all such transfers. It adds market earnings, the cash equivalent of noncash transfers, and cash transfers to calculate family incomes. But it does not include

cash transfers: money allocated away from one group in society to another

in-kind transfers: the allocation of goods and services from one group in society to another

[1] *Economic Report of the President, 1992,* p. 143.

TABLE 1   Average Income Poverty Cutoffs for a Nonfarm
Family of Four in the United States, 1959–1993

YEAR	POVERTY LEVEL	YEAR	POVERTY LEVEL
1959	$2,973	1982	$ 9,862
1960	3,022	1983	10,178
1966	3,317	1984	10,609
1969	3,743	1985	10,989
1970	3,968	1986	11,203
1975	5,500	1987	11,611
1976	5,815	1988	12,090
1977	6,191	1989	12,675
1978	6,662	1990	13,359
1979	7,412	1991	13,924
1980	8,414	1992	13,950
1981	9,287	1993	14,764

SOURCES: U.S. Bureau of the Census, *Current Population Reports*, series P-60, no. 174 (Washington, D.C.: U.S. Government Printing Office, 1992); *Social Security Bulletin*, Spring 1995.

food stamps, aid to families with dependent children (AFDC), or housing subsidies. In sum, the poverty measure is arbitrary. It is an arbitrary level of income, and income is an arbitrary measure of the ability to purchase necessities.

Table 1 lists the average poverty levels of income for a nonfarm family of four since 1959. Families with incomes above the cutoffs would be above the poverty level, in the eyes of the federal government.

Where does the arbitrary poverty income level come from? A 1955 study found that the average family in the United States spent about one-third of its income on food, so when the government decided to begin measuring poverty in the 1960s, it calculated the cost to purchase a meal that met a predetermined nutritional standard and multiplied that cost by 3. That is where it drew the poverty line. Since then, the official poverty-line income has been adjusted for inflation each year. In 1993, a family of four whose income, measured as noted above, fell below $14,764 was defined as being in poverty.

Poverty Distribution and Economic Trends How many Americans fall below the poverty line? In 1994, more than 39 million U.S. residents received incomes that were lower than the cutoff. Figure 1 compares the number of people living in poverty and the percentage of the total population living in poverty (the incidence of poverty) for each year from 1960 to

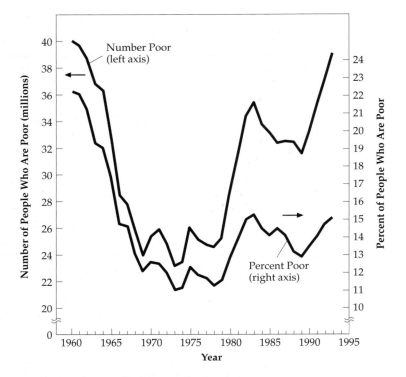

FIGURE 1 The Trends of Poverty Incidence The number of people classified as living in poverty is measured on the left vertical axis. The percentage of the population classified as living in poverty is measured on the right vertical axis. The number and the percentage declined steadily throughout the 1960s, rose during the recessions of 1969, 1974, 1981, and 1990 and fell during the economic growth between 1982 and 1990. Sources: U.S. Bureau of the Census, *Current Population Reports* (Washington, D.C.: U.S. Government Printing Office, 1994); *Economic Report of the President, 1995.*

1994. From 1960 to the late 1970s, the incidence of poverty declined rapidly. From the late 1970s until the early 1980s, the incidence of poverty rose; it then began to decline again after 1982. Small upswings in the incidence of poverty occurred in 1968 and 1974, and a large rise occurred between 1978 and 1982. It then fell until 1990, when the U.S. once again dipped into recession. It has continued to rise even as the economy grew in 1993 and 1994.

The health of the economy is a primary determinant of the incidence of poverty.

A major factor accounting for the incidence of poverty is the health of the economy. The economy grew at a fairly sustained rate between 1960 and 1969 and from 1982 through 1990. During both growth periods, the poverty rate fell. But from 1992 to 1994, the rate rose even as the economy improved. This surprised the U.S. Census Bureau officials who said, "This is somewhat surprising." They had expected the rate to fall.[2]

People are generally made better off by economic growth. Economic stagnation and recession throw the relatively poor out of their jobs and into poverty. Economic growth increases the number of jobs and draws people out of poverty and into the mainstream of economic progress.

Four recent recessions have had important impacts on the numbers of people thrown into poverty. The recession of 1969–1970 was relatively mild. Between 1969 and 1971, the unemployment rate rose from 3.4 to 5.8 percent, and the total number of people unemployed rose from 2,832,000 to 5,016,000. This recession halted the decline in poverty rates for two years. When the economy once again began to expand, the poverty rates dropped. The 1974 recession brought on another bout of unemployment that threw people into poverty. The 1974 recession was relatively serious, causing the unemployment rate to rise to 8.3 percent by 1975 and the number of unemployed to rise to 7,929,000. Once again, however, the poverty rate declined as the economy picked up after 1975. The recession of 1980–1982 threw the economy off track again. In 1979, the total number of people unemployed was 6,137,000; by 1982, a whopping 10,717,000 were without jobs. As the economy came out of this recession, the poverty rate began to decline, and it continued to decline as the economy grew throughout the 1980s. However, the poverty rate rose as the economy fell into recession in 1990 and struggled into 1992. The poverty rate of 14.2 percent in 1991 was the highest level in nearly three decades; the number of people living in poverty grew to 35.7 million.[3] Somewhat surprising was that the number of people in poverty and the incidence of poverty both grew in 1993 and 1994, years of economic growth. Some people point to this as evidence that the poverty measure is flawed, that it does not give an accurate indication of who and how many do not get proper nutrition and health care. Some argue that the poverty rate is really not nearly as high as these figures indicate; that government transfers and programs are not properly taken into account. Others argue that it is an indication that government programs must be increased, that not enough care is taken to

[2]"Number of Poor Rises Despite Recession's End," M. L. Usdansky, *USA Today,* October 7, 1994, p. 1A.
[3]U.S. Bureau of the Census, *Statistical Abstract of the United States, 1994* (Washington, D.C.: U.S. Government Printing Office, 1994). *Social Security Bulletin, Annual Statistical Supplement,* 1994.

Incomes are unequally distributed in every nation. In less developed nations, the distinction between rich and poor is greater than in the industrial nations, although the per capita income is significantly less in the LDCs. For instance, although the per capita income in Nigeria is only 7 percent of the per capita income in the United States, the wealthy in Lagos, Nigeria, live very well, with large houses, servants, expensive clothes, and other accouterments of wealth. During the 1970s, many Nigerians became very wealthy as the price of oil surged and Nigerian oil production rose. Economic crisis and the collapse of oil prices since the late 1970s has led to a decline in Nigeria that wiped out the gains of the previous twenty years.   © M. BERTINETTI / PHOTO RESEARCHERS, INC.

provide for the poor. Still others point to the increase in the number of people working full time who do not earn more than the poverty level. Nearly 18 percent of the nation's full-time workers earned less than $14,000 in 1994 while only 12 percent were less than that figure (in real terms) in 1980. These numbers indicate how the pay for unskilled jobs has declined over the last decade.

There are many controversies over the poverty measure. The measure makes no distinction between the needs of a three-month-old and a fourteen-year-old or between a rural family in a cold climate and an urban family in the subtropics. It draws no distinction between income and purchasing power. A welfare mom living on $400 a month is treated identically to a graduate student who earns $400 a month at a part-time job and borrows an additional $1,500 from her parents. Nor does it consider the problem of income from the underground economy — the income not reported or measured in income statistics. Nevertheless, the measure is used to determine how federal government money is to be allocated among states and regions and is used to support or not support anti-poverty programs.

— *William Boyes and Michael Melvin*

1. What does Table 1 show? _____

_____

_____

2. If a family of four earned $13,925 in 1991, how would the government view their status on the poverty line? _____

_____

3. Why do the writers present this poverty information in table form? _____

_____

_____

_____

4. Why do the writers call the definition of poverty arbitrary?

_____

_____

_____

5. What does the graph in Figure 1 represent? _____

_____

_____

_____

6. In 1994, how many people did the government place in the poverty category? What percentage of the population fit the

poverty category? _____

_____

_____

7. Why — despite the criticism and controversy — is the poverty measure so important? _____

_____

_____

_____

8. Why do the writers represent the poverty information in graph form (Figure 1)? _____

_____

_____

_____

_____

9. Why do the writers provide text paragraphs as comments on the graph? _____

_____

10. What does the photograph on page 104 illustrate? _____

_____

_____

_____

Critical Thinking in Writing

What have you learned about poverty from the selection you have just read? Use information from the graph and table as well as from the text to write a paragraph or so on what you learned.

Visual Aids

In the space provided, write the letter of the correct answer. Use the map on page 109 to complete the sentences that follow it. Count 20 points for each correct answer.

_____ 1. The map shows

    a. changes in Israel's borders.
    b. changes in Israel's weather.
    c. occupation of Israel by different nations.
    d. Middle East trade routes.

_____ 2. The nation of Israel before 1967 is represented by

    a. the striped area.
    b. the dark area.
    c. the dark and white areas.
    d. the white area.

_____ 3. The dots on the map represent

    a. places of interest.
    b. cities.
    c. towns.
    d. airports.

_____ 4. The stars on the map represent capital cities. The capital of Jordan is

    a. Beirut.
    b. Damascus.
    c. Amman.
    d. Aqaba.

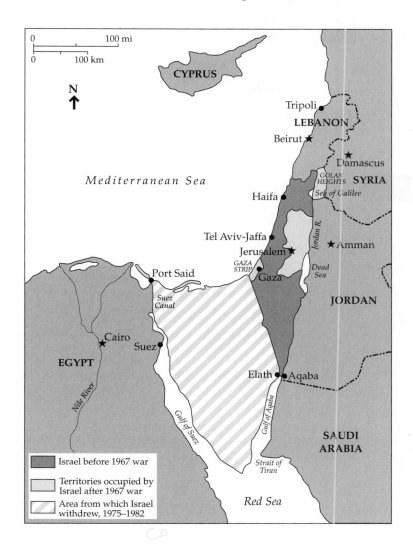

_____ 5. The area from which Israel withdrew in the late 1970s is

a. the Dead Sea.
b. the Golan Heights.
c. the Sinai Peninsula.
d. Haifa.

Score: _____ correct × 20 points each = _____

5

Reading for the Main Idea

5a ## Key Ideas in Sentences

Although a sentence can give a great deal of information, it usually offers one key idea. Readers must be able to find key ideas in order to understand sentence meanings clearly.

The key idea of a sentence usually tells

■ who a person or what an object is.
■ what a person or an object is doing.

> Toshio, in a clean white suit, slowly sat down on the leather chair outside the door of Miss Sanchez's office.

This sentence tells about Toshio. We know that he sat down. All the information about his appearance, about where he sat, and about whose office he sat near adds details. These are helpful in completing the scene for the reader, and very often we need to rely on details to make the main text more clear. But the key idea, the main thought, in the sentence is simply *Toshio sat down*.

Here is how to find key ideas in sentences:

■ Ask *who* or *what* the sentence is about.
■ Ask what the person or object is doing or what is happening to that person or object.
■ Learn to separate minor details from the main idea. Many words in sentences describe things about the subject of the sentence; they simply add details around it. If you ask *when, what kind, where, how,* or *why,* you will find details. This makes it easier to separate the key idea.

>   *(why)*   *(what kind)*
> As a result of new guidelines, many students
>   *(where)*   *(when)*
> on college campuses can now receive financial benefits
>   *(how)*
> by meeting special government standards.

110

Who or what is the sentence about? *Students.* What do the students do? *Receive benefits.* The key idea is *students receive benefits.*

Of course, you cannot always easily decide which details are simply descriptive and which contribute markedly to the key idea. You'll have to make your own decision about how various elements influence sentence meanings. In stating a key idea, you may have to shift words in the sentence around, summarize parts of the sentence, or put some of the writer's words into your own words.

The starting point for determining the key idea in a sentence, however, is finding who or what the sentence is about and what that person or object is doing.

EXERCISES

1. Key Ideas in Sentences

In each of the following sentences, underline the words that help give the key idea. Here is an example:

Children who play on city streets face dangers regularly, even when they are supervised.

1. Our nation's health care system must move to redress the inadequate attention paid to women's health concerns.

— *Leonard Abramson*

2. Because food is one of the great pleasures Taiwan has to offer, we go to one of the local restaurants such as Ching Ye that serve Taiwanese specialties.

— *Cho-Liang Lin*

3. The greater visibility of Hispanics in the cultural landscape is a reminder that the roots of Spanish culture go deep into American life, especially in that spawning ground of the national self-image, the West.

— *Time*

4. Without the guidance and comfort of the wives and mothers, life on the Llaho would have been unbearable, and a great debt is owed to the brave pioneer women who ventured into the cruel life of the plains, far from contact with the outer world.

— *Fabiola Cabeza deBaca*

5. Voters in thirty-nine California counties encountered ballots in Spanish and Chinese for the first time in the elections of 1980, much to their surprise, since authorizing legislation had been passed by Congress with almost no public discussion.

    — S. I. Hayakawa

2. Key Ideas in Textbooks

The following sentences come from basic college textbooks. On the lines, in your own words, write the key idea of each statement.

1. *American History*
    In response to growing protests that black citizens were being denied full rights, Congress in 1957 passed the first civil rights law since Reconstruction.

    — Henry F. Graff

    _____

    _____

2. *Psychology*
    There is a high correlation between the prejudices of parents and those of their children, because parents often consciously or unconsciously (through modeling) train their children to be prejudiced.

    — Clifford T. Morgan, Richard A. King, and Nancy H. Robinson

    _____

3. *Business*
    Economists had complained that the regulation of the trucking industry since 1935 by the Interstate Commerce Commission had resulted in gross inefficiencies.

    — Mansel G. Blackford and K. Austin Kerr

    _____

4. *Biology*
    Most of the information ultimately controlling cellular processes resides in *chromosomes*, the main nuclear organelles.

    — Paul B. Weisz and Richard N. Keogh

    _____

5. *Educational Psychology*
Many psychological researchers have ventured beyond familiar Western middle-class locations to study learning in widely
different settings, both in different countries and in the United
States.

— *N. L. Gage and David C. Berliner*

5b   Topics and Main Ideas in Paragraphs

A *paragraph* is a group of sentences about some related subject
or topic. Each sentence states some idea about the *topic*, and all
those ideas add up to an overall *main idea* of the paragraph.

A main idea is not simply a topic. A topic is just the general
subject that a paragraph deals with. A main idea is the statement
the paragraph makes about the topic. You often can state a topic
in a single word; but to state a main idea clearly, you usually
need a sentence. The topic of the following paragraph is, simply,
"Mexican Americans"; but you would have to state the main
idea more fully: "As Mexican Americans grow in number and
become more aware of their ethnic identity, they are turning the
Southwest into another Mexico."

Be aware that a main idea is not a statement of absolute fact.
Writers usually project their opinions about a topic in the main
idea statement. Good readers learn to see the writer's opinion
as part of the main idea; they look within the paragraph for the
facts and details that support that opinion (see **6a** and **12a**).

In the following paragraph it is the writer's *opinion* that the
Southwest is becoming another Mexico. Some people might disagree with that opinion; others might support it. In any case, the
opinion is part of the paragraph's main idea.

> Too little known, Mexican-Americans also are too often misun-
> derstood. But that is changing. In a decade they have become
> a phenomenon to be reckoned with. As their numbers swell
> and their ethnic awareness grows, they are transforming much
> of the U.S. Southwest into Mexico U.S.A.
>
> — *Griffin Smith, Jr.*

To understand the meaning of a paragraph, readers must
identify, first, the topic of the paragraph and, next, the main idea
being presented about that topic. The topic may be stated in only
a word or two, naming a thing, person, or event discussed

throughout the paragraph. The main idea, however, is a more complete statement that ties all the ideas and information in the paragraph together.

In a paragraph, the main idea may be stated directly in a sentence or may only be implied in the overall message of all the sentences. When the main idea is stated directly, you need only locate the main idea sentence. When the main idea is implied, you must figure out the topic of the paragraph and the idea being stated about that topic. Later in this chapter you will see examples of paragraphs with both stated and implied main ideas. For now, however, practice seeing the difference between a topic and a main idea.

EXERCISES

Topic and Main Idea

For each of the following selections from textbooks, state the topic and then the main idea. Use a separate sheet of paper.

1. Sherlock Holmes likened the brain to the attic of a house, in which we store all the things we know. The fictional detective, who was a master of memory, emphasized that to be able to find the information we need, we must stock our brain attic with great care. What Holmes referred to as the "brain attic" is what psychologists today call long-term memory — and, more specifically, declarative memory. Research has shown that Holmes was right in recommending that we stock the attic carefully. Unless information is carefully coded and filed, it will be impossible to retrieve the information when we need it. The task would be like trying to find a book in a large library where the volumes are arranged randomly and the card catalogue is disorganized.
    — *Zick Rubin, Letitia Anne Peplau, and Peter Salovey*

Topic: _____

Main idea: _____

_____

2. Many people want to live and work in this country because they see it as a land of opportunity, a place where they can

find work to help them support their families. Immigrants generally enter the United States in one of three ways. Most people enter legally with permission from the INS. Trained doctors, engineers, and professional people are usually allowed to immigrate if they have jobs waiting for them. Others may have to wait before they may enter. Other immigrants enter under special circumstances, for example, as political refugees. Many people from Cuba, Vietnam, and Haiti have entered the United States as political refugees. Last of all, some people enter the country illegally, slipping across our borders undetected by the border guards. Others may enter the country legally as migratory farm workers, and then decide to stay here illegally.

— *Betty J. Brown and John E. Clow*

Topic: _____

Main idea: _____

3. From 1860 until approximately 1875, dime novels cost ten cents, ran about 100 pages in small format (about seven by five inches), and were aimed at adults. By 1875, publishers discovered that boys were the most avid readers, though adults, too, bought them. Thereafter, publishers concentrated on the younger audience, dropping the price to a nickel (though the public continued to call them dime novels, mostly out of habit) and cutting costs. The result was a nickel (or half-dime) novel of sixteen or thirty-two pages, usually part of a series and featuring one fictional hero, Diamond Dick, Fred Fearnot, Buffalo Bill, or some other equally fascinating and impossible character. The cover portrayed in lurid black and white (color came later) some heroic act of derring-do or a villainous performance of darkest evil.

— *Kenneth L. Donnelson and Aileen Pace Nilsen*

Topic: _____

Main idea: _____

_____

_____

4. Physical science texts tend to assume that you have a working understanding of scientific inquiry. These texts assume that

you know how basic laws, facts, and principles are discovered and that you understand the relationship between basic principles and their supporting proofs. In addition, authors typically assume that you have background knowledge from previous chapters in their book, from high-school courses, or from other college courses. These assumptions make reviewing a vital part of studying scientific material. Finally, science texts assume that you can quickly decode new and unusual words and understand their meaning. Authors often use a new word in the very next sentence to define yet another word.

— *Sherrie L. Nist and William Diehl*

Topic: _____

Main idea: _____

_____

5.   Left-handed people — about 10 percent of people in all cultures and throughout history (Coren, 1992) — present a paradox. On the one hand (if you can forgive the pun), left-handers have often demonstrated special talents. Left-handers have been great painters (Leonardo da Vinci, Picasso), outstanding performers (Marilyn Monroe, Jimi Hendrix), and even presidents (Ronald Reagan, George Bush). (As these examples suggest, left-handedness is considerably more common among males than among females.) And left-handedness has been reported to be twice as common among children who are mathematical prodigies as it is in the overall population (Benbow, 1988). On the other hand, left-handers have often been viewed as clumsy and accident-prone. They "flounder about like seals out of water," wrote one British psychologist (Burt, 1937, p. 287). The very word for "left-handed" in French — *gauche* — also means "clumsy." Because of such negative attitudes toward left-handedness, in previous decades parents and teachers often encouraged children who showed signs of being left-handed to write with their right hands.

— *Zick Rubin, Letitia Anne Peplau, and Peter Salovey*

Topic: _____

Main idea: _____

_____

> **Critical Thinking in Writing**
> If you're left-handed, discuss in a paragraph how you feel about being left-handed — whether it's a problem or something you're proud of. If you're right-handed, describe in a paragraph how suddenly turning into a left-hander might affect your life.

5b(1) Stated Main Ideas

Often one sentence in a paragraph tells the reader exactly what the rest of the paragraph deals with and therefore gives the main idea. This *main idea sentence* (often called a *topic sentence* or *topic statement*) can appear in one of several places.

Main Idea in the Beginning

The present inability of black political and civil rights leaders to cope with the persistent and deepening problems of American racism has many causes. Within the last decades there has been an abrupt loss of most of the major and charismatic black leaders. Martin Luther King, Jr., was assassinated just as he was seeking more effective methods to deal with the bedeviling problems of Northern and urban racism. Whitney M. Young, Jr., of the National Urban League, died suddenly as he was developing plans to make corporate leaders more sensitive and responsive to their pragmatic self-interest in seeking the goals of racial justice. Roy Wilkins retired after a long and productive tenure as leader of the N.A.A.C.P., and his successor, Benjamin Hooks, has not demonstrated a similar capacity. With the retirement of James Farmer, the Congress on Racial Equality soon became a separatist cult virtually indistinguishable from the racists whom the organization had fought so courageously. Malcolm X was murdered as he was seeking a way to become a rational and effective ally of other civil rights leaders.

— *Kenneth B. Clark*

The main idea of this passage is that *there are many causes underlying the inability of black leaders to cope with racism.* All the sentences in the paragraph illustrate that idea by providing lots of details.

Main Idea in the Middle

Your description must create sense impressions for your readers. Remember that there are still five senses, even though our civilization may have dulled their keenness. Most of us tend to be visually minded, thinking of description primarily in terms of what we see. *But the sensations of sound and scent, touch and flavor, can be essential in descriptions.* Imagine trying to tell a foreigner about the fun of an American country fair. If you described only what you saw, you would have to omit much of the experience — the shouts of the barkers at the amusement concessions and the clatter of the machinery for the various rides; the odors from the food stands, the barns, and the crowd; the spicy flavor of the hot dogs and the intense sweetness of the cotton candy; and everywhere the grittiness of the dust stirred up by hundreds of feet.

— *Louise E. Rorabacher*

The main idea of this paragraph is that *sound, scent, touch, and flavor can be essential in descriptions.*

Main Idea at the End

During the Cold War, a small group of men reportedly infiltrated Point Mugu Naval Air Weapons Station and bivouacked on the beach under cover of night. The next morning, the Navy took them by surprise. In a textbook two-pronged assault, an amphibious landing craft crashed through the surf while jeeps rolled across the sand. Outgunned and outflanked, the men surrendered. *And the base was once again safe from surfers.*

— *Jeff Meyers*

The main idea of the paragraph is that *the base was once again safe from surfers.* The entire paragraph tells about an incident that is summed up and given a point by this final sentence. By saving the main point until the end, the author builds to a surprise conclusion.

Main Idea in More Than One Sentence

Citizens do help to determine the ends, purposes, and objectives of policy through elections and other processes of influence. Public anger over contaminated foods induced Congress to pass the initial legislation in 1906 prohibiting adulterated foods in interstate commerce. After a number of books and articles in the 1950s pointed out the increasing content of DDT and other insecticides in human foods, public opinion supported further regulation: in due time Congress responded with the 1958 amendments. *But citizens' knowledge of the specific means that will best serve their ends is often inadequate.* Thanks in part to bureaucratic expertise, Congress and the president can supply some of the needed knowledge in formulating policies to achieve these ends. Sometime before the 1958 amendments were passed, a special House committee spent two years holding hearings on pesticides and food additives; the members thereby acquired unusual expertise on these subjects. The FDA in turn employed laboratory findings about the effects of saccharin in order to arrive at a judgment that it was a dangerous food additive.

— *Robert A. Dahl*

The main idea in this paragraph appears in two sentences. Although the first sentence of the selection says that citizens help set public policy, only part of the paragraph gives details to support that idea. Other details in the paragraph show that citizens do not always know enough to get what they want. An accurate statement of the main idea would have to include the information in both of the marked sentences: *Citizens help set public policy, but they do not always know the specific means to serve their ends.*

EXERCISES

Stated Main Ideas

For each of the following paragraphs, underline the sentence that tells the main idea. On the blank lines, write the main idea in your own words.

1. Yes, mastering multiplication is hard. So is learning to swing a bat level. Throughout a lifetime it's handier to know that 6 times 8 is 48 than to know you should keep your elbows up before the pitch. We don't need to pretend that school is fun, fun, fun, but we do need to convince kids that the work of school is worthwhile. Ten-year-olds can't afford our living-for-the-weekend mentality when they'll be competing for jobs with eager students from around the world in just a few years. We keep saying our schools need reforming; think what reforming our attitude about school would accomplish.

— *Marie Faust Evitt*

_____

_____

2. "Mommy, I want to be white." Imagine my wife's anguish and alarm when our beautiful brown-skinned three-year-old daughter made that declaration. We thought we were doing everything right to develop her self-esteem and positive racial identity. We overloaded her toy box with black dolls. We carefully monitored the racial content of TV shows and videos, ruling out *Song of the South* and *Dumbo,* two classic Disney movies marred by demeaning black stereotypes. But we saw no harm in *Pinocchio,* which seemed as racially benign as *Sesame Street* or *Barney,* and a good deal more engaging. Yet now our daughter was saying she wanted to be white, to be like the puppet who becomes a real boy in the movie. How had she got that potentially soul-destroying idea and, even more important, what should we do about it?

— *Jack E. White*

Critical Thinking in Writing

What reasons can you imagine that someone would have for wanting to be of a different race, ethnic group, or other category of people? Do you know anyone who would like to change his or her group identity? Write a paragraph or two in which you discuss this issue.

3. Jorge Zamora's grades at Oliver Hazard Perry Middle School in Providence, R.I., were low this past year because he read chess magazines in class. He's the best chess player in the United States under 16, and he comes by the title almost genetically. His father and brother are both masters, and by the time Jorge was 7, he was too good to play against other kids. "Chess is like falling in love for me," he says — but it's not a smooth romance. In 1990 his family moved from Honduras to the United States so he could compete at a higher level. Now they move him to New Jersey so Jorge can be closer to tournaments in New York. Yet at the same time, says Jorge, "my Dad gets mad and says I'm smart, I should get A's. I think he's right. When I study for 15 minutes, the next day I do get A's." It's clear that Jorge is torn. At 14, he wants to be like everyone else, so the kids won't laugh at him — and he wants to stand out as a champion. But he sees the pressures of that life. "To be an engineer of computers or a doctor, you don't have to be the

best to make a living," he says. "But to make a living at playing chess, you have to be really at the top."

— Seth Resnick

_____

_____

4. There are stories in every room of the South End townhouse that has been Sara Lawrence Lightfoot's home for 18 years. On the top floor of the five-story bow-front Victorian, the Harvard professor of sociology has her "dream office," where she wrote *Balm in Gilead,* the award-winning biography of her *mother,* child psychiatrist Dr. Margaret Lawrence. The book, which was made possible by a grant from the MacArthur Foundation, has brought Lightfoot a broader recognition than her academic books and articles about the sociology of education or her position as the lone tenured African-American woman on the Harvard faculty.

— Anita Diamant

_____

_____

5. Computers don't forget, unless they blow a chip or encounter a programming bug. And they never tire of the endless drills necessary to impart a basic principle or lesson. Thus, it's no surprise that early and enthusiastic prophesies about the computer predicted that teaching would be among its primary functions. To some extent, these prophesies have been correct. Computers are widely used to teach at nearly all levels of education. But they haven't replaced the textbook, as some had predicted. Nor does it appear likely that they ever will.

— Ronald E. Anderson and David R. Sullivan

_____

_____

6. The process of industrialization began in western Europe for a number of reasons. Western Europe was wealthier than much of the world, and its wealth was spread across more classes of people. Contributing to the accumulation of capital was the rapid expansion of trade, both overseas and on the Continent, during the sixteenth and seventeenth centuries (the commercial revolution). This expansion resulted from an aggressive search for new markets and tapped the wealth of a

much larger area of the world than the Mediterranean lands accessible to earlier generations. Thus, the resources, both human and material, of the New World and of Africa fueled Europe's accumulation of wealth.

— *Marvin Perry*

---

7. It is curious, but till that moment I had never realized what it means to destroy a healthy, conscious man. When I saw the prisoner step aside to avoid the puddle I saw the mystery, the unspeakable wrongness, of cutting a life short when it is in full tide. This man was not dying, he was alive just as we are alive. All the organs of his body were working — bowels digesting food, skin renewing itself, nails growing, tissues forming — all toiling away in solemn foolery. His nails would still be growing when he stood on the drop, when he was falling through the air with a tenth-of-a-second to live. His eyes saw the yellow gravel and the grey walls, and his brain still remembered, foresaw, reasoned — reasoned even about puddles. He and we were a party of men walking together, seeing, hearing, feeling, understanding the same world; and in two minutes, with a sudden snap one of us would be gone — one mind less, one world less.

— *George Orwell*

---

8. Ethnic newspapers battle not only the mainstream dailies, but also each other. Such a war was waged for much of 1988 and 1989 in Little Italy and other Italian-American enclaves in the city. One protagonist was *Il Progresso,* founded in 1880, which proclaimed itself, on a line under the masthead, "the first and greatest Italian daily newspaper in the United States." During the 1930s, its circulation had surpassed 500,000. But in 1988, its readership shrinking, the paper fired striking employees represented by the Newspaper Guild. Resuming publication with nonunion labor, *Il Progresso* soon faced competition: an Italian-language daily called *American Oggi.* Twenty of the dismissed workers had pooled their funds — $5,000 each — to create the upstart.

— *Michael Dorman*

5b(2) *Implied Main Ideas*

Sometimes paragraphs do not state exactly what the main idea is. Instead, you must decide what it is yourself. To do that, you must add up all the details the writer gives and then state the main idea in your own words.

When the writer has not stated a main idea exactly but instead *suggests* the idea to you through information in the paragraph, the idea is *implied*. An *implied main idea* is one that is suggested. Here is an example:

> *Einstein* was four years old before he could speak and seven before he could read. *Isaac Newton* did poorly in grade school, and *Beethoven*'s music teacher once said of him, "As a composer he is hopeless." When *Thomas Edison* was a boy, his teachers told him he was too stupid to learn anything. *F. W. Woolworth* got a job in a dry goods store when he was 21, but his employers would not let him wait on a customer because he "didn't have enough sense." A newspaper editor fired *Walt Disney* because he had "no good ideas." *Caruso*'s music teacher told him, "You can't sing. You have no voice at all." The director of the Imperial Opera in Vienna told *Madame Schumann-Heink* that she would never be a singer and advised her to buy a sewing machine. *Leo Tolstoy* flunked out of college; *Wernher von Braun* flunked ninth-grade algebra. *Admiral Richard E. Byrd* had been retired from the Navy as "unfit for service" until he flew over both Poles. *Louis Pasteur* was rated as "mediocre" in chemistry when he attended the Royal College. *Abraham Lincoln* entered the Black Hawk War as a captain and came out as a private. *Louisa May Alcott* was told by an editor that she could never write anything that had popular appeal. *Fred Waring* was once rejected for high school chorus. *Winston Churchill* failed the sixth grade.
>
> — *Milton E. Larson*

Here is one way to state the main idea of this paragraph: *People do not always recognize creative and imaginative men and women.* No one sentence makes that point. Instead, we must add up the details that the writer gives us in order to state the main idea in our own words. In this case, we read about various creative geniuses — Einstein, Edison, and Disney, for example — and see how their talents were not always acknowledged. Putting all the information together, we conclude that this writer is trying to show us that talented people do not always get the recognition they deserve.

Here is how to state the main idea in your own words:

- Try to figure out what *all* the details in the paragraph, not just a few of them, are trying to show.
- Make a complete sentence that (1) names a person or an object and (2) tells what a person or an object is doing.
- Do not look at just a few sentences in the paragraph to find out the main idea. If you stopped after the first sentence in the Larson selection, thinking it was the main idea, you would believe the paragraph is only about Einstein. It would be incorrect to say that the sentence *Einstein learned to speak and read rather late* is the main idea of the paragraph. The sentence is true; we know that from reading the whole paragraph. But the sentence is not the *main* idea; it is only one narrow idea that helps us build the main idea sentence: *People do not always recognize creative and imaginative men and women.*
- Do not specify as the main idea a statement that is *too general.* For example, it would be incorrect to say that the main idea of the paragraph is *All people have unrecognized talents.* The author of the paragraph might agree with this statement. But no details in the paragraph suggest that the writer is talking about people in general. Rather the author is talking about those talented people who later distinguished themselves and earned fame. The main idea should be stated in these terms: *Creative and imaginative people do not always receive the recognition that they should.*

EXERCISES

1. Implied Main Ideas

Read each of the following brief passages. Add up all the details in your mind to figure out the implied main idea. Then, on the lines provided, write a sentence that states the main idea.

1. Neither asked why I wanted to know mechanics. Only the occasional curious customer did that. To Harvey and Bud, it was self-evident. They respected their own expertise; of course anyone with intelligence would want to know how cars worked. And of course apprenticeship was the best way. After all, that's how they both learned. Harvey started at age 13, Bud at age 8. So far as they were concerned, I was just a late developer.

    — *Lesley Hazleton*

———————————————————————————————

———————————————————————————————

2. Lee Iacocca, president of Chrysler Corporation, who became internationally famous as the man who saved the company from almost certain bankruptcy in 1981, made this observation: "I'm constantly amazed by the number of people who can't seem to control their own schedules." The way we use time — or waste it — is largely a matter of habit. It is not easy to change old habits, but if they are bad habits, they put a ceiling on achievement. For example, a professional baseball player with a poor batting stance can become a good hitter, up to a point. Unless he improves his stance, however, progress beyond that point is doubtful. To change and begin almost all over again — to break a bad habit and make a good one — takes determination and will, but the decision to change brings the chance for success. If you find that you need more time for all your studies and other activities, consider scheduling your time in order to gain time.

    — Walter Pauk

    _____

    _____

3. Role models operate on more than one level. Parents and teachers are the guiding lights for everyday reality. Star athletes and other celebrities — the Muhammad Alis and Babe Ruths, the Jordans and Barkleys — are the models in daydreams. They represent an impossible dream, perhaps, but something to grow on. Yet as press coverage of sports becomes less and less worshipful, these fantasy figures begin to look less than ideal. "They're womanizers, they're gamblers . . . they spit," says Carol Lorente, a Bolingbrook, Ill., magazine editor who has conflicting feelings about her 9-year-old son Paul's dreams of becoming a major-league player. "I don't expect my son to do those things because he's heard they do them. On the other hand, he wants to be one of those guys." In fact, there's little evidence in social-science literature that children actually adopt the behavior of athletes they adore. When Michael Jordan began wearing long shorts, young basketball enthusiasts everywhere suddenly began turning up in the knee-length look. But that doesn't mean they will model their lives on Jordan's.

    — David Gelman

    _____

    _____

> **Critical Thinking in Writing**
> Which sports figure or other celebrity do you or someone you know look up to as a role model? In one or two paragraphs, describe and explain the person's influence.

4.   Most students are pointed toward goals, and many of them have the idea that achieving those goals (and rewards) will make them happy. For these students, goals exist somewhere out there in the future. They think that when they get to that place out there called future, they will be satisfied. They rarely are. In fact, high numbers of students don't make it to graduation.

— *David B. Ellis*

5.   About 2 percent of the population may be diagnosed as schizophrenics at some time in their lives, but about 10 percent of all high school students seen in psychiatric clinics suffer from depression. Common symptoms of depression include self-deprecation, crying spells, and suicidal thoughts and attempts (Masterson, 1967). Additional symptoms of depression found in adolescents below the age of seventeen involve fatigue, hypochondriasis, and concentration difficulty (Weiner, 1980, p. 455). High school students who experience such symptoms typically try to ward off their depression by restless activity or flight to or from others. They may also engage in problem behavior or delinquent acts carried out in ways that make it clear they are appealing for help. (A depressed fifteen-year-old boy may carry out an act of vandalism, for instance, at a time when a school authority or police officer is sure to observe the incident.) Adolescents over the age of seventeen who suffer from depression are likely to show little self-confidence and feel worthless and discouraged. To combat such feelings, they may join antiestablishment groups, manifest a "what's the use of it all?" attitude, or turn to sex and drugs.

— *Robert F. Biehler and Lynne M. Hudson*

2. Main Ideas in Paragraphs: A Review

In the following paragraphs, the main idea is either stated or implied. [See **5b(1)** and **5b(2)**.] Try to determine the main idea of each selection and then write it in your own words in the space provided.

1. My family came to America in 1985. No one spoke a word of English. In school, I was in an English as a Second Language class with other foreign-born children. My class was so over-crowded that it was impossible for the teacher to teach English properly. I dreaded going to school each morning because of the fear of not understanding what people were saying and the fear of being laughed at.

    — *Yu-Lan (Mary) Ying*

    _____

    _____

2. Years ago, students who performed well in school were recognized with a coveted spot on the honor roll or a shiny gold star on a spelling test. Now, good work or behavior brings material as well as psychic payoffs: a Dodger T-shirt, a free pass to Disneyland or a coupon for a hamburger.

    — *Catherine Gewertz*

    _____

    _____

3. It was Monday, the first week of November. The grape season was over and I could now go to school. I woke up early that morning and lay in bed, looking at the stars and savoring the thought of not going to work and of starting sixth grade for the first time that year. Since I could not sleep, I decided to get up and join Papá and Roberto for breakfast. I sat at the table across from Roberto, but I kept my head down. I did not want to look up and face him. I knew he was sad. He was not going to school today. He was not going tomorrow, or next week, or next month. He would not go until the cotton season was over, and that was sometime in February. I rubbed my hands together and watched the dry, acid stained skin fall to the floor in little rolls.

    — *Francisco Jimenez*

_____

_____

_____

_____

Critical Thinking in Writing

Were you or was anyone you know ever prevented by family or financial circumstances from going to school? Write a page in which you describe the experience. If you never have been prevented from going to school, suppose you were. What would you do?

---

4. Anyone can become a leader. Abraham Lincoln and Harry S. Truman rose from humble beginnings and hardship to become U.S. presidents. Exceptional athletes such as Arthur Ashe and Cal Ripken overcame enormous odds to become all-American heroes and spokespersons for worthy causes. Corporate executives have worked their way up from the sales force (Ross Perot) and secretarial pools (Ardis Krainik, General Director of the Lyric Opera of Chicago) to become chief executive officers. Yet, as inspiring as these examples may be, leaders are not necessarily the hardest workers or the smartest employees. The path to a leadership position can be as easy as being in the right place at the right time or being the only person willing to take on a difficult job. Becoming the leader, chairperson, or president of a group occurs in many different ways.

    — *Isa N. Engelberg and Diana R. Winn*

_____

_____

5. "It's a misconception that some people are born to draw. Anybody can draw as well as do anything else," believes Philip Ortiz, a character artist for the Walt Disney Company. "Nothing is impossible." Ortiz's career has proved that. Before Disney, he worked as a background designer on Saturday morning cartoons and the prime time hit *The Simpsons*, where he

designed everything from Springfield's nuclear power plant to Bart's bedroom. "My dream is to sell my own characters," says Ortiz as he presents a grouping of his own characters for a new animated series he's developing. Ortiz started as a designer at Hanna-Barbera in 1978, a few weeks before graduating from junior college. He advises aspiring animators to build a portfolio. "Keep everything you draw." You can be sure this successful animation designer does.

— *Pamela Kleibrink Thompson*

_____

_____

6. The Constitution grants the President authority to appoint people to fill federal government offices and positions. Presidential appointments to most major government positions must be approved by a majority vote of the Senate. Appointments that require the Senate's "advice and consent" include ambassadors, Supreme Court justices, other federal judges, heads of Cabinet departments and regulatory commissions, federal marshals, and high-ranking White House officials such as the Budget Director. In addition, Congress may permit the President to appoint "inferior officers" without Senate approval. Examples are bureau chiefs, military officers, and most White House staff members.

— *Richard J. Hardy*

_____

_____

7. The World War II relocation-camp experience was painful. The U.S. government ordered thousands of first-, second-, and even third-generation Japanese-Americans to leave their homes, abandon their businesses, and crowd into temporary quarters set up in places like the Tanforan racetrack near San Francisco and at Topaz, Utah, with very little advance warning. No less painful, however, was the earlier immigrants' suffering from racial discrimination at the hands of white Americans — the Bret Hartes, and the Kearneys, and the nondescript and unnamed neighborhood white boys who chanted "Ching Chong Chinaman" and "Fat Jap." Time and gradual socio-cultural enlightenment have modified much of the bitter hatred, but the scars are there to remind many Asian-Americans of an identity

somehow separate from the mainstream of the white Americans.

— *Kai-yu Hsu and Helen Palubinskas*

_____

_____

_____

_____

8. Personality is unbelievably complex. It is the result of a lifetime of experiences and influences, the product of both physical and social forces. However, there is a thread running through all our acts that ties our conduct and thinking together into a pattern. After we have been observed to act in a certain way in several sets of circumstances, someone who knows us has a fairly good idea of what we will do in a new situation. If we fail to do as expected, our friends are surprised. We are expected to be somewhat the same sort of individual over time, despite changes that we experience. "He isn't the fellow he used to be" is a statement that expresses bewilderment over inconsistent behavior in a person. Personality is the total picture of a person's behavior, especially as it can be defined by his or her fellow human beings in a consistent way.

— *Bruce Shertzer*

_____

_____

3. Topics and Main Ideas: A Longer Selection

Read the selection below and then answer the questions that follow.

Big Dreams in "Little Havana"

1   For three decades, Cuban exiles in southern Florida have clustered in front of coffee stands in Miami's Little Havana and talked about returning to their homeland. "Next year in Havana" is the common slogan. But suddenly, the wishful talk has become decidedly confident. Inspired by changes sweeping Eastern Europe and Central America, some of southeast Florida's estimated 700,000 Cuban exiles say that they are no

longer wondering if Fidel Castro will ever fall, but euphorically planning for the day that he does. They are taking guerrilla training, drawing up new economic policies and deciding how to cash in on a free Cuban market. Few of the exiles openly recognize the reality: that Castro remains firmly in power, and that their plans may be highly premature.

2   For the Cuban-Americans who fled from the island after Castro took power in 1959, virulent anti-communism is a way of life. Spanish-language radio broadcasters in Dade County routinely refer to Cuba as a slave island and to Castro as a tyrant. One commentator has launched a contest: pick the date when Castro will fall. According to a recent TV poll of exiles, 44 percent of respondents believe that Castro will be overthrown within a year. One out of five said that they would return to Cuba if democracy were to replace communism.

3   But some experts question the validity of the poll. They say that many exiles have grown comfortable and affluent in the United States and responded only out of deep-seated patriotism. "You have to say you are going back," said Eduardo Padron, a Cuban exile and college administrator. "People believe that's what every patriot should do."

4   Still, on Sundays, up to four dozen exiles practice ambushes and amphibious assaults in the Everglades. One Cuban-American group recently tried a more bizarre tactic: releasing hundreds of helium-filled balloons containing packets of coffee, disposable razors and comics showing an emaciated Castro at the end of a hangman's rope. (There is no indication of how many of the balloons made it from Florida to Cuba.)

5   The largest political group, the 6,000-member Cuban American National Foundation, has drafted political and economic policies for transitional rule after Castro's era ends. Exiled business owners say that they plan to open restaurants and to export machinery to Cuba when the market opens. Said Domingo Moreira, a seafood importer: "There's going to be some very intense economic activity." But some experts urge the exiles to curb their optimism. Said University of Miami historian Jaime Suchlicki: "I tell people to buy your suitcase, but don't pack your clothes yet — because they'll just get wrinkled."

— *Tim Johnson*

1.   What is the topic of this selection?

_____

_____

_____

2. In your own words, what is the main idea of the selection as a whole?

    _____

    _____

    _____

3. In your own words, what is the main idea of each of the paragraphs?

    a. Paragraph 1: _____

    _____

    _____

    b. Paragraph 2: _____

    _____

    _____

    c. Paragraph 3: _____

    _____

    _____

    d. Paragraph 4: _____

    _____

    _____

    e. Paragraph 5: _____

    _____

    _____

Reading for the Main Idea

In the space provided, write the letter of the correct answer. Count 4 points for each correct answer.

Key Ideas in Sentences

A. Each main sentence has a set of four sentences following it. In each set, choose the letter of the sentence that best tells the key idea of the main sentence. Write your answer in the space provided.

_____ 1. Without warning, sixty enormous whales beached themselves on the California coastline between San Diego and Los Angeles.

    a. Whales give no warnings.
    b. A coastline exists between San Diego and Los Angeles.
    c. Whales are beached.
    d. Whales are enormous.

_____ 2. The United States government ordered thousands of first-, second, and third-generation Japanese-Americans to leave their homes, abandon their businesses, and crowd into temporary quarters set up in places like the Tanforan racetrack near San Francisco and at Topaz, Utah, with very little advance warning.

                            — *Kai-Yu Hsu and Helen Palubinskas*

    a. Japanese people moved to Topaz, Utah.
    b. The U.S. government ordered Japanese-Americans to abandon homes and businesses and live in temporary quarters.
    c. Little advance warning was given to Japanese-Americans forced to move near San Francisco.
    d. People should not be forced to give up their homes and businesses.

133

_____ 3. Not everyone was in favor of a land route between England and France, but the Chunnel, a tunnel under the English Channel, was opened in the summer of 1994 with great fanfare.

    a. Some people objected to the Chunnel.
    b. The Chunnel was opened in 1994.
    c. The Chunnel is a tunnel under the English Channel that connects England and France.
    d. Great fanfare marked the opening of the Chunnel.

_____ 4. Magnificent flowers with unusual blossoms grow throughout the desert in Arizona and New Mexico.

    a. Magnificent flowers grow in the Southwest.
    b. Deserts appear in Arizona and New Mexico.
    c. Blooming flowers are magnificent.
    d. Blossoms are unusual.

_____ 5. Explanations vary from the increasingly poor quality of network shows to the rising popularity of video equipment, but the fact remains that we are owning more TV sets but enjoying them less.

    a. Network shows are of poor quality.
    b. Video equipment is increasingly popular.
    c. We are owning more TV sets but enjoying them less.
    d. Explanations vary.

Topics and Main Ideas

B. Read each selection. Then identify the topic of the paragraph and the main idea, as directed, from the choices given. Write the letter of your choice in the space provided.

Americans have one of the fattiest diets in the world; about 37 percent of all calories consumed today come from fats. Most of this fat intake occurs at the expense of carbohydrates. The chief sources of fat in the diet include meats, poultry, and dairy products, as well as vegetable oils and shortenings. Most nutritionists recommend that only 30 percent of our total daily calories come from fat and that we should try to get more of these calories from plant sources or fish, rather than animal sources.

— *The Wellness Encyclopedia*

_____ 1. The topic of this paragraph is

    a. the chief sources of fat.
    b. the importance of carbohydrates.
    c. what nutritionists recommend.
    d. the American diet.

_____ 2. The main idea of this paragraph is

    a. Americans need to change from a fatty diet to a more healthful one.
    b. plant products and fish are better for us than animal products.
    c. the chief sources of fat are meats, poultry, dairy products, vegetable oils, and shortenings.
    d. nutritionists recommend that we get 30 percent of our total calories from fat.

(1) Summer employment can be very useful in areas besides financial ones. (2) Both summer and part-time jobs are opportunities for you to try out what it means to work, to experience what it means to have other people rely on you and to develop an understanding of why others behave as they do. (3) In addition, part-time and summer jobs provide firsthand experience to add to information obtained through books, newspapers, family, friends, and counselors. (4) Probably the most difficult thing about a summer job is finding it. (5) Although more summer jobs are available during good economic times than bad, there never seem to be enough for all the students who want them.

— *Bruce Shertzer*

_____ 3. The topic of this paragraph is

    a. family, friends, and counselors.
    b. obtaining job information from books.
    c. summer jobs.
    d. what it means to work.

_____ 4. The main idea of this paragraph is

    a. the most difficult thing about a summer job is finding it.
    b. summer jobs teach you many things in addition to offering you money.
    c. part-time summer jobs provide firsthand experience.
    d. working in the summer is important.

_____ 5.   The sentence that best expresses the main idea is

    a.   sentence 1.
    b.   sentence 2.
    c.   sentence 3.
    d.   sentence 5.

Stated Main Ideas

C.   Read the selection. In the space provided, write the letter of the phrase that best completes each sentence.

(1) The idea of birthstones came from old superstitions about precious stones. (2) Certain stones were thought to bring health and long life. (3) Others were supposed to make the wearer brave and strong. (4) Some other stones would protect you from fire and lightning. (5) By wearing a special stone for their month of birth, people thought they would have special luck or qualities.

_____ 1.   The main idea of this paragraph is expressed by

    a.   sentence 1.
    b.   sentence 5.
    c.   sentence 3.
    d.   sentence 2.

(1) Once you know the general topic, you should be able to state the *main idea* of a paragraph. (2) The main idea holds the paragraph together. (3) Each sentence relates to the main idea and helps build the paragraph's meaning. (4) The main idea of a paragraph is more than the general topic. (5) To find the main idea, you start with the topic, of course; but you must figure out what the paragraph is saying about the topic.

_____ 2.   The main idea of this paragraph is expressed by

    a.   sentence 1.
    b.   sentence 5.
    c.   sentence 3.
    d.   sentence 2.

Surprisingly, many liars are betrayed by their words because of carelessness. It is not that they couldn't disguise what they said, or that they tried to and failed, but simply that they neglected to fabricate carefully. The head of an executive search firm described a fellow who applied to his agency under two different names within the same year. When asking the fellow which name should he be called, "The man, who first called himself Leslie D'Ainter, but later switched to Lester Dainter, continued his prevaricating ways without skipping a beat. He explained that he changed his first name because Leslie sounded too feminine, and he altered his last name to make it easier to pronounce. But his references were the real giveaway. He presented three glowing letters of recommendation. Yet all three 'employers' misspelled the same word."

— *Paul Ekman*

_____ 3.　The main idea of the paragraph is

    a.　Liars cannot disguise what they say.

    b.　Spelling a former employee's name wrong in a reference letter is a real giveaway.

    c.　Experienced executive search firms detect liars easily.

    d.　Many liars give themselves away because they are careless.

For the most part we think of portable radios as a post–World War II phenomenon. From the cheap plastic models of the 1950s to today's elaborate Walkmans, they have been among the most visible examples of the electronics revolution. But portable radios did not start with the invention of the transistor; their history stretches back more than two decades earlier. The 1920s gave birth to the boom box, but the boom box boom quickly went bust.

— *Michael Brian Schiffer*

_____ 4.　The main idea of the paragraph is

    a.　Portable radios came into existence after World War II.

    b.　In portable radios we see evidence of the electronic revolution.

    c.　The history of portable radios really begins in the 1920s.

    d.　The boom box did not last very long.

America owes its progress as an industrial nation in large part to its ability to produce tremendous quantities of steel. Railway rails and cars, automobiles, all sorts of machinery, and huge buildings are only a few of the things which are made from steel. For centuries, steel was known to have qualities of strength and toughness not found in iron. But steel was too expensive to be widely used. Impurities had to be removed from iron to make steel, and no cheap method of removing these impurities was known. Then, in the 1850s, an En-glishman, Henry Bessemer, and an American, William Kelly, each discovered a startling fact. Working on the same problem separately, they found that a blast of air directed at melted iron would remove its impurities. This new process of making steel was so cheap and easy that steel could be produced in large quantities and at low cost.

— *Wilder, Ludlum, and Brown*

_____ 5. The main idea of the paragraph is

    a. Producing large amounts of cheap steel made America progress as an industrial nation.
    b. Impurities must be removed from iron to make steel.
    c. William Kelly and Henry Bessemer discovered how to remove impurities from iron.
    d. Many important objects, such as rails, cars, and machinery, are made from steel.

Implied Main Ideas

D. In each paragraph below, the main idea is implied. Read the paragraph and then choose the statement that best expresses the main idea. Write the letter of your answer in the space provided.

_____ 1. Dust in the air makes people sneeze and cough, especially those with allergies. Dust makes extra work for those who have to clean homes or offices. You have seen the layer of dirt that forms when dust settles on tables, chairs, and other surfaces. However, dust is a necessary feature of our environment. Without it we would have no rain or snow. Dust also is one of the key ingredients in color. When we see blue skies, rainbows, and bright yellow and orange sunrises, dust is largely responsible.

    a. Dust in the air is harmful.
    b. Dust may be harmful, but it is also an important part of air.
    c. Dust is a major ingredient in rain or snow.
    d. People get annoyed when they have to clean dust off their desks and furniture.

_____ 2. My day begins officially at 7:00, when all inmates are required to get out of bed and stand before their cell doors to be counted by guards who walk along the tier saying, "1, 2, 3 . . ." However, I never remain in bed until 7. I'm usually up by 5:30. The first thing I do is make up my bed. Then I pick up all my books, newspapers, etc., off the floor of my cell and spread them over my bed to clear the floor for calisthenics. In my cell, I have a little stool on which I lay a large plywood board, about 2½ by 3 feet, which I use as a typing and writing table. At night, I load this makeshift table down with books and papers, and when I read at night I spill things all over the floor. When I leave my cell, I set this board, loaded down, on my bed, so that if a guard comes into my cell to search it, he will not knock the board off the stool, as had happened before. Still in the nude, the way I sleep, I go through my routine: kneebends, butterflies, touching my toes, squats, windmills. I continue for about half an hour.

— *Eldridge Cleaver*

   a.   Prison guards knock over makeshift tables in prison.
   b.   Prison life is cruel.
   c.   Cleaver performs a number of activities after he wakes up each morning in his cell.
   d.   He must clear the floor of all reading materials before he does his calisthenics.

_____ 3.   Early in our country's history there was no money. Instead of buying or selling products, people exchanged or traded goods. For example, if you wanted a saddle and harness for your horse, you might trade an old donkey for them. If you worked for someone, your salary might be a bushel of wheat or corn instead of silver or gold coins. However, as our population grew and grew, people had to trade more and more, and the system soon was much too complicated. A demand for money was strong. Thus, a law to coin shillings, sixpences, and three-pences was passed. Captain John Hull was made mint-master, and he first minted, that is made, silver coins from old cups, buckles, and buttons. Each coin had the date 1652 on it.

   a.   Coins were first made in 1652 by John Hull.
   b.   Money is important for a successful society.
   c.   In the early days of our country people traded things instead of buying or selling them.
   d.   The early trading system in our country soon gave way to a system of money.

_____ 4.   Clad in T-shirts and sweat pants or skin-tight spandex, they break into rhythmic jumping jacks, bouncing and flapping like recruits at boot camp. In a slightly malodorous room across the hall, men and women pedal stationary bicycles or labor on rowing machines, computerized to calculate the calories burned with each stroke — one slice of chocolate cake down, another to go. Others sprawl on benches, straining against pulleys laden with stacks of weights, or hoist barbells as they study themselves shamelessly in floor-to-ceiling mirrors, which, in the critical eye of the beholder, are not always kind.

— *Maclean's Magazine*

a. Not happy with their weight or how they look, people try to improve their bodies by exercising strenuously at health clubs.

b. Health clubs are great places for men and women to meet.

c. Although people can take aerobics classes at health clubs, they can also exercise alone using stationary bikes, rowing machines, and weights.

d. People generally are not satisfied with their bodies.

_____ 5. Naturally, before the true nature of the movements and orientation of the Earth was understood, there could be no confidence that in any one particular year, the sun, as it lowered toward the winter solstice, might not continue to lower indefinitely, disappear, and bring all life to an end. Thus, in the Scandinavian myths, the final end is heralded by the "Fimbul winter" when the sun disappears and there is a terrible period of darkness and cold that lasts three years — after which is Ragnarok and the end. Even in sunnier climes where faith in the perpetual beneficence of the sun would naturally be stronger, the time of the winter solstice, when the sun ceased its decline, turned, and began to ascend the heavens once more, was the occasion of a vast outpouring of relief.

— *Isaac Asimov*

a. Confidence in the sun's reappearance should have been greater in warmer places than it was in Scandinavia.

b. Even in warm countries, ancient people were happy when the sun began its ascent in the sky.

c. Scandinavian myths conclude with a long winter, followed by the end.

d. Before people understood planetary movement, they were in constant fear that the sun might vanish forever.

Score: _____ correct × 4 points each = _____

6

Reading for Information

The first step in reading for specific information is to look for the main idea. (See Chapter 5.) In a one-paragraph selection, you add up all the sentences to find the main idea. In a longer work, you add up the main ideas of the various paragraphs in order to figure out the main idea (or thesis) of the whole selection.

But the main idea does not give you all the information you need. Facts and details that appear in the paragraphs help develop the main ideas. These facts and details may paint a more complete picture, give examples to help you understand the ideas better, prove a point, or show how each idea relates to other ideas. To make the best use of these facts and details, you have to be able to

■ find important facts and remember them.
■ separate major facts and details from minor facts and details.

A course that requires several books may demand different kinds of reading for those several books. Is one book the basic text for the course? Is another book merely a supplement, something added to thorough class instruction? Does a third book repeat the lectures you hear each day? If you ask yourself — and your instructor — some of these questions, you'll know what to do with your text for a given class.

Often your syllabus or course outline tells you just how to approach a book. Spend time figuring out how to read each book required by your courses. And in books that you own, use underlining (see **2a**) to help you identify essential information.

6a Fact-Finding

To find and remember important facts, you must be an active reader. Here are nine ways to locate facts:

141

■ Have a definite purpose for reading. Are you reading the newspaper out of general interest or for a specific research project? Are you reading a page of your biology book to find out how the eye works? Are you reading a chapter of a political science text to learn the meaning of *democracy*? Or are you reading only because an instructor made an assignment?

■ Learn to read for the main idea. If you recognize the main idea easily, the facts supporting that idea will stand out.

■ Know that not all facts and details are equal in importance. Look only for the facts that relate to the main idea.

■ Look for information in groups or units. Facts often appear together in clumps.

■ Look for the way the paragraph is put together. How is the information arranged? Has the writer organized the material into a pattern that is easy to see?

■ Learn to keep an author's *opinions* separate from the *facts* offered in the writing.

■ Question yourself as you read. Stop to think and to let facts sink in before you rush on to other information. Ask yourself "What does that mean?" or "What does this information tell me?" or "Why is this information here?"

■ Use the five *W*s when you read to ask yourself specific questions about the facts.

1. Ask yourself *Who*? Then look for the name of someone or something.
2. Ask yourself *When*? Then look for a date (a day, a month, a year) or a time of day or year.
3. Ask yourself *Where*? Then look for words that show a location or name a place.
4. Ask yourself *What*? or *What happened*? Then look for some action.
5. Ask yourself *Why*? Then look for an explanation of some act or event.

■ Think about the kinds of questions someone might ask you about the information you have read. Go back after you have finished to reread quickly and review any facts you have learned. Try to summarize the important facts in your mind.

Look at the following selection about how a Korean woman related to one of her American neighbors early in the twentieth century. Read to find the main idea, to see how the information is organized, and to answer the five *W*s. The notes in the margin show where the answers to these questions appear in the reading.

The residents of Anaheim were mostly German- — *Who?*
Americans, and they did not think much of Orien-   *Where?*
tals. When I first moved there, I was surprised to — *What hap-*
see the "For Whites Only" signs everywhere in   *pened?*
town. One afternoon as I was preparing to close up,
a young man came in, obviously very drunk. He — *Information*
slapped me hard on the back and said, "Hi Mary!"   *about a spe-*
in a loud voice. I was so surprised and annoyed that   *cific person*
I turned around and hit him as hard as I could on — *What hap-*
his back and said, "Hi Charlie!" He replied angrily,   *pened?*
"My name's not Charlie!" Then he staggered over — *What the*
to the lunch counter in the middle of the market,   *person did*
saying what he thought of the "so and sos."
   Two days later, he came in, apologized, and said, — *More infor-*
"Something bothers me. Why did you call me   *mation*
Charlie?" I replied, "Why did you call me Mary?"   *about the*
He said, "I thought all you Jap women were Mary."   *person and*
That really got to me. "How stupid can you be?" I   *what he*
asked. "Do you mean to tell me that all the women   *said*
in Japan have the same name? Even animals have a
different grunt for each other and birds have different
chirps and songs. Why should humans who can talk
have the same names? The reason I called you Charlie -- *Why the*
is because people like you always call all Oriental   *woman said*
men by that name. Isn't that true?" He nodded yes.   *what she*
"Also, you call all black men 'boy' — young and old.   *said*
White people always say 'Hey boy!'" He had to
admit that was also true, and that he hadn't thought
about it and had just gone along with whatever others
were doing. He was nice enough to admit he was — *How the*
wrong and stupid. We became good friends after   *man felt*
that. Every time he came in, he wanted to know more
about Oriental people and Asian countries.
                                    — *Mary Paik Lee*

EXERCISES

1. Fact-Finding: A Review
Reread the selection on this page.

1. What is the main point of the selection?

_____

_____

_____

2. What are two questions someone might ask about the selection?

    _____

    _____

    _____

3. Write down three of the most important facts.

    a. _____

    b. _____

        _____

    c. _____

        _____

        _____

4. How did the man's attitudes change?

    _____

    _____

Did you have a purpose in reading? Did you use the words *how a Korean woman related to one of her American neighbors* in the instructions to help you read for special information? Did you ask yourself these questions as you read: What is the main idea? How is the information arranged? Which facts are most important? What questions might someone ask about this selection?

Critical Thinking in Writing

Mary Paik Lee confronted prejudice and stereotyping directly by speaking with the offending person. What other strategies can we use to educate people about stereotyping and prejudice? Write your response in about a page.

---

2. Reading for Facts

Read the following paragraph about the struggle of civil rights leaders against discrimination. Look for the main idea and for information about steps taken by the courts to overcome segregation.

> In the 1940s, civil rights leaders began a struggle against discrimination and segregation. Leaders of the movement turned to the federal courts, and, in a series of cases beginning in 1941, the Supreme Court ruled against various forms of segregation. A Supreme Court decision in 1954 — *Brown* v. *Board of Education of Topeka* — overturned an 1896 Court decision that allowed "separate but equal" schools for black students. The court ordered schools to end segregation with "all deliberate speed." Resistance to this decision forced President Eisenhower to send federal troops to Arkansas in 1957 to protect black students. In the early 1960s, President Kennedy used federal marshals in Mississippi and National Guard units in Alabama to ensure that black students were allowed to enter state universities.
>
> — *Marvin Perry et al.*

1. What is the main idea of this paragraph?

   _____

   _____

2. What facts did you learn about

   a. when the court struggles began?

   _____

   b. separate but equal schools?

   _____

   _____

   c. which states resisted the 1954 ruling?

   _____

d. how President Eisenhower enforced the court's ruling?

_____

e. how President Kennedy protected black students at state universities?

_____

3. Reading with a Purpose

Read the advertisement on the next page about Alice Harris's contribution to her community. Then answer these questions.

1. What is the main idea of this advertisement?

_____

_____

2. Which details help you see the main point?

_____

_____

_____

_____

3. What facts support the idea that the community needed emergency medical facilities?

_____

_____

4. What kinds of programs are provided by POW?

_____

_____

_____

Alice Harris
— A Dream Maker —

"Sweet Alice" and the Watts Crusade

They had come to this poor section of Los Angeles to rebuild a community. As urban planners, these men were outsiders who believed that a mix of trees, stores, a hotel and a large dose of goodwill could bring the city's Watts area back from one of the nation's most devastating riots.

But Alice Harris, a Watts resident who watched these professionals at work, had other concerns.

Long before the 1965 riots, basic medical services were hard to find in Watts. There was the boy who was hit by a car and died in the street hours before an ambulance could arrive. There were the women—Harris was one of them—who gave birth at home because they had no easy way of getting to the nearest hospital.

So when the planners began talking of revitalizing Harris' riot-scarred community, she decided to raise her hand and speak her mind. "I told them who I was, and I asked them to please listen to me," she recalls. "You might not do anything about it, but let me tell you how we're suffering down here and how our children are suffering."

By the time she had finished, one of the planners had penciled in a diagram for an emergency health center, which was built within the year. Since then, Harris has continued to speak up, and people have listened.

As the founder of Parents of Watts (POW), Harris oversees a community organization that operates 15 programs including emergency food aid, help for the homeless, health seminars, voter registration and an educational program for teen mothers. POW's supplemental education programs have sent more than 100 "problem" youngsters to several colleges across the nation.

Harris admits that after nearly 30 years of grassroots community work, she is close to realizing her dream for the people of Watts. "We can do all things through God," she says. "I just want to plant that [idea] in others now. I want to build up their hopes, to show them because you have a lot of doubting Thomases out here."

Known in Watts as "Sweet Alice," Harris would be the first to tell you that as a child, she hardly qualified for the lofty title of

"Don't come in here telling me that you're pitiful because you're homeless. You just made a mistake, and you need some help. Ain't nothing pitiful about that."

"Sweet Alice" Harris

community role model. Born in Birmingham, Ala., in 1937 and raised in Detroit, she had the first of her nine children at 13. She was homeless briefly three years later.

Many people look down on a background of teen pregnancy and homelessness. However, Harris uses it to motivate her many clients. "Don't come in here telling me that you're pitiful because you're homeless," she says. "You just made a mistake, and you need some help. Ain't nothing pitiful about that [being homeless]. You come in here rejoicing because you finally met the help you need."

Help is something she has given since she arrived in Los Angeles in 1959 and moved into the Jordan Downs Housing Project, a clean community that didn't quite match the neighborhood's seedy reputation.

Although the lack of essential government services and medical facilities led to the formation of POW in 1982, Harris' greatest task continues to be convincing her neighbors that Watts deserves better. "People have become conditioned," Harris says. "They are satisfied with the status quo. They say it's all right, and I'm saying it's not all right. Our children deserve better."

Reprinted with permission of Amway Corporation and Johnson Publishing Company, Inc.

6b   Major Details, Minor Details

It's obvious that not all facts in a paragraph have the same importance. In the selection on pages 130–131, for example, the names of the Cuban exile and college administrator, the seafood importer, and the University of Miami historian are among the less important details. Because you do not need those details to understand the selection, the information they give is minor. Minor details help round out the paragraph and often hold our attention to make the material we are reading more interesting. Still, we can ignore minor details if our goal is a quick understanding of what we've read. Details that give major information about the main idea, however, are very important.

Here is how to find major details:

- State the main idea in your own words.
- Look only for information that supports the main idea.
- Read quickly over the words or sentences that give information that is not relevant to the main idea.
- Look for signal words like *most important, first, finally, the facts are*, and so on.
- Underline the major details when you locate them.

Here is how one student separated the major details from the minor details in a passage she was reading to learn about a product's price for her course in marketing.

Although we generally assume that price is a significant issue for buyers, the importance of price depends on the type of product and the type of target market. For example, buyers, in general, are probably more sensitive to cigarette prices than to luggage prices. R. J. Reynolds introduced the first American low-price cigarettes in Japan when trade barriers were lifted, making the Japanese market a target for increased U.S. importation. The cigarettes, called Islands, sell for approximately 10 percent less than most Japanese brands. The lower cigarette price gives Reynolds a major advantage over Japan Tobacco, Inc., which has 90 percent of all the market's cigarette sales. Another advantage is that 30 percent of all cigarettes and 40 percent of foreign cigarettes are sold through vending machines; smokers buying Islands need only two coins instead of the four that are required for Japanese brands.[1] By assessing the target market's evaluation of price, a marketer is in a better position to know how much emphasis to place on price. Information about the target market's price evaluation may also help a marketer <u>determine how</u> far above the competition <u>a firm can set its prices.</u>

[1] Christine Donahue, "Low Price Brand Launched in Japan," *Adweek's Marketing Week,* Feb. 1, 1988, p. 5.

— *William M. Pride and O. C. Ferrell*

Notice that by underlining, the student focuses only on details that help explain the main idea directly. (See Chapter 5.) Two of these details are the cost of American-made cigarettes in Japan and their price advantage in vending machines.

Also notice those details the student passes over as not so important. Some unimportant details are the comparison between luggage prices and cigarette prices and the lifting of trade barriers.

EXERCISES

1. Separating Major and Minor Details

Read the following selection about a game some businesses use to promote diversity on the job. Then answer the questions that follow.

To help supervisors understand how diversity can work for them, an Atlanta nonprofit research organization developed a game that simulates a production line.

During two-day seminars organized by the American Institute for Managing Diversity, participants split into teams and compete to manufacture a product. The product is a signal box with a corrugated cardboard frame and flashing lights regulated by electric wires and switches. The boxes are simple enough that they don't require special skills to make, but complicated enough that team members must follow directions precisely and organize the work efficiently. Teams are rated on how many boxes they produce while meeting quality standards.

In order to reach peak production, the game requires teams to draw from a pool of "unemployed" people of diverse ethnic and educational backgrounds — portrayed by institute employees. The idea is that the team that can best integrate the new hires into a cohesive unit will produce the most boxes.

Some players try to circumvent the diversity constraints. Terry Kruzan, executive director of the institute, recalls one team made up entirely of white women — except for one man.

The women ignored the man, eventually forcing him off the team, and they resisted hiring the "unemployed."

"They got off to a fast start," Kruzan said, but soon arguments began erupting over who was doing the most work and who was slacking off. The bickering caused production to stall and the team to fall behind.

— Tom Mulligan

_____ 1. The main idea of the selection is that
   a. the American Institute for Managing Diversity, an organization based in Atlanta, uses a game that simulates a production line.
   b. the team that best integrates new-hires into a cohesive unit produces the most boxes.
   c. a production line simulation can teach people about diversity.
   d. women feel more comfortable working with only other women.

2. Write *maj* beside major details and *min* beside minor details.

_____   a. The American Institute for Managing Diversity is a non-profit organization.

_____   b. A game helps supervisors understand diversity.

_____   c. The game was developed by a research organization in Atlanta.

_____   d. The game simulates a production line.

_____   e. Teams compete to manufacture a product.

_____   f. The product is a signal box.

_____   g. The signal box is made of corrugated cardboard and flashing lights.

_____   h. Making boxes does not require special skills.

_____   i. Making boxes requires following directions and efficient organization.

_____   j. Both the quality and the quantity of production are rated.

_____   k. To reach peak production, teams need diverse workers.

_____ l. Workers are represented by institute employees.

_____ m. Some players try to avoid diversity.

_____ n. Terry Kruzan tells a story about a team made up of all women except for one man.

_____ o. The team of women resisted hiring unemployed workers.

_____ p. Arguments erupted in the team that tried to avoid diversity.

_____ q. After a fast start, the team that tried to avoid diversity fell behind.

2. Finding Major and Minor Details

Read the following selection about bilingual education and answer the questions that follow.

Bilingual education, which provides instruction in their native language for students not proficient in English, has been expanding in U.S. public schools. In 1968, Congress passed the Bilingual Education Act, and in 1974 the Supreme Court ruled unanimously in *Lau* v. *Nichols* that the schools must take steps to help students who "are certain to find their classroom experiences wholly incomprehensible" because they do not understand English. Congressional appropriations for bilingual education increased from $7.5 million in 1969 to more than $200 million in 1995. Although the federal and state governments fund bilingual projects for more than sixty language groups speaking various Asian, Indo-European, and Native American languages, the large majority of children served by these projects are Hispanic.

— *Allan C. Ornstein and Daniel V. Levine*

_____ 1. Which sentence best states the main idea?
   a. The government funds many bilingual programs.
   b. Bilingual programs have been expanding for students not skilled in English.
   c. Some students cannot comprehend classroom instruction in English.
   d. Congress supports bilingual education.

2. Write *maj* beside each major detail in the paragraph and *min* beside each minor detail.

_____   a. Bilingual education provides native language instruction to students not proficient in English.

_____   b. *Lau* v. *Nichols* was a Supreme Court case that supported bilingual education.

_____   c. The federal and state governments fund bilingual projects for more than sixty language groups.

_____   d. Congress appropriated $7.5 million to bilingual education in 1969.

_____   e. In 1995 the government provided about three times more funding for bilingual programs than it did in 1969.

_____   f. Bilingual programs largely serve Hispanic children.

_____   g. The Bilingual Education Act was passed in 1968.

3. Major and Minor Details: A Review

Read the following selection about a winner of the National Book Award. Then answer the questions on major and minor details.

Author Charles Johnson
Wins National Book Award

Author Charles Johnson recently became the first black man to win the prestigious National Book Award since Ralph Ellison won in 1953.

Johnson, 42, a professor of English at the University of Washington in Seattle, won the award for *Middle Passage,* which chronicles the journey of a freed African slave returning to his homeland. The book won in the fiction category. The historical novel takes place in 1830 and tells the story of a terrifying voyage taken by a slave en route to his native Africa on a clipper ship. The title refers to the crossing of the Atlantic to America from Africa by slave ships.

Exclaimed Johnson after winning the award, "I've been waiting my entire life for this moment."

Ellison, who won the award for his classic *Invisible Man*, attended the awards ceremony at the Plaza Hotel in New York.

Other Black winners of the award in the past include women writers Alice Walker and Gloria Naylor.

Also winning the National Book Award this year was author Ron Chernow for his *The House of Morgan: An American Banking Dynasty and the Rise of Modern Finance.* The book won in the non-fiction category.

— *Jet*

1. In your own words, state the main point of the selection. Where in the selection is the main point stated?

   _____

   _____

   _____

2. What are some major details?

   _____

   _____

   _____

   _____

   _____

3. What are some minor details?

   _____

   _____

   _____

CHAPTER **6** REVIEW TEST

Reading for Information

In the space provided, write the correct answer. Count 5 points for each correct answer.

Fact Finding

A. Read the selection below about women's wages in the 1960s. Then follow the instructions.

The Woman as Worker: The 1960s

In England women form 38 percent of the workforce; in the U.S.A. the proportion is only slightly smaller, around 35 percent. This means that in both countries half the women between the ages of sixteen and sixty-four work outside their homes. Of the seventeen million married women in the U.S. who go out to work, ten million have children under the age of seventeen. The average wage of an Englishwoman doing administrative, technical or clerical work is less than £12 ($28.80) a week, while men in the same industries earn an average wage of £28 a week. Male manual workers earn an average wage of £20 week; women, £10. The same disparity between the earnings of the sexes is visible right across the board in the United States, where male professionals and technicians can expect to earn $9,370 annually and females, $5,210. Male clerical workers can expect to earn $6,380, women $3,844. While a sales*man* can live on a respectable $6,814, his female counterpart must do with $2,116. The skilled operator, who is nearly always a man, nets about $7,224 annually; skilled women may expect $3,826. Men in the service industries get paid an average wage of $4,532 annually for more important work than the women waitressing, cleaning and answering the telephone for the starvation wage of $2,076. The average male employee in the United States earns $6,610 a year; his sister $3,157, less than half.

— *Germaine Greer*

154

_____ 1. In the blank space write the letter of the sentence that best states the main idea of the paragraph.

    a. Women earn less than half as much as their male counterparts.

    b. Although women in England and the United States make up a large part of the work force, they are underpaid compared to men.

    c. Women work hard and should be men's equals on the job no matter what the job is.

    d. Male and female clerical workers are paid equally poorly both in England and the United States of America.

Put a plus sign (+) next to the statements that are facts, based on the paragraph and a minus sign (−) next to the statements that are not facts.

_____ 2. Women do not work outside their homes.

_____ 3. An Englishwoman who did clerical or administrative work in the 1960s earned less than half of what an Englishman in the same position earned.

_____ 4. In the United States male professionals in the 1960s earned about $5,200 while female professionals earned about $9,400.

_____ 5. In the United States in the 1960s the average male worker earned more than twice what the average female worker earned.

_____ 6. In the 1960s the women's workforce in the U.S. was slightly higher than the workforce of women in England.

_____ 7. A female manual worker in England earned about £10 a week.

_____ 8. Sales*men* earned about twice what sales*women* earned.

_____ 9. Waitresses in the United States were paid just about as well as service industry workers.

_____ 10. United States wages for women were generally better than women's wages in England.

Major Details, Minor Details

B.   Read the paragraph below and then answer the questions that follow.

> A classic example of how public relations can "rehabilitate" an image is that of Richard Nixon, who resigned from the presidency in disgrace in 1974. Through skillful public relations, he has rebuilt his image over nearly two decades. After a long absence, and after publishing several books, Nixon re-emerged in the 1980s as an expert on foreign policy and a senior statesman. He bravely spoke before the American Society of Newspaper Editors and what is now the Newspaper Association of America — journalists' organizations with whom he had notably bad relations during his presidency. He appeared in a widely disseminated photo with Katherine Graham, publisher of the *Washington Post,* the newspaper credited with hastening his ouster from office. Thus, as a result of a carefully orchestrated communications strategy, the new Nixon seemed statesmanlike, brilliant, and even responsive to criticism. His eventual place in history doubtless will be positively affected by his creative use of public relations.
>
> *— Melvin L. DeFleur and Everette E. Dennis*

_____ 1.   Write the letter of the sentence that best states the main idea of the paragraph.

   a.   Nixon will have a positive place in history.
   b.   Skillful public relations are essential for United States presidents.
   c.   The example of Richard Nixon shows how public relations can help change a negative image.
   d.   Senior statesmen are made by newspapers like the *Washington Post.*

2.   Write *maj* beside each major detail in the paragraph and *min* beside each minor detail.

_____   a.   Nixon resigned the presidency in disgrace.

_____   b.   Katherine Graham was the publisher of the *Washington Post.*

_____   c. Nixon spoke with two newspaper groups with whom he had had bad relations during his presidency.

_____   d. The two groups he addressed were the American Society of Newspaper Editors and the Newspaper Association of America.

_____   e. Nixon spoke bravely to the newspaper groups.

_____   f. The new Nixon seemed like a brilliant statesman responsive to criticism.

_____   g. Nixon resigned in 1974.

_____   h. Creative public relations will ensure Nixon's positive place in history.

Score: _____ correct × 5 points each = _____

7

Recognizing Paragraph Patterns

Paragraphs are important units of thought in your reading. Each paragraph fits ideas and information together into a web of meaning. Writers often help you discover this meaning by arranging information or ideas into patterns that are easy to recognize. If you miss the pattern and don't see how the details fit together, the paragraph may seem a jumble of ideas or facts to you. Once you are familiar with these patterns, you will be able to spot them when you read.

For example, when you are able to recognize *time order*, you immediately will know how to put the details together in your mind. You also will know that each new sentence answers the question "What happens next?" When you recognize a *comparison-contrast* pattern, you will know that the writer is presenting double information — details for each of the two things being compared. You then will be careful to match up every detail with its proper subject. You also will look to see how the sets of details match up with each other, point by point.

Writers rarely use basic paragraph patterns in a rigid way. They often shift, overlap, and combine patterns. Sometimes they invent new ones. A paragraph that begins by following place order to set a scene may shift to time order to let the writer tell a story. When an order of importance emerges, the writer is conveying opinions about the material.

Recognizing paragraph patterns will help you read more smoothly. Look for patterns in everything you read.

7a Ordering Ideas

7a(1) *Time Order (Chronology)*

Some paragraphs present information in time order. In these cases, you must keep in mind the *sequence*: One idea follows another and relates to an event or idea that comes before. This order often is used to tell a story or to explain how to do or make something.

> The dimly lit place where I sat in a tub lodged between two boards was the room that served as both kitchen and bath in the house where my father was born. My mother had been about to give me a bath, but first she put me in the tub of hot water and went into the next room to take off her kimono. Suddenly she heard me start wailing at the top of my lungs. She rushed back and found me spilled out of the tub on the floor crying. The painfully bright, shiny thing overhead, my mother explained, was probably a hanging oil lamp of the type still used when I was a baby.
>
> — *Akira Kurosawa*

7a(2) *Place Order*

Some paragraphs provide details arranged according to their place in a room, a building, or an outdoor scene. These details follow a direction that traces movement from one part of a scene to another. A writer, especially when describing something, may give details from left to right, from near to far, from east to west, or in some other clear place order.

> In a little while we had come to the top of the ridge where, looking to the east, you can see for the first time the monument and the burying ground on the little hill where the church is. That is where the terrible thing started. Just south of the burying ground on the little hill a deep dry gulch runs about east and west, very crooked, and it rises westward to nearly the top of the ridge where we were. It had no name, but the Wasichus sometimes call it Battle Creek now. We stopped on the ridge not far from the head of the dry gulch. Wagon-guns were still going off over there on the little hill, and they were going off again where they hit along the gulch. There was much shooting

down <u>yonder,</u> and there were many cries, and we could see cavalrymen scattered <u>over the hills ahead</u> of us. Cavalrymen were riding <u>along the gulch</u> and shooting <u>into it,</u> where the women and children were running <u>away</u> and trying to hide <u>in</u> <u>the gullies</u> and the stunted pines.

— *Black Elk*

7a(3) *Order of Importance*

Some paragraph details are put together so that we know which ideas the writer thinks are more important than others. In this kind of paragraph the least important idea generally comes first, and the writer tells the other details in order of growing importance.

By 1905 there were several score of these cafés, or, as they were sometimes called, coffee-and-cake parlors, on the East Side. Each café had its enthusiasts claiming it was the true center of Yiddish intellect. For the early playwrights and actors, it was Schreiber's café on Canal Street. For the serious young poets of 1907–1908 who called themselves *Di Yunge* (The Young Ones), it was Goodman and Levine's on East Broadway. For the radicals, as the veteran socialist Louis Waldman remembered, it was the Monopole at Second Avenue and Ninth Street, where Leon Trotsky once appeared in the flesh. But the <u>most famous</u> center for writers, actors, philosophers, and *kibitzers* who took pleasure in staring at the great, was the Café Royale on Second Avenue and Twelfth Street. For a dime (and a nickel tip) you could get a glass of tea and a piece of coffee cake while sorting out the celebrities of Yiddish culture and listening to the gypsy fiddler Ferenc Miklos, who played, said the critic Samuel Chotzinoff, "with a sumptuous tone that a great artist might envy."

— *Irving Howe*

Once you know the way the writer orders details, you can follow the sequence more easily. In time order, events come one after the other. In place order, objects appear in relation to other objects. In order of importance, you learn the writer's opinion about which ideas are more crucial than others.

> How to See Paragraph Arrangement
> - Certain words in paragraphs give you hints about how the ideas are arranged.
> - For *time order* look for words that tell time, such as *when, then, first, second, next, last, after, before, later, finally, suddenly.*
> - For *place order* look for words that locate, such as *there, beside, near, far, above, below, next to, under, on top of, over, alongside, beneath, by, behind, on, east, west, north, south.*
> - For *order of importance* look for words that help us judge importance, such as *first, next, last, less, least, most important, major, greatest, in the first place.*

EXERCISES

1. Ordering Ideas

1. In the example of *time order* (page 159), circle the words that help you see that paragraph details are arranged in time order.
2. In the example of *place order* (pages 159–160), circle the words that help you see that paragraph details are arranged in place order.
3. In the example of *order of importance* (page 160), circle the words that help you see that paragraph details are arranged in order of importance.

2. Understanding Sequence

Look at the following details from the example of time order (page 159). Arrange the details in correct chronological order by putting a *1* in front of the first event that happened, a *2* in front of the second, and so on.

_____   a. The mother takes off her kimono.

_____   b. The mother is about to bathe the child.

_____   c. The child is crying on the floor.

_____   d. The mother explains what the bright shiny thing is overhead.

_____   e. The mother puts the child in a tub of hot water.

_____   f. The child spills out of the tub.

3. Understanding Sequence
1. Reread the example of place order (pages 159–160). Put a *1*
next to the item described first in the paragraph, a *2* next to
the item described second, and so on.

_____   a. the wagon guns

_____   b. women and children running to hide

_____   c. the top of the ridge

_____   d. cavalrymen scattered over the hills

_____   e. a dry gulch called Battle Creek

_____   f. cavalrymen riding along the gulch

_____   g. the monument, burying ground, and church

_____ 2. In what order are the details mainly arranged?
a. top to bottom
b. left to right
c. inside to outside
d. large to small

_____ 3. What word best sums up the scene described by the
writer?
a. cheerful
b. terrible
c. amusing
d. silent

4. Understanding Sequence

The following details all are about the places named in the example on page 160. Put an *X* next to the place that is most important in the paragraph. Put an *L* beside the statement that comes latest in the paragraph.

_____ a. Goodman and Levine's hosted *Di Yunge*.

_____ b. Early playwrights and actors visited Schreiber's café.

_____ c. Writers, actors, and philosophers visited the Café Royale on Second Avenue and Twelfth Street.

_____ d. Leon Trotsky once appeared at the Café Monopole at Second Avenue and Ninth Street.

5. Understanding Sequence

Read this paragraph about the kitchen that a writer remembers from his youth. Then answer the questions that follow.

The kitchen held our lives together. My mother worked in it all day long, we ate in it almost all meals except the Passover *seder,* I did my homework and first writing at the kitchen table, and in winter I often had a bed made up for me on three kitchen chairs near the stove. On the wall just over the table hung a long horizontal mirror that sloped to a ship's prow at each end and was lined in cherry wood. It took up the whole wall, and drew every object in the kitchen to itself. The walls were a fiercely stippled white-wash, so often rewhitened by my father in slack seasons that the paint looked as if it had been squeezed and cracked into the walls. A large electric bulb hung down the center of the kitchen at the end of a chain that had been hooked into the ceiling; the old gas ring and key still jutted out of the wall like antlers. In the corner next to the toilet was the sink at which we washed, and the square tub in which my mother did our clothes. Above it, tacked to the shelf on which were pleasantly ranged square, blue-bordered white sugar and spice jars, hung calendars from the Public National Bank on Pitkin Avenue and the Minsker Progressive Branch of the Workmen's Circle; receipts for the payment of insurance premiums, and household bills on a spindle; two little boxes engraved with Hebrew letters. One of these was for the poor, the other to buy back the Land of Israel.

— *Alfred Kazin*

_____ 1. The details in the paragraph are arranged primarily in which order?
a. time order
b. place order
c. order of importance
d. a combination of all three

2. Number the correct sequence by putting a *1* next to the item named or described first in the paragraph, a *2* next to the item named or described second, and so on.

_____ a. the electric bulb on the ceiling

_____ b. the mirror

_____ c. the sink and tub

_____ d. the calendars hanging from the shelf

_____ e. the bed of chairs

_____ f. the gas ring and key

_____ g. the painted walls

_____ h. the shelf of spice jars

_____ i. the toilet

_____ j. the kitchen table

Critical Thinking in Writing

In what way does the kitchen (or some other room) in your house hold your family's lives together? Write a paragraph or two to describe this room and its central role in the life of your family.

7b   Listing Details

Information in a paragraph sometimes appears just as a series of facts or details. Though all statements relate to the main idea, each fact is not expanded. The paragraph presents a listing of information.

In the following paragraph about wildlife getting loose, notice how the writer lists a series of details to support the topic.

> Imported wildlife getting loose also contributes to the growth of our new urban jungle. In Florida, where the climate is hospitable, about 50 such exotic species have been recorded, according to the National Geographic Society. These escaped species include giant Colombian iguanas, walking Siamese catfish (creatures with stiff fins that permit them to "walk" across roads), and the Amazon flesh-eating piranha fish, brought into Florida under strict control but freed by careless handlers. Rhesus monkeys were imported for early Tarzan films and later freed; today they survive in Florida swamps. Many Western jackrabbits used in Florida training farms for racing greyhounds escaped in 1940. Today they plague the state's cattle ranches. Armadillos also roam the Florida countryside and ruin lawns by boring into them. These armadillos are descendants of escapees from a private zoo in Cocoa Beach that was destroyed by a hurricane in 1924.
>
> — *Christopher Nyerges*

EXERCISES

1. Listing Details

Reread the paragraph above and answer these questions.

_____ 1. What is the main idea of the paragraph?
   a. Armadillos are descendants of escapees from a Cocoa Beach zoo.
   b. Wildlife causes problems.
   c. The National Geographic Society records species of animals.
   d. Wild animals that have escaped from care contribute to the growth of a new urban jungle.

2. What are some of the animals mentioned to support the main point?

_____

_____

2. Listing Details in a Longer Selection

Read this selection on job interviews from a textbook on career planning. Notice the listing of details throughout. Then answer the questions that follow.

Job Interviews

1   Job interviews are never easy for an applicant. Most people get anxious about interviews, particularly if they are seriously interested in the job. They are afraid that they will not do well.

2   The style of the interviewer may vary from warm and interested to cold and aloof or even rude. Some interviewers expect the applicant to make only brief remarks; others encourage or expect you to do most of the talking. You should not be surprised by occasional silence from the interviewer.

3   Employers and personnel officers will sometimes ask questions that you do not expect, because they are interested in how you react and respond. Table 9.1 presents questions frequently asked during job interviews. Before you go to an interview, think about the responses you would make if you were asked these or similar questions.

4   From the point of view of the organization, an interview is conducted (1) to obtain information and impressions about applicants, and (2) to give applicants information about the organization. Many interviewers seem to be most concerned about ruling out undesirable candidates, so negative information gained from the applicant often carries more weight than positive information.

5   The average interview is fairly brief, lasting about twenty to thirty-five minutes. Decisions to employ are often based on subjective factors such as intuition, attitudes, and ideas about a good employee. Your objective as an applicant in a job interview is to present yourself honestly, but in such a way that the interviewer develops a positive impression based on subjective factors unrelated to job performance. For example, the employ-

TABLE 9.1   Questions Frequently Asked During
Job Interviews

1. What led you to choose your academic major or field? What do you like about it? What don't you like about it?
2. In what kinds of positions are you most interested?
3. Would you identify or describe any summer or previous employment in this or a related field?
4. What have you learned from previous work experience?
5. In choosing a job, what are your most important considerations?
6. What courses have you taken that you think helped prepare you for this occupation? How did you do in them?
7. Why are you interviewing with our organization?
8. Do you have any geographical preferences about where you work?
9. What do you expect to be doing five years from now? Ten years from now? What are your long-range goals?
10. If you are married, how does your spouse view your working?
11. How important is your family and personal life compared with your work?
12. What are your father's and mother's occupations?
13. How do you spend your leisure time?
14. What would you say is your strongest attribute? Weakest?
15. What are your ideas on salary? How much money do you want to be earning five years from now?
16. Were you ever fired from a job? Did you ever quit? Why?
17. What can you contribute to this organization?
18. Do you have any questions you want to ask?

ment interview is not the place to talk about personal problems, family problems, or previous job problems. Never lie about leaving previous jobs, for contradictions will show up when personnel officers do reference checks. If you were fired, be honest with the interviewer and say you didn't have the skills or understand the responsibility. Also say you are looking for ways to grow and to overcome such problems in the future. No matter what happened, don't criticize your former employer or the people you worked with — if you do, you will probably lose the job. If the interviewer asks about personal weaknesses, always speak of your weaknesses as potential areas of development. You might say, for example, "I haven't had management experience yet, but that's what I find appealing about this job. I think it will give me the opportunity to get some experience." Or turn your weakness into a strength, saying, for example, "I'm a perfectionist."

6   Most interviewers look for a pleasant, friendly person who has positive attitudes toward working. They expect the appli-

cant to be prepared to discuss his or her skills and experiences and how he or she would fit the job being sought. The positive person who has been involved in career planning and has some idea of where he or she wants to be in five or ten years has a jump ahead of the person shopping for a job.

7   Here are some suggestions for handling job interviews:

1. *Make an appointment.* Be on time for the appointment. Some evidence is available that being on time is even more important than appearance in making a positive first impression. If you are going to be the least bit late, call ahead. When you arrive, apologize immediately for your tardiness and explain what delayed you. Treat the secretary or others in the outer office with courtesy and respect.

2. *Go alone.* Don't take a friend or a parent. The employer is interested in you. If a friend or parent accompanies you, the employer may wonder if you are mature or serious enough to handle a job.

3. *Before you go, think about the questions you may be asked.* Although interviewers vary in the questions they ask, most of them want to know what experience you have had, what education you have had and where you received it, what you are like, what your plans for the future are, what you can do well, the state of your health, and the like. You can prepare by asking yourself these questions and planning your answers. (See Table 9.1.) For example, if you are asked why you left your last job, there are several good reasons you can name, all of them positive: "I needed more opportunity for growth," or "I'm looking for professional advancement."

    If your long-range goal is to go into business for yourself, you may want to avoid saying so. You certainly will not encourage an employer by indicating that you will give the company the privilege of training you for a year or two, but then plan on going on your own to compete with it.

4. *Be aware of your physical appearance.* Two factors are particularly important in influencing an interviewer's initial impression of you. These are dress and physical attractiveness. You should avoid extremes in appearance that divert the interviewer's attention. For men, a business suit always is appropriate, but stay away from leisure suits. Excessive facial hair tends to create a negative impression; long hair produces the strongest negative reaction, beards the next strongest. Mustaches seem to produce little negative reaction, and sideburns seem to have a neutral effect. For women, short skirts, low necklines, and, in some in-

stances, pantsuits create unfavorable impressions. Dress conservatively. The work setting will determine the appropriate attire. Don't smoke or chew gum during the interview.

5. *Be attentive.* Remain standing until you are invited to sit down. Listen to what the interviewer is saying. Talk clearly (that does not mean loudly) and directly to the interviewer. Answer questions factually, fully, and directly. If you do not hear something the interviewer has said, ask him or her to repeat it. Many interviewing experts consider communication and interpersonal skills as the single most important factors in the interview. Nonverbal behaviors such as eye contact, smiling, and attentive posture also are influential.

6. *Show interest.* Before an employer hires you, he or she must know what you can do and must feel confident that you can do it. Many employers who interview young people say that they often show no interest in the job or what it can lead to in the future. All too often, these employers say that young people are only interested in the money and the hours of employment. You need not and should not claim that you know everything about the job, but you must show that you are eager to learn and improve as you go along.

You may be able to state your abilities more clearly if you plan beforehand how you might describe them to an interviewer. Also show an interest in the company as a whole, not just in the particular job. To do so, research the company before the interview, finding out what it does, its history, future plans, etc. Statements that indicate cooperation, dependability, trustworthiness, and motivation help to counter negative impressions. The interviewer looks for a pleasant, socially aware individual who is enthusiastic about work and career.

To maintain an interviewer's attention on objective factors, you need to discuss your special qualifications for the position both at the beginning and at other times. Mentioning specific and relevant skills, work experience, and educational background demonstrates both your strength as a candidate and your understanding of the skills the job requires.

7. *Write down questions you want to ask the interviewer.* You can show your interest in the job and the company by asking questions. The interview is the place to become informed about the company. Too many applicants close up and can't remember the questions they have, so write them down and

use the list to ask what you want to know. Here are some questions you may want to ask:

a. Is there a written job description you can see?

b. What are usual working hours? policy on overtime?

c. Is there any probationary period for a new employee? If so, how long is it and who makes the decision?

d. Is a pre-employment physical examination required by the company? Does the company pay for it?

e. Is there a policy on vacation time? sick leave? How many vacation days and sick time hours are accrued in what length of time?

f. Are there company sports teams? physical fitness facilities?

g. Does the company offer a retirement plan? Do employees contribute to it? How long must you work before you become eligible for the plan?

h. Does the firm publish its salary schedule? Are there policies about cost-of-living increases? merit raises, bonuses?

i. How and when will you be notified whether you have the job?

Write your questions and put them in order of importance to you. You may want to jot down the answers you receive from the interviewer. The important thing is to know what you want to ask and ask it.

8. *Do not prolong the interview.* Once the interviewer indicates that it is over, leave promptly unless you have something relevant to say. If you do, tell the interviewer what you want to say. Most interviewers have other appointments to keep, but they want to be sure that you have presented everything that should be said in your behalf. Ask for the privilege of returning or calling in a few days to find out whether you have the job. Be sure to express your appreciation for the interview.

Unless you have been told that you have or do not have the job, return occasionally to inquire as to whether there is an opening. Do not let the firm forget you, but do not make a nuisance of yourself. Ask your questions courteously, but do not linger after you have a reply. If you have an unsuccessful interview, analyze the whole experience and plan how you could present your case better next time.

8   If, after an interview, you fail to get the job, do not always assume that you made a bad impression. Employers often have so many qualified applicants that they must turn down many who could handle the job well. The person they finally employ may have some chance advantage over the other applicants —

a personality that matches those of the other workers in the organization, for example — that you could not possibly guess at. So if you fail to get a job, try not to worry about it. Go on to the next interview, and do the best you can.

— *Bruce Shertzer*

1. What is the main idea of this selection?

    _____

2. What is the main idea of paragraph 4? What does the writer list to support his point?

    _____

    _____

    _____

    _____

3. Write down three important details listed in paragraph 5 about how to present yourself in an interview.

    _____

    _____

    _____

4. How does the writer present information in Table 9.1? Why?

    _____

    _____

5. The writer lists a number of suggestions for handling job interviews. Which three do you find most important? Why?

    _____

    _____

    _____

Critical Thinking in Writing

Write a one-page letter to a high school student preparing for a first job interview. Drawing on what you read by Bruce Shertzer, give the student advice on how to succeed at the interview.

7c Classification

In some paragraphs different details relating to a topic are arranged in categories, or groups. This paragraph pattern identifies categories and shows how various examples in the same category are either alike or different. Classification also can show how a large subject can be broken up into different parts. In reading paragraphs that use classification, notice the kinds of categories that separate the specifics into groups.

The following paragraph from a textbook classifies the kinds of resolutions (formal statements) that the U.S. Congress takes up.

> In addition to bills, Congress sometimes considers resolutions. A resolution is a formal statement expressing a legislative decision or opinion. There are three types of congressional resolutions. A *simple resolution* concerns the rules or opinions of just one chamber of Congress — for instance, changing the jurisdiction of a subcommittee or congratulating the U.S. Olympic team. Simple resolutions do not require the approval of the other house or of the President and do not have the force of law. A *concurrent resolution* expresses opinions or rule changes agreed to by both the Senate and House. Like simple resolutions, they neither have the force of law nor require presidential approval. Finally, a *joint resolution* must be passed by both houses of Congress and signed by the President. Like bills, joint resolutions have the force of law, but they usually deal with very special matters, such as making an invitation to a foreign government or correcting an error in a bill previously sent to the President. Constitutional amendments are also proposed in the form of joint resolutions.
>
> — *Richard J. Hardy*

EXERCISES

1. Classification

Reread the preceding paragraph and answer these questions.

1. What is the first category of resolutions? Give some examples of it.

    _____

    _____

2. What is the second category? What kinds of issues does it deal with?

    _____

    _____

3. What is the third category of resolutions? Explain and give examples.

    _____

    _____

    _____

    _____

2. Classification

The following report of survey research on Hispanic voters suggests that it may be too easy to categorize people by ethnic group. Then the report goes on to use the survey data to suggest a more complicated set of classifications that can be used to understand this group of voters. Read the selection and then answer the questions that follow.

> The term "Hispanic voters" rolls easily off the tongues of pollsters and politicians, suggesting a monolithic ethnic group whose members share the same values.
>
> But in the first broad analysis of the political attitudes and practices of Mexicans, Puerto Ricans, and Cubans, who comprise a large majority of all Hispanics, the Latino National Po-

litical Survey (LNPS) reveals differences that defy conventional wisdom about the nation's fastest-growing major population group.

Filling a void in national voting and polling studies, which generally have overlooked this group, the survey indicates that it is misleading to think any label can encompass Hispanic behavior or political preference. According to the survey, Mexicans, Puerto Ricans, and Cubans prefer their national identity to terms like "Hispanic," "Latino," or "Spanish American." In fact, a majority in all three groups prefer to identify themselves as "American."

LNPS respondents — who included non-Hispanic "Anglos" living in cities with large Hispanic populations — also see themselves as distinct culturally and politically. When asked to place themselves on a scale ranging from very liberal to very conservative, the largest portions of all three Latino groups as well as the Anglos put themselves on the conservative side of the spectrum; 51% of Cubans, 47% of Puerto Ricans, and 39% of Mexicans and Anglos perceive themselves as "very conservative," "conservative," or "slightly conservative." On the other hand, those regarding themselves as "moderate, middle of the road" include 23% of Cubans, 25% of Puerto Ricans, 32% of Mexicans, and 35% of Anglos. Those in the "very liberal," "liberal," and "slightly liberal" categories include 23% of Cubans, 28% of Puerto Ricans, 29% of Mexicans, and 26% of Anglos.

— *Lynne Duke*

1. In what way could the classification "Hispanic voters" be considered a mistake?

2. The political attitudes and practices of three subgroups were surveyed. What are these three groups, and how were they chosen?

3. How would the people in these groups prefer to classify themselves? In what category would they place themselves?

4. What categories do most not prefer?

   _____

5. On the basis of this survey what conclusions can you draw about how Hispanic voters actually vote?

   _____

   _____

   _____

7d   Comparison and Contrast

The technique of relating one object to another by showing how they are alike and how they are different is called *comparison and contrast*. To describe an unfamiliar object or idea, an author sometimes relates the unfamiliar object to a familiar one.

In the following paragraph, the writers compare the changes that occur in a child's physical development between ages two and five. Notice that the writers describe the behaviors of the younger child first and of the older child second. In this kind of comparison and contrast, called the *block method*, the writer presents one subject and explains it fully and then presents the next subject and explains it fully.

> The most direct way to get a clear picture of changes in physical development during the years from two to five is to visit a nursery school and watch the children at play. Differences between two- and five-year-olds are apparent not only in physical size, but also in coordination of both small and large muscle activities. Most two-year-olds have a well-coordinated walk, but they run with difficulty. If they get on a tricycle, they may use only one pedal at a time. Great effort and concentration may be required to get food on a spoon, and spills at the dining table are common. When getting dressed, they may help by pushing their arms and legs into shirt sleeves and pants, but they cannot get into these garments by themselves. They negotiate stairs one step at a time, putting down first one foot and then the other before moving to the next step. Most five-year-olds, by contrast, can run easily and use play equip-

ment with considerable skill. They can handle tricycles with proficiency and may also be able to ride a bicycle (with or without training wheels). They can handle spoons and forks well (although knives may still be a problem), and spills while eating are more likely to be due to carelessness than to lack of coordination. They can dress themselves easily, although tying shoe laces may still be a problem. They can go up and down stairs by alternating feet and climb with agility.

— *Robert F. Biehler and Lynne M. Hudson*

In another type of comparison and contrast, called the *point-by-point* (or *alternating*) *method,* the writer states one point and discusses *both* ideas or objects in relation to it. Then the writer states another point and discusses both ideas or objects in relation to *that* point, and so on, one point at a time.

In this selection from a composition textbook, see how a student writer discusses the various qualities of her two roommates.

Different Roommates

I am amazed myself at how little trouble it is living with and liking two such different roommates. Their physical appearances differ greatly. With small brown eyes and straight black hair to her shoulders, Julie is tall, lean, and statuesque. Pat, on the other hand, is tiny. Under five feet tall, she keeps her blond hair short and fluffy. Looking out over a small nose, her large grey eyes are "funny looking," according to her. "They're all right if you like cats," she says grinning. These two girls also have different kinds of interests. Julie likes reading or relaxing quietly in front of the television set. She likes talking too; she will speak to me for hours about a feature in *People Magazine* or about a Marx Brothers' film she watched on Channel 4 until dawn. Her voice quivers with excitement. "Just listen to this," she will say, her eyes glowing, her warm fingers pressed to my palm to hold my attention. But for Pat the outdoor life holds more interest than books or screens. At six each morning, in a bright orange sweat suit, she is jogging merrily down University Drive, crunching through leaves for her usual four miles. She swims. She plays tennis. She is a terror at paddleball, smashing shots I have to groan to return. However, the most interesting difference between them is their approach to schoolwork. Julie grows tense before an exam. At her desk a small fluorescent lamp throws a pale light on her face as she sits for hours glaring nervously at a page in her biology book. She underlines words noisily and scrawls notes to herself in the margin with a yellow felt pen. Her lips say over and over some key words she wants to memorize. Because only "A" grades satisfy her, she works tirelessly. Pat, on the contrary, takes everything easy, and exams are no exception. Sprawled on the red and white print couch, she surrounds herself with cola, corn chips, chocolate bars, apples, and salted nuts. She jabbers endlessly and jumps up every few minutes to stare out the window, to do a few sit-ups or to splash herself with spicy cologne. Without much effort or anxiety she crams enough data into her head to earn grades that keep her happy. Since I can live in harmony with my two roommates in spite of their differences, I am confident that I will be able to get along with most people anywhere.

— *Cecilia Richardson**

How to Recognize Comparison-and-Contrast Patterns

- Look for key words that help relate the two objects or ideas. These words point to like ideas:

similarly	*in addition*	*in the same way*
also	*further*	*likewise*

These words point to ideas that differ:

but	*on the other hand*	*still*
although	*in contrast*	*in spite of*
however	*yet*	*even so*
nevertheless	*conversely*	*nonetheless*

- Look for a sentence that tells just what is being compared to what.
- As you read, keep in mind the two ideas that the writer is comparing or contrasting. Ask yourself: What things are being compared? Why are they being compared? How are the things alike or different?

---

*Richardson, Cecilia, "Different Roommates." From Harvey S. Wiener, *Creating Compositions*, 5/e, pp. 133–134. Copyright 1987. Reproduced with permission of the publisher, McGraw-Hill, Inc.

EXERCISES

1. Comparison and Contrast

Reread the selection about two- and five-year-olds on pages 175–176. Then answer these questions.

1. What is the main idea of this paragraph?

_____

_____

2. What are some physical qualities of two-year-olds?

_____

_____

_____

3. What are some physical qualities of five-year-olds?

_____

_____

_____

_____

4. Why do you think the writers used comparison and contrast here?

_____

_____

_____

2. Comparison and Contrast

Reread the paragraph on pages 176–177 about the writer's two roommates. Then answer these questions.

1. What is the main idea?

    _____

    _____

2. In what three ways does the writer compare Pat and Julie?

    _____

    _____

3. How are the details arranged in this paragraph? (See **7a.**)

    _____

    _____

4. What are Julie's main interests? Pat's?

    _____

    _____

5. How are Julie and Pat different in the way they study?

    _____

    _____

3. Comparison and Contrast

The selections below use comparison-and-contrast strategies. For each example, state the main idea and explain what is being compared. Also point out some of the similarities or differences between the objects being discussed in each case.

1. San Antonians think that they have much to teach the rest of the nation about how Anglo and Hispanic cultures can meld. In other North American cities, Hispanics tend to form their own communities of little Havanas or little San Juans. San Antonio is different. In politics and business, in the arts and language, in clothes and food, San Antonio is well ahead of the rest of the country in what the Spanish call *mestizaje* — the

gradual merging of two peoples into one. "What you find here in San Antonio is the embryo of a new mestizo culture, with each side taking from the other," observes John Leeper, who is the director of the McNay Art Museum.

— *Kenneth Woodward*

a. What is the main idea?

_____

_____

_____

b. What is being compared?

_____

_____

c. What are some similarities or differences?

_____

_____

_____

2. There are two Americas. One is the America of Lincoln and Adlai Stevenson; the other is the America of Teddy Roosevelt and the modern superpatriots. One is generous and humane, the other narrowly egotistical; one is self-critical, the other self-righteous; one is sensible, the other romantic; one is good-humored, the other solemn; one is inquiring, the other pontificating; one is moderate, the other filled with passionate intensity; one is judicious and the other arrogant in the use of great power.

— *J. William Fulbright*

a. What is the main point?

_____

_____

b. What is being compared?

_____

_____

c. What are some similarities or differences?

_____

_____

_____

_____

_____

_____

3. The most salient features of many disabled persons are bodily traits similar to skin color, gender, and other attributes that have been used as a basis for differentiating people for centuries and without which discrimination probably could not occur. In fact, in a recent survey, 45 percent of disabled Americans said that they considered themselves "a minority group in the same sense as . . . Blacks and Hispanics." Unlike other minorities, however, disabled men and women have not yet been able to refute implicit or direct accusations of biological inferiority that have often been invoked to rationalize the oppression of groups whose appearance differs from the standards of the dominant majority. Since most disabled children and adults have been raised by nondisabled parents or guardians, they also lack a sense of generational continuity that might otherwise allow the legacy of their experience to become an important solace in an uncaring and inhospitable world. Perhaps even more significantly, people with disabilities have been forced to bear a stigma that virtually defines them as "not quite human."

— *Harlan Hahn*

a. What is the main idea?

_____

_____

_____

b. What is being compared?

_____

_____

c. What is one similarity?

_____

_____

d. What are some differences?

_____

_____

_____

_____

7e   Cause and Effect

In this kind of paragraph, you learn either *why* something happened or what happened *as a result* of something. The writer may explain conditions or events that *cause* a certain situation or discuss conditions or events that *result* from a situation.

Cause and effect are important in much of the scientific and technical material you will read in college. As those of you who study science already know, many scientific discoveries were made because a scientist studied cause and effect in natural events. In the passage you just read, you saw how educators studied two *effects* — boys suffering in elementary school classrooms and girls performing poorly on later tests — to see if they could discover some possible *causes* for them.

In our everyday life we frequently consider causes. For instance, we avoid eating food that smells bad or touching some-

> ## How to Recognize Cause-and-Effect Patterns
> - If the writer tells why something happened, what happened because of something, or what might happen because of something, you can expect reasons to explain causes or effects.
> - Look for word clues: *because, as a result, therefore, consequently, so.*
> - Remember that many causes can contribute to a single situation and that many effects can grow from a single cause.

thing that is glowing hot because we know the effect tainted food or red-hot objects have on us. So, too, when we read a passage, we can look for reasons (causes) behind the events described (effects).

The following selection from a sociology textbook explains causes. It tells why young boys, but not young girls, feel comfortable with both male and female activities.

> Why have boys become comfortable with both traditionally female and male activities while girls have not? Apparently, boys have become more comfortable with dolls and cooking because many now have mothers who work outside the home and fathers who change diapers. However, while mothers may be developing careers in male-dominated occupations, they often continue to perform traditional female roles at home, which accounts in part for their daughters' preference for house play and similar activities (Hellmich, 1985:D3).
>
> — *Richard T. Schaefer**

EXERCISES

1. Cause and Effect

Reread the paragraph on this page and answer the questions.

1. How can you tell from the first sentence that the writer will be explaining causes?

_____

_____

_____

*From *Sociology*, 5/e, by Richard T. Schaefer, copyright 1995 McGraw-Hill, Inc. Reproduced by permission of McGraw-Hill, Inc.

2. Why have boys become more comfortable with dolls and cooking?

   _____

   _____

3. Why are girls more comfortable with "house play" than with male-oriented games?

   _____

   _____

2. Cause and Effect

Read this paragraph about a student's efforts to understand his past. Then answer the questions that follow.

> When I try to understand my years of failure in school, I can come up with some answers now that I'm finally in college and serious about my work. In the first place, things were not easy at home. Five of us lived in a dingy three-room apartment on Sutter Avenue, where not much privacy encouraged study and reading. My father died when I was five, and my mother's energy after a day packing chemicals at a local factory was too low for her to keep after me. After dinner she would stretch out on an old brown sofa in front of the television, and my sisters and I would sit beside her on the floor. At report card time, though, she'd complain bitterly; I could tell from her tired eyes that she knew she hadn't kept after me enough. Also, my friends were just not the studying kind. On spring afternoons we would skip high school classes regularly, smoking and rapping in my friend Jerry's old Ford or swatting softballs on the diamond at Hillcrest Park. A recent survey by the United States Office of Education may have shown that fewer than two-thirds of America's high school students ever graduated, but in my group of eight friends not one of us received a diploma. And we couldn't have cared less! But the most important reason for my not doing well in school, I think, was that I never saw a connection between what we did at our creaky wooden desks at Jefferson and what was waiting for us beyond school. I don't think I ever believed that Mrs. Allen's pages of algebra homework or Mr. Delaney's boring lectures on the Civil War had any real meaning for me. But then after school I tried find-

ing a job. I worked for five years as a stock boy without getting anywhere. Lugging up cartons of Coke and boxes of toilet tissue from the basement at Foodtown was not my idea of a future. I tried finding other jobs without success. When I finally decided to take my high school equivalency test, I passed it the first time around. As a business major at LaGuardia Community College, I know that there are no guarantees about my life from now on, but at least a college degree will open doors that people slammed in my face before.

— *Richard S. Smith*

1. What is the main point of this selection?

2. In what order does the writer arrange the information (see Section **7a**)? How do you know?

3. List the three main causes for the writer's failure in school.

3. Combined Paragraph Patterns

Read this selection about what affirmative action meant to one writer. As you read, keep in mind the various paragraph patterns you have examined. After you read, answer the questions that follow.

1   My plan to become a professor of English — my ambition during long years in college at Stanford, then in graduate school at Columbia and Berkeley — was complicated by feelings of embarrassment and guilt. So many times I would see other

Mexican-Americans and know we were alike only in race. And yet, simply because our race was the same, I was, during the last years of my schooling, the beneficiary of their situation. Affirmative Action programs had made it all possible. The disadvantages of others permitted my promotion; the absence of many Mexican-Americans from academic life allowed my designation as a "minority student."

2   For me opportunities had been extravagant. There were fellowships, summer research grants, and teaching assistantships. After only two years in graduate school, I was offered teaching jobs by several colleges. Invitations to Washington conferences arrived and I had the chance to travel abroad as a "Mexican-American representative." The benefits were often, however, too gaudy to please. In three published essays, in conversations with teachers, in letters to politicians and at conferences, I worried the issue of Affirmative Action. Often I proposed contradictory opinions. Though consistent was the admission that — because of an early, excellent education — I was no longer a principal victim of racism or any other social oppression. I said that but still I continued to indicate on applications for financial aid that I was a Hispanic-American. It didn't really occur to me to say anything else, or to leave the question unanswered.

3   Thus I complied with and encouraged the odd bureaucratic logic of Affirmative Action. I let government officials treat the disadvantaged condition of many Mexican-Americans with my advancement. Each fall my presence was noted by Health, Education, and Welfare department statisticians. As I pursued advanced literary studies and learned the skill of reading Spenser and Wordsworth and Empson, I would hear myself numbered among the culturally disadvantaged. Still, silent, I didn't object.

4   But the irony cut deep. And guilt would not be evaded by averting my glance when I confronted a face like my own in a crowd. By late 1975, nearing the completion of my graduate studies at Berkeley, I was so wary of the benefits of Affirmative Action that I feared my inevitable success as an applicant for a teaching position. The months of fall — traditionally that time of academic job-searching — passed without my applying to a single school. When one of my professors chanced to learn this in late November, he was astonished, then furious. He yelled at me: Did I think that because I was a minority student jobs would just come looking for me? What was I thinking? Did I realize that he and several other faculty members had already written letters on my behalf? Was I going to start act-

ing like some other minority students he had known? They struggled for success and then, when it was almost within reach, grew strangely afraid and let it pass. Was that it? Was I determined to fail?

5   I did not respond to his questions. I didn't want to admit to him, and thus to myself, the reason I delayed.

6   I merely agreed to write to several schools. (In my letter I wrote: "I cannot claim to represent disadvantaged Mexican-Americans. The very fact that I am in a position to apply for this job should make that clear.") After two or three days, there were telegrams and phone calls, invitations to interviews, then airplane trips. A blur of faces and the murmur of their soft questions. And, over someone's shoulder, the sight of campus buildings shadowing pictures I had seen years before when I leafed through Ivy League catalogues with great expectations. At the end of each visit, interviewers would smile and wonder if I had any questions. A few times I quietly wondered what advantage my race had given me over other applicants. But that was an impossible question for them to answer without embarrassing me. Quickly, several persons insisted that my ethnic identity had given me no more than a "foot inside the door"; at most, I had a "slight edge" over other applicants. "We just looked at your dossier with extra care and we like what we saw. There was never any question of having to alter our standards. You can be certain of that."

7   In the early part of January, offers arrived on stiffly elegant stationery. Most schools promised terms appropriate for any new assistant professor. A few made matters worse — and almost more tempting — by offering more: the use of university housing; an unusually large starting salary; a reduced teaching schedule. As the stack of letters mounted, my hesitation increased. I started calling department chairmen to ask for another week, then 10 more days — "more time to reach a decision" — to avoid the decision I would need to make.

8   At school, meantime, some students hadn't received a single job offer. One man, probably the best student in the department, did not even get a request for his dossier. He and I met outside a classroom one day and he asked about my opportunities. He seemed happy for me. Faculty members beamed. They said they had expected it. "After all, not many schools are going to pass up getting a Chicano with a Ph.D. in Renaissance literature," somebody said laughing. Friends wanted to know which of the offers I was going to accept. But I couldn't make up my mind. February came and I was running out of time and excuses. (One chairman guessed my delay was a bar-

gaining ploy and increased his offer with each of my calls.) I had to promise a decision by the 10th; the 12th at the very latest.

9   On the 18th of February, late in the afternoon, I was in the office I shared with several other teaching assistants. Another graduate student was sitting across the room at his desk. When I got up to leave, he looked over to say in an uneventful voice that he had some big news. He had finally decided to accept a position at a faraway university. It was not a job he especially wanted, he admitted. But he had to take it because there hadn't been any other offers. He felt trapped, and depressed, since his job would separate him from his young daughter.

10   I tried to encourage him by remarking that he was lucky at least to have found a job. So many others hadn't been able to get anything. But before I finished speaking I realized that I had said the wrong thing. And I anticipated his next question.

11   "What are your plans?" he wanted to know. "Is it true you've gotten an offer from Yale?"

12   I said that it was. "Only, I still haven't made up my mind."

13   He stared at me as I put on my jacket. And smiling, then unsmiling, he asked if I knew that he too had written to Yale. In his case, however, no one had bothered to acknowledge his letter with even a postcard. What did I think of that?

14   He gave me no time to answer.

15   "Damn!" he said sharply and his chair rasped the floor as he pushed himself back. Suddenly, it was to *me* that he was complaining. "It's just not right, Richard. None of this is fair. You've done some good work, but so have I. I'll bet our records are just about equal. But when we look for jobs this year, it's a different story. You get all of the breaks."

16   To evade his criticism, I wanted to side with him. I was about to admit the injustice of Affirmative Action. But he went on, his voice hard with accusation. "It's all very simple this year. You're a Chicano. And I am a Jew. That's the only real difference between us."

17   His words stung me: there was nothing he was telling me that I didn't know. I had admitted everything already. But to hear someone else say these things, and in such an accusing tone, was suddenly hard to take. In a deceptively calm voice, I responded that he had simplified the whole issue. The phrases came like bubbles to the tip of my tongue: "new blood"; "the importance of cultural diversity"; "the goal of racial integration." These were all the arguments I had proposed several years ago — and had long since abandoned. Of course the offers were unjustifiable. I knew that. All I was saying amounted

to a frantic self-defense. I tried to find an end to a sentence. My voice faltered to a stop.

18   "Yeah, sure," he said. "I've heard all that before. Nothing you say really changes the fact that Affirmative Action is unfair. You see that, don't you? There isn't any way for me to compete with you. Once there were quotas to keep my parents out of certain schools; now there are quotas to get you in and the effect on me is the same as it was for them."

19   I listened to every word he spoke. But my mind was really on something else. I knew at that moment that I would reject all of the offers. I stood there silently surprised by what an easy conclusion it was. Having prepared for so many years to teach, having trained myself to do nothing else, I had hesitated out of practical fear. But now that it was made, the decision came with relief. I immediately knew I had made the right choice.

20   My colleague continued talking and I realized that he was simply right. Affirmative Action programs *are* unfair to white students. But as I listened to him assert his rights, I thought of the seriously disadvantaged. How different they were from white, middle-class students who come armed with the testimony of their grades and aptitude scores and self-confidence to complain about the unequal treatment they now receive. I listen to them. I do not want to be careless about what they say. Their rights are important to protect. But inevitably when I hear them or their lawyers, I think about the most seriously disadvantaged, not simply Mexican-Americans, but all those who do not ever imagine themselves going to college or becoming doctors: white, black, brown. Always poor. Silent. They are not plaintiffs before the court or against the misdirection of Affirmative Action. They lack the confidence (my confidence!) to assume their right to a good education. They lack the confidence and skills a good primary and secondary education provides and which are prerequisites for informed public life. They remain silent.

21   The debate drones on and surrounds them in stillness. They are distant, faraway figures like the boys I have seen peering down from freeway overpasses in some other part of town.

— *Richard Rodriguez*

1.   What is the main point of this selection?

_____

_____

_____

_____

2. What is the main point of the first and second paragraphs? What general paragraph pattern does the writer use there?

_____

_____

3. What reason (cause) does the writer give for his embarrassment? What effects of affirmative action programs in his own life does he describe?

_____

_____

_____

_____

4. Number the sequence of events in paragraphs 4 through 7 in correct order by putting a *1* beside the first event, a *2* beside the second, and so on.

_____   a. The professor yells at his student.

_____   b. The writer fears his inevitable success as a job applicant.

_____   c. The writer applies to several schools for jobs.

_____   d. The writer does not apply to any schools for jobs.

_____   e. The professor asks if the student wants to fail.

_____   f. The writer receives many job offers.

_____   g. The writer explains in his letters that he is not disadvantaged.

_____   h. The writer flies to job interviews.

5. Where does the writer use comparison and contrast?

_____

_____

_____

_____

_____

_____

6. What details are listed in paragraph 17 to explain the value of affirmative action?

_____

_____

Critical Thinking in Writing

Write about a page in which you present the advantages and disadvantages of affirmative action policies for students. Draw freely from Rodriguez's essay as well as from your own experience or other reading.

Recognizing Paragraph Patterns

In the space provided, write the correct answer. Count 4 points for each correct answer.

Ordering Ideas

A. Read the paragraph below. Then answer the questions that follow.

> It is August 6, 1945. A lone aircraft flies over Hiroshima, Japan, and releases a single bomb. Seconds later, the bomb explodes. A huge mushroom-shaped cloud forms, and grows until it fills the sky. Within hours, approximately 75,000 are dead. During the next 30 years, an additional 800,000 people are to die of various diseases caused by the radiation from the bomb. The world has catapulted into a new era, the atomic age.
>
> — *A. Sherman et al.*

1. The following details from the paragraph above are *not* arranged in the correct order. Put a *1* next to the first thing that happened, a *2* next to the second, and so on.

   _____ a. A huge mushroom-shaped cloud forms.

   _____ b. 75,000 are dead.

   _____ c. A lone aircraft releases a single bomb.

   _____ d. An additional 800,000 people die.

_____ 2. In the blank space put the letter of the most important statement in the paragraph.

   a. The world has catapulted into a new era, the atomic age.
   b. During the next 30 years, an additional 800,000 people

are to die of various diseases caused by the radiation from the bomb.

   c. It is August 6, 1945.

   d. Seconds later, the bomb explodes.

Basic Paragraph Patterns

B. Read the paragraphs below and write the letter of the correct choice in the space.

Sometimes people suffer from an excess of certain vitamins. Some people think that if one vitamin capsule daily is healthy, four or five might be even better. Actually, such a daily overdose might be quite harmful. While the body appears to handle a moderate overdose of the B and C vitamins, surpluses of the fat-soluble vitamins are not easily excreted. An excess of vitamin D can cause weight loss, nausea, diarrhea, and eventually, mineral loss from the bones and calcification of soft tissues, including heart, blood vessels, and kidney tubules. One common result is renal disease. In children 2,000 units or more a day results in growth retardation, and high doses of vitamin D taken by pregnant women have been linked to mental retardation in the developing child. Overdosage of vitamin A results in skin ailments, slow growth, enlargement of liver and spleen, and painful swelling of long bones.

— *P. W. Davis and E. P. Solomon*

_____ 1. Which pattern of development does the paragraph represent?

   a. cause and effect

   b. chronological order

   c. listing of details

   d. comparison and contrast

_____ 2. What is the main idea of the paragraph?

   a. Vitamins are bad for you.

   b. Sometimes people take too many vitamins.

   c. It is impossible to "overdose" on vitamins.

   d. Too many vitamins may cause renal disease.

   3. Put a plus sign (+) beside any results of taking excess vitamins. Put a minus sign (−) beside any results not indicated in the selection.

_____ a.   Retardation in babies

_____ b.   High blood pressure

_____ c.   Mineral loss

_____ d.   Soft tissue calcification

C. Hot dogs are the great equalizer. It's hard to be taken seriously when you're stuffing a silly, sloppy, delicious frankfurter into your mouth. New York bankers slurp sauerkraut-topped street dogs while running between meetings. Home cooks add substance to supper soups with a few cut-up franks. Medical residents subsist on microwaved hot dogs and buns from hospital vending machines, and NASA even included hot dogs on Apollo and Skylab flights. When desperate for ideas, newspaper food sections still suggest bizarre "international hot dogs," using ingredients like Chinese sweet-and-sour sauce and pineapple, for the kind of teenage parties that went out with *Bye Bye Birdie.*

— *Food and Wine*

_____ 1.   Which pattern of development does the paragraph represent?

a.   cause and effect
b.   classification
c.   comparison and contrast
d.   listing of details

_____ 2.   The main idea of this paragraph is

a.   People do not know what to cook for teenage parties.
b.   New York bankers eat hot dogs between meetings.
c.   Americans in all walks of life love to eat hot dogs.
d.   Astronauts had frankfurters on Apollo and Skylab flights.

3.   Look at the information listed below. Put an *S* beside each example that supports the main idea. Put an *N* beside each example that does not support the main idea or that does not appear in the paragraph.

_____ a.   Some teenage parties went out of style with the musical comedy *Bye Bye Birdie.*

_____ b. New York bankers eat hot dogs between meetings.

_____ c. Doctors buy microwaved hot dogs and buns.

_____ d. Hot dogs originated in Germany.

D. Computers use binary numbers in everything they do, so programmers must understand some things about binary numbers. Because all number systems have certain things in common, knowledge of the decimal system helps us learn the
binary system. Both systems have place values that can be expressed as positive or negative powers of the base, and through
the use of place values either system can express any number,
no matter how large or how small. We can convert binary numbers to decimal, or decimal to binary, easily if we remember
the place values in both systems.

— *Gary Popkin and Arthur Pike*

_____ 1. Which pattern of development does the paragraph represent?

a. cause and effect
b. listing of details
c. comparison and contrast
d. classification

_____ 2. The paragraph deals with

a. computers and programmers.
b. the binary system and the decimal system.
c. positive powers and negative powers.
d. place value and base.

_____ 3. Binary and decimal number systems have

a. certain things in common.
b. place values that can be expressed as positive or negative powers of the base.
c. the ability to express any number, no matter how large
or small.
d. all of the above.

_____ 4. Programmers must understand the binary number system because

    a. they seek positive powers.
    b. binary numbers can be converted to decimal numbers.
    c. computers use binary numbers in everything they do.
    d. knowledge of the binary system helps us learn the decimal system.

E. (1) College money from sources other than parents or relatives can be divided into two basic categories: loans and grants. (2) A student loan is money advanced by the government, a bank or financial institution, or the school itself that must be repaid at a set interest rate over a specific term of years. (3) Payments on some loans for school begin immediately; on others, payments are deferred until after completion of college or when the student quits school. (4) Loans are of two types — those that are made directly to students and those that are made to parents for use on a student education for which the parents must qualify and are responsible for repayments. (5) A grant is money given to a student to cover specific school expenses and need not be paid back. (6) Scholarships are a form of grant. (7) As you might suspect, loans are far easier to get than grants. Don't believe the ads and hype that there are thousands of grants going to waste. (8) True, there are thousands of grants, but many are never used primarily because of the extreme requirements that must be met.

— Charles J. Givens

_____ 1. Which pattern of development does the paragraph represent?

    a. comparison and contrast
    b. listing of details
    c. classification
    d. cause and effect

_____ 2. Which sentence best expresses the main idea of the selection?

    a. Sentence 1
    b. Sentence 2
    c. Sentence 5
    d. Sentence 8

_____ 3. Loans

    a. are never made directly to students.
    b. don't usually have to be paid back.
    c. are harder to get than grants.
    d. must be repaid with interest over a given time period.

_____ 4. Grants

    a. are one of the two forms of loans.
    b. usually have no requirements attached.
    c. cover specific school expenses.
    d. never include scholarships.

_____ 5. Payments on some loans

    a. are the responsibility of the student's parents.
    b. are canceled if the student does well in college.
    c. need never be made.
    d. are met by scholarship money.

Score: _____ correct × 4 points each = _____

UNIT 2 REVIEW TEST

Read the following selection about special education programs for schoolchildren. Then write the answers in the blanks as indicated. Count 5 points for each correct answer.

Education for Students with Disabilities

Some of the major developments in education in the past twenty years have involved schooling for children with disabilities. Large gains have been made in providing and improving special-education services for these students. (Placement in "special education" usually means that a disabled student receives separate, specialized instruction for all or part of the day in a self-contained class or a resource room.) Table 11.3 shows the numbers of students with disabilities served in

TABLE 11.3   Number of Students Receiving Public Special-Education Services, by Type of Disability, 1977 and 1993

TYPE OF DISABILITY	1977	1993
Speech or language impaired	1,302,666	1,000,159
Mentally retarded	969,547	533,713
Learning disabled	797,213	2,369,382
Emotionally disturbed	283,072	402,668
Other health impaired	141,417	66,059
Hearing impaired	89,743	60,896
Orthopedically impaired	87,008	52,920
Visually handicapped	38,247	23,811
Deaf-blind and other severe or multihandicapped	NA*	124,073
Other general or unspecified	NA*	536,561
Total	3,708,913	5,170,242

*NA = Not an applicable category in 1977.

SOURCE: U.S. Department of Education, "To Assure the Free Appropriate Education of All Handicapped Children" (Washington, D.C.: U.S. Department of Education, 1994), Table 1.4, p. 9; other U.S. Department of Education sources.

or through public education in 1977 and 1993. As indicated, the total number served during this time increased by nearly a million and a half children and youth. Analysis conducted by the U.S. Department of Education indicates that about 70 percent of students with disabilities receive most or all of their education in regular classes (with or without assignment to part-time resource rooms); approximately 25 percent are in self-contained classes; and the rest are in special schools or facilities.

The growth of special education has been associated with the civil rights movement and its concern with equal educational opportunity. The U.S. Supreme Court's 1954 decision in *Brown* v. *Board of Education,* which addressed the segregation of African American children in separate schools, also served as a precedent in establishing the rights of students with disabilities. This right was explicitly affirmed in 1974 when a U.S. district court ruled in *Pennsylvania Association for Retarded Children, Nancy Beth Bowman et al.* v. *Commonwealth of Pennsylvania, David H. Kurtzman* that the state had an "obligation to place each mentally retarded child in a free, public program of education and training appropriate to the child's capacity."

The Pennsylvania case and similar judicial decisions reflect federal laws based on the Fifth and Fourteenth Amendments to the Constitution, which state that no person can be deprived of liberty and of equal protection of the laws without due process. Federal requirements for the education of students with disabilities were enumerated systematically in the **Education for All Handicapped Children Act** of 1975 (often known by its public law number, PL 94-142) and in the **Individuals with Disabilities Education Act** (IDEA) of 1990. The basic requirements spelled out in these acts, as well as by other laws and judicial interpretations, are as follows:

1. Testing and assessment services must be fair and comprehensive; placement cannot be based on a single criterion such as an IQ score.
2. Parents or guardians must have access to information on diagnosis and may protest decisions of school officials.
3. Individualized education programs (IEPs) that include both long-range and short-range goals must be provided.
4. Educational services must be provided in the **least restrictive environment,** which means that children with disabilities may be placed in special or separate classes only for the amount of time judged necessary to provide appropriate services. If a school district demonstrates that placement in

Effective mainstreaming of students with disabilities into regular classroom settings requires a variety of special resources, relatively small classes, and educators skilled in and dedicated to creating an effective learning environment and acceptance for all students.   (© PAUL CONKLIN/PHOTO EDIT)

a regular educational setting cannot be achieved satisfactorily, the student must be given adequate instruction elsewhere, paid for by the district.

Although there now are more than 5 million students receiving special-education services, much progress still needs to be made in expanding participation in many school districts that tend to have high percentages of students with mental retardation, learning disabilities, and emotional problems. For example, recent reports have indicated that tens of thousands of children with disabilities are on waiting lists for placement in special education programs, and that federal and local monitoring and enforcement activities are weak and inadequate. Various analyses also indicate that the disability laws have been implemented much more successfuly in some locations than in others, and that implementation in big cities has been particularly inadequate.

— *Ornstein and Levine*

1.   What is the topic of this selection?

_____

2. What is the main idea of the selection? Write it in your own
    words.

    _____

    _____

    _____

    _____

_____ 3. Which sentence from the selection best states the main idea?

    a. "Some of the major developments in education in the
       past twenty years have involved schooling for children
       with disabilities."
    b. "Individualized education programs (IEPs) that include
       both long-range and short-range goals must be pro-
       vided."
    c. "Parents or guardians must have access to information
       on diagnosis and may protest decisions of school offi-
       cials."
    d. "Large gains have been made in providing and improv-
       ing special-education services for these students."

4. What is the main idea of paragraph 1?

    _____

    _____

    _____

5. What is the main idea of paragraph 2?

    _____

    _____

    _____

6. What is the main idea of paragraph 4?

   _____

   _____

_____ 7. The photograph and caption indicate

   a. the value of playing card games in special education classrooms.
   b. the importance of informal special education class settings such as children sitting on the floor to learn.
   c. the value of integrating students with disabilities into regular classrooms that have special resources.
   d. the importance of mainstreaming boys into classes that usually have mostly girls.

8. What does Table 11.3 illustrate?

   _____

   _____

_____ 9. According to the table, which type of disability showed the greatest increase in services received from 1977 to 1993?

   a. learning disabled
   b. speech or language impaired
   c. hearing impaired
   d. emotionally disturbed

10. Write *maj* beside each major detail and *min* beside each minor detail.

   _____ a. Nancy Beth Bowman represented the Pennsylvania Association for Retarded Children.

   _____ b. The Supreme Court case of *Brown* v. *Board of Education* was a precedent in establishing the rights of students with disabilities.

   _____ c. Testing and assessment services must be fair and comprehensive for students with disabilities.

_____ d. The Education for All Handicapped Children Act was passed in 1975.

_____ e. The lawyer for the Commonwealth of Pennsylvania in U.S. District Court was David H. Kurtzman.

_____ f. PL 94-142 enumerates requirements for children with disabilities.

_____ g. Districts must provide services to special education students in the least restrictive environment.

_____ h. By 1993 special education services for disabled children and youth increased by 1.5 million.

11. What contrast does the writer refer to in the first paragraph?

_____

_____

_____

12. What order does the writer use to arrange details in paragraph 2?

_____

13. What pattern does the writer use to provide the basic requirements established by the federal government for children with disabilities?

_____

Score: _____ correct × 5 points each = _____

Unit Three

Reading and Critical Thinking

Making Inferences

Inference is a process by which readers use hints to gather information. In making inferences, you go beyond the stated information. You "read between the lines" to get more details.

Factual details in what you read are the basis of knowledge. But not every bit of information is stated clearly. You may have to build on hints or suggestions provided by the writer, with your own knowledge and experience, to understand something fully. You cannot always be certain that what you supply is absolutely right. But if you follow hunches that are based on evidence, you can be fairly sure about your conclusions.

Of course, a page of writing does not offer the only opportunity you have to learn more about something through hints or suggestions. In understanding human behavior, you've been using your inference skills throughout most of your life.

In particular you "read" people's faces — their eyes, their lips, the angle of their heads — and their body language to infer information about them. For example, someone you know pretty well — your mother or a friend, let's say — pushes open the door to the house at 7:30 on a hot July evening. Her face is pale; her dress is stained with sweat at the waist and back and armpits; her pocketbook trails on the floor beside her. She moves straight past you without saying a word and shuffles into the kitchen. You hear ice tinkle in a glass and water running.

What do you infer from this person's behavior? Clearly she has had an exhausting day. You add up all that you see and infer that information. You know she's hot and tired and thirsty and not in the mood for conversation. Let's say that you need a favor from this person. Maybe you want her to help you move furniture, listen to a paper you wrote for history class, or lend you $20. Your built-in inference machine tells you to hold off, not to ask. You know that this is not the right moment to be any trouble to anyone who looks the way she does! From her movements, her attitude, her body language, you know that she needs space and time alone, time to cool off and relax. No one has to tell you these things; you just "know." Here is inference in action. You read the hints and signs and figure things out without having to be told.

In making inferences you have to be careful not to go too far beyond the information at hand. Otherwise your inferences might not be correct. For example, could you assume that the person we have described was exhausted because she had trouble with her car? Not at all. Nothing in what you saw or observed suggested that. On the other hand, you might have heard her mumble an angry remark to herself about her old Ford as she passed by you. Or you might know for a fact that she struggles regularly with a failing car air conditioner, and that when it broke at the end of another summer's day her behavior resembled the behavior she displayed this evening. Then you might safely say to yourself, "Well, I guess the old Ford is acting up again!" The point, of course, is that inferences must be based on available information, not simply on vague suspicions or wild guesses.

Look at the picture on page 209. In a sentence explain the point of the picture — that is, what you think it is about. Include information about who is in the picture, what the person is doing, and where the action takes place.

You probably wrote something like *A young woman is studying something under a microscope in a laboratory.* Think for a moment about how you arrived at your statement. How did you know that the person in the picture is a young woman rather than a man? How did you know that the object she is looking through is a microscope instead of a camera? How did you know that she is in a laboratory, at school perhaps, and not in her bedroom or in a shop that sells microscopes? The photograph does not provide definite answers to these questions. You arrived at your answers by inferring from the details in the photograph.

In the space below, write down some of the clues that helped you infer that the person is a young woman.

_____

_____

_____

FRANK WARD/© 1991 AMHERST COLLEGE

Most likely the haircut, the general features of the face, and the earrings told you that the person is a woman. We often use hair style, facial expression, and clothing to judge a person's gender. Also, from the person's face and size you guessed that she is about eighteen; you knew that she isn't six or seven, or forty or fifty. The hints in the picture enabled you to reject the extremes and infer that the woman is a teenager.

From what clues did you infer that the woman is looking through a microscope? Write them in the space below.

_____

_____

_____

Was it that you've seen a microscope before and that the object in the picture matches your memory of one? Or maybe it is the look of concentration on the woman's face and the way she's squinting. Or was it a combination of these clues? In any case, you knew that the object is not a camera: People don't use conventional cameras in the way shown in the photograph.

In the space below, write down some of the clues that helped you infer that the scene is in a laboratory, probably in a school.

_____

_____

_____

Several factors probably gave you the impression of a laboratory. You've seen labs before; they often have low tables and display cases of the kind you see in the background of the photograph. The woman is dressed casually and she is not wearing a lab coat, which suggests that she is at a school rather than a professional laboratory in a hospital or in private industry. It's unlikely that the scene is the girl's bedroom; most bedrooms don't look like this. Also, it is not likely (although it is possible) that the scene is a microscope shop. We don't get enough clues from the picture to make that inference.

The clues we do get, however, help us go beyond the information given. We infer meanings from what we actually see and then take those meanings further. Inference helps us complete the details and fill in important information.

In reading, too, inference is an important skill. Inference helps us fill in information that a writer only suggests. Read the paragraph below and use your inference skills to answer the questions that follow.

The world wants what Taiwan makes, and the cash pouring in has brought its economy to critical mass. With it has come prosperity and growth. The Taiwan I go back to now is flush with success and full of self-confidence, much of it thanks to the energy and plain hard work of its citizens. Until just recently, a lack of money, coupled with an isolation from the rest of the world, severely limited opportunities for talented individuals. It's not at all unusual to find people from Taiwan studying or working in the United States. If I had stayed, I probably would not have become a violinist or even a musician.

— *Cho-Liang Lin*

———— 1. We can infer that one of Taiwan's economic strengths is
   a. international banking.
   b. knowing what materials to produce for world use.
   c. scholarship support for artists and musicians.

What clues in the passage helped you infer your answer?

_____

_____

———— 2. We can infer that the writer
   a. was born in Taiwan but studied music in the United States.
   b. was born in the United States but studied music in Taiwan.
   c. lives in Taiwan but cannot find work there.

What clues in the passage helped you infer your answer?

_____

_____

———— 3. We can infer that musicians in Taiwan today
   a. have severely limited opportunities.
   b. cannot become violinists.
   c. would have more opportunities than in the past.

What clues in the passage helped you infer your answer?

_____

_____

To answer these questions about the paragraph, you had to use inference skills. The sentences about Taiwan only hint at the answers to the questions. No one answer is stated exactly.

If you picked *b* for question 1, how did you know that Taiwan succeeded economically by producing materials for world use? You inferred that Taiwan's strength comes from the country's economic vision — that is, from its ability to see needs clearly and to make what people want. The very first sentence supplies the information needed to make that inference. If the world wants what Taiwan makes and pays lots of cash for it, you can infer that the country has a knack for meeting global needs and that this knack leads to economic success. Furthermore, neither *a* nor *c* is supported in the paragraph. That is, neither international banking nor the subject of scholarships is mentioned there.

If you chose *a* for question 2, how did you know that the writer was born in Taiwan and studied in the United States? You used clues from the paragraph. "The Taiwan I go back to now" suggests that the writer has been there before. Also, the last sentence of the paragraph helps you infer that the writer left the country. And the writer's name, clearly Asian, may suggest a national origin other than the United States — even though many native-born Americans also have Asian names. In addition, choice *b* cannot be right. The writer, a violinist, talks about limited opportunities in the Taiwan of years past. You can infer, then, that he is like other people "from Taiwan studying or working in the United States." Nor is choice *c* supported by information in the paragraph. Artists and musicians had limited opportunities in the past, but nothing in the paragraph backs up the idea that Cho-Liang Lin cannot find work in Taiwan today.

That brings us to question 3. If you chose *c*, how did you know that musicians in Taiwan today have more opportunities than they did in the past? You used your inference skills. You inferred from words such as *prosperity, growth, success,* and *self-confidence* that today's Taiwan is very different from the country of Cho-Liang Lin's youth. Also the words "until just recently" help you infer that conditions in the past may have limited artists' chances, but that the Taiwan of the 1990s might treat its citizens differently. You could not choose *a*; nothing in the paragraph suggests limited opportunities for musicians today. Also *b* is incorrect. Years ago, perhaps, a talented violinist could not have developed in Taiwan's environment, but we cannot infer that a Taiwanese musician cannot become a violinist today.

Building Inference Skills
- Read beyond the words. Fill in details and information based on the writer's suggestions and your own experiences.
- Question yourself about your reading: Why is this person doing what she is doing? What can I infer from the scene? Supply the answers on the basis of the writer's hints and your own knowledge.
- If a writer describes a person, try to understand the person from how she moves, what she says, what she looks like. You can infer things about character from the way a person behaves. Build a picture of the person in your mind; base your picture on the writer's description of how she acts and what she looks like.
- If you cannot easily answer a question about what you have read, remember to use inference skills. Return to the part of the reading where you would expect to find the answer. Then see if the writer suggests something that you yourself have to supply more explicitly.

EXERCISES

1. Inferring Details from Cartoons

Look at the cartoon on page 214. Use your inference skills to answer the following questions.

_____ 1. We can infer that the cartoon portrays a
   a. television interview.
   b. private party.
   c. meeting at a restaurant.
   d. court trial.

_____ 2. We can infer that the first mouse to speak is
   a. a good friend of the other.
   b. famous.
   c. an interviewer.
   d. being interviewed.

DON WRIGHT/© 1992 *THE PALM BEACH POST*, TRIBUNE MEDIA SERVICES

_____ 3. We can infer that Dr. Furr E. Tail is concerned about
   a. people's enjoyment of poetry.
   b. the productivity of mice.
   c. all stereotypes.
   d. what people think of mice.

_____ 4. We can infer that Dr. Tail
   a. has no prejudices.
   b. is prejudiced against mice.
   c. holds no grudges.
   d. is prejudiced against reindeer.

2. Making Inferences

Answer the questions below after you read the following selection about a Spanish custom in the Old Southwest — asking for the bride. ("New Possessions" refers to the Spanish-owned territories in America.)

The Spaniard is dramatic in his love affairs. When a son of a *patrón* [master or boss] wished to become engaged, his father

and uncles made a visit to the father of the girl to ask for the parent's consent to an engagement, following the old custom as expressed in the Spanish law of 1766, that no young people could marry without the consent of their parents. This law was to prevent marriages between people of different social positions. It was the intention of Spain to perpetuate the ruling class in the New Possessions. The father and uncles on arriving at the home of the young girl were received most formally. This was an occasion when the formal reception room was made ready in advance, for a visit of this nature was never a surprise, although convention required that it seem so. After an exchange of courtesies, the father of the would-be groom presented a letter which was received but not read. After a social visit, with wine and cookies served, the men departed, knowing only that a return visit would be made to deliver the answer before the month was over.

— *Niña Otero*

1. Write the main idea of this selection in your own words.

_____

_____

_____

_____ 2. We can infer that the parents of the girl
a. were truly shocked when the would-be groom's relatives arrived.
b. only pretended to be surprised when the would-be groom's relatives arrived.
c. disliked the old custom.
d. invited the would-be groom's relatives at a set time for the meeting.

_____ 3. We can infer that in the Old Southwest Spanish society, if a boy wanted to marry a girl from a social class different from his own,
a. the boy's parents would have to visit the girl's parents.
b. the girl's parents would visit the boy's parents.
c. the boy and girl would be required to marry outside the church.
d. the Spanish law of 1766 would have prevented it.

_____ 4. Suppose that the bride's parents were named Señor (Mr.) Rafael Gonzalez and Doña (Mrs.) Merna Gonzalez. What can we infer might be an English version of the greeting used by the boy's relatives during their visit?
   a. "Hi there, folks!"
   b. "Hello, Rafael and Merna."
   c. "Hi, Raf and Mern."
   d. "Good evening, Señor and Doña Gonzalez."

_____ 5. We can infer that the purpose of the letter is to
   a. inform the girl's parents that the boy wants to marry their daughter.
   b. explain the boy's financial worth.
   c. express the boy's love for the girl.
   d. thank the girl's parents for their hospitality.

Critical Thinking in Writing

What customs do members of your social, ethnic, or religious group observe regarding marriage? What "rules" do men and women and their families have to follow before the wedding?

---

3. Making Inferences from Poetry

Read the following poem, using your inference skills to determine who is speaking in the poem, with whom the speaker is speaking, and what the other person or people are saying. Then answer the questions after the selection.

Sure You Can Ask Me
a Personal Question

How do you do?
    No, I am not Chinese.
No, not Spanish.
    No, I am American Indi-uh, Native American.
No, not from India.
    No, not Apache.
No, not Navajo.
    No, not Sioux.

No, we are not extinct.
     Yes, Indian.
Oh?
     So that's where you got those high cheekbones.
Your great grandmother, huh?
     An Indian Princess, huh?
Hair down to there?
     Let me guess, Cherokee?
Oh, so you've had an Indian friend?
     That close?
Oh, so you've had an Indian lover?
     That tight?
Oh, so you've had an Indian servant?
     That much?
Yeah, it was awful what you guys did to us.
     It's real decent of you to apologize.
No, I don't know where you can get peyote.
     No, I don't know where you can get Navajo rugs real
     cheap.
No, I didn't make this. I bought it at Bloomingdale's.
     Thank you. I like your hair too.
I don't know if anyone knows whether or not Cher is really
Indian.
     No, I didn't make it rain tonight.
Yeah. Uh-huh. Spirituality.
     Uh-huh. Yeah. Spirituality. Uh-huh. Mother
Earth. Yeah. Uh'huh. Uh'huh. Spirituality.
     No, I didn't major in archery.
Yeah, a lot of us drink too much.
     Some of us can't drink enough.
This ain't no stoic look.
     This is my face.

— *Diane Burns*

1. Who is speaking in this poem?

   _____

2. With whom is the speaker speaking? In what kind of situation?

   _____

   _____

   _____

3. What are some of the statements you can infer are being made by the other people?

    _____

    _____

    _____

    _____

    _____

4. What do you infer is the attitude of the other people toward the speaker?

    _____

    _____

5. What do you infer the speaker feels in reaction to what the other people say?

    _____

    _____

6. Look up the word *stoic* in a dictionary. What can you infer about the writer's feelings from the closing lines: "This ain't no stoic look. / This is my face"?

    _____

    _____

    _____

7. What is the implied main idea of the poem?

    _____

    _____

    _____

> **Critical Thinking in Writing**
>
> Write your own poem called "Sure You Can Ask Me a Personal Question," in which you explore your own heritage by asking and answering questions as Burns has.

4. Inferences in a Longer Selection

Read the following selection. Then, using your inference skills, answer the questions that follow. The selection gives the author's opinions about politically correct speech on campus — that is, whether language that is offensive to groups or individuals should be discouraged.

Who's Afraid of Political Correctness?

A simple concept is at the heart of the intellectual debate about "political correctness" on college campuses — respect. A disturbing lack of mutual respect among human beings for others of different genders, races, cultures, and sexual orientations is manifesting itself in a new generation of Americans. In an attempt to combat the cancers of sexism, racism, and homophobia that this lack of respect inevitably produces, an idealistic few have taken up the banner of political correctness and seek to impart to this generation a sensitivity that will allow it to avoid repeating the atrocities carried out by previous ones.

If Americans are genuinely concerned with making their young people more respectful of one another, there is much work to be done, as recent incidents suggest.

In Albuquerque, New Mexico, students from a predominantly white middle-class high school traveled across town for a basketball game with a predominantly Mexican American school. For a well-orchestrated joke, some of the white students brought with them several bags of tortillas. During the game, they flung the tortillas with laughter and indiscretion across the gymnasium floor and toward the opposing bleachers where the Mexican students were sitting.

In Salinas, California, four white students on the yearbook staff of Salinas High School were suspended by school officials because they substituted for the names of a group of Mexican American students terms related to various kinds of Mexican food. In the yearbook, *El Gabrilian*, specific phrases substituted for students' names included *carne asada, quesadilla,* and *rosita chiquita.*

These racially insensitive excesses of youth may be excused by some with the shrugged-shoulder admission that kids will be kids. We convince ourselves that by the time children become adults, they will have outgrown racial hatred — forgetting that it is from adults that children learn such hatred in the first place.

Still, we trust, attending a university whose glossy recruitment brochure boasts of campus cultural diversity will save our children. There they can learn Spanish and share their roommates' *tamales* mailed parcel post from the Southwest. Yet, unfortunately, as a student packs his bags for college, sometimes racial insensitivity sneaks into his suitcase and stows away like the family cat. The university presidents who greet us on our first day with idealistic rhetoric about the "new world" that we are about to enter are disappointed to find in our young hearts and minds ugly remnants of the old world — remnants that make it hard, if not impossible, for those students to "play nice" with one another. And so, we concede that bigotry — once dismissed as a toy for the ignorant — can go to college too.

At the University of California, Berkeley, a largely white fraternity sponsored a "Border Party" that guests entered by crawling underneath a barbed-wire fence, presumably to mock the journey of Mexican immigrants crossing the border.

At Pennsylvania State University, someone distributed mock job applications for minorities with suggested sources of income: theft, relief, welfare, and unemployment. The applications also asked for a place of birth: charity ward, cotton field, back alley, free clinic, and zoo.

Over the last five years, the National Institute Against Prejudice and Violence has tabulated more than 250 incidents of racial and sexual harassment at more than 200 colleges. *The Washington Post* has editorialized: "The college campus, which a quarter of a century ago spawned the civil rights movement, now seems to be breeding a new and especially distasteful racism."

In these difficult times, a generation of young Americans searches for moral leadership and is disappointed to find none. Last year, during a speech at the University of Michigan, President Bush attacked not the epidemic of racism and sexism on our campuses but instead the idealism that seeks to end it by bringing racial and gender sensitivity to the halls of academia.

What the President and others who attack political correctness are most afraid of is change. The sort of change that, thirty years ago, allowed James Meredith to withstand a flood of angry and violent opposition to become the first African American enrolled at the University of Mississippi is necessary so that a new generation of female and minority students can take the next step toward educational opportunity, unhindered by racially insensitive acts intended to intimidate and humiliate them.

And it is change that James Meredith and scores of young people after him were lured to the university to precipitate, in the hope that its idealistic juices would flow over into society at large: that being the very nature of that elusive entity called progress.

— *Ruben Navarrette, Jr.*

_____ 1. The main idea of this selection is that
    a. students who are concerned about political correctness do not respect others.
    b. students who are concerned about political correctness are trying to increase people's respect for one another.
    c. many racist incidents still occur on campus.
    d. we forgive racist incidents on campus too easily, by saying that students are not yet adults.

_____ 2. The author, Ruben Navarrette, Jr., probably is a
    a. professor.
    b. university administrator.
    c. student activist.
    d. political conservative.

_____ 3. We can infer that the incidents at an Albuquerque high school basketball game and a Salinas high school were
    a. typical of what happens at every high school.
    b. meaningless jokes that all the students found amusing.
    c. intended to start violent riots.
    d. offensive to Mexican American students.

_____ 4. We can infer that the incidents at the University of California, Berkeley, and Pennsylvania State University
    a. were similar to the high school incidents.
    b. reflected the views of most of the students at those two campuses.
    c. were not as offensive as the high school incidents.
    d. were just the work of a few cranks.

_____ 5. We can infer that
   a. no university students outgrow the racist attitudes they held in high school.
   b. the students at the universities mentioned in the selection are more racist than are students at other universities.
   c. there are few minority students at Berkeley and Penn State.
   d. a substantial number of bigoted students attend the universities mentioned in the selection and other universities.

_____ 6. We can infer that the teachers and officials at the high schools and universities mentioned in the selection
   a. found the incidents funny.
   b. do not care whether racist incidents take place at their schools.
   c. would like to stop racist incidents but have not been totally successful.
   d. are able to control racist incidents successfully.

_____ 7. We can infer that the author believes President Bush
   a. was bigoted.
   b. was not courageous enough to fight bigotry.
   c. supported students who want to increase people's sensitivity.
   d. was an outspoken, courageous leader.

_____ 8. We can infer that the author believes that students who are concerned about political correctness
   a. are justified in their concerns
   b. have been highly successful in educating others.
   c. cannot change the opinions of people who are afraid of change.
   d. are inviting attacks on themselves.

Critical Thinking in Writing

Write a paragraph describing your thoughts about how we should treat people who use insensitive or discriminatory language. Should we ignore them? oppose them? punish them?

CHAPTER **8** **REVIEW TEST**

Making Inferences

A. Read this selection about El Hoyo, a section of downtown Tucson, Arizona. In the space provided answer the questions that follow. Count 10 points for each correct answer.

From the center of downtown Tucson the ground slopes gently away to Main Street, drops a few feet, and then rolls to the banks of the Santa Cruz River. Here lies the section of the city known as El Hoyo. Why it is called El Hoyo is not very clear. In no sense is it a hole as its name would imply; it is simply the river's immediate valley. Its inhabitants are Chicanos who raise hell on Saturday night and listen to Padre Estanislao on Sunday morning. While the term *Chicano* is the short way of saying *Mexicano*, it is not restricted to the paisanos [country people] who came from old Mexico with the territory or the last famine to work for the railroad, labor, sing, and go on relief. *Chicano* is the easy way of referring to everybody. Pablo Gutiérrez married the Chinese grocer's daughter and now runs a meat department; his sons are Chicanos. So are the sons of Killer Jones who threw a fight in Harlem and fled to El Hoyo to marry Christina Méndez. And so are all of them. However, it is doubtful that all these spiritual sons of Mexico live in El Hoyo because of its scenic beauty — it is everything but beautiful. Its houses are simple affairs of unplastered adobe, wood, and abandoned car parts. Its narrow streets are mostly clearings which have, in time, acquired names. Except for some tall trees which nobody has ever cared to identify, nurse, or destroy, the main things known to grow in the general area are weeds, garbage piles, dark-eyed chavalos [slang for *boys* or *young men*], and dogs. And it is doubtful that the Chicanos live in El Hoyo because it is safe — many times the Santa Cruz has risen and inundated the area.

— *Mario Suárez*

_____ 1. The main point of this selection is that
a. El Hoyo is the region of downtown Tucson that slopes down to Main Street and the banks of the Santa Cruz River.
b. American cities have different personalities depending on the varied people who live and work there.
c. *Chicano* is the short way of saying *Mexicano.*
d. In El Hoyo, Chicanos are a varied group who live in a defined community.

_____ 2. We can infer that in El Hoyo, *Chicano* is a term used for
a. Mexicans who live there.
b. anyone who lives there.
c. children of mixed marriages.
d. paisanos and chavalos.

_____ 3. We can infer that many Mexicans in El Hoyo
a. migrated in phases from Mexico.
b. married the children of Chinese immigrants.
c. do not appreciate Padre Estanislao.
d. live on the river banks.

_____ 4. The selection suggests that the Chicanos who "raise hell" on Saturday night and go to church the next morning
a. are very religious.
b. are just trying to have a good time on the weekends.
c. come to church under the influence of alcohol.
d. have both a fun-loving and a serious side to their personalities.

_____ 5. We can infer that people live in El Hoyo because
a. it is beautiful.
b. the economy is good there.
c. they are bonded together in a community.
d. Mexicans like living with people with the same ethnic background as their own.

B. Read the following selection about the development of magazines and newspapers in America. In the space provided answer the questions that follow.

The impact of the American periodical press also has been technological and social. The large, mass-circulation magazines have influenced the smaller magazines, which in many instances seek to imitate their appearance and to emulate the high quality of their printing, layout, and make-up. They also have influenced magazines around the world. Europe, for example, is given to publishing magazines resembling *Life* and *Look*, and almost no heavily industrialized country is without its imitator of *Time* (*The Link* in India, *Elseviers* in the Netherlands, *Tiempo* in Mexico, *Der Spiegel* in Germany, and *L'Express* in France, for example). The social effect has to do with the discharge or failure to discharge its social responsibilities. These responsibilities the magazine press shares with all communications media, printed or electronic. They include the obligation, in a political democracy such as in the U.S.A., to provide the people with a fair presentation of facts, with honestly held opinions, and with truthful advertising. All but the subsidized periodicals hold — or seek to hold — to these goals within a certain framework: that of the business order, the private initiative, profit-making system.

— *Roland E. Wolseley*

1. In your own words write the point that the writer makes about the impact of American magazines and newspapers (see **7b**).

   _____

   _____

_____ 2. We may infer that the responsibilities of the media and the media's business interests
   a. prevent the magazines from meeting their social goals.
   b. can work together in a cooperative manner.
   c. restrict mass-circulation magazines from succeeding in the marketplace.
   d. challenge technological and social objectives.

_____ 3. We can infer about news magazines like *Life, Look,* and *Time* that
   a. they are resented in European countries.
   b. they sell very well throughout the world.
   c. they are respected as models for foreign magazines.
   d. they do not discharge social responsibilities.

_____ 4. The writer believes that magazines
    a. must make a profit at any cost.
    b. should not compete with television for advertising.
    c. should imitate European models.
    d. should not accept untruthful advertising.

_____ 5. We can infer about the author's knowledge of the subject that
    a. he knows very little about Asian or African periodicals.
    b. he knows a great deal about European and American
        magazines.
    c. he knows a great deal about European magazines but not
        much about American magazines.
    d. he has worked as a magazine layout editor.

Score: _____ correct × 10 points each = _____

9

Understanding Figurative Language

To make language clearer, more interesting, and more vivid, we all use expressions that are not literally true. We make comparisons in speaking and writing. *Figurative language* –– language that compares — paints a picture.

People frequently use figurative expressions when they speak:

1. "I worked *like a dog* last night!"
2. "Either spend that fifty dollars or put it in the bank. You can't *have your cake and eat it too.*"
3. "I told him to stop *bugging me.*"

None of these expressions is literal — that is, not one means *exactly* what it says. The speakers are not really talking about dogs, cake, or bugs.

In example 1, the speaker wants to show how hard she worked and how it made her feel. So she compares herself to a dog.

In example 2, the speaker wants to say that it's impossible to both use something up and keep it to use later. In using a familiar figurative expression, he's comparing the listener's conflicting wishes with those of someone who wants to eat a piece of cake and, at the same time, to save it for later.

In example 3, the speaker compares someone to an insect, even though she really is talking about a person. The expression "bugging me" suggests that the person is behaving like an annoying bug — a mosquito, perhaps, or an ant.

These informal figurative expressions are so familiar that they are unlikely to bring pictures to your mind. But writers who use *original* figurative language expect you to picture the comparisons they have made so that you can see something more easily. Look at these two statements:

227

1. A yellow light was slanting over the high walls into the jail yard.
2. A sickly light, like yellow tinfoil, was slanting over the high walls into the jail yard.

— George Orwell

In example 1, the writer certainly has painted a picture for the reader. You can see the jail yard, the high walls, and the yellow light slanting over them. There are no figurative expressions here; the description is literal. But in example 2, because of figurative language, the picture is much more vivid. You know that light cannot be ill or in bad health (only living things like people or animals can get sick). Yet by calling the light *sickly*, by comparing it to a living thing, Orwell makes us see unhealthfulness in the scene. Then he makes the picture even clearer by comparing the light to yellow tinfoil. Of course, there is no tinfoil here: You would not expect there to be any on the walls outside a prison. But by means of the comparison, the writer is trying to paint an original picture in your mind. If you have ever seen (or can imagine) yellow tinfoil, you can picture the kind of light Orwell wants you to see as it slants over the jail yard walls.

Writers have many different ways of using figurative language to create vivid pictures. Sometimes they give nonhuman things human features. This kind of comparison is called *personification*.

1. The sun *yawned* through the trees. (The sun is being compared to a person yawning.)
2. An idea *spoke* within him, *racing through* his mind. (The idea has the quality of a living thing: It speaks and races.)

Sometimes we make comparisons using the word *like* or the word *as*. This kind of figurative expression is called a *simile*.

3. The tree bent in the wind *like an old man praying*. (A tree is being compared to an old man at prayer.)
4. The moon looked *as white as a skull*. (The moon's color is being compared to the color of a skull.)

Sometimes writers only suggest comparisons. They say one of two objects they are comparing *is* the other object; but in reality the two things are different from each other. Implied comparisons like those that follow are called *metaphors*.

5. His *blackberry* eyes darted nervously. (The eyes are being compared to blackberries so that you can picture them as small and black.)

6. A brown, *withered leaf of a hand* fluttered gently on her lap and then lifted up to wipe a tear away. (The hand is being compared to a withered leaf so that you can picture a frail person approaching the end of life.)

For special effects, writers exaggerate some comparisons. A figurative expression that exaggerates is called *hyperbole.*

7. He roared with the force *of a thousand lions.* (The force of his roar is exaggerated so that you can picture his fierceness and imagine how loud he sounded.)

In newspapers, magazines, and textbooks, you can expect to find figurative language to make a point clearer or more lively, and often both. In poetry and other forms of creative writing, writers often use figurative language in subtle and complex ways. As a reader, you must recognize figurative expressions so that you can understand a writer's point fully.

Understanding Figurative Language

- Make sure you are aware that the writer is making a comparison. In example 6, the writer is talking about a woman's hand. By introducing the idea of a leaf, the writer has not changed the topic suddenly to a discussion of leaves. The writer simply is making the description more vivid by comparing the hand to something else.
- Keep clearly in your mind just what is being compared to what. Don't lose the basic point by getting confused about the comparison and forgetting what the writer is explaining in the first place. In example 3, you are supposed to see the tree better because it looks like an old man at prayer; you should not, however, expect to read anything further about religion or praying. (There are *extended metaphors*, which carry the implied comparisons further. Especially in poetry, you should watch for words that continue and extend a simple comparative theme.)
- Look for such words as *like* and *as*, which often introduce comparisons.
- Try to figure out why the writer has made the comparison. Why, in example 1, is the sun compared to a person yawning? Why, in example 4, is the moon compared to a skull?

EXERCISES

1. Understanding Figurative Language

Each of the following extracts makes a comparison. In your own words, identify the objects being compared and the meaning of the comparison. Also tell why you think the writer is making the comparison. Use a separate sheet of paper.

1. Bear in mind
    That death is a drum
    Beating forever

    — Langston Hughes

2. Let us be still
    As ginger jars are still
    Upon a Chinese shelf

    — Gwendolyn Bennett

3. It's March, off season, the sun
      A pale coin burnt on the horizon's
      wash of clouds.

    — Daniel Tobin

4. The Yucatán crater now becomes far and away the largest known celestial blemish to mar the Earth's surface.

    — William J. Broad

5. What you said keeps bothering me
    keeps needling, grinding
    like toothache
    or a bad
    conscience.

    — Gloria T. Hull

2. Common Figurative Expressions

We often use figurative language in our everyday talk, as the following expressions illustrate. On a separate sheet of paper, explain the meaning of the figurative expressions that appear in italics.
1. Why are you such a *pain in the neck*?
2. He's just not *tuned in* to what I say.
3. We'd like to get *input* and *feedback* from you on this project.
4. When Flora saw all that ice cream, she was in *hog heaven.*
5. I wanted help, but all he gave me was *static.*

3. Understanding Figurative Language in Poetry

In this selection, "Dream Deferred" by Langston Hughes, the poet uses a variety of figurative images to show what happens to a dream that is deferred — put off, in other words. Read the poem with an eye toward understanding how each figurative expression helps you understand what Hughes is talking about. Then answer the questions.

Dream Deferred ("Harlem")

What happens to a dream deferred?

Does it dry up
like a raisin in the sun?

Or fester like a sore —
And then run?
Does it stink like rotten meat?
Or crust and sugar over —
like a syrupy sweet?

Maybe it just sags
like a heavy load.

Or does it explode?

          — *Langston Hughes*

1. What is the first comparison the poet makes?

   _____

   _____

2. Explain the image of something drying up "like a raisin in the sun."

   _____

   _____

3. In the fourth line, Hughes says that something deferred can "fester like a sore." What does *fester* mean? How can a dream be like a festering sore?

   _____

   _____

4. Why does Hughes think it is necessary to give the reader so many different pictures of a deferred dream? Why isn't one enough?

_____

_____

_____

Critical Thinking in Writing
What kinds of deferred dreams dry up, fester, or explode? Write a paragraph in which you explain a dream that you or someone you know had to defer.

5. Figurative Language in a Speech
The following excerpt from Martin Luther King, Jr.'s, "I Have a Dream" speech uses many figurative expressions. On a separate sheet of paper, list several examples of those expressions and explain in each case what is being compared to what.

> Five score years ago a great American in whose symbolic shadow we stand today signed the Emancipation Proclamation. This momentous decree came as a great beacon light of hope to millions of Negro slaves who had been seared in the flames of withering injustice. It came as a joyous daybreak to end the long night of their captivity. But one hundred years later the Negro still is not free. One hundred years later the life of the Negro is still sadly crippled by the manacles of segregation and the chains of discrimination. One hundred years later the Negro lives on a lonely island of poverty in the midst of a vast ocean of material prosperity.
>
> — *Martin Luther King, Jr.*

6. Figurative Language in an Advertisement
On a separate sheet of paper, explain the uses of figurative language in the following advertisement, which appeared in *Ebony* magazine.

The opportunity to get ahead isn't always a matter of red or green. Historically, it's often been a question of black and white.

Luckily, Garret A. Morgan didn't see color as an obstacle. Instead, this son of a former slave overcame tremendous prejudice to become one of the most important American inventors of this century. His creations ranged from a hair-straightening cream to the gas mask which saved thousands of lives during World War I.

But it was Mr. Morgan's development of the traffic signal which perhaps best symbolizes his life. In 1923, automobiles were increasing in number, and so, unfortunately, were automobile accidents.

After witnessing one down the street from his house, he developed and sold his patent for a traffic safety light to General Electric—the forerunner of the traffic light we see on practically every corner in the world.

It typified his concern for the safety of people everywhere. His perseverance. And his refusal to let the color of his skin color anyone's perception of his ability.

Which brings us the true lesson of Garret A. Morgan. He may have invented the traffic signal. But he never saw a red light.

Amtrak

How do you see the road in front of you?

COURTESY OF AMTRAK AND THE GARRETT A. MORGAN, SR. FOUNDATION

Understanding Figurative Language

Read the following stanza of poetry. In the space provided, write the letter of the word or phrase that best completes each sentence. Count 20 points for each correct answer.

I love bright words, words up and singing early;
Words that are luminous in the dark, and sing;
Warm lazy words, white cattle under trees;
I love words opalescent, cool, and pearly,
Like midsummer moths, and honeyed words like bees,
Gilded and sticky, with a little sting.

— *Elinor Wylie*

_____ 1. The images the poet creates enable us to see words as each of the following *except*
   a. worms.
   b. cattle.
   c. bees.
   d. moths.

_____ 2. The poet's figurative language helps us to understand that words
   a. may be used as tools.
   b. are people's greatest gift.
   c. are more powerful than weapons.
   d. have great variety.

_____ 3. Words having the quality of moths are described as
   a. bright.
   b. gilded.
   c. opalescent.
   d. sticky.

_____ 4. Words having the quality of birds are described as all *except*
   a. up and singing early.
   b. luminous in the dark.
   c. bright.
   d. honeyed.

_____ 5. When the poet says she loves "words . . . with a little sting"
   she means that she
   a. enjoys hurting people.
   b. accepts the idea that only those who experience pain can
      appreciate pleasure.
   c. sees nothing wrong with obscenity.
   d. values language that gets a reaction from the reader.

Score: _____ correct × 20 points each = _____

10

Drawing Conclusions
and Predicting Outcomes

Careful readers *interpret* what they read; that is, they try to explain and to understand the ideas they come across in their reading. One way to build your skill at interpreting is to try to draw conclusions from what a writer tells you.

A reading selection gives you information about a topic. Good readers are able to use that information on their own to know what to expect next.

Paragraphs or longer readings present information to support a topic, but they do not always state all the possible results of the events the writer discusses. In fact if you have to answer questions after you read, those questions often involve conclusions you must draw on your own.

But before you think of larger units like paragraphs or whole essays, it's useful to think about drawing conclusions from parts of individual sentences. Sometimes you can predict the outcome of a sentence — that is, you can make a reasonably accurate guess as to how the sentence will end. You can use this skill to help you see how to draw conclusions and predict outcomes in longer works.

Which word group would you select to complete the following sentence?

If you keep reading books with small print in such dim light,
a. you'll never pass your exam.
b. you may not learn the meaning of important words.
c. you may strain your eyes.
d. you should play some music on the radio.

We can reasonably guess that *c* is the correct ending for the sentence. In fact the only sound selection we can make from the choices given here is *c*.

We can tell from the word *if* that the writer is setting up

236

conditions that will affect the outcome of the sentence. From the words in the sentence and from our own experiences, we know that small print and dim lighting can lead to eyestrain. Although we cannot be absolutely certain that the writer had that point in mind, choice *c* would be a safe one.

Even though there may be some truth in the other choices, none of them logically develops from the rest of the sentence. Choice *a* is not as good a choice as *c* because some people could pass an exam even though they read small print in poorly lit rooms. Similarly you'd have to reject *b*: Although you might have to squint, you could determine the meanings of words. Also, nothing in the first part of the sentence helps us predict that music has anything to do with what the writer is aiming for. True, dim lighting and music sometimes go together, but in this example playing music is not a logical outcome, so choice *d* would be incorrect.

If you followed this explanation, you have some idea about the kind of thinking that goes into drawing conclusions or predicting outcomes, even in paragraphs and longer selections. You have to put together facts and details logically in your own mind to draw correct conclusions. You have to think ahead to events or ideas that might come from information the writer gives, information that forces you to *predict* how things will come out. Even though you might not know for sure, you have to use evidence from your reading to forecast what will happen.

Read this selection by an Asian American who returns to the small town in Taiwan where he grew up. Then answer the questions that follow. These questions involve drawing conclusions and making predictions.

There is a famous Chinese proverb that mocks a careless man who, while crossing a river, accidentally drops his sword overboard. Unfazed, he slices a notch in the wood along the vessel's side marking the exact spot, so he can come back later and find it. Trying to find the Taiwan of my youth today would be as futile as his marking the side of that boat, because things there have been changing so rapidly during the last decade.

I grew up in a little town in central Taiwan called Hsinchu, on a street lined with bicycle repair shops and noodle parlors. Over the years, Hsinchu has become another Silicon Valley of sprawling research parks. The bicycle shops now sell imported luxury cars; the noodle parlors have given way to boutiques

bent on quenching a nearly insatiable thirst for the best things
money can buy.

— *Cho-Liang Lin*

_____ 1. The careless man will
    a. find his sword when he comes back.
    b. never come back to the river.
    c. never find the same boat when he comes back.
    d. never find his sword when he comes back.

_____ 2. The careless man
    a. knows how to correct his mistakes.
    b. is foolish.
    c. has learned his lesson.
    d. is from Taiwan.

_____ 3. The town of Hsinchu
    a. has changed.
    b. is the same as before, only more modern.
    c. is familiar.
    d. has remained poor.

_____ 4. The author probably
    a. will return to Hsinchu frequently to remember his child-
       hood.
    b. plans to meet with the old owners of the bicycle shops
       and noodle parlors.
    c. will set up business in Hsinchu.
    d. feels that the place of his childhood has vanished forever.

Because the notch on the side of the boat moves with the
boat, we can predict that the mark will not help the man find
his sword. And because the man has nothing to help him locate
the sword, we can predict that he will not be able to find it. Answer *d*, therefore, is correct for question 1.

Because the careless man thinks the notch will help him, even
though we can easily predict it will do him no good, we can
conclude that the man is foolish. The correct answer for question
2 is *b*.

Many clues tell us that the town has changed greatly. All
the shops have changed, the town has grown, high-technology
industry has developed, and wealth has come to the town. More-

over, the author himself, through the comparison with the story from the proverb, lets us know that he cannot find the place of his youth there. So the correct answer to question 3 is *a*.

So much has changed in the town that we can no longer be sure that the author will want to return there or that he can meet his old acquaintances. Nor can we predict that he will want to profit from the changes themselves. All we can safely predict is that he will no longer look for his childhood in this changed town. The correct answer to question 4 is *d*.

How to Form Conclusions and Predict Outcomes

- Be sure you know the main idea of the selection.
- Be sure you understand all the facts or details that the writer gives to support the main idea.
- Check difficult vocabulary. Did you use context clues (**3a**) to figure out that *insatiable* meant "not able to be satisfied"?
- Follow the logic of the action. Does it follow a sequence (**7a**)? Did you put events together in the right order of time or place to help you predict what would happen?
- Look at the way people are described. Can you tell from their personalities — from the way they think and feel — just how they might act?
- After you read, ask yourself "What will happen as a result of these actions or events?"
- Be careful to build your conclusions on evidence you find in what you read, not exclusively on your opinions, likes, and dislikes. Of course you have to rely on your own experience to help you figure out how things happen. But most of your conclusions should be based on what you read in the selection.

EXERCISES

1. Predicting Outcomes of Sentences

Try to determine the outcome for the following statements. In your own words, write what you feel would be a logical ending for each sentence. Be prepared to defend your choice.

1. Janna usually did not like spicy foods, but when she tried

    chile verde for the first time, ————————————————

    ———————————————————————————————————————

2. After eating five portions of fried chicken, dirty rice, and

    greens, Samuel decided that ———————————————

    ———————————————————————————————————————

3. If you are looking for Thai food in Abilene, Kansas,

    ———————————————————————————————————————

    ———————————————————————————————————————

4. In Hong Kong, the best restaurants serve ——————————

    ———————————————————————————————————————

    ———————————————————————————————————————

5. You can find the best fresh seafood in cities that

    ———————————————————————————————————————

    ———————————————————————————————————————

6. If you walk into a McDonald's or Burger King anywhere in

    the world, you can expect ————————————————

    ———————————————————————————————————————

    ———————————————————————————————————————

2. Drawing Conclusions and Predicting Outcomes

Read the following selection to see what kind of instruction children may need to learn to read. Then answer the questions that
follow.

> A child takes great pleasure in becoming able to read some
> words. But the excitement fades when the texts the child must
> read force him to reread the same word endlessly. Word recog-
> nition — "decoding" is the term used by educational theo-

rists — deteriorates into empty rote learning when it does not lead directly into the reading of meaningful content. The longer it takes the child to advance from decoding to meaningful reading, the more likely it becomes that his pleasure in books will evaporate. A child's ability to read depends unquestionably on his learning pertinent skills. But he will not be interested in learning basic reading skills if he thinks he is expected to master them for their own sake. That is why so much depends on what the teacher, the school, and the textbooks emphasize. From the very beginning, the child must be convinced that skills are only a means to achieve a goal, and that the only goal of importance is that he become literate — that is, come to enjoy literature and benefit from what it has to offer.

— *Bruno Bettelheim and Karen Zelan*

_____ 1. As the writers use it, the word *decoding* means
  a. figuring out secret languages.
  b. rote learning.
  c. theorizing about education.
  d. recognizing individual words.

_____ 2. From the writers' point of view, we can conclude that a child who reads mainly by rote decoding will
  a. learn how to read intelligently.
  b. never learn how to read.
  c. not enjoy or get satisfaction from reading.
  d. come to enjoy literature later in life.

_____ 3. We can conclude from this selection that as a skill, decoding is
  a. worthless.
  b. important only as a part of a larger effort to enjoy literature.
  c. the most important reading skill.
  d. still being explored as a new area for teaching reading.

_____ 4. If the writers examined a children's reading text that read "Run, Jim, run. Run to Tim. Tim and Jim run to Tom," we could predict that they would
  a. disapprove quite strongly.
  b. approve enthusiastically.
  c. have no real opinion one way or the other.
  d. want teachers and parents to read the text aloud to children.

Critical Thinking in Writing

What were your attitudes toward reading and/or reading instruction when you were a young child? Write a paragraph to respond to these questions.

3.   Drawing Conclusions and Predicting Outcomes

Read the following selection about housing problems faced by a disabled person. Answer the questions that follow by writing the correct letter in the space provided.

It's easy to let yourself be discriminated against when you are disabled. I hear references all the time to the disabled as "special" people with "special" needs. I always ask myself, "What's so special about having to go to the bathroom or wanting to cross the street?" Steps discriminate against anyone who uses a wheelchair to get around in this world. Yet building with fewer of them does not lessen the problem. It only takes one step to discriminate.

After coping with the steps in my former house, I moved four years ago to a house where I occupied the lower flat. No steps — no problem. Did I have it made in the shade? I had a ramp built to act as my bridge from the sidewalk to my front door. It turns and slopes over four steps, is three feet wide, and is built pier style (so the wood can breathe in the summer) out of treated lumber (which can be textured with sand in the sealer to prevent wheels from slipping).

I soon learned that mere elimination of steps was not the total solution to my problems. I thought I could call this house "home" because my wheelchair could fit in the bathroom, unlike the bathroom at my previous house. But very soon I realized that, once in the bathroom, there was not enough space to do anything. Once again the cry rings out . . . HELP!

Further, the apartment's pea-green carpet had inches of padding. Maneuvering through the rooms was exhausting — I felt like I was in the middle of an Easter basket.

Usually, most residential doors are too narrow to qualify as barrier-free. My chair is 24″ wide, but with my hands on the push-rims, the measure is 26½″ knuckle to knuckle. There were two 27″ doorways on either side of my kitchen sink — ouch!!! — and the sink itself was totally unapproachable.

I got mad, and then I made a lot of changes.

The carpet went. Hardwood floors and mop boards and

elimination of thresholds and door jambs make the best surface for moving around. Any door that was not absolutely needed came off. Doors needed to cover closets and close bathrooms and bedrooms were changed to sliding doors. These can slide open to the desired width without creating the clearance problem common to all conventional, hinged swing-out doors.

The unapproachable sink went next, being replaced by a double-basin corner sink mounted not in the corner but facing straight out from a flat wall at its normal height. A swiveling, high goose-necked faucet was used and the two together resulted in success. The sink, mounted in the wall and not to the floor, provides access for the wheelchair and makes the room look more spacious.

— Patty Hayes

_____ 1. We can conclude that the author feels that buildings
   a. today are being made more accessible for those with disabilities.
   b. are designed with disabled people in mind.
   c. are not designed with disabled people in mind.
   d. present obstacles to those with disabilities that cannot be overcome.

_____ 2. We can conclude that the author believes disabled people
   a. have special needs that are very difficult to meet.
   b. have the same basic needs as everyone else.
   c. find it impossible to have their needs met.
   d. have simple needs.

_____ 3. We can predict that if the author found it hard to reach light switches from her wheelchair, she would
   a. leave the lights on all the time.
   b. ask someone for help.
   c. regularly curse the person who installed the switches.
   d. have the switches changed to a more convenient location.

_____ 4. We can conclude that the author
   a. has solved all the problems with her living arrangements.
   b. will continue to improve her environment.
   c. is not concerned about the needs of other people with disabilities.
   d. has taken on the job of designing apartments for people with disabilities.

_____ 5. We can predict that the author will tell other people in wheel-
chairs that they should
a. try to change their environment to fit their needs.
b. expect special help because they are disabled.
c. not expect other people to understand their special needs.
d. learn carpentry.

Critical Thinking in Writing

How has your school or community made services available to people with disabilities? What further steps might improve these services further? Write a paragraph to explain your answer.

---

4. Drawing Conclusions from Textbook Selections

Read each of the following selections from textbooks and answer the questions that follow by drawing conclusions and predicting outcomes.

Government

As in other areas of civil rights, the first major legislative efforts to prohibit job discrimination based on sex came in the 1960s. The Equal Pay Act of 1963 forbids using different pay scales for women and men who do equal work under similar conditions. The bill's coverage, though, effectively excluded millions of women and permitted wage differences for a number of reasons. Until it was amended in 1972, the law applied only to large interstate companies.

Many of these shortcomings were addressed in the Civil Rights Act of 1964. . . . Title VII of this act prohibits sex (as well as racial) discrimination in employment. This provision was not in the bill first introduced in Congress. Southern Congressmen — the principal opponents of the Civil Rights Act — introduced an amendment on sex discrimination in hopes of weakening its chances of passage. Both the act and the amendment passed, bringing about the first comprehensive legislation on sex discrimination.

Following these new laws, many cases of sex discrimination in the workplace came before the Supreme Court in the 1970s.

For example, it ruled against a corporation that would not hire women with preschool-age children, though it employed men with young children (*Phillips* v. *Martin Marietta Corp.*, 1971). The Court also rejected arbitrary height and weight requirements that effectively barred women from jobs as prison guards (*Dothard* v. *Rawlinson*, 1977). It also outlawed company policies in which maternity leave was treated differently from other types of leave in calculating seniority benefits (*Nashville Gas* v. *Satty*, 1977).

— Mary Beth Norton et al.

_____ 1. We can conclude from this selection that sex discrimination
   a. no longer occurs.
   b. has been declared illegal in all its forms.
   c. is a political issue.
   d. has been declared illegal in some specific ways.

_____ 2. We can conclude that the Supreme Court has
   a. been active in banning sex discrimination throughout this century.
   b. been concerned with sex discrimination in recent decades.
   c. not been concerned with sex discrimination as a problem.
   d. been the only government body concerned with sex discrimination.

_____ 3. We can conclude from this selection that sex discrimination
   a. has been eliminated most effectively from the workplace.
   b. is only a matter of job discrimination.
   c. has been eliminated in many areas of life.
   d. is a simple matter to eliminate.

Anthropology

The Manus baby is accustomed to water from the first years of his life. Lying on the slatted floor he watches the sunlight gleam on the surface of the lagoon as the changing tide passes and repasses beneath the house. When he is nine or ten months old his mother or father will often sit in the cool of the evening on the little verandah, and his eyes grow used to the sight of the passing canoes and the village set in the sea. When he is about a year old, he has learned to grasp his mother firmly about the throat, so that he can ride in safety, poised on the back of her neck. She has carried him up and down the long house, dodged under low-hanging shelves, and climbed up and down the rickety ladders which lead from house floor down to the landing verandah. The decisive, angry gesture with which he was reseated on his mother's neck whenever his grip tended to slacken has taught him to be alert and sure-handed. At last it is safe for his mother to take him out in a canoe, to punt or paddle the canoe herself while the baby clings to her neck. If a sudden wind roughens the lagoon or her punt catches in a rock, the canoe may swerve and precipitate mother and baby into the sea. The water is cold and dark, acrid in taste and blindingly salt; the descent into its depths is sudden, but the training within the house holds good. The baby does not loosen his grip while his mother rights the canoe and climbs out of the water.

— *Margaret Mead*

1. Without using a dictionary, try to determine the definitions of the following words. Refer to the line in which the word appears for hints to its meaning.

    a. lagoon (line 3) _____

    b. verandah (line 6) _____

    c. rickety (line 12) _____

    d. slacken (line 15) _____

    e. punt (line 17) _____

    f. precipitate (line 20) _____

    g. acrid (line 21) _____

_____ 2. The main idea of this paragraph is
    a. to show how the Manus babies learn about water.
    b. to show how the Manus mothers raise their children.
    c. to show how to survive the dangers of the sea.
    d. to show how the Manus families pass their time.
    e. all of the above.

_____ 3. The Manus houses are built
   a. in the mountains.
   b. in bush country.
   c. on slats above a lagoon.
   d. with shells from the sea.
   e. by the villagers at a festival.

_____ 4. We can conclude that a Manus child who falls by accident
   into the sea with the mother
   a. probably will drown.
   b. probably will be all right.
   c. probably will be attacked by sharks.
   d. will be rescued by the father.
   e. will swim to safety.

_____ 5. The Manus mothers probably take their children onto the
   water after they reach the age of
   a. five weeks.
   b. eleven weeks.
   c. nine months.
   d. ten months.
   e. one year.

_____ 6. When traveling with his or her mother, the Manus baby
   a. rides in a backpack.
   b. sits in a straw carriage.
   c. hangs from the mother's neck.
   d. paddles a canoe.
   e. all of the above.

_____ 7. As rowers along the lagoon, the Manus mothers are
   a. not as good as the fathers.
   b. inexperienced.
   c. capable.
   d. usually involved in accidents.
   e. unable to dodge low-hanging shelves.

Government

The promotion of equality has not always been a major objective of government. It has gained prominence only in this cen-

tury, in the aftermath of industrialization and urbanization. Confronted by the contrast of poverty amid plenty, some political leaders in European nations pioneered extensive government programs to improve life for the lower classes. Under the emerging concept of the **welfare state**, government's role expanded to provide individuals with medical care, education, and a guaranteed income, "from the cradle to the grave." Sweden, Britain, and other nations adopted welfare programs aimed at reducing social inequalities. This relatively new purpose of government has been by far the most controversial. Taxation for public goods (building roads and schools, for example) is often opposed because of its cost alone. Taxation for government programs to promote economic and social equality is opposed more strongly on principle.

— *Kenneth Janda, Jeffrey Berry, and Jerry Goldman*

_____ 1. The main idea of this selection is that
    a. a welfare state is the greatest good toward which a government can move.
    b. the governments of Sweden and Britain are very successful.
    c. people oppose taxes to fund public works and to promote equality.
    d. promoting equality, a relatively new goal for government, still causes controversy.

_____ 2. If a modern government proposed new taxes for job training for the poor, we can predict that people would
    a. support the idea in principle.
    b. oppose the idea in principle.
    c. oppose the idea because of its high cost.
    d. not care one way or the other.

_____ 3. According to this selection, if industry expands and the growth of cities continues in the next century, we can predict that
    a. life will be very difficult for most citizens.
    b. governments will continue to promote equality.
    c. governments will no longer be interested in promoting equality.
    d. governments will tax political leaders.

English Composition

When you talk, you say your words and sentences once, and that's it — you can't go back and change what your listener has already heard. But when you write, you have plenty of time and plenty of chances to work on your words before your reader sees them. In your rough drafts (a **draft** is an early, working copy of writing) you can change your mind: you can put in things you left out the first time, you can try to make your message clearer, and you can even stop for a while to collect your thoughts. The reader of your final copy sees only the neat results — not the messy work that went into making them.

— *Charles Bazerman and Harvey S. Wiener*

_____ 1. The main idea of this selection is that
    a. you can't change what your listener already has heard.
    b. writing is difficult.
    c. you can alter your thoughts before presenting a final version of something you've written.
    d. it is important that the final version of something you've written be neat.

_____ 2. We can conclude that if you omit something important from a draft you are writing, you should
    a. start again.
    b. just insert it in the appropriate place.
    c. forget it because you'll run out of time.
    d. not tell your reader about it.

_____ 3. We can conclude that a messy draft
    a. can be done over and over again with no offense to the reader.
    b. means a messy mind.
    c. should be avoided at all costs.
    d. is of great interest to readers.

_____ 4. You can predict that if you showed a messy effort as a final draft to a reader, he or she would be
    a. delighted.
    b. surprised.
    c. indifferent.
    d. hopeful.

Drawing Conclusions
and Predicting Outcomes

Read the selections below and in the space provided write the letter of the correct answer. Count 10 points for each correct answer.

A. In 1934, when Disney announced his intention of making the first feature-length animated cartoon — perhaps costing as much as $250,000 — his sincerest well-wishers told him he was crazy. In the first place, there was a Hollywood truism that fantasies were failures at the box office. In the second place, the public wouldn't sit through so long a cartoon. In the third place, an adult audience wouldn't even go to see a fairy tale. And in the fourth place, the juvenile audience wasn't large enough to pay for the cost of production.

Disney, who always said that self-confidence was the most important element of success, listened politely and made the feature anyway — at a final cost of $1.5 million in mostly borrowed dollars. *Snow White and the Seven Dwarfs* had its premiere in Hollywood on December 21, 1937, and promptly grossed $8 million in its first release — at that time, the most money a film had ever made. It played in 41 countries and soon had soundtracks in 10 different languages.

— *John Culhane*

_____ 1. In regard to filming *Snow White* we may conclude that Walt Disney
    a. needed financial support from many of his friends.
    b. chose it instead of Cinderella.
    c. did not pay much attention to his friends' opinions.
    d. did not want to make it into a full-length film.

_____ 2. About Disney's personality we may conclude that he
    a. believed in his own abilities.
    b. had many self-doubts.

   c. was very childlike.

   d. was interested only in becoming a millionaire.

_____ 3. About filming *Snow White,* it is obvious that the advice of Disney's well-wishers was

   a. wrong.

   b. right.

   c. weird.

   d. mean.

_____ 4. What advice may we safely predict that Disney would give to a young producer who wanted to make a full-length cartoon fantasy?

   a. Stay out of the movie business.

   b. Borrow all the money you can from your friends.

   c. The public won't sit through a very long cartoon.

   d. Have confidence in your own ideas.

_____ 5. About the money needed for producing *Snow White,* we may conclude that Disney

   a. knew exactly how much he'd have to borrow to make the film.

   b. thought the film would cost more than it actually did.

   c. thought the film would cost less than it actually did.

   d. did not expect to be able to pay back what he borrowed from his friends.

B. My family came to America in 1985. No one spoke a word of English. In school, I was in an English as a Second Language class with other foreign-born children. My class was so overcrowded that it was impossible for the teacher to teach English properly. I dreaded going to school each morning because of the fear of not understanding what people were saying and the fear of being laughed at.

At that time, my mother, Tai-Chih, worked part time in a Chinese restaurant from late afternoon till late in the night. It was her unfamiliarity with the English language that forced her to work in a Chinese-speaking environment. Although her job exhausted her, my mother still woke up early in the morning to cook breakfast for my brother and me. Like a hen guarding her chicks, she never neglected us because of her fatigue.

So it was not surprising that very soon my mother noticed

something was troubling me. When I said nothing was wrong, my mother answered: "You are my daughter. When something is bothering you, I feel it too." The pain and care I saw in her moon-shaped eyes made me burst into the tears I had held back for so long. I explained to her the fear I had of going to school. "Learning English is not impossible," my mother said. She cheerfully suggested that the two of us work together to learn the language at home with books. The confidence and determination my mother had were admirable because English was as new to her as it was to me.

That afternoon I saw my mother in a different light as she waited for me by the school fence. Although she was the shortest of all the mothers there, her face with her welcoming smile and big, black eyes was the most promising. The afternoon sun shone brightly on her long, black hair creating an aura that distinguished her from others.

My mother and I immediately began reading together and memorizing five new words a day. My mother with her encouraging attitude made the routine fun and interesting. The fact that she was sacrificing her resting time before going to work so that I could learn English made me see the strength she possessed. It made me admire my mother even more.

Very soon, I began to comprehend what everyone was saying and people could understand me. The person solely responsible for my accomplishment and happiness was my mother. The reading also helped my mother learn English so that she was able to pass the postal entrance exam.

It has been seven years since that reading experience with my mother. She is now 43 and in her second year at college. My brother and I have a strong sense of who we are because of the strong values my mother established for herself and her children. My admiration and gratitude for her are endless. That is why my mother is truly the guiding light of my life.

— *Yu-Lan (Mary) Ying*

————— 1. The main idea of this selection is that
a. a Chinese family has had difficulties in the United States since 1985.
b. Tai-Chih works part-time in a Chinese restaurant.
c. a mother's determination and support helped her daughter learn English.
d. learning English requires strong values in the home.

_____ 2. We can predict that if Yu-Lan had needed help in mathematics, her mother would have
a. found her a tutor.
b. worked together with her daughter so that they both could learn.
c. said that it didn't matter because Yu-Lan is a girl.
d. asked her son to help Yu-Lan.

_____ 3. We can safely conclude that if Yu-Lan had some other routine task to perform, she would
a. avoid it.
b. ask her mother to help with it.
c. ask her teacher for help.
d. find a way to make the routine enjoyable and challenging.

_____ 4. We can conclude that Tai-Chih
a. loved her daughter very much.
b. was annoyed with her daughter.
c. objected to giving up resting time to help her daughter learn English.
d. favored Yu-Lan over Yu-Lan's brother.

_____ 5. We can conclude that Tai-Chih
a. benefited from helping her daughter.
b. thought education in China was better than in America.
c. found learning English almost impossible.
d. wished that her son could learn English.

Score: _____ correct × 10 points each = _____

11

Generalizing

Another way to help you interpret what you read and to get deeper meanings from it is to develop skills in generalizing. When you generalize, you extend meanings beyond the specific ideas you read about. Generalizing allows you to apply information you've learned in a broader, less specific sense. You add up facts and details and draw from that particular information some general ideas or principles.

In Chapter 10 you learned about drawing conclusions and predicting outcomes. These skills are closely related to generalizing. *Generalizing* carries you a step beyond a conclusion you can draw about a specific set of details. It's almost as though *you* develop a concept or a rule based on the material you've read.

Read the following selection about the difficulties some men have shaving because of the type of hair they have. Then try to answer the questions that follow.

> For millions of men with coarse, curly hair there is no such thing as a smooth clean shave. For these men, shaving is painful because they develop razor bumps on the face and neck from the closely cut ends of hairs that imbed themselves to irritate and scar the skin.
>
> Although they occur among men of other races, the bumps are particularly common among black men. And they are a particular problem for them too, because the skin of blacks tends to form large scars known as keloids more easily than that of whites.
>
> The easiest and most effective treatment is simple: Grow a beard or use clippers to leave a stubble and a permanent 5 o'clock shadow.
>
> Yet the prescription is often difficult, if not impossible, to fill because of social pressures to be clean-shaven. Some organizations, like police departments or airlines, demand that men be clean-shaven. Many other employers informally make it clear that the corporate image requires a smooth shave. Some have been criticized for harassing bearded workers.
>
> — *Lawrence K. Altman*

_____ 1. The social expectation that all men should shave is
  a. a necessity for civilized behavior.
  b. annoying but not a serious problem.
  c. unfair to men with coarse, curly hair.
  d. unfair to all men.

_____ 2. Because of this problem — which is particularly common among black men — police departments, airlines, and other organizations ought to
  a. allow all black men to grow beards.
  b. allow only black men to grow beards.
  c. make black men follow the same shaving regulations as everyone else.
  d. allow all individuals with this problem, whatever their race, to grow beards.

_____ 3. Medical science
  a. recommends that men with coarse, curly hair avoid the problem.
  b. does not understand why certain men get razor bumps.
  c. has found a cure for razor bumps that allows all men to shave.
  d. is not concerned about social pressures that force men to shave.

This passage tells us that many men with coarse, curly facial hair develop razor bumps that can scar and that social pressures force these men to shave. So we can say that social pressures cause these men pain. That these men suffer just to meet an organizational standard certainly does seem unfair. Answer _c_, then, is the correct answer to question 1. Answer _b_ is clearly wrong because razor bumps are more than annoying to the men who can be scarred by them. Answers _a_ and _d_ are wrong because the reading provides no information about whether social pressures for shaving present problems for people other than this group of men. And to say that society's preference for clean-shaven men is inappropriate based on this one problem would be over-generalizing.

In question 2 we must go beyond the direct evidence in the passage about who experiences this problem and generalize to arrive at a fair solution. Although the problem most often affects black men, it does not affect black men _only_. So any solution that is directed only to black men is clearly a case of overgeneralizing. Answers *a, b,* and *c* concern black men only; only answer *d* generalizes a solution appropriate for the entire group of people affected by the problem of razor bumps.

Without stating it outright, the reading implies that medical science has not found a simple cure for razor bumps. If it had found such a cure, the "most effective treatment" would not be to grow a beard. So answer *c* is wrong. And although the recommendation not to shave conflicts with social pressures, we cannot generalize that medical science is not concerned about those pressures. Medical science may be well aware of the pressures but still believe the best solution is not shaving. So answer *d* is wrong. Medical science does seem to understand the problem because it recommends a solution. So answer *b* is wrong too. The solution — not shaving — does avoid the problem rather than cure it. Therefore *a* is the correct answer.

How to Generalize

- Make sure that you understand the main idea and key details from the reading.
- Make sure that you can draw conclusions or predict outcomes based on information you have read.
- Think about how you might apply the writer's ideas in different situations.
- When you try to generalize, don't go *too* far beyond the information the writer gives. Avoid making statements that are too broad in scope.
- Avoid overgeneralizing. Don't conclude that statements apply to *all* members of one group or *only* to members of one group before you check to see whether they apply just to some members of the group or include members of other groups. Make sure your statements refer only to those people or things that they really apply to.
- When you state a generalization, be particularly careful of words that do not allow exceptions. Words such as *always, never, must, certainly, absolutely,* and *definitely* can rule out possibilities for any challenge to the general statement.

EXERCISES

1. Practice with Generalizing

Read the following passage about how different mice are treated differently. Then put a checkmark next to the numbered statements that are correct generalizations based on the passage.

The University of Tennessee's Walters Life Sciences Building is a model animal facility, spotlessly clean, scrupulous in obtaining prior approval for experiments from an animal-care committee. Of the 15,000 mice housed there in a typical year, most give their lives for humanity. These are "good" mice and, as such, warrant the protection of the animal-care committee.

At any given time, however, some mice escape and run free. These mice are pests. They can disrupt experiments with the pathogens they carry. They are "bad" mice, and must be captured and destroyed. Usually, this is accomplished by means of "sticky" traps, a kind of flypaper on which they become increasingly stuck. Mice that are not dead by morning are gassed.

But the real point of this cautionary tale, says animal behaviorist Harold A. Herzog Jr., writing in the June issue of *American Psychologist,* is that the labels we put on things can skew our moral responses to them. Using sticky traps or the more lethal snap traps would be deemed unacceptable for good mice. Yet the killing of bad mice requires no prior approval. "Once a research animal hits the floor and becomes an escapee," writes Herzog, "its moral standing is instantly diminished."

In Herzog's own home, there was a more ironic example. When his young son's pet mouse, Willie, died recently, it was accorded a tearful ceremonial burial in the garden. Yet even as they mourned Willie, says Herzog, he and his wife were setting snap traps to kill the pest mice in their kitchen. With the bare change in labels from "pet" to "pest," the kitchen mice attained a totally different moral status. Something of the sort happens with so-called feeders — mice raised to be eaten by other animals. At the Walters facility, no approval is needed for feeding mice to laboratory reptiles that subsist on them. But if a researcher wants to film a mouse defending itself against a predator, the animal-care committee must review the experiment, even though the mouse will often survive. The critical factor in the moral regard of the mouse is whether it is labeled "subject" or "food."

— *David Gelman*

_____ 1. Some mice are more deserving of good treatment than others.

_____ 2. We treat mice differently depending on the label we attach to them.

_____ 3. Animal laboratories have too many restrictions on how they treat experimental animals.

_____ 4. We need to treat all animals better.

_____ 5. Some mice get treated better by humans than others.

_____ 6. Our principles of morality are always fair and well thought through.

_____ 7. "Bad" mice ought to be exterminated.

_____ 8. "Bad" mice are unwanted mice, so they are exterminated.

_____ 9. Labels are silly and of no importance.

_____ 10. Labels affect how we treat animals.

Critical Thinking in Writing

Gelman raises the point that what we call something — the label we give it — influences our moral responses to it. Do you agree or disagree? Consider one or more of these sets of terms as you write about a paragraph to address the issue:

- *Killing* versus *sacrificing* animals
- *Depression* versus *recession* versus *economic slowdown*
- *Vagrant* or *bum* versus *homeless person*
- *Retarded* children versus *special* or *exceptional* children

2. Generalizing

What kind of authority should a father have in his family? Read the following selection and then answer the questions that fol-

low. Most of the questions are based on your ability to generalize.

> In adapting the principle of democratic government to the fam-
> ily, we run into some obvious difficulties. The child does not
> elect his parents and he is not a responsible and functioning
> citizen in the society of his family. His father cannot be guided
> by the popular will of an electorate or a governing body to
> whom he is responsible. He cannot be guided by the popular
> will of his children, either, unless he is prepared to lose his
> sanity and his life's savings. If he is an earnest, democratic fa-
> ther, he may go in for family councils and such things, but this
> is likely to become a hoax in the name of democracy which
> any five-year-old can spot in a minute.
> We need to rescue the American father from the unreason-
> able and false situation into which we have put him in the
> name of democracy. We will have no tyrants either, for author-
> ity does not mean tyranny. And authority of the kind I speak
> does not require physical force or the exercise of power for the
> sake of power. It is a reasonable and just authority (as authority
> must be in a democratic society) exercised confidently as the
> prerogative of a father, deriving its strength from the ties of
> love that bind a parent and child.
>
> — *Selma H. Fraiberg*

1. What generalization can we draw about the author's view
   of a father's authority?

   _____

   _____

2. What generalization can we draw about the author's view
   of the role of democracy in the family?

   _____

   _____

3. What generalization can we draw about the author's view
   of a child's role in family discipline?

   _____

   _____

4. Put a checkmark next to those statements with which the author probably would agree.

_____   a. Authority does not depend on physical strength.

_____   b. The ties of love do not allow the use of authority.

_____   c. Only responsible functioning citizens should have the rights of democracy.

_____   d. Obeying children's will always forces parents to become insane.

_____   e. Problems in adapting principles of democratic government to families can be overcome easily.

3. Generalizing from a Textbook

The following passage comes from a textbook on marriage and the family. Read the selection and then answer the questions that follow, most of which are based on your ability to generalize.

Exploration of bodies, "playing doctor," and other forms of sex play are quite common in childhood, but they seem to have more to do with curiosity about oneself and the parts adults regard as taboo than they do with satisfying a primordial urge. A good deal of behavior concerning sex roles is learned during childhood. But sexual experience as such begins at adolescence with the biological events of puberty. The timing of puberty varies, but girls generally undergo these changes between the ages of 12 and 14, and boys go through puberty about two years later. The complex changes of puberty begin in the brain with the signal to release certain hormones. Over a period of about two years, the reproductive organs mature, and adolescents develop sex characteristics, which give them the physical attributes of men or women. Although the physical events and sexual experiences of adolescence are quite different for male and female, the sense of oneself as a sexual being — a *sexual identity* — is part of the overall sense of individual identity that develops during the teenage years. The experience of socializing with the opposite sex and feeling desirable or undesirable, the events that surround sexual arousal, and the combination of guilt, anxiety, and satisfaction that accompanies such feelings — these are some of the elements that shape this new sense of sexual identity.

— *Diane I. Levande, Joanne B. Koch, and Lewis Z. Koch*

_____ 1. The main idea of this selection is
   a. to provide a comprehensive view of puberty.
   b. to outline the requirements of socializing with the oppo-
      site sex.
   c. to define "playing doctor" among young children.
   d. to explain the elements of sexual identity.

_____ 2. It is safe to generalize from this passage that a young child
   who engages in sex play
   a. will develop a strange sexual identity.
   b. is merely exploring.
   c. may require psychiatric counseling in adulthood.
   d. is following a normal biological urge to satisfy sexual feel-
      ings.

_____ 3. We can generalize that a girl who undergoes puberty at the
   age of 15 is
   a. abnormal.
   b. not typical of most girls, but is not abnormal.
   c. never going to catch up fully with her peers in terms of
      sexual development.
   d. generally more mature and therefore more attractive to
      the opposite sex.

4. Examine the statements below and put a checkmark next to
   those that on the basis of the passage are correct generalizations.

_____   a. Girls are more dependable than boys.

_____   b. Guilt and anxiety are normal consequences of early sexual
              arousal.

_____   c. Both boys and girls form sexual identities in their teens.

_____   d. Only girls develop adequate sexual identities.

_____   e. Adolescent boys and girls generally have similar sexual
              experiences.

_____   f. People develop a sense of their sex roles with the onset
              of puberty.

_____   g. Sexuality involves both physical and emotional changes.

_____   h. Children should not socialize too early with the opposite sex.

_____   i. The start of sexual experiences is related to biological events.

_____   j. Sexual identity is an important part of a larger individual identity.

4. Generalizing from a Public Service Advertisement

Read the advertisement on page 263, placed by the Mobil Oil Corporation, which describes some of Mobil's educational support programs throughout the country. Then answer the questions that follow.

_____ 1. The word *defense* in the title refers to teachers being able to help America
   a. fight ignorance among those who are illiterate.
   b. gain a competitive edge in the next century.
   c. advance its military skills.
   d. keep its children from being violent.

_____ 2. "Global battlefield of technology," "potent weapons are math and science literacy," and "young technology troops" are all examples of
   a. figurative language.
   b. battle strategies.
   c. generalizations.
   d. ideas from Pegasus Award teachers.

3. Put a checkmark beside any generalization that you can safely make from this selection.

_____   a. Education needs the support of industry to help improve basic instructional programs.

_____   b. Children in other industrial countries have better math skills than do American children.

_____   c. Military boot camps are doing a poor job teaching basic mathematics to recruits.

Teachers:
Our best and last defense

Teachers. They're the best and last defense if America hopes to remain competitive in the future. But will they be able to get America's children ready for the stiff competition on tomorrow's global battlefield of technology when some of the most potent weapons are math and science literacy?

A study by professors at the University of Michigan and the University of California suggests America's young technology troops need to learn a whole lot more math at boot camp if they're going to be ready for a high-tech workplace. The professors tested math skills of 1st through 11th graders and found Americans were outscored by their counterparts from competitive countries.

This trend is distressing because America's economic future hinges on our children's ability to grasp the fundamentals of technology. There's no one answer to the problem. Nationwide, companies are trying a number of strategies to help schools bring America's young troops up to speed.

At Mobil, we're forging partnerships with teachers across America to try to enhance students' technical skills early.

In New Jersey, we cosponsor an intensive three-week summer program for 6th- to 12th-grade teachers called the South Jersey Summer Institute. The program gives science, social studies, history and economics teachers an inside look at business while building a network between education and industry.

Through plant tours and frank talk with industry and government leaders, teachers get real-life examples of what students need to know today to fill our jobs tomorrow.

In Beaumont, Texas, we're working with the superintendent of schools to introduce a pilot program called "Operation Breakthrough!" It's designed to enhance a teacher's ability to boost students' math and science skills whether they plan to seek technical jobs right out of high school or pursue a college degree. Employers will work with a team of teachers, parents and school administrators to try to change the way students learn math and science by creating a seamless stream of effective instruction from kindergarten through 12th grade.

In Dallas, Texas, Bakersfield, California, and several other cities, we offer Pegasus Award grants to teachers at inner-city schools. We fund dozens of teacher proposals for such innovative classroom ideas as laser disc instruction for 6th graders, and we provide needed materials like calculators, multicultural textbooks and laboratory equipment.

We're providing teachers with learning materials to promote better critical thinking skills among students at nearly 24,000 high schools across America.

And in Fairfax, Virginia, we sponsor a middle-school program called "Expanding Visions" to help an interdisciplinary teaching team build on each other's specialties to spark early interest among 7th graders in engineering, math and science careers.

It makes sense to us to help teachers, because the children in America's classrooms today are the scientists, engineers, technicians, plant operators and skilled craftspeople we'll need one day to help run our business. We want them well-armed for the technology battle ahead.

We're convinced programs like these are worth the investment. And, while a number of businesses have launched public-school partnerships, America needs more. That's why we encourage your business to consider helping your local school system. If you're interested in finding out more about our efforts, write to us at: Mobil Education Programs, P.O. Box ER, 3225 Gallows Road, Fairfax, VA 22037-0001.

Teachers shouldn't be the only ones in the trenches.

_____   d. Teachers should learn to defend themselves in the
              trenches through military training.

_____   e. Technology will play a major role in the economic future
              of our country.

_____   f. Some companies believe that it is worth their time and
              money to help educate young people.

_____   g. To better prepare their students, teachers should under-
              stand what skills and knowledge students will need to fill
              jobs.

_____   h. The objective of a pilot program in Texas is to replace
              classroom teachers with instructors from industry.

_____   i. Students must be well armed because the technology bat-
              tle ahead will be extremely violent.

_____   j. Industrial support for mathematics instructors includes
              providing equipment, special instruction, programs for
              students and teachers, and awards for innovation.

_____ 4. Mobil probably placed this ad in the newspaper because
              a. it wants a competitive edge over other oil companies.
              b. it wants to impress readers.
              c. it wants to encourage other businesses to support educa-
                 tion.
              d. all of the above.

Generalizing

Read the following paragraph. Then examine the statements after the selection and put a plus (+) next to each general statement with which the author probably would agree and a minus (−) next to each general statement with which the author probably would disagree. Count 10 points for each correct answer.

> During the 1952–1953 period when I was preparing the screenplay, I was fully aware that the wholesale crimes of the waterfront were not to be explained merely by the prominence of certain gentlemen from Sing Sing and Dannemora in positions of authority on the docks. The shipping companies and the stevedore management had accepted — in some cases encouraged — the thugs for years, and in many cases city politicians were nothing less than partners of the longshore union racketeers. It was this unhealthy axis, I knew, that made it so difficult to bring any real democratic reform to the graft-ridden docks. I even discussed with my film collaborators scenes that would dramatize this civic plight. Those scenes were not eliminated through any cowardice or fear of censorship, as some critics have suggested. No, it was another tyrant, the ninety-minute feature form, that lopped off their heads.
>
> — *Budd Schulberg*

_____ 1. The form a writer uses affects his or her message.

_____ 2. Social problems are usually due to a variety of causes.

_____ 3. Authority is always corrupt.

_____ 4. Film makers operate out of cowardice and fear of censorship.

_____ 5. Fiction can influence life.

_____ 6. Writing screenplays is very difficult.

_____ 7. Unions and management can contribute to crimes in business.

_____ 8. Writers have difficulty in reforming corruption.

_____ 9. Corrupt politicians created the crime conditions on the waterfront.

_____ 10. The required format of an artistic work can prevent a writer from including all essential information.

Score: _____ correct × 10 points each = _____

12

Evaluating Ideas

The skills described in Chapters 1 through 11 help you understand and interpret what you read. But effective reading is more than just understanding. You must be able to read in a *critical* way — which means that you have to *evaluate* ideas once you understand them. When you evaluate a writer's ideas, you judge the worth of what you read.

Here are some important questions to ask yourself in evaluating what you read:

- Does the author carefully separate fact from opinion?
- Does the passage present the facts completely, specifically, and accurately?
- Does the author seem reliable? What strengths or experiences qualify the author to write about the topic?
- Does the author make any claims that seem outrageous or insupportable?
- Does the author make the intent or point of view clear?
- Does the author take into account other points of view on the topic?
- Does the author try to appeal more to your emotions than to your reason and common sense?
- Do your emotions get in the way of your ability to judge the author's statements fairly?
- Does it seem that the author is slanting information to prejudice your ideas? Is the author using propaganda?

The following sections will help you sharpen your critical reading.

12a   Fact and Opinion

Most reading samples contain ideas based on fact *and* opinion. Of course, a writer can combine the two in such a way that you do not always notice where fact ends and opinion begins. In a philosophy course you might spend much time discussing just what makes a fact different from an opinion. But in most instances you simply want to distinguish between two types of statements as you read.

Facts are statements that tell what really happened or really exists. A fact is based on direct evidence. It is something known by actual experience or observation.

Opinions are statements of belief, judgment, or feeling. They show what someone thinks about a subject. Solid opinions, of course, are based on facts. However, opinions are still somebody's view of something; they are not facts themselves.

Look at the following statements, which come from Dee Brown's *Bury My Heart at Wounded Knee: An Indian History of the American West*:

1. In 1848 gold was discovered in California.
2. In 1860 there were probably 300,000 Indians in the United States and Territories, most of them living west of the Mississippi.
3. Now, in an age without heroes, the Indian leaders are perhaps the most heroic of all Americans.

In sentence 1 we read a statement of fact. We have evidence of the discovery of gold in California in 1848. If we checked sources, we would see that the statement is true.

The use of numbers, dates, and geography in sentence 2 creates a sense of fact. But the word *probably* suggests some doubt, so we cannot accept the statement as completely factual. That doesn't make it wrong or untrue. It just makes it partly an opinion. Because Dee Brown is a scholar in American Indian history, most people would accept this statement as fact. But it is still his educated judgment that 300,000 Indians lived in the United States in 1860. The writer's education and background tell us to rely on his statement, so we accept it as true without much thought. It is possible, though, that some people have other views on this subject.

In sentence 3 we have a clearer example of the author's opinion. The statement is not wrong; it just is not a statement of fact. The word *perhaps* tells us that the author himself believes other ideas are possible. It is true that many people would agree that Indian leaders are the most heroic. Others might say, however, that leaders during World War II or leaders of this country in times of crisis were the most heroic. Still others might say that leaders on Vietnam battlefields were the most heroic. None of these statements is incorrect. All, however, are opinions.

To judge a writer's work you must be able to distinguish opinion from fact. Often writers mix fact and opinion even within the same sentence, with some words representing facts and others representing opinions. Think about the following sentences:

> Compact discs reproduce truer sound than records. They cannot skip or scratch the way records do. Despite this, there will always be a market for record players because many people don't like to change things they're used to for new gadgets they can't understand.

The first part of this statement is factually true. Compact disc players use digital computers, which reproduce sound more faithfully than old-fashioned records do. And because compact disc players use lasers and not needles, they can't damage discs or cause skips or scratches.

The next part of the statement is a prediction based on two beliefs that may or may not be true. First, "people don't like to change things they're used to" is not a fact. It isn't true in all cases. For instance, one hundred years ago people traveled by horse and buggy, but today hardly anyone would consider it more practical to travel by horse rather than in an automobile. New inventions take time to become accepted. Elevators, computers, televisions, and airplanes have all been accepted by most people, and someday maybe everyone will own a compact disc player. The second opinion expressed, that people can't understand new gadgets, is invalid for similar reasons. Years ago people were unfamiliar with calculators, automatic teller machines, microwave ovens, and many other "gadgets." While some people avoid devices they find difficult to operate or understand, many people discard old ones and adapt to new ones. The fact of the matter is that no one knows for certain whether "there will always be a market for record players."

Keeping Fact and Opinion Apart

- Look for words that *interpret*. In the first of the following sentences, we have details that describe facts — without any evaluation of these facts. In the second sentence, the writer interprets the details for us.

  The man leaning against the fence had brown eyes and black hair touching his shoulders.
  A handsome man leaned against the fence.

  It's somebody's opinion that the man is handsome. Other words that interpret — there are countless examples — are *pretty, ugly, safe, dangerous, evil, attractive, well dressed,* and *good.*

- Look for words that serve as clues to statements of opinion. Some words like *probably, perhaps, usually, often, sometimes,* and *on occasion* are used to limit a statement of fact, to indicate the possibility of other opinions. Other words — for example, *I believe, I think, in my opinion, I feel,* and *I suggest* — say clearly that an opinion follows.

- Before you accept a statement of fact and before you agree with a statement of opinion, question the author's authority. Is he or she reliable? Why should you take his or her word?

- Test the writer's opinion by asking whether a different opinion is possible. You do not have to agree with the different opinion (or with the author's, for that matter). You just have to be able to see if there is another point of view.

- Some authors include statements from other writers or authorities in order to illustrate their own ideas ("According to Maria Rodriguez, the latest data show . . ."). Make sure you can identify the source of any statement that appears in what you read.

When you have a mixture of fact and opinion in a single statement, you must decide whether the main point of the statement is essentially fact or opinion. In the compact disc example, the main point of the statement was to make a prediction, so it basically offers an opinion, even though it contains many facts. Consider another example:

Marta Bahia was in a hopeful mood as she arrived in San Francisco for the first time. She felt that in this new city she would be able to get a better job and meet new people and start a new life. Soon, however, she would have to look at her situation realistically.

In the first sentence, the word *hopeful* tells us something about Bahia's view of the future; however, the main point of the sentence is to announce her arrival and tell us what her mood was at the time, both of which are facts. The second sentence is similar. It again expresses Bahia's hopes about her future, but its main point is to report her specific feelings. The last sentence, however, expresses the *writer's* opinion that she was being unrealistic and would soon have to think differently.

EXERCISES

1. Fact and Opinion

Write *F* before each sentence that basically represents a fact; write *O* before each statement of opinion.

_____ 1. Baseball is the most American of all sports.

_____ 2. Baseball is based on the British game of rounders.

_____ 3. More Americans play baseball than soccer or tennis.

_____ 4. Japanese professional baseball players are good enough to play in the American major leagues.

_____ 5. Taiwan has won more Little League World Series championships than any other country in recent years.

_____ 6. Most major league ball parks use artificial turf.

_____ 7. Baseball should be played on natural grass, not artificial turf.

2. Fact and Opinion

Read this letter to the editor of the *New York Times* to discover the writer's views on bilingual education. Then answer the questions that follow on the use of facts and opinions in the letter. *Bilingual education* refers to the instruction of a child who has recently come to this country in both English and the child's native language until the child develops good skills in English.

To the Editor

I was appalled by the full-page advertisement by the advocacy group U.S. English (July 25), which implied that bilingual education for people of limited English proficiency or none at all will subject them to a life of menial jobs ("children will be forced to study all subjects in their native languages, with very limited instruction in English"). To the contrary, bilingual education is essential to millions across the country who wish to live and prosper in America.

The ad responded to the New York Education Department Board of Regents' much-lauded decision to provide equal education opportunity for all the state's residents, including those for whom English is not a native language. By providing bilingual education opportunities, New York is taking the lead in insuring that everyone has an equal chance to succeed. Such programs teach English and American culture, using a person's native language. In doing so, the students, mostly children, learn to speak English, adapt to the surrounding customs and culture, and become integrated into their community without abandoning their heritage.

The implications made by the U.S. English advertisement are untrue and unfounded. Bilingual education courses will help insure that children whose native language is not English will be assimilated into the schools, will be better prepared for the job market and will be able to join the mainstream of America. Children will not be forced to study all subjects in their native languages, with very limited instruction in English. Rather, a majority of the classes will be taught in English.

Such disregard for the truth and misrepresentation of facts should not go unnoticed. It is important that the public knows the facts about bilingual education and the positive effects it will have on American society. America must realize the great potential of its cultural diversity and strive to become as open-minded as possible. We must accept others with different backgrounds and cultures, learn from them, and give them an equal opportunity to succeed.

I hope that the people of New York examine the merits and benefits of bilingual education before they make judgments against such a valuable program.

— *Robert Garcia*

1. The opening sentence of this letter makes several statements of fact and opinion. In the following breakdown of those statements, place an *F* before those that are fact and an *O* before those that are opinion.

_____ a. An advertisement appeared in the newspaper on July 25.

_____ b. U.S. English sponsored the ad.

_____ c. U.S. English is an advocacy group.

_____ d. Bilingual education will subject children to a life of menial jobs.

_____ e. Children in bilingual programs will not get enough instruction in English.

_____ f. The ad stated that "children will be forced to study all subjects in their native languages, with very limited instruction in English."

_____ g. The ad is appalling.

_____ 2. Overall the first sentence presents
   a. primarily facts.
   b. the writer's opinions only.
   c. U.S. English's opinions only.
   d. the writer's reaction to U.S. English's opinions.

3. Put a checkmark before each statement below that accurately reflects the writer's opinion.

_____ a. As a result of bilingual education, children will not be brought into the American mainstream.

_____ b. Bilingual education is essential for millions who want to prosper in America.

_____ c. The Board of Regents has decided to provide bilingual education.

_____   d. New York is taking the lead in equal-opportunity education.

_____   e. A majority of the classes in a bilingual education program are taught in English.

_____   f. Children will not be forced to study all subjects in their native languages.

_____   g. The advertisement disregarded the facts.

_____   h. It is our choice to recognize our cultural diversity, become open-minded, and provide equal opportunity.

_____   i. Bilingual education is a valuable program.

_____ 4. Overall the letter presents
         a. facts that disprove U.S. English's opinions.
         b. opinions that oppose U.S. English's opinions.
         c. facts and opinions that support U.S. English's opinions.
         d. a balanced view, accepting all opinions.

Critical Thinking in Writing

Should children whose first language is not English be taught in their native language as well as in English? Write a paragraph or two in which you explore your views.

---

5. Fact and Opinion in an Essay

Read this selection from an essay called "This Land Is Your Land," which appeared in *Newsweek* magazine. The writer is a grain and livestock farmer in Harlan, Iowa, who is unhappy about America's farm policy. After you read, answer the questions that follow.

> Four dollars for a bowl of cereal! Moscow, right? No, it's what I paid for oatmeal at a hotel in Washington, D.C., recently. I have to grow nearly four bushels of oats to get paid $4. I'm an Iowa farmer, and I had been invited by the United States Department of Agriculture to participate in a Grain-Users Ad-

visory Workshop recommending how agricultural-research money should be spent. I was so angry, I practically choked on my oatmeal. Angry not at the price of the cereal but by what's happened to agriculture, farms and rural America, and society's ignorance and indifference. As Mary Lease, a fiery 19th-century populist said: "You farmers need to raise less corn — and more hell."

There are fewer farmers every year. Our average age keeps going up, and so does the average size of our farms. For the past 20 years, I've kept a "Family Farms" file of newspaper clips — many full of politicians' rhetoric, espousing the values of, and the need to save, family farms. In 1940 there were 6 million farms; now there are 2 million, and the prediction is that there will be fewer than 1 million by the year 2000. The 400 largest farms in the country represent only about .02 percent of the nation's farms, but they account for about 15 percent of total farm income. Ours, a medium-size farm of 480 acres, which I work with the help of my wife and one employee, is doing well — for the moment. But we are concerned for our three sons, ages 6, 8 and 10, should they choose to farm.

This country has lost the capability even to recognize the needs of rural America. Many "enlightened and educated" people haven't the foggiest idea of what is happening, nor do they care. Even farmers have been brainwashed into thinking little can be done: technology and big business's control of agriculture are just too powerful to counter, they figure. And as long as food is relatively cheap and abundant, the consumer doesn't seem to care how it's produced.

Small family farms are worth saving, and not for nostalgia's sake. We can never go back to the romantic scenes of Currier and Ives. But it appears the path we're following continues to dry up small- and medium-size family farms and the small towns and community values that go along with them. It's happening in the name of free enterprise and efficiency. Farm programs, initiated in the 1930s to help small farmers, have, over time, resulted in a major portion of the program going to large-scale agribusinesses. This encourages environmentally damaging practices on fragile lands. The more corn planted, the greater the subsidy. Some program modification is needed. We have a "cheap food policy," but is it cheap in its implications? What are the environmental and health costs of modern agriculture with its heavy dependence on pesticides?

Some small farmers are fighting for something called "sustainable agriculture," which simply means a system of agriculture that will last. In Iowa we call it "practical farming." With it, farmers are seeking environmentally sound and profitable farming techniques that rely more on management and labor skills than on pesticides, expensive technology, high capital outlay and big debts. We are not organic purists; we are trying to find a happy medium where pesticides are used sparingly. It means making a decent living on the small- and medium-size farms, not looking longingly over the neighbor's fence hoping his or her place will come up for sale.

— *Ronald L. Rosmann*

In the statements below, put an *F* beside those that are fact and an *O* beside those that are opinion.

_____ 1. Farmers need to raise less corn and more hell.

_____ 2. Society is ignorant about and indifferent to agriculture, farms, and rural America.

_____ 3. Since 1940 the number of farms in America has dropped by 4 million.

_____ 4. Our country cannot even recognize the needs of rural America.

_____ 5. The country's 400 largest farms account for 15 percent of total farm income.

_____ 6. As long as food is cheap, consumers don't care how it is produced.

_____ 7. Farmers have been brainwashed.

_____ 8. Technology and big business control agriculture.

_____ 9. The agricultural policy we now have is drying up small- and medium-sized farms.

_____ 10. *Sustainable agriculture* means a system of agriculture that draws on profitable farming techniques and relies more on management and labor skills than on pesticides, expensive technology, and big debts.

12b Evidence

Sometimes when writers state their opinions, they just assert their points of view without providing any support. In these cases you have no particular reason to believe their opinions unless you trust them as authorities or experts. In fact, you probably shouldn't believe any writer — even an "expert" — who states opinions without giving supporting evidence.

More often, writers try to convince readers to share their opinions by presenting various facts or evidence, just as a lawyer presents evidence in court to support the opinion that the accused is innocent or guilty of a crime. Just as a jury must evaluate the evidence carefully to decide whether to accept a lawyer's opinion about the accused, so must you evaluate the evidence presented in what you read to decide whether to accept a writer's opinion.

The following questions will help you evaluate any evidence offered in support of an opinion you find expressed in your reading:

■ Can you trust the facts? Why do you think so?
■ Are the facts given in an objective way? What makes you say so?
■ Do the facts really support the opinion being expressed? How can you tell?
■ Are the facts relevant to the point being made? Why do you think so?
■ Has the writer left out unfavorable or negative points? Which? Why?
■ Do the facts prove the writer's opinion, or do they suggest only that the opinion is reasonable? How can you tell?

If two writers give opposite opinions, you should judge which one gives better evidence. Whose facts are more reliable, more complete, and expressed more objectively? Whose facts support the opinion more fully?

Many times, writers try to convince you to share their opinions. They use all their persuasive skills to make you believe that tall people make better presidents, that Michael Jackson is the greatest male vocalist, or even that people who use crack should be shot. Only a careful reader can avoid falling for an emotional or poorly reasoned argument.

EXERCISES

1. Evidence Backing Up Statements

Before each of the following statements, write *E* if the statement is backed up properly by evidence, write *N* if there is no supporting evidence, and write *I* if there is evidence but it is used improperly.

_____ 1. Anyone who studies a foreign language in college is just wasting time.

_____ 2. Because English is the most commonly used language in international business, there is no business advantage to be gained from learning a foreign language.

_____ 3. Because college courses in computer programming are more popular than language courses, computer programming is far more useful to learn than any foreign language.

_____ 4. Asian languages, like Japanese and Chinese, will be important to learn in the future.

_____ 5. French and German have contributed so many words to English that studying these languages can develop your English vocabulary.

_____ 6. You learn a foreign language best when you have a real need to use it every day.

_____ 7. The fact that more American students study Latin than Russian, Chinese, and Japanese combined shows that Americans are not preparing themselves to communicate in the modern world.

_____ 8. As the global economy expands, people who know foreign languages may be about to expand business into new territories.

2. Opinion and Evidence in a Textbook Selection

Read this selection on Native Americans' civil rights from a government textbook. As you read, evaluate which statements are backed up by evidence and which represent judgments of the authors or other people. Then answer the questions that follow.

During the eighteenth and nineteenth centuries, the U.S. government took Indian lands, isolated Native Americans on reservations, and denied them political and social rights. The government's dealings with the Indians were often marked by violence and riddled with broken promises. The agency system for administering Indian reservations kept Native Americans poor and dependent on the national government.

The national government switched policies at the turn of the century, promoting assimilation instead of separation. The government banned the use of native languages and religious rituals; it sent Indian children to boarding schools and gave them non-Indian names. In 1924, Indians were given U.S. citizenship. Until that time, they were considered members of tribal nations whose relations with government were subject to treaties made with the United States. The Native American population suffered badly during the Depression, primarily because the poorest people were affected most, but also because of the inept administration of Indian reservations. Poverty remained on the reservations well after the Depression was over, and Indian lands continued to shrink through the 1950s and into the 1960s — in spite of signed treaties and the religious significance of portions of those lands. In the 1960s, for example, a part of the Hopi Sacred Circle, which is considered the source of all life in tribal religion, was strip-mined for coal.

Anger bred of poverty, unemployment, and frustration with an uncaring government exploded into militant action in November 1969, when several American Indians seized Alcatraz Island, an abandoned island in San Francisco Bay. The group cited an 1868 Sioux treaty that entitled them to unused federal lands; they remained on the island for a year and a half. In 1973, armed members of the American Indian Movement seized eleven hostages at Wounded Knee, South Dakota — the site of a tragic battle in 1890 between the Sioux and U.S. cavalry troops. They remained there, occasionally exchanging gunfire with federal marshals, for seventy-one days.

In 1946, Congress had passed legislation establishing an Indian claims commission to compensate Native Americans for land that had been taken from them. In the 1970s, the Native American Rights Fund and other groups used that legislation to win important victories. Lands were returned to tribes in the Midwest and in the states of Oklahoma, New Mexico, and Washington. In 1980, the Supreme Court ordered the national government to pay the Sioux $117 million plus interest for the Black Hills of South Dakota, which had been stolen from them a century before. Other cases, involving land from coast to coast, are still pending.

The fight continues for survival of ancient native culture and control over lost lands. The preservation of Native American culture and the exercise of Native American rights, however, sometimes create conflict with the interests of the majority. For example, Chippewa Indians in northern Wisconsin engage in an annual battle with local fishermen on the shores of Lake Minocqua. The Indians wish to exercise their acknowledged right to spearfish for walleyed pike. Fishermen fear that the Indians will deplete the stock and drive sport fishermen away. The Chippewas voluntarily limit their annual catch, but they are offended that their ancestral claims are envied as government concessions when their stake rests on legal rights.

In other instances, economic necessity may overwhelm ancient ways. One Alaskan tribe desperate for funds has been forced into unsettling choices: Sign away logging rights, permit oil drilling in a wildlife area, or allow the construction of an airfield in a vast habitat for Kodiak bears. Some tribes have allowed the use of their reservations for dumps and waste disposal only to face land and water contamination as a consequence.

Throughout American history, Native Americans have been coerced physically and pressured economically to assimilate into the mainstream of white society. The destiny of Native Americans as viable groups with separate identities depends in no small measure on curbing their dependence on the national government. Litigation on behalf of Native Americans may prove to be their most effective weapon in the march toward equality.

— *Kenneth Janda, Jeffrey Berry, and Jerry Goldman*

In the spaces after each statement below, indicate what evidence in the selection, if any, backs up the statement. If you find no evidence for the statement, write *opinion* in the space.

1. The government's dealings with the Indians often have been marked by violence and riddled with broken promises.

_____

_____

2. The agency system for administering Indian reservations kept Native Americans poor and dependent on the national government.

   _____

   _____

3. The national government switched policies at the turn of the century, promoting assimilation instead of separation.

   _____

   _____

4. The Native American population suffered badly during the Depression.

   _____

   _____

5. Indian lands continued to shrink in the 1950s and 1960s in spite of the religious significance of portions of the land.

   _____

   _____

6. Anger exploded into militant action.

   _____

   _____

7. The fight continues to preserve the ancient native culture and to regain control over lost lands.

   _____

   _____

8. Preserving rights for Native Americans can create conflict with majority interests.

_____

_____

9. Throughout American history Native Americans have been coerced physically and pressured economically.

_____

_____

10. The survival of Native Americans as a group with separate identities depends on curbing their dependence on the national government.

_____

_____

12c The Writer's Technique

Be aware of the writer's technique in any selection you read. Once you know what the writer is doing with the material — once you know what effect the writer is trying to create — you can judge the issues more fairly and clearly.

12c(1) Style

In general, *style* is the way a writer picks words and puts them together. The style usually tells you who the writer expects to read the work. If the sentences are long and the words are difficult, the writer is writing for an educated reader. If the language is rich in slang expressions and current phrases, the writer is talking to a more general group. If the words are very technical, the writer is aiming for a special audience that knows the language of the subject being discussed. Some writers pick words with deep emotional appeal in order to urge their readers to act. Other writers choose a more impartial style.

A writer who wants to convince you of the urgency of his or her message might use short sentences so that as you read along, you become wrapped up in the fast pace. During World War II, Winston Churchill said, "We shall fight them on the beaches. We shall fight them street by street. We shall never give up." He used repetition and short sentences effectively to show how committed England was to keep on fighting. If he had said, "We shall fight them on the beaches and in the streets and never give up," he would have delivered the same basic message, but the style would not have fired up his listeners' emotions.

12c(2) Tone

Tone is the attitude a writer takes toward a subject. Writers may write about something they respect or about something they hate. A writer may be angry or impatient. A writer may take a humorous view of a subject. Or a writer may be ironic — say one thing but really mean the opposite.

Oscar Wilde was asked by a judge during his trial, "Are you trying to show contempt for this court?" and Wilde replied, "On the contrary, I'm trying to conceal it." The tone of his response was much more effective than if he had said, "Yes, I am." Wilde's use of irony made his contempt — that is, disrespect and scorn — appear so strong that he could not restrain it.

12c(3) Mood

Mood is a state of mind or feeling at a particular time. Often writers create a mood so that they can make you respond in a certain way.

Edgar Allan Poe said that sibilants (words that contain the *s* sound, such as *snake, sinister,* and *shadow*) help create a mysterious mood, and he used sibilants often: "And then did we, the seven, start from our seats in horror, and stand trembling, and shuddering and aghast."

12c(4) *Purpose*

Writers write for a *reason*. Some want to give information. Some want to persuade you to believe something. Others try to push you into taking action on an issue that is important to them. Some write to amuse or entertain.

Advertising is a good example of writing with a purpose — to make you buy a certain product. And editorials in newspapers aim at gaining public support for a political position.

12c(5) *Point of View*

Our beliefs and ideas often determine our views of a subject. In this sense, *point of view* means "opinions" or "attitudes." Although there are several other meanings for the term, we are concerned here with the way a writer's interests and beliefs influence his or her work. A communist, for example, would look at the Cuban government differently from a person who believes in democracy. A Catholic's view on religious ceremonies would be different from that of a Protestant or a Jew. And a black person might have much stronger views on the treatment of sickle cell anemia than a white person. Sometimes a writer's point of view forces him or her to *slant* the writing. Slanted writing leans toward one way of looking at a problem and leaves out ideas that might disagree.

Of course, writers often blend these techniques. Often it's impossible to separate style and tone: both clearly relate to purpose and point of view. Also, the writer's style often creates a mood.

Furthermore, a writer's technique frequently yields a range of effects. For example, writing can be both humorous and ironic. Or a writer may want to give information to persuade you to do something and so may write in a very emotional style.

Mark Twain once said, "Man is the only animal that blushes, or needs to." This is a much more effective way to communicate his point of view than if he had said, "People, unlike animals, do things that they are ashamed of." As Twain and other humorists have discovered, people will listen to any argument if it is entertaining.

The point in seeing a writer's technique is to help you notice that *what* an author wants to say relates to *how* he or she says it.

EXERCISES

1. The Writer's Technique

Read the following statements. Below the statements a series of questions appears. In the blank space, write the letter of the statement that answers the question. You can use the same letter more than once and more than one letter for each answer.

a. The high impact of this audio–video system could change your whole lifestyle. Because this system produces images so vivid and sounds so real, you're transported into a whole new era of home entertainment.

b. If you have received a mailing label from us, please use it. Make sure information on the label is correct. If it isn't, cross out what is wrong and mark corrections directly on the label. If you have not received a label, print or type your name, address, and social security number.

c. Instead of teaching liberty, the U.S. foreign relations apparatus has chosen to teach the world coups d'état, assassination, duplicity, torture, and state control. If the U.S. would show the world a different face, one that accords with the precepts by which we have built our own society, we would begin to succeed where we now fail.

— *Jonathan Kwitny*

d. The shadow-puppet play exists or has existed in an extensive but fairly narrow strip of territory stretching from China in the East to Morocco and Western Europe in the West.

— *Amin Sweeney*

e. 1945. A year to remember. Sure, there were some slightly interesting occurrences during the year, like FDR's death, and the end of World War II. However, these events pale into insignificance when compared with the one truly great news story of that year: the birth of Steve Martin. Stephen Martin was born unto Glenn and Mary Lee Martin in August 1945, in Waco, Texas. ("Waco," incidentally, is pronounced "Way-co," not "Wacko." Since the name stands for the birthplace of Steve Martin, the city fathers may consider changing the pronunciation.)

— *Grey Lenburg, Randy Skretvedt, and Jeff Lenberg*

f. Even before his death, George mentioned that several times he had heard mysterious music coming from the organ in the projection room. As a test he locked the door and disconnected the electric apparatus that worked the organ. Still the music continued. But as soon as he entered the room, it stopped.

g. If you love things Italian wait until you've tasted them in Italy. There's so much more to love and life. The fashion, the food, the wines, the music, the scenery, the architecture, the works of art . . . it's more than a holiday, it's a celebration of life itself. But don't just come to Italy. Come to Alitalia's Italy. We can show you Romeo and Juliet's balcony in Verona; let you sigh on the Bridge of Sighs in Venice; gaze in awe at Michelangelo's "David" in Florence; sit where Roman Emperors sat in ancient Rome; point you in the direction of the most elegant boutiques.

— *Italiatour!Inc.*

h. Mother Cat is taking Huckle and Lowly to the city. What do you think they are going to do there? They have to take the train. Mother Cat sits in the passenger coach. Huckle and Lowly sit with the engineer in the locomotive. TO-O-O-O-T! Lowly pulls the whistle.

— *Richard Scarry*

i. It is no secret that organized crime in America takes in over $40 billion a year. This is quite a profitable sum, especially when one considers that the Mafia spends very little for office supplies. Reliable sources indicate that the Cosa Nostra laid out no more than six thousand last year for personalized stationery, and even less for staples. Furthermore, they have one secretary who does all the typing, and only three small rooms for headquarters, which they share with the Fred Persky Dance Studio.

— *Woody Allen*

_____ 1. Which statement is written in a style suitable for children?

_____ 2. Which statement is designed to make you do something?

_____ 3. Which piece uses humor?

_____ 4. Which one creates a mood of excitement?

_____ 5. Which statement uses a precise tone?

_____ 6. Which one gives instructions?

_____ 7. Which statement is written from a critical point of view?

_____ 8. Which statement is written from an admiring point of view?

_____ 9. Which one has an unemotional tone?

_____ 10. Which piece creates mystery?

_____ 11. Which statement uses surprise and offers unexpected information?

2.   Style

As you read each of the following selections, figure out from the writer's style what kind of person is writing and who the intended audience is. Describe the writer and the audience in the spaces after each selection, and then write down your impressions of the style.

1. The black clouds swirled over the Gauntlet. Morak the Evil One cackled in glee as he watched a brave and powerful warrior try to retrieve the long lost Sacred Orb — only to be defeated in the most hideous way. But unless some warrior can rescue the Orb, all mortals are helpless against Morak's evil magic. Can you survive the Gauntlet's 9 missions to discover the magical Orb to win? Choose between Thor the Warrior or Shyra the Valkyrie to help defeat Morak's vicious henchmen, and his evil slew of ghosts, demons, grunts and evil sorcerers. So try to find the Orb if you dare, but watch your power bar because once your energy level reaches zero you're in the hands of the evil ones forever . . . or at least until the next game begins.

Writer: _____

Audience: _____

2. If a mother nags in a house full of kids, does she make a sound? Probably not. Children, like all of us, have selective hearing, and a constant barrage of commands and directives is likely to be tuned out. So how do you keep your kids' feet off the table, stop your daughter from biting your son, or save the

family car from a midnight rendezvous on the local strip? Well, let's talk about it.

Writer: _____

Audience: _____

3. I am delighted to see each of you here tonight in spite of a storm warning. You reveal that you are determined to go on anyhow. Something is happening in Memphis, something is happening in our world.

Writer: _____

Audience: _____

4. Happiness, then, being an activity of the soul in conformity with perfect goodness, it follows that we must examine the nature of goodness. When we have done this we should be in a better position to investigate the nature of happiness. There is this, too. The genuine statesman is thought of as a man who has taken peculiar pains to master this problem, desiring as he does to make his fellow-citizens good men obedient to the laws. Now, if the study of moral goodness is a part of political science, our inquiry into its nature will clearly follow the lines laid down in our preliminary observations.

   Well, the goodness we have to consider is human goodness. This — I mean human goodness or (if you prefer to put it that way) human happiness — was what we set out to find. By human goodness is meant not fineness of physique but a right condition of the soul, and by happiness a condition of the soul. That being so, it is evident that the statesman ought to have some inkling of psychology, just as the doctor who is to specialize in diseases of the eye must have a general knowledge of physiology.

Writer: _____

Audience: _____

4. Tone and Purpose

Look at the cartoon on page 289. Then answer the following questions.

"It's one thing for the National Commission to comment on the quality of teaching in our schools. It's another thing entirely for you to stand up and call Mr. Costello a yo-yo."

DRAWING BY STEVENSON; © 1983 THE NEW YORKER MAGAZINE, INC.

1. What is the difference in tone between the critical comments of the National Commission on Education and the critical comments of the boy in the principal's office?

_____

_____

_____

2. What is the commission's purpose in making its comments, and what is the boy's purpose in calling his teacher a name?

_____

_____

3. Why are the commission's criticisms, but not the boy's, acceptable to the principal?

_____

_____

_____

4. Judging from the principal's tone, what is his purpose in speaking to the boy?

_____

_____

12d Techniques That Twist the Truth

As a critical reader, you have to be able to judge the fairness of writing. If the purpose of a piece of writing is to convince you to adopt a certain opinion about a subject, the author may not be completely truthful. *Propaganda* (ideas forced on the public by organizations with special interests) often uses unfair arguments and logic. Any information that leaves out or alters facts in order to press a special point of view is called *biased, prejudiced,* or *slanted.*

Be on your guard for propaganda.

■ Look out for words that are used for emotional effect: *commie, bleeding heart, right-winger, geek, airhead, druggie.*
■ Look out for words that have special connotations (see **3c**).
■ Try to recognize the following methods of propaganda:

1. The writer tries to combine a famous person's name with an idea so that people, liking the person, will like the idea too.

   Reggie Jackson plays the field in Murjani jeans.

2. The writer quotes a famous person who approves of or agrees with an idea so that the reader will approve of it too.

Jacques Martin, the famous French chef, says, "Margarine is just as good as butter." Why are *you* still using butter?

3. The writer says that everyone is doing something (or thinking in some way), so you should do it (or think it) too.

Every farmer, every hard-working city resident knows the dangers of the welfare system.

4. The writer uses only very positive words and broad general statements to present an idea.

Every driver loves this stunning, efficient, and completely safe automobile. Add a bit of sunshine to your life — take a ride in a glamorous, high-fashion car!

5. The writer "stacks the deck" by presenting only those facts that tend to make you agree with him or her.

There's nothing wrong with drinking before driving. Not one person at our party was hurt on the way home — and believe me, not too many people there were sober!

6. The writer attaches a negative label to a person or product.

Only a fool like Lorna would buy an imported car. Those things look like wind-up toys.

7. The writer describes someone by using a group stereotype rather than paying attention to that person's individual characteristics. Stereotypes, which often are applied to people from specific ethnic or racial groups, ignore the great variation among all individuals, even those who share a country of origin or a skin pigment.

She's just like every other welfare cheat; she has no self-respect and never wants to work.

We can see the effect of slanted writing in the following statements:

There is no point in working. The money just goes to the no-good government and the cheating landlord. You break your back to make the boss rich.

Look, you do the best you can. Taxes are high and rent is impossible. But if you do not work, you give up your pride and the few comforts you have. Of course, the boss has to make a

fair profit from your work; otherwise, you would not be hired.
You just have to live on what is left over.

Every American should be proud to work and support the system. Your taxes go to making this country great. And by helping the landowners and the factory owners make money, you are strengthening the backbone of the nation. Hard work makes good Americans.

The first version is slanted against work by telling only part of the story and by name-calling — making it appear that everybody is out to take advantage of the poor worker. The third version slants the case in the opposite direction, "stacking the deck" in favor of those who benefit from the worker's labor, by using only positive language and by pressuring the reader to follow a group. Only the second version gives a balanced, truthful view.

EXERCISES

1. Slanted Writing

Read the following sentences. Write *T* before those sentences that use only truthful methods. Write *S* before those sentences that use slanted writing techniques.

_____ 1. That shiftless teenager has been ripping off this neighborhood for years.

_____ 2. He was arrested three times on burglary charges, but he was never brought to trial because of lack of evidence.

_____ 3. He hangs out with the worst crowd, so you can bet he is into something illegal.

_____ 4. He is a good guy. He has never done anything bad when he has been with me.

_____ 5. He is the most popular guy on the block; everyone likes him and he is always helping out his friends. How can you say he's done anything bad?

_____ 6. I don't really know what this guy is like, but he has been very kind to me.

2. Persuasive Techniques in Advertisements

Identify the technique (from the numbered list on pages 290–291) used in each of these slogans from advertisements to persuade you to use a product that you might not otherwise use.

1. "Accept no cheap imitations."

2. "The ultimate driving machine."

3. "Join the Pepsi generation."

4. "Diamonds. Just because you love her."

5. "The commanding presence of champion Nancy Lopez. And her Rolex."

3. Stereotyping

Each ethnic or racial group has been subject to stereotyping, which usually is negative but sometimes is positive. Identify three stereotypes that have been applied to your ethnic or racial group by other people; then give examples of individuals you know to whom the stereotype does not apply. Use a separate sheet of paper. Afterward you may want to compare your answers with those of your classmates in a class discussion.

Evaluating Ideas

In the space provided, write the correct answer. Count $3\frac{1}{3}$ points for each correct answer.

A. Fact and Opinion

Read each of the following statements and in the space provided write the letter of the phrase that best completes each sentence.

_____ 1. The Environmental Protection Agency (EPA) announced, "A new dumping site will be designated 106 miles at sea off the continental shelf." This statement is
   a. a guess.
   b. a fact.
   c. the opinion of someone who should know.
   d. the opinion of the EPA only.

_____ 2. The candidate said, "It is clearly a two-man race and it is very close." This statement is
   a. a reliable fact.
   b. a guess.
   c. the opinion of someone who should know.
   d. the only opinion anyone could possibly have on the subject.

_____ 3. The freed prisoner attested, "I am the father of a new nationalism." This statement is
   a. the only opinion anyone could possibly have on the subject.
   b. a guess.
   c. a reliable fact.
   d. the opinion of someone who is not an expert on the subject.

_____ 4. The agency reported, "Initial research suggests that safe levels in fruit are similar to those set for grain." This statement is
  a. a guess.
  b. a reliable fact.
  c. the only opinion anyone could possibly have on the subject.
  d. an opinion that should not be believed without further evidence.

_____ 5. The senator alleged, "The President is the captive of the Washington lobbies." This statement is
  a. a guess.
  b. a fact.
  c. the opinion of the senator.
  d. the only opinion anyone could possibly have on the subject.

B. Evidence

For each of the following statements write *E* if the statement is backed up properly by evidence, write *N* if there is no supporting evidence, and write *I* if there is evidence but it is improperly used.

_____ 1. Carmen bought a car last week. She's been driving around in a bright red Neon and taking people wherever they want to go.

_____ 2. Carmen bought a car last week.

_____ 3. Carmen bought a car last week. She made a down payment of $2,000 for a used Neon and got her license plate from the Department of Motor Vehicles the same day.

_____ 4. Carmen bought a car last week. She bought it from her neighbor, who gave her the service receipts for the past four years.

_____ 5. Carmen bought a car last week. Her mother and father didn't want her to buy a car until she finished school.

C. The Writer's Technique

Read statements a–h, all quoted from the *New York Times Magazine*. Then answer questions 1–10 by writing the letter of the quotation to which the question best applies. You may use the same letter more than once.

a. "... a new approach to skin care has been formulated especially for the life style a contemporary woman lives. It is the ultimate survival plan for your skin."

b. "... the new man is sensitive. He is not cruel. The previous man was cruel, but the new man is sensitive. He realizes that 'the only man' is a coarse phrase which cruel men sometimes use when speaking irreverently of their fathers."

c. "After the destruction of their economy in World War II, the Japanese adopted a technological strategy born of necessity."

d. "The world champion Baltimore Orioles were in town for their first meeting with the league-leading Tigers."

e. "Heat the oil in a skillet and add the mushrooms, garlic, thyme, salt and pepper. Add the parsley and toss to blend."

f. "Amid views of two tranquil ponds, a trout-filled brook, and timbered woodlands is this 4,000-square-foot designer Contemporary."

g. "The way we build furniture, it's suitable for combat."

h. "... an orderly environment conducive to improved academic performance."

_____ 1. Which statement sets a peaceful mood?

_____ 2. Which statement is designed to appeal to the point of view of a modern woman?

_____ 3. Which statement explains a phenomenon of world trade?

_____ 4. Which statement serves the purpose of telling the reader what to do?

_____ 5. Which statement is designed to reassure?

_____ 6. Which statement is written in a humorous tone?

_____ 7. Which statement establishes a mood of excitement?

_____ 8. Which statement uses warlike language to deal with domestic concerns?

_____ 9. Which statement requires the reader's careful attention?

_____ 10. Which statement appeals to a parent's point of view?

D. Techniques That Twist the Truth

For each of the following statements, write *T* if the statement uses only truthful methods; write *S* if the statement is slanted as a result of bias, prejudice, or propaganda.

_____ 1. No research has really proved that smoking is harmful. Everybody I know smokes, and no one has gotten lung cancer.

_____ 2. People who shop in clothing discount stores can't afford to buy clothes anywhere else.

_____ 3. Most of the fat in a traditional Mediterranean diet comes from olive oil.

_____ 4. Everybody who is anybody has an American Express card. If you don't have one, you're out of touch with the world around you.

_____ 5. There are a million reasons why you should apply for that job.

_____ 6. You always get better information from television news than from daily newspapers.

_____ 7. There's no proof that saturated fats are harmful. My grandparents put butter on everything, and they lived to a ripe old age.

_____ 8. Smoking kills 420,000 Americans a year.

_____ 9. Everybody knows that hockey is the most dangerous sport among competitive team events.

_____ 10. This is going to be the party of the century. If you didn't get an invitation, you'll never make it in the business world.

Score: _____ correct × 3⅓ points each = _____

13

Making Connections

Critical readers and thinkers develop an independent view of what they read.

As a critical reader you should be able to show how your own view differs from or agrees with what you read. You must provide reasons or evidence for holding your point of view. You must relate the ideas you read and think about to the ideas you have read or heard about elsewhere. And finally, you should be able to express your ideas about what you have read to others. Much of the earlier material in this book — particularly Chapter 12, "Evaluating Ideas" — can help you read critically. This chapter provides you with some additional techniques.

13a Personalizing

Critical reading starts with making a connection between what you read and think and what you have experienced. On the one hand, your experiences may be so powerful and your opinions about certain subjects so strong that any writer will have a hard time changing your mind. On the other hand, your experiences and opinions about other subjects may have opened you up to questions, so that you find new ideas and information interesting. In order to evaluate fairly the ideas expressed in a piece of writing, then, you must first be aware of your own opinions, experiences, and reactions.

13a(1) Notes in the Margin

One way to keep track of your ideas and personal connections as you read is to make marginal notes — at least in the books you own. This procedure is similar to one of the study techniques described in **2a**; but instead of just noting what you think the writer finds important, write down your *own* thoughts and associations in the margin of the page you are reading. When you own a book, show that it is really yours by adding your ideas to it.

In the following example, notice how one student responded to the opening of an article about the risks some professional athletes take to gain the rewards of success. Also notice how the student's notes not only express opinions but also make connections to the writer's experience.

Should Athletes Risk Death for Money?

There always has been some risk involved in athletic competition. Whether it is the man-on-man competition in boxing, where the object of the sport is to injure someone's brain to the point of rendering him unconscious, or the singular sport of road racing, where it is man and machine versus the track, where the next turn could be your last, the risk of injury, even death, is always there.

— *Jet*

Now that sport makes no sense!

Someone always seems to get hurt on pro teams, but also when we play "friendly" games. I guess that's what makes it exciting.

13a(2) *A Reading Journal*

Another way to sort out your thinking is to keep a reading journal, a kind of diary of your thoughts about your reading. Every time you finish reading a selection, write out your thoughts and reactions to it. You should not summarize or simply repeat what the reading states. Instead you should say whether you like or agree with the passage and why. If there are any ideas you object to, you might give reasons for your objections. If the reading reminds you of something you have experienced, describe that experience and how it is related to the reading. If other facts you know or ideas you hold support the writer's opinions, discuss them. And if you dislike the writer's attitude or manner of looking at the subject, explain exactly what is wrong with his or her approach.

What you say about the reading is not as important as putting down your ideas and developing them. Don't be satisfied with expressing an opinion in a single sentence or two. Go on to describe your ideas, to give examples, to explain why you feel as you do. Think your thoughts through in any way that strikes you. After writing your ideas down and discussing them for a while, you may end up changing your mind — or you may find yourself even more firmly committed to your original position.

This sample from a reading journal presents a student's reaction to the selection on page 299 about risks for athletes.

I never thought about the risks involved in athletic competition. As a member of varsity football in high school, sure I picked up my share of cuts and bruises. But if you like sports, you have to take risks. Money isn't the sole motivation. I didn't get any money for playing on the team. It was the excitement of play, the fun of racing across the field, the joy of working together with teammates to move the ball forward. ''The risk of injury, even death''--well I suppose it's always there. But life is full of risks. I mean you can get knocked over by a car when you're walking through the campus parking lot! I think that people involved with sports accept the risks involved. Maybe money keeps people in the game, professionals I mean, longer than they should stay. Still, I think that risks are part of the attraction of athletic competition.

Do you see how the writer of this journal doesn't just repeat the ideas he read but reacts to them? He talks about his own experiences in school, which leads him to question one of the premises in the short reading. He defines risks not as a questionable element in athletic competition but as a basic feature of the activity. The reading stimulated a personal response.

EXERCISES

1. Make marginal notes expressing your thinking about the article on pages 219–221 on the controversy over political correctness.
2. Set aside a notebook to use as a reading journal for the rest of the semester. Every time you have a reading assignment, write down and develop your thoughts in response to your reading by making an entry in the journal. At the end of the semester, read through your entire journal and in the final entry write your observations on how the journal helped you, how your thinking developed through the journal, or how your use of the journal changed during the semester.

3. Read the following passage and then write down your thoughts in your journal. You may want to develop your ideas on how John Holt's views about learning apply to you. Do you know when you do not know something? How do you know you know something? Can you think of any ways to decide better whether you know something?

How can we tell whether children understand something or not? When I was a student, I generally knew when I understood and when I didn't. This had nothing to do with marks; in the last math course I took in college I got a respectable grade, but by the end of the year I realized I didn't have the faintest idea of what the course was about. In Colorado, I assumed for a long time that my students knew when they did, or did not, understand something. I was always urging them to tell me when they did not understand, so that with one of my clever "explanations" I could clear up everything. But they never would tell me. I came to know by painful experience that not a child in a hundred knows whether or not he understands something, much less, if he does not, why he does not. The child who knows, we don't have to worry about; he will be an A student. How do we find out when, and what, the others don't understand?

— *John Holt*

13b Connecting Ideas

Skilled readers try to connect their reading with a variety of other elements in their lives. They link what they read in one selection to what they read in others. They connect the ideas they read about in books, newspapers, and magazines to ideas in other readings, as well as to ideas in movies, television editorials, talk shows, song lyrics, and so on — in short, to the widest range of human thought and expression.

As your reading skills advance, you should attempt to link the issues in the books, articles, and stories that you read with other elements in your life. Make comparisons. Describe contrasts. Such efforts will enrich your understanding. When you are able to see how different thinkers and writers treat a related subject, you can develop new insights into that subject. You also can expand your thinking about an issue by seeing it within many different contexts. A government report, a newspaper article, a sociology textbook, a novel, a poem, a movie, a play, or a television program about poverty will all provide many different views on the topic. The more views you are aware of, the deeper your understanding.

How to Make Reading Connections

- Linking what you read often means little more than saying to yourself "Where did I read or see or hear about something like this before?" Ask that question as you read and after you read a selection. Use your response to make comparisons and contrasts.
- Use your skill at identifying the topic to make reading connections. Once you state the topic, you can run it through your mind. What else have you read or seen or heard on the same or a related topic? Where? How do the other sources treat the topic?
- Use your skill at stating the main idea in order to connect what you have read. Usually a main idea expresses the writer's opinion or attitude. How is this writer's opinion similar to or different from that of another writer, say, or of a film director, an actor, or a newscaster?
- Test the generalizations you develop from one reading against generalizations in other areas. (Review the topic of generalizing in Chapter 11.) For example, you might conclude from reading the textbook excerpt on special education (page 181) that minority students are treated unfairly in educational settings. Yet Richard Rodriguez's piece on pages 185–189 will give you other insights into this issue. Perhaps you will want to qualify your generalization by stating: "Many minority students are treated unfairly by our education system, but others get advantages and privileges." The ability to state, reshape, and refine generalizations is an important element in critical thinking. You don't have to agree with the generalizations, but you should be able to state them clearly.
- Write down the relations you see among different presentations of ideas. Writing always helps you see more clearly what you think about an issue. Pointing out comparisons and contrasts in a few sentences will focus your thinking about what you have read.

EXERCISES

Read the three articles below on the issue of how to deal with illegal guns. On a separate sheet of paper, answer these questions: How do the ideas in these pieces relate to one another? What is the topic of each? What is the main idea? What comparisons and contrasts can you make among them? What generalization could you make that applies to all three pieces?

Teach Kids to "Talk It Out"

"They could have just talked it out." Those were the words of the friend of a 15-year-old who was fatally shot outside his junior high school in a dispute over a girl who was slapped. Today, many adolescent arguments — over coats, jewelry, or dirty looks — end in death.

Can talking it out really be a viable alternative for a generation of youths weaned on violence? They see it on television and in the movies, and sometimes in their homes. They see cops and criminals in their neighborhoods carrying more powerful guns. The message that violence solves problems surrounds them. Gun control alone won't help; there are always weapons of some sort available.

We have to teach our youth to resolve their problems with words and compromise, not guns and murder. Since 1983, Project Smart — School Mediators' Alternative Resolution Team — has had students in 15 high schools mediating disputes ranging from lunchroom brawls to interracial incidents, from fights between gangs to conflicts between students and teachers. Mediation agreements drawn up and signed by students are honored 90 percent of the time.

Students introduced to mediation as disputants often become mediators, proud of their skill. Suspensions for fighting in participating schools have decreased by up to 72 percent.

Peer conflict resolution should be the fourth "R" in all of our schools at every grade level. Far from being a utopian approach, it is a practical solution to the violence that wracks our city. The way to keep kids from reaching for guns is by teaching them from the first grade on that "talking it out" works.

— *John Feinblatt, deputy director, Victim Services Agency*

Use a Gun, Do Federal Time

Guns abound on New York City streets because they are so easy to obtain in other states. A 1988–89 government study showed that more than two-thirds of the guns seized from criminals in the city were traceable to legally authorized sellers in Virginia, Texas, Florida, Georgia, and Ohio, and that fewer than 1 in 20 originated in New York State. Gun traffic from the South has grown with the northbound stream of drugs.

The old ways of dealing with this traffic — generally at the state level — do little. While Congress has made laws that attach heavy penalties to use of guns in *federal* offenses, the problem in New York City is gun use in state offenses like stickups, drive-by shootings, and drug deals. Legislation making it a federal felony to commit a *state* crime while armed with a gun brought across state lines would give potential gun offenders a new punishment to ponder.

At present, thugs manipulate New York's overburdened courts so that, if they do any time at all, they serve short terms in local jails. I propose passage of a federal law that would make long terms in distant federal penitentiaries — like those in Atlanta or Marion, Ill. — an additional and probable consequence of gun crime.

Such a law, which would supplement rather than replace state and local prosecutions, would force states whose lax laws bring violence to New York cities to bear some of the costs of prosecuting and housing gun criminals. Although the gun lobby finds an unconstitutional conspiracy behind every legislative proposal, such a law might even placate the most ardent Second Amendment supporters: It would affect only armed *felons*, not armed law-abiding citizens.

— *James J. Fyfe, former New York City police lieutenant, professor of justice, American University*

Trace Illegal Firearms

The first step in getting guns off the streets of New York City is to collect identifying information on the last 200 guns confiscated by the New York police.

Through the serial numbers on the guns, federal authorities can determine where and when these illegal guns were first sold at retail and to whom. Most of the guns confiscated in New York will have a readily identifiable history to the point of first retail purchase. This information can pinpoint where the major illegal gun supply pipelines are located, particularly for recently made guns.

State and local police can assist in the search, but only the Federal Bureau of Alcohol, Tobacco and Firearms has the jurisdictional reach and investigative resources to seek out the major channels of illegal supply. Studies conducted over 25 years indicate that about 80 percent of the guns used for crime in New York came from out of state, and the great majority entered the city in violation of federal law.

Thus, most guns on the streets arrived as a result of a federal crime that can and should be investigated. The B.A.T.F. must focus its resources on the very small number of cities where almost every gun on the street crossed a state border.

Interdiction of the interstate movement of guns is neither easy nor cheap. But the techniques available to trace ownership make the intelligence part of gun enforcement easier than that of drug interdiction.

If the government committed the equivalent of 2 percent of our $10 billion drug control budget to gun interdiction, it would be the best hope of getting guns off the New York City's streets.

— *Franklin E. Zimring, professor of law,*
University of California at Berkeley

Critical Thinking in Writing

Write a letter to the editor of your local newspaper expressing your views on gun control. Draw freely on the selections you have just read as well as on your personal observations and experiences.

13c Collaboration

Researchers across the country have found that collaborative learning is an effective way to improve reading skills and critical thinking. Collaborative learning is a method of study that gives you responsibility for your own learning. After gathering in small groups to discuss academic issues in a limited time frame, you try to come to a rough agreement about some issue — although everyone in the group is not required to agree absolutely with everyone else.

Many teachers use collaborative techniques to improve students' understanding of reading selections. They organize students into small groups during class and talk about what they have read. Each group then reports to the whole class. Many students, seeing the benefits of these sessions, set up informal study groups after class in the library or cafeteria. These focused discussions with classmates generally shed new light on the essays, stories, poems, novels, or textbook selections they have read.

Use the suggestions below to guide your collaboration in the classroom.

Collaborating on a Reading Assignment: Pointers for Successful Small-Group Discussion

- *Frame a statement or question about the reading that your group can react to.* Your teacher can help you develop clear statements or questions to set the groups' tasks. You may want to address the main idea of the reading or some of the key points. You also might debate a generalization (see Chapter 11) from the reading. Alternatively, the members of each group can develop their own generalizations or conclusions about what they've read. Keep in mind that all groups can focus on the same task; or the instructor can assign one of several tasks to each group.
- *Always write your personal response to the task before holding group discussions.* Thinking on paper will help you see where you stand on the issue addressed by the reading. In group work you often will modify that stand. By beginning with something written, you have a starting point for collaboration and will be able to keep the discussion in focus.
- *Form productive groups and establish time limits.* Groups of three to five people generally produce the best results because each member can have his or her say in a limited time. Depending on the task at hand, you may want to allot from fifteen to twenty-five minutes for a full discussion of an issue. In addition, observe group discussion etiquette: Allow everyone to speak; don't dominate the conversation; and listen thoughtfully to the points being made.
- *Select a recorder/reporter.* The recorder / reporter writes down the group's main responses to the task and then reports back to the rest of the class.

- *Try to reach consensus on the issues.* Reaching a consensus requires negotiation. Use the give and take of discussion to develop a position that most people in the group consider acceptable. Include any strong opposing views as objections to the group's consensus.
- *Compare your responses with those of other groups.* What thinking patterns do you observe? Which points support one another? Which points contradict one another?

EXERCISES

Reread the selections on pages 303–305 about illegal guns. Then form groups under your teacher's supervision. Within each group, address the following question: How should we deal with the issue of illegal guns? Follow these steps:

1. Before forming groups, each person must write *three* recommendations in response to the question. Use what you read as the basis for your thinking.
2. Each group should discuss the various responses and decide by consensus on any *two* recommendations supported by the group members.
3. The recorder/reporter of each group should then relate the two recommendations to the rest of the class.
4. Write all of the recommendations on the chalkboard or on an overhead projector transparency. Discuss similarities and differences.

Critical Thinking in Writing

How do you feel about working in groups? What positive or negative elements have you seen in group work? Explore your thoughts in a paragraph.

Making Connections

Count 10 points for each correct answer.

1. Identify five qualities of critical readers and thinkers.

   a. _____

   b. _____

   c. _____

   d. _____

   e. _____

2. Identify five ways to make connections between and among readings.

   a. _____

   _____

   b. _____

   c. _____

   _____

   d. _____

   _____

   e. _____

Score: _____ correct × 10 points each = _____

Read the following selection about a young mother's efforts to deal with illness and loss in her family. Then write answers to the questions in the space provided.

Role Reversal

In the middle of dinner my son suddenly remembers the dead pigeon we saw last week in the park. "What happens after we die?" he asks. I repeat the question, stalling. "No one really knows." He knows. He has an arsenal of answers: We get born again, we grow new skin, we still talk to each other, we'll still see each other, right? Right?

"No one really knows," I repeat. He says he wants to live forever. I say part of us does live forever — our spirit. He wants to know what that is. It's what people remember about us. He hates this. He swats away my answers; rejects them like bad milk.

Four, the experts tell me, is the age of phobias, when children bounce off the opposite feelings of power and powerlessness as recklessly as a hard-hit squash ball. "I wish I were He-Man," my son announces on the way home from a movie he found scary, "because then I wouldn't be afraid." I assure him that everyone feels fear. I try to hug him. But four has also seen the dawn of some new feelings about me. No longer does he return my every hug, no longer does he automatically melt into my arms during a snuggle. Now he pushes me away, scowling, his little body hard and muscular. "Not here, Ma."

So, I am thinking of loss too, and not for the first time do I feel as if my son and I are navigating the same developmental waters together.

"Trees die in winter," my son announces during his bath, thinking I don't know what he's up to, "and are born again in spring, right?" I assure him that he is. "And people die when they are very old, and are born again, right?" I tell him that I really don't know for sure. "But you have to be really old," he says, and I wonder whom he is thinking of — his great-grandmother?

Her son, my father, was recently diagnosed as having can-

309

cer. My grandmother calls me every week about it. "Don't worry," I tell her, "he's in good hands."

"Don't worry?" she cries, this matriarch who has survived 87 rough years, with whom I feel a painful stab of empathy. "How can I not worry? He's my son."

Last week, at a street fair, my son and I lost each other. He had wanted to go on a trolley ride. I saw him get on the car, and when it returned from its two-minute trip, didn't see him get off. I waited until the car had emptied and a few moments more, uncomprehendingly. I grabbed one of the men steering the ride. "What is he wearing?" he asked.

That's when I began my mad rushing through the sunny crowd of parents and children as if it were a cave I had to claw my way out of. The panic was unlike any I had previously experienced. Breathing not air but lethal panic, I screamed inwardly, "No, it can't happen," knowing with dead certainty that it could. When I finally stumbled into the clown, the only person I could find with a megaphone, she said, "Calm down, it won't help to be hysterical; he's only the fifth one today who's been lost and we found them all." She started calling his name. Trailing behind her, imagining calling my husband, calling my parents, my in-laws, I pictured my son's empty room, his closet full of clothes; I felt the enormity of the city and the tininess of my son, dressed in nothing more remarkable than jeans and a T-shirt.

Suddenly amid a swell of voices I heard a man calling, "Yes, over here, we have him."

There he was, standing impassively on the steps of the school, and when I ran and hugged him and sobbed uncontrollably he jammed both his hands over my mouth.

"I thought you didn't keep your word," he said. I assured him that I had been waiting for him, that we just missed each other, that it was no one's fault. He worried that he had done something wrong, but, in fact, he had done everything exactly right: When he didn't see me, he went to a man in a blue shirt and said, "I can't find my Mommy."

He only referred to the experience once more, a day later, when he sat up in bed during our good-nights and said, "We were *separated*," as if the words finally were joined to an experience that we had talked about, rehearsed many times before.

But I think of it more often than I'd like: doing the laundry, teaching a class, I am inexplicably back in the impossible darkness of his absence. How could I have survived losing him?

I take a cab home from the hospital the evening after my father's most recent operation, and the driver turns into Central Park. Weaving from the snow-covered, silent, remote interior to the perimeter where buildings are ablaze with lights, with families busy living and dying, I think of what I will try to tell my son about spirit. Shamelessly borrowing from a conglomerate of religous beliefs, I thought I had concocted a spiritualism I felt comfortable with, yet now it seems indistinguishable from a heartfelt injunction to remember. I wish I had an orthodoxy to fall back on as my father found in his middle years — a messianic vision to comfort my son with. But he doesn't need mine; he seems to have been born believing in the doctrine of reincarnation. Whatever its origin, he draws from it effortlessly.

Walking home from nursery school, clutching a chocolate pop, my son comes up with a new worry. What would happen, he wants to know, if I left him outside the house at night? Who would take him inside? I tell him this would never happen. He insists on knowing what would happen if it did. We are at a stalemate.

He breaks it: "Just hold on to my hand really tight when we walk home from school tomorrow." His voice quivers, his eyes brim with whatever horror he can conjure up.

"I'll never leave you," I say, "I'll always be here." And then I am furious with myself. How can I promise that? Mothers leave, sometimes by their own will, sometimes against; mothers die.

"Call me in the middle of the night if you need me," my friend says when I tell her of my father's deteriorating condition. I know she means it. We have been through many losses together. "After all, it's your daddy."

For the first time in his illness, which has spanned several months, I am in tears. To others I talk about my father, but to me, in the voice I use to myself, he is Daddy: *Daddy*, who took us to the beach carrying the red-and-white-striped canvas umbrella that he ground into the sand, and that kept us protected all afternoon. Daddy, Mommy — these primitive syllables, our anchors to the world, our hope for the worlds we can only imagine and fear.

Most people postpone having a child until they feel entrenched as adults. But for me the challenge came from an opposite direction: I found myself being called upon to become a child again, and this entailed far more responsibilities than having dinner on the table or clean clothes folded in drawers. Sometimes when I kiss my sleeping child goodnight I let my lips linger on his cheek and think that I am in bed and my father is beside me, or my father's in his sickbed and I'm beside him, and we're all pleading with the same voice. We'll still see each other, we'll still be able to talk to each other, right? Right?

— *Roberta Israeloff*

_____ 1. The main idea of this selection is that the
   a. writer feels as lost and helpless as her own child when she is faced with her father's death.
   b. writer feels guilty that she cannot always keep track of her child's whereabouts.
   c. writer's son is confused and insecure about death.
   d. writer's grandmother is very disturbed about her son's illness.

_____ 2. We can infer from the fact that the son has so many answers about what happens when we die that the boy
   a. understands much about death.
   b. has studied many theories about death.
   c. does not fully understand the meaning of death.
   d. is trying to cheer his mother up.

_____ 3. We can infer that the boy is not satisfied with his mother's answers about death because he
   a. knows his mother is wrong.
   b. wants simple, reassuring answers.
   c. wants his mother to feel better.
   d. is not worried about death.

_____ 4. The view of the four-year-old as a squash ball (paragraph 3) is an example of
   a. personalizing.
   b. evidence.
   c. figurative language.
   d. twisting the truth.

_____ 5. Overall the tone of this essay is
   a. desperately uncertain.
   b. quietly confident.
   c. sad.
   d. strong in the face of adversity.

_____ 6. The essay ends with the words "right? Right?" The author uses the repetition
   a. for strong emphasis.
   b. to make the reader ask the question.
   c. to underscore her desperate need for reassurance.
   d. to be unusual.

_____ 7. We can conclude that the writer
   a. is on the edge of panic at the thought of her father's death.
   b. will be able to answer all her son's questions eventually.
   c. always plays the part of a responsible adult.
   d. has come to terms with her father's death.

_____ 8. We can predict that the writer's son will
   a. no longer cry when he gets lost.
   b. not feel the loss of his grandfather because of the child's belief in reincarnation.
   c. get lost many more times before he becomes an adult.
   d. continue to bring up new fears and worries to his mother.

9. For each of the following statements from the selection, put an *F* if the statement is a fact and an *O* if the statement is an opinion.

_____ a. "In the middle of dinner my son suddenly remembers the dead pigeon we saw last week in the park."

_____ b. "Most people postpone having a child until they feel entrenched as adults."

_____ c. "We get born again, we grow new skin, we still talk to each other."

_____ d. "Last week, at a street fair, my son and I lost each other."

_____ e. "I take a cab home from the hospital the evening after my father's most recent operation, and the driver turns into Central Park."

_____ f. "I saw him get on the car, and when it returned from its two-minute trip, didn't see him get off."

10. Put a plus (+) in the blank space next to each generalization that you think the writer would agree with. Put a minus (−) next to each generalization that she would not agree with.

_____   a. Young children have many questions about death.

_____   b. Parents should avoid discussing death with their young children.

_____   c. It's hard for a very young child to understand the finality of death.

_____   d. Losing one's child, even for a few minutes, is one of the most horrible moments of panic in a parent's life.

_____   e. Everyone must learn to deal with loss.

_____   f. Religious background offers no help for people facing the death of a loved one.

Score: _____ correct × 5 points each = _____

Reading
Selections

Introduction

We have chosen these selections carefully to represent the wide range of cultures that define the modern American college and university. The selections will allow you to practice the reading skills you've learned thus far. The questions that accompany each selection will test your understanding of what you have read. In some cases you will be able to answer the questions without returning to the selection. In other cases you will want to return quickly to specific passages before you choose an answer. Returning to the selection to check *every* response will slow you down, so try to retain as much information as you can when you read each piece for the first time.

You'll notice that numbers in parentheses appear at the end of most questions. These numbers refer to the chapter and section in the first part of the book in which the skill required to answer the question is explained. If you are still stumped for an answer after you've checked the selection again, turn to the appropriate section of the handbook and review your skills.

Two approaches can help you learn new words in each selection. The most difficult words appear with definitions in a section called Word Highlights right before the selection. When a difficult word appears in the selection, you can look it up easily in this section. In addition, a vocabulary exercise appears at the end of the questions on each piece. These exercises require that you answer questions about the uses and meanings of new words. You will want to add the new words to your reading, writing, and speaking vocabularies as soon as possible. That means writing the words down, using them in sentences, and following the other guidelines given in Chapter 3. You also should keep a list of other words you don't know in each selection. Check their meanings and learn them too.

The Connecting Ideas and the Critical Thinking in Writing activities provided for each selection will help you understand what you have read in relation to ideas in other selections and in the world around you. At the end of each group of selections, questions in a section called Putting Thoughts Together help you think about how the selections relate to each other and to your life.

The works chosen for this anthology will teach you, amuse you, and make you more aware of the multicultural riches of our society. You'll find articles, essays, and sections of books, including textbooks, newspapers, and magazines. You'll find short stories and biographies. In short, the anthology provides a varied program of college study.

Coming to America

A New Dawn   *Sam Moses*

The Business of Selling Mail-Order Brides   *Venny Villapando*

Hearts of Sorrow   *James M. Freeman*

Immigrants   *Aurora Levins Morales*

A New Dawn

Sam Moses

Lester Moreno Perez, a bold seventeen-year-old, windsurfed to freedom at night over rough waters from Cuba. Read about his daring escape.

Prereading

Write a journal entry in which you imagine what it would be like to windsurf at night alone, knowing that you risked severe punishment if you were caught. **(9a)**

Word Highlights

boom   a horizontal handle gripped by the sailor and surrounding the sail

destined   fated; predetermined

durable   strong; able to last

Fidel Castro   revolutionary leader of Cuba who turned the country's government to Communism

infrared   radiation with wavelengths greater than those of visible light and shorter than those of microwaves

regime   government in power

rigged   equipped with sails; attached sails to masts and booms

sleek   smooth and lustrous; glossy

I n the annals of great escapes, the flight by 17-year-old Lester Moreno Perez from Cuba to the U.S. surely must rank as one of the most imaginative. At 8:30 on the night of Thursday, March 1, Lester crept along the beach in Varadero, a resort town on the north coast of Cuba, and launched his sailboard into the shark-haunted waters of the Straits of Florida. Guided first by the stars and then by the hazy glow from concentrations of electric lights in towns beyond the horizon, Lester sailed with 20-knot winds, heading for the Florida Keys, 90 miles away.

2   Two hours past daybreak on Friday, Lester was sighted by

318

the Korean crew of the *Tina D,* a Bahamian-registered freighter. The boom on his craft was broken, and he was just barely making headway, 30 miles south of Key West. The astonished crew pulled Lester aboard, fed him spicy chicken and white rice, and then radioed the U.S. Coast Guard, which sent the patrol boat *Fitkinak* to take him into custody. After five days in the Krome Detention Center in Miami while paperwork was being processed, he was issued a visa by U.S. immigration officials and released into the welcoming arms of his relatives.

3   Except for his rich imagination and broad streak of courage, Lester could be any 17-year-old who decides to leave home. He was raised in the shoreside town of Varadero, the second-oldest of five children in his family. "As soon as I started thinking a little bit — when I was seven or eight years old — I wanted to come to America," he says. Independent thinking ran in the family; his grandfather, Urbino, had been imprisoned for attending a counterrevolutionary meeting early in Fidel Castro's regime and spent nearly five years in jail. Furthermore, Lester's sister Leslie, who had been on the national swim team and had traveled to several foreign countries, had told intriguing tales of life outside Cuba. Lester also did not like the idea of serving three years in the Cuban army and then facing the possibility of having his career chosen for him by the Communist Party. There was also trouble at home; he and his stepfather, Roberto, were at odds, mostly over politics. So Lester decided he wanted to go to America, not Angola.

4   When he was 10 years old, Lester taught himself to windsurf by hanging around the European and Canadian tourists who rented boards on the beach at Varadero. "If you made friends with them, they would sometimes let you use their equipment," he says. As he grew older and got better at the sport, he found he liked the isolation and freedom of the sea. "Sometimes I would sail for eight hours without stopping, and go very far out," he says. His windsurfing to freedom seemed destined.

5   Recently, Lester sat in a big easy-chair in the Hialeah, Fla., apartment of Ana and Isidro Perez, the great-aunt and great-uncle who took him in. Lester is so skinny — 5'6", 130 pounds — that it seems there is room for two or three more of him in the chair. On his head he wears Walkman earphones, which he politely removes when a visitor enters the room. He has been in America only a few weeks, but he has already been interviewed several times and has been chauffeured all over Miami in a limo

on a radio station–sponsored shopping spree. The tops of his feet are still covered with scabs, the result of the hours he spent in the sailboard's footstraps; but his hands show no blisters, only hard, white calluses.

6   As he waits for a translator to arrive, Lester rocks back and forth in the chair like a hyperactive child. He clicks the television on with the remote control, passes a Spanish-language station and stops at a morning show on which a man is explaining, in English, how to prevent snoring by placing a Ping-Pong ball between your shoulder blades, a move that forces one to sleep face-down. When a visitor demonstrates this to Lester through gestures and snores, the young man rolls his dark eyes, smiles, and says in perfect English, "People are all crazy here."

7   A few minutes later, the translator, who owns a windsurfing shop in Miami, arrives, and Lester begins to tell his story through him.

8   "I had only been thinking of making the trip on a sailboard for about a month," he says. "Before that, I'd been thinking of leaving the country by marrying a Canadian girl — every couple of months a few would come that were pretty nice-looking. But I decided to sail because I was training hard and was confident I would be able to make the trip easily. I had windsurfed in bad weather, and even surfed during Hurricane Gilbert, so I was already out in really rough conditions and wasn't worried about it.

9   "Right before I left, I was watching the wind patterns. A cold front had passed by and it was pretty strong, so I waited until it subsided a little. Usually after a cold front passes, the wind shifts to the east, and it's just a straight reach to the U.S., so I waited for that. Then I told two of my friends, who said they would help me. I wasn't hungry, but I ate a lot — three or four fried eggs, some rice and half a liter of milk — so I would be strong for the journey." His friends also persuaded him to take along some water, a can of condensed milk, and a knife.

10   At 7:00 on the evening of March 1, Lester, who had said nothing to his family, slipped out of his house and went down to the Varadero beach, where he worked at a windsurfing rental booth by day, while attending high school at night. Earlier that day, he had carefully rigged the best mast and strongest boom he could find with a big 5.0-square-meter sail. Then he had lashed the sail rig in the sand with the rental boards. Under cover of darkness, he unlocked the shed where the privately owned

boards were kept and removed his sleek and durable Alpha model. It had been a gift to him from a man who sympathized with his plight — a generous East German whom Lester called Rambo for the camouflage hat he always wore. Lester fastened the sail rig to the board and carried it to the water. He waded into the ocean until he was knee-deep, glanced over his shoulder to make sure he hadn't been seen, and stepped onto the board. His ride on the wind to freedom had begun.

11   "I wasn't nervous," he says. "I had to be very clear minded once I decided to go; otherwise they would catch me and I would be in a lot of trouble. It would have meant three or four years in prison if I had been caught. No lie about what I was doing was possible."

12   About one and a half blocks away from the beach was a tower usually manned by guards with infrared binoculars. Lester, who was sailing without lights, also had to keep an eye out for freighters and pleasure boats that would be cruising in the busy Straits of Florida.

13   "At first I wasn't able to get my feet in the footstraps," he says, "because there wasn't enough wind for my sail. But as I got farther out and was able to get fully powered up, I began feeling more confident. The swells were very steep, maybe four or five meters, and I was going so fast I had no choice but to jump them."

14   As he recalls the moment, Lester rises from his chair, plants his bare feet on the tile floor and extends his thin arms, grasping an imaginary boom. He begins in English, "Wind coming, coming, coming . . . out, out, out . . . is very strong." He's hanging in his invisible harness now, arms stretched wide, eyes lit up, flying over the waves. "Whoosh!" he cries. "Is good!"

15   For 10 hours he rode the wind, never once fearing failure, or drowning. He thought of his family and how worried they would be when they discovered he was missing. But he wasn't alone out there. "Ever since I left, I could see the sharks coming out and in, coming up on the board. I was hoping and thinking they were dolphins, but when the sun came up, I could see there was no way they were dolphins."

16   Around daybreak, the aluminum boom broke, separating the connection to the mast like pieces of a wishbone. He tried fixing the boom with his knife but couldn't, so he sailed on, clutching the pieces of the broken sail. This made control of the board extremely difficult, and he couldn't rest in the harness he had

rigged. "My arms and hands were getting really tired, but by then I could already see the big kites of the fishermen, so I wasn't really worried. When I saw the freighter, I tried to point [into the wind] as much as I could and sail toward it."

17   A similar crossing was made in January 1984, by Arnaud de Rosnay, a Frenchman who boardsailed from Key West to Cuba as a personal challenge and a publicity stunt. De Rosnay, one of the best boardsailors in the world, had sailed in daylight with a chase boat. His trip included two stops for repairs and two stops to rest, and he completed the crossing in about seven hours. (In November of the same year, de Rosnay vanished while trying to cross the Straits of Formosa.) But only a month before Lester's odyssey, another young Cuban had perished attempting to reach the Keys in a raft.

18   Not surprisingly, Hollywood has come knocking on Lester's door. "The story is a natural," says Paul Madden, the president of Madden Movies. "It's *Rocky* and *The Old Man and the Sea* in one. If this picture is done right, by the end of it the audience will be standing up in the theater and cheering."

19   Lester has handled the movie offers and the media blitz with uncommon courtesy and self-assurance. A new acquaintance has even invited him to spend the summer at Hood River, Ore., where he will be able to jump the formidable swells of the Columbia River. This sounds good to Lester. But right now, one of his teenage friends has invited him to go sailing off Miami Beach. That sounds like the most fun of all.   ❑

EXERCISES

Comprehension

_____   1.   The topic of this selection is **(5b)**
a. adjusting to life in America.
b. how to windsurf.
c. how one young man escaped from Cuba by windsurfing.
d. political oppression in Castro's Cuba.

_____   2.   The main idea of the selection is that **(5b)**
a. Lester Moreno Perez taught himself how to windsurf with the help of friendly tourists.

    b. determination leads to success even against great odds.

    c. Lester Moreno Perez risked great danger by escaping to Florida from Cuba on a sailboard.

    d. life in Cuba is difficult for teenagers.

_____ 3. The main idea of paragraph 3 is to **(5b)**

    a. compare Lester to other teenagers.

    b. describe the shoreside town of Varadero.

    c. sketch in details of Lester's personal life.

    d. explain why Lester decided to leave Cuba.

4. In your own words, write the key idea of this sentence from paragraph 2 **(5a):**

The astonished crew pulled Lester aboard, fed him spicy chicken and white rice, and then radioed the U.S. Coast Guard, which sent the patrol boat *Fitkinak* to take him into custody.

_____

_____

_____ 5. At present, Lester lives in **(6a)**

    a. Hialeah with his great-aunt and great-uncle.

    b. Varadero with his four brothers and sisters.

    c. Miami Beach with his sister Leslie.

    d. Hood River, Oregon, with a new acquaintance.

_____ 6. Which of the following was *not* among the dangers Lester faced on his ride to freedom? **(6a)**

    a. freighters and pleasure boats

    b. his lack of experience windsurfing

    c. tower guards with infrared binoculars

    d. sharks

_____ 7. Which of these options for leaving his country tempted Lester before his daring escape? **(6a)**

    a. running away with his sister Leslie

    b. going into the surfboard business with Rambo, his generous East German friend

    c. joining Arnaud de Rosnay in a windsurfing stunt from Cuba to Key West

    d. marrying an attractive Canadian girl

_____ 8. Lester "wasn't alone out there" on the water because **(6a)**
a. his sister was with him.
b. dolphins were with him.
c. Arnaud de Rosnay was with him.
d. sharks were with him.

9. Order the events in the correct sequence by placing the number *1* beside the first event in time, *2* beside the second, and so forth. **(7a)**

_____   Lester sits in an easy chair in the Perez's apartment.

_____   Lester retrieves his Alpha model surfboard.

_____   The aluminum boom breaks.

_____   Lester learns to windsurf.

_____   Lester wades into the ocean.

_____   Lester rides the wind for ten hours.

_____   Lester watches the wind patterns.

_____   Lester sails for the freighter.

_____   Lester rigs the mast and boom.

_____   The *Fitkinak* takes Lester into custody.

_____   Lester is issued a visa.

10. Put *maj* next to major details and *min* next to minor details. **(6b)**

_____   a. Independent thinking runs in Lester's family.

_____   b. Lester has a sister named Leslie.

_____   c. Varadero is a resort town.

_____   d. Lester was wearing earphones.

_____ e. A man on television is explaining how to prevent snoring.

_____ f. Lester said nothing to his family.

_____ g. Lester took off under cover of darkness.

_____ h. The *Tina D* is a Bahamian-registered freighter.

_____ i. Lester was not nervous.

_____ j. Lester did not want to serve in the Cuban army.

Reading and Critical Thinking

_____ 1. The Korean crew of the *Tina D* was astonished because they probably **(8)**
a. had never seen a boy windsurfing before.
b. did not expect to see someone on a broken-boomed craft 30 miles south of Key West.
c. did not expect to see Lester without his friend Rambo.
d. had never seen anyone eat so much before.

_____ 2. We can infer from the selection that Lester's grandfather Urbino **(8)**
a. opposed Castro's government.
b. supported Castro's government.
c. had no opinion about Castro's government.
d. fought in Castro's army.

_____ 3. The words *New Dawn* in the title are figurative for **(9)**
a. the sleek and durable surfboard.
b. the calm Lester felt on his escape.
c. the start of a new life in America.
d. the sun rising each morning.

_____ 4. We can infer from the selection that leaving Cuba is **(8)**
a. against the law.
b. ignored by the guards watching the Straits of Florida.
c. a goal of all teenagers in that country.
d. legal for windsurfers.

_____ 5. Hollywood has come knocking on Lester's door because **(8)**
a. he is very good looking.
b. his life is so typical of Cuban teenagers.
c. he wants to see *Rocky* and *The Old Man and the Sea.*
d. the story of his life should have wide audience appeal.

_____ 6. We can infer from the story of the young Cuban who had
perished trying to reach the Keys on a raft that **(8)**
a. he did not know how to windsurf.
b. the boy did not rig his craft right.
c. escape from Cuba is very dangerous.
d. Hollywood plans to film his story.

_____ 7. We can safely predict that if the freighter *Tina D* had not
seen Lester, he would **(10)**
a. have returned to Cuba and tried again in a few weeks.
b. not have ended his journey safely.
c. have swum to land.
d. have stopped for rest on a nearby island before going
on.

_____ 8. We can conclude from the last paragraph that Lester **(10)**
a. has been hurt psychologically by his ordeal.
b. is working very hard to get the best possible movie deal
that he can.
c. is eager to leave his new home in Hialeah, Florida.
d. seems surprisingly well adjusted considering his ordeal.

9. Put an *F* beside each statement that is a *fact;* put an *O* beside
each statement that is an *opinion.* **(12a)**

_____   a. Canadian girls who visited Cuba were pretty nice
looking.

_____   b. People in the United States are all crazy.

_____   c. Lester tells his story through a translator.

_____   d. The audience for the movie of Lester's life will stand up
and cheer.

_____   e. Arnaud de Rosnay vanished while crossing the Straits of Formosa.

_____   f. Lester is uncommonly courteous and self-assured.

_____ 10. We can infer from the selection that **(8)**
a. no one likes to go to Angola.
b. Lester's stepfather lived in Angola.
c. Cuban soldiers are sent to Angola.
d. Communist party leaders are trained in Angola.

11. Put a checkmark beside any valid generalizations that can be drawn from the selection. **(11)**

_____   a. Oppressed people everywhere should try to escape from their countries.

_____   b. Courage and determination can produce success even against great odds.

_____   c. Political oppression can lead people to take drastic measures.

_____   d. Hollywood filmmakers believe adventure stories are well received by audiences.

_____   e. Living in a new country can be very difficult, especially when you don't know the language very well.

_____   f. All Cubans oppose Fidel Castro's regime.

Connecting Ideas

If you were making a movie called *Lester Moreno Perez's Great Escape,* what features of Lester's life would you portray? What sequence of events would you follow? Draw on other escape movies you have seen to help you highlight exciting elements in Lester's story.

Critical Thinking in Writing

1. Assume Lester Moreno Perez's identity and write a letter to

your family in Cuba in which you describe your great escape and give some impressions of what life is like for a teenager in America.

2. Leaving home and family for a new life is a drastic step; yet many people take it. What conditions in your home, social, political, or economic environment might compel you to "escape" to a new life without your immediate family? Write an essay in which you analyze what might lead you to take such an action.

Vocabulary

1. All the words below contain word part clues that can help you determine meanings. In Column A write the parts of the word; in Column B write your own definition. Do not use a dictionary. **(3b)**

	A	*B*
1. shark-haunted	_____	_____
	_____	_____
2. sailboard	_____	_____
	_____	_____
3. shoreside	_____	_____
	_____	_____
4. counter-revolutionary	_____	_____
	_____	_____
5. windsurf	_____	_____
	_____	_____
6. earphones	_____	_____
	_____	_____

7. footstrap   _____ _____

    _____ _____

8. hyperactive   _____ _____

    _____ _____

9. knee-deep   _____ _____

    _____ _____

10. self-assurance _____ _____

    _____ _____

2. Use context clues to develop your own definitions for the words in italics. Refer to the reading if you have to. Write your definitions in the space provided. **(3a)**

1. in the *annals* of great escapes _____

2. told *intriguing* tales _____

3. until it *subsided* a little _____

4. sympathized with his *plight* _____

5. *swells* were very steep _____

6. only a month before Lester's *odyssey* _____

7. another young Cuban had *perished* _____

8. he was *outbid* for the rights _____

9. the media *blitz* _____

10. to jump the *formidable* swells _____

The Business of Selling Mail-Order Brides

Venny Villapando

This selection is a sociological description of an unusual practice: men's selecting wives through the mail. The men are usually white, and the women are usually poor Asians from underdeveloped countries. Read to understand why this practice continues and what it means for the women who become mail-order brides.

Prereading

After reading the title and subheads in the selection, write down all the questions you have about mail-order brides. Also write down what you think are the main ideas in this selection. **(1a)**

Word Highlights

beset   troubled
denounced   spoke against; severely criticized
erroneously   in error; by mistake
exploitation   unjust use of another person for advantage
intimidating   frightening; threatening
prevail   continue; survive
resurgence   a return to activity or importance
unabashedly   without disguise or embarrassment

T he phenomenon is far from new. Certainly in the Old West and in other frontier situations such as the labor camps at the sugar farms in Hawaii, the colonization of Australia, or even in the early Irish settlements of New York, there were always lonely men who would write to their homeland for a bride. These women would come on the next train or on the next boat to meet their husbands for the very first time.

2   For Japanese immigrants traditional marriages were arranged in Japan between relatives of the man and the prospective bride. Information was exchanged between the two families

about the potential union, and photographs were exchanged between the couple. If both parties agreed, then the marriage was legalized in the home country, and the bride came to America.

3   While these marriages occurred in less than ideal situations, a number of them were successful. For example the Japanese sugar worker who once waited on the Honolulu pier for the arrival of his picture bride today enjoys the company of a family clan that spans at least two generations. That is indeed an achievement considering the picture bride of yesteryear, just like the contemporary mail-order bride, has always been at a disadvantage. She comes to the marriage from far away, without the nearby support of her family or a familiar culture. The distance that she has traveled is measured not so much in nautical as in emotional miles. She is not quite the happy bride who has been courted and wooed, freely choosing her groom and her destiny.

4   Today's mail-order brides are products of a very complex set of situations and contradictions. They are confronted by far more complicated conditions than the picture brides of years past. They do not quite fit the simple pattern of a marriage between a lonely man stranded in a foreign land and a woman who accepts him sight unseen.

5   In the present matches brides-to-be are generally Asian and husbands-to-be are Caucasians, mostly American, Australian, and Canadian. A majority of the women are poor and because of economic desperation become mail-order brides. Racial, as well as economic, factors define the marriage, however. The new wife is relegated to a more inferior position than her picture bride counterpart. Plus the inequity of the partnership is further complicated by the mail-order bride's immigrant status. Consequently, she is a foreigner not only to the culture, language, and society, but to her husband's race and nationality as well.

6   **Why Men Choose Mail-Order Brides**   "These men want women who will feel totally dependent on them," writes Dr. Gladys L. Symons of the University of Calgary. "They want women who are submissive and less intimidating." Aged between thirty and forty, these men grew up most likely before the rise of the feminist movement, adds Symons. She partially attributes the resurgence of the mail-order bride to a backlash against the 1980s' high-pressure style of dating.

7   Dr. Davor Jedlicka, a sociology professor from the University of Texas, notes in his study of 265 subscribers of mail-order bride

catalogues that "very many of them had extremely bitter experiences with divorce or breakups or engagements." His research also shows the median income of these men to be higher than average — 65 percent of them had incomes of over $20,000. According to Jedlicka, the average age was thirty-seven, average height five feet seven inches, and most were college educated. Only five percent never finished high school.

8   The Japanese American Citizens League, a national civil rights group, confirms this general profile of the typical male client and adds other findings. According to its recent position paper on mail-order brides, the group found that the men tend to be white, much older than the bride they choose, politically conservative, frustrated by the women's movement, and socially alienated. They experience feelings of personal inadequacy and find the traditional Asian value of deference to men reassuring.

9   In her interview in the Alberta Report, Symons points out that the men are also attracted to the idea of buying a wife, since all immigration, transportation, and other costs run to only about two thousand dollars. "We're a consumer society," says Symons. "People become translated into commodities easily." And commodities they are.

10   **Gold at the End of the Rainbow**   Contemporary traders in the Asian bride business publish lists sold for twenty dollars for a catalogue order form to twenty thousand dollars for a deluxe videotaped presentation. Perhaps the most successful company is Rainbow Ridge Consultants run by John Broussard and his wife, Kelly Pomeroy. They use a post office box in Honakaa, Hawaii. Explains Broussard:

> Basically, we just sell addresses. . . . We operate as a pen pal club, not a front for the slave trade, although some people get the wrong idea. We're not a Sears catalogue from which you buy a wife. You have to write and win the heart of the woman you desire.

For providing this service, Broussard and Pomeroy reported a net profit in 1983 of twenty-five thousand dollars, which catapulted to sixty-five thousand in 1984.

11   Rainbow Ridge Consultants distribute three different publications, of which the top two are *Cherry Blossoms* and *Lotus Blossoms*. These differ from the Sears catalogue only because an issue is only twenty-eight pages long, not several hundred, and photos

are black and white, not glossy color. A typical entry reads: "If you like 'em tall, Alice is 5'9", Filipina, social work grad, average looks, wants to hear from men 25–40. $4." For the stated dollar amount, interested men can procure an address and a copy of her biographical data.

12   Broussard and Pomeroy's sister publication *Lotus Blossoms* has twice the number of names, but Broussard admits that *Lotus* is a "second string" brochure, offering pictures of women who do not have the same looks as those in *Cherry Blossoms.*

13   Six months of subscription to the complete catalogues of Rainbow Ridge will cost the wife-seeker $250. A special service will engage Broussard and Pomeroy in a wife hunt at the rate of $50 per hour and includes handling all details, even writing letters and purchasing gifts when necessary. Should the match succeed, the business pockets another fee of $1,000.

14   Kurt Kirstein of Blanca, Colorado, runs Philippine–American Life Partners, which offers one thousand pictures of Filipino women looking for American men. Louis Florence of the American Asian Worldwide Service in Orcutt, California, provides men with a similar catalogue for $25; another $630 will permit the bride-seeker to correspond with twenty-four women, of whom any fifteen will be thoroughly investigated by the service. The California business reports an annual gross income of $250,000.

15   Selling Asian women is a thriving enterprise because the number of American men who seek Asian brides continues to grow. Broussard estimates the total number of daily inquiries is five hundred. In 1984 the Gannett News Service reported that seven thousand Filipino women married Australians, Europeans, and Americans. The *Wall Street Journal* noted that in 1970, only thirty-four Asians were issued fiancée-petitioned visas, while in 1983, the figure jumped dramatically to 3,428.

16   Broussard says that he receives one hundred letters a day from Asian and other women. He publishes about seven hundred pictures every other month in his catalogues. Still, Broussard reports that the chances of a man finding a wife through his service is only about one in twenty.

17   When he receives a letter and the appropriate fees from a prospective groom, Broussard sends off a catalogue. One of his correspondents describes the process: "I selected fourteen ladies to send introductory letters to. To my amazement, I received fourteen replies and am still corresponding with twelve of

them." One of the reasons why letters so often succeed is the detailed coaching both parties receive. For instance, Broussard and Pomeroy publish a 130-page pamphlet entitled "How to Write to Oriental Ladies." There is also one for women called "The Way to an American Male's Heart."

18   The Japanese American Citizens League points out the disadvantage to women in these arrangements because of the inequality of information disseminated. Under the traditional arranged marriage system, family investigation and involvement insured equal access to information and mutual consent. Now only the women must fill out a personality evaluation, which asks very intimate details about their life style and history, and is then shared with the men. Prospective grooms do not have to submit similar information about themselves. Some companies, in fact, even discourage their male clients from disclosing certain types of personal facts in their correspondence, including such potentially negative characteristics as being black or having physical disabilities.

19   **The Economics of Romance**   Coaching or no coaching, the mail-order brides business succeeds partly because it takes advantage of the economic deprivation faced by women in underdeveloped Asian countries. The Broussard brochure categorically states:

> We hear lots of stories about dishonest, selfish and immature women on both sides of the Pacific. Perhaps women raised in poverty will have lower material expectations and will be grateful to whoever rescues them and offers a better life.

20   One Caucasian man who met his wife through the mail says: "They don't have a whole lot of things, so what they do have they appreciate very much. They appreciate things more than what the average American woman would." In other words, they are properly grateful for whatever the superior male partner bestows on them.

21   "Filipinas come because their standard of living is so low," asserts Pomeroy. In 1984 the per capita income in the Philippines was $640. "Most of the women make no secret of why they want to marry an American: money." An Australian reporter who has studied the influx of Filipino mail-order brides to her country agrees: "Most Filipinas are escaping from grinding poverty." Indeed, most Asian governments that are saddled with chronic

unemployment, spiraling cost of living, malnutrition, and political turmoil are faced with the problem of emigration and a diminishing labor force. In contrast, Japan, the economic and technological leader of Asia, has very few women listed in mail-order catalogues.

22   The *Chicago Sun-Times* describes Bruce Moore's visit to the family home of his mail-order bride, Rosie, in Cebu, Philippines:

> "All of a sudden, we were driving through the jungle. There was nothing but little huts. I really started worrying about what I got myself into." . . . The house turned out to be an unpainted concrete building with no doors, plumbing or electricity. . . . Rosie had worked in a factory, eight hours a day, making 75 to 80 cents a day.

23   Because the Filipinas who avail themselves of mail-order bride service may not have much, Broussard's instructional brochures advise men to use caution in describing their financial status. The woman may turn out to be "a con artist after your money or easy entry into the United States." Despite the poverty, though, many of the women are truly sincere in their responses. The Broussard customer who is still writing to twelve of the fourteen women who wrote him notes:

> They all appeared genuine, and not one has asked me for money or anything else. In fact, in two instances, I offered to help with postage, and in both cases, it was declined. One of the ladies said she could not accept postal assistance, as that would lessen the pleasure she felt in the correspondence.

24   Regardless of the sincerity of the parties involved, one women's rights group in the Philippines has denounced the promotion of relationships through "commerce, industry, negotiation or investment." Their protests, however, do not seem to affect the business.

25   **Racial Images and Romance**   Added to economic exploitation, a major cornerstone of the mail-order bride business, is the prevalence of racial stereotypes. They have a widespread effect on the treatment of women and influence why so many men are attracted to mail-order romance. "These men believe the stereotypes that describe Oriental women as docile, compliant, and submissive," says Jedlicka. His 1983 survey showed that 80 percent of the respondents accept this image as true.

26   One Canadian male, who asked not to be identified, was quoted as saying: "Asian girls are not as liberated as North American or Canadian girls. They're more family-oriented and less interested in working. They're old-fashioned. I like that."

27   The California-based American Asian Worldwide Service perpetuates the stereotypes when it says in its brochure: "Asian ladies are faithful and devoted to their husbands. When it comes to sex, they are not demonstrative; however, they are not inhibited. They love to do things to make their husbands happy."

28   This company began after owner Louis Florence began his search for a second wife. He says that friends had touted how their Asian wives "love to make their men happy" and finally convinced him to find a wife from Asia.

29   Another mail-order pitch describes Asian women as "faithful, devoted, unspoiled, and loving." Broussard confirms this popular misconception by saying these women are "raised to be servants for men in many Oriental countries." Referring to the Malaysian and Indonesian women who have recently joined his list of registrants, Broussard insists: "Like the Filipinas, they are raised to respect and defer to the male. . . . The young Oriental woman . . . derives her basic satisfaction from serving and pleasing her husband."

30   Virginity is a highly sought virtue in women. Tom Fletcher, a night worker in Ottawa, Canada, who dislikes North American women because they "want to get out [of the house] and work and that leads to break-ups," is especially appreciative of this sign of purity. "These women's virginity was a gift to their husbands and a sign of faithfulness and trust." One mail-order service unabashedly advertises virginity in a brochure with photos, home addresses, and descriptions of Filipino women, some of whom are as young as seventeen. "Most, if not all are very feminine, loyal, loving . . . and virgins!" its literature reads.

31   Many of the Asian countries affected by the revived mail-order bride business have a history of U.S. military involvement. Troops have either fought battles or been stationed in Korea, the Philippines, and countries in Southeast Asia. During their stays, the soldiers have often developed strong perceptions of Asian women as prostitutes, bargirls, and geishas. Then they erroneously conclude that Asian American women must fit those images, too. Consequently, the stereotype of women servicing and serving men is perpetuated.

32   The Japanese American Citizens League objects to the mail-order bride trade for that very reason. "The marketing tech-

niques used by the catalogue bride companies reinforce negative sexual and racial stereotypes of Asian women in the U.S. The negative attitude toward Asian women affects all Asians in the country." Further, the treatment of women as "commodities" adds to the "non-human and negative perception of all Asians."

33   **Romance on the Rocks**   A marriage made via the mail-order bride system is naturally beset by a whole range of problems. In her testimony before the U.S. Commission on Civil Rights, professor Bok-Lim Kim, then with the University of Illinois, noted that negative reactions and attitudes toward foreign Asian wives "exacerbates marital problems," which result in incidences of spouse abuse, desertion, separation, and divorce. In addition, writes an Australian journalist, most of the men they marry are social misfits. "Many of them drink too much; some beat their wives and treat them little better than slaves."

34   The Japanese American Citizens League asserts:

> Individually, there may be many cases of couples meeting and marrying through these arrangements with positive results. We believe, however, that for the women, there are many more instances in which the impetus for leaving their home countries and families, and the resulting marriage relationships, have roots and end results which are less than positive.

35   Many of the Caucasian men who marry what they believe are stereotypical women may be in for some surprises. Psychiatry professor Joe Yamamoto of the University of California at Los Angeles says: "I've found many Asian women acculturate rather quickly. These American men may get a surprise in a few years if their wives pick up liberated ways."

36   One legally blind and hard-of-hearing American, married to a Korean woman, was eventually bothered by the same problems that plague other couples: in-laws and lack of money. "She gets frustrated because I don't hear her," complains the man about his soft-spoken Asian wife. In response, she says, "The main problem is [his] parents. I can't adapt to American culture. I was going to devote my life for him, but I can't."

37   Another area which specifically affects foreign-born brides is their immigrant status. According to the Japanese American Citizens League, "these foreign women are at a disadvantage." This civil rights group targets the women's unfamiliarity with the U.S. immigration laws as one of the most disturbing aspects of the business. "As a result [of the ignorance], they may miss

an opportunity to become a naturalized citizen, forfeit rights as a legal spouse, or live under an unwarranted fear of deportation which may be fostered by their spouse as a means of control."

38   **Conclusion**   Despite the constant stream of criticism, the mail-order bride system will prevail as long as there are consumers and profit, and as long as underdeveloped countries continue failing to meet the economic, political, and social needs of their people. Indications show the business is not about to collapse now.

39   Erroneous ideas continue to thrive. An Asian woman dreams she will meet and marry someone rich and powerful, someone to rescue her and free her from poverty-stricken bondage. She hopes to live the rest of her life in a land of plenty. An American man dreams he will meet and marry someone passive, obedient, nonthreatening, and virginal, someone to devote her entire life to him, serving him and making no demands. Only a strong women's movement, one tied to the exploited underdeveloped country's struggle for liberation and independence, can challenge these ideas and channel the aspirations and ambitions of both men and women in a more positive and realistic direction.   ❏

EXERCISES

Comprehension

_____ 1. The main idea of this selection is that **(5b)**
a. Philippine women have hard lives.
b. U.S. military involvement in Asia has led to sexist and racist stereotyping of Asian women.
c. the mail-order bride business serves the needs of both husband and wife.
d. the business of mail-order brides is based on economic and racial exploitation.

_____ 2. The first three paragraphs of the selection give a **(5b)**
a. justification for the mail-order bride industry.
b. brief history of the mail-order bride business.
c. history of the development of the American west.
d. physical description of the countries the brides come from.

_____ 3. The mail-order bride of yesteryear typically was **(6a)**
   a. of the same race as her husband.
   b. better informed about her husband than is today's mail-order bride.
   c. still at an emotional disadvantage, having left her home and culture.
   d. all of the above.

_____ 4. Today's men who choose mail-order brides primarily want **(6a)**
   a. assertive career women.
   b. submissive and nonintimidating women.
   c. women who are very tall and athletic.
   d. women to help them with their businesses.

5. Put a checkmark next to all of the characteristics below that match the profile of the men who choose mail-order brides. **(6a)**

_____ 6 feet tall, on average

_____ politically liberal

_____ thirty-seven years old, on average

_____ higher-than-average income

_____ much older than bride

_____ Asian

_____ politically conservative

_____ Caucasian

_____ college educated

_____ 5 feet, 7 inches tall, on average

_____ like idea of buying mate

_____ socially alienated

_____   have had a bitter breakup

_____   frustrated by feminist movement

_____   feelings of personal inadequacy

_____   work as a doctor or engineer

_____ 6. The Japanese American Citizens League believes that the mail-order bride industry **(6a)**
   a. helps promote good relations between the United States and Asian nations.
   b. provides Asian women with good husbands and a more prosperous way of life.
   c. reinforces negative sexual and racial stereotypes of Asian women.
   d. should give a percentage of its profits to the governments of developing Asian nations.

   7. Place *maj* before major details and *min* before minor details. **(6b)**

_____   a. Companies produce catalogs that show photographs of and give information about Asian women.

_____   b. The Asian mail-order bride business makes a lot of money.

_____   c. The demand for Asian mail-order brides is increasing.

_____   d. A six-month subscription to the Rainbow Ridge catalog costs $250.

_____   e. Kurt Kirstein runs Philippine–American Life Partners.

_____   f. Two of the catalogs are called *Cherry Blossoms* and *Lotus Blossoms.*

_____   g. Mail-order brides do not get very much information about prospective grooms.

_____ h. One man wrote to fourteen "ladies" and got fourteen replies.

_____ i. Many women in underdeveloped Asian nations live in extreme poverty.

_____ j. In a 1983 survey of men using a mail-order bride service, 80 percent of respondents described Asian women as docile and submissive.

_____ k. Many countries in which prospective mail-order brides live have a history of U.S. military involvement.

8. Many mail-order marriages exhibit a wide range of problems. Check all those that apply. **(6a)**

_____ a. alcoholism

_____ b. physical abuse

_____ c. career conflicts

_____ d. parenting conflicts

_____ e. lack of money

_____ f. the community's negative reactions toward the wives

_____ g. decisions about vacations

_____ h. in-laws

_____ i. constant arguments

_____ 9. One factor that prospective grooms don't seem to consider is that their mail-order brides might **(6a)**
a. leave them when they discover they have been lied to.
b. bring their families with them.
c. quickly adopt the more liberated attitudes of other women in the United States.
d. want to love and take care of them always.

Reading and Critical Thinking

_____ 1. We can infer that many of the women who offer themselves
            as brides **(8)**
            a. have lots of options and take this one for the adventure
               of it.
            b. know exactly what to expect when they get to their new
               country.
            c. are well educated.
            d. believe they will get out of poverty and have a better
               life.

_____ 2. We can infer that many Asian women who participate in
            the mail-order bride business **(8)**
            a. have no idea that most of the potential grooms are social
               misfits.
            b. make a lot of money on the initial transaction.
            c. end up starting their own businesses.
            d. already have children.

_____ 3. We can infer that some men are disappointed with their
            mail-order brides because **(8)**
            a. they cannot cook well.
            b. their brides are not as submissive as they expected.
            c. they do not look anything like their picture in the cat-
               alog.
            d. the process ends up costing a lot more than they thought
               it would.

_____ 4. The article concludes that the mail-order bride business **(10)**
            a. will die a natural death in a few years.
            b. will continue as long as there are consumers and profit
               and poverty.
            c. is likely to be shut down by the U.S. government.
            d. is a program that benefits both brides and grooms.

_____ 5. We can conclude that the mail-order bride business **(10)**
            a. meets the needs only of the people who run the agencies.
            b. meets the needs of all grooms and brides.
            c. satisfies some grooms and brides and therefore is good.
            d. meets certain needs for some grooms and brides, but in
               ways that are unjust.

_____ 6. We can conclude that until sexist and racist attitudes change, **(10)**
   a. the mail-order bride business will flourish.
   b. America will continue to be a world power.
   c. we will have equality among the sexes and races.
   d. the mail-order bride business will fail.

_____ 7. We can conclude that until underdeveloped Asian countries become independent and economically stable, **(10)**
   a. Hawaii will be the center of the mail-order bride trade.
   b. Japan will continue to supply most of the mail-order brides.
   c. the mail-order bride business will continue.
   d. the mail-order bride business will continue to lose money.

_____ 8. We can generalize that the mail-order bride business is based on a common stereotype that views **(11)**
   a. mail-order businesses as sleazy.
   b. marriage as an evil.
   c. America as the land of opportunity.
   d. women as commodities.

_____ 9. The author believes that today's mail-order bride business is more **(12a)**
   a. sensitive to women than it is to men.
   b. oppressive for women than it was in the past.
   c. important in creating jobs for Asian women than we think.
   d. positive than any of the surveys indicate.

_____ 10. The author's opinion of the mail-order bride business is **(12a)**
   a. that it is no problem.
   b. that the women are being exploited.
   c. that it is based on sexism and racism.
   d. both *b* and *c*.

_____ 11. The evidence in this selection is taken primarily from **(12b)**
   a. books written by women who were mail-order brides.
   b. newspaper articles and census data.
   c. interviews and studies done by sociologists.
   d. the author's speculation.

Connecting Ideas

1. Read the selection "They Treat Girls Differently, Don't They?" (pages 391–396). While the treatment of young women described in that selection isn't as extreme or painful as the treatment described in this selection, discuss whether both reflect similar or different attitudes toward women that make these problems possible.
2. Discuss with your classmates whether the mail-order bride business bears any similarity to other current social practices that affect either relations between the sexes or economic relations between rich and poor nations.

Critical Thinking in Writing

1. How do you feel about the fact that there is such a thing as a mail-order bride business? Would you ban it if you had the opportunity, or would you support it? Explain your opinion in a paragraph or two.
2. The existence of a mail-order bride business is related directly to society's view of marriage. What elements in our view of marriage contribute to the success of the mail-order bride business? How are minority women seen in marriage roles? How about minority men and majority men? Explore your views in a paragraph or two.

Vocabulary

1. The following exercise pertains to words used in the selection that have very similar meanings. In the space provided write the best definition for the word in italics. Use a dictionary if you have to. **(3a)**

_____ 1. women who are *submissive*
   a. willing to surrender to others' wishes
   b. dogmatic in personal beliefs
   c. assertive
   d. caring

_____ 2. traditional Asian value of *deference* to men
   a. concern for your own well-being above all else
   b. respect for someone you consider to be superior or who is older than you
   c. lack of consideration
   d. childishness

_____ 3. describe Oriental women as *docile*
a. energetic
b. having respect for an elder
c. talking a great deal
d. quietly obedient

_____ 4. describe Oriental women as docile, *compliant,* and submissive
a. willing to give in
b. disorganized
c. complaining
d. disrespectful

_____ 5. the stereotype of women servicing and serving men is *perpetuated*
a. ended immediately
b. caused to continue
c. weakened
d. started up; begun

_____ 6. *reinforce* negative sexual and racial stereotypes
a. strengthen
b. rework entirely
c. let alone
d. weaken

_____ 7. *exacerbates* marital problems
a. ignores
b. weakens
c. solves
d. makes worse

_____ 8. happy bride who has been *courted* and wooed
a. pursued by a potential mate
b. named in a lawsuit
c. taken before a judge
d. called on the telephone

_____ 9. happy bride who has been courted and *wooed*
a. left alone
b. the subject of gossip
c. actively sought after with affection
d. treated unfairly

2. Next to each word in Column A, write the letter of the correct definition in Column B. You may need to refer back to the selection for context clues. The number of the paragraph in which the word appears is in parentheses. **(3a)**

A	*B*
_____ 1. nautical (3)	a. given out
	b. adapt to new customs
_____ 2. consequently (5)	c. given citizenship in a new country
_____ 3. attributes (6)	d. get
	e. state of being without
_____ 4. backlash (6)	f. without cause; inexcusable
_____ 5. catapulted (10)	g. forced removal from a country
_____ 6. procure (11)	h. associated with the ocean
_____ 7. petitioned (15)	i. as a result of
	j. identifies the cause
_____ 8. prospective (17)	k. likely; expected
	l. sudden backward movement
_____ 9. disseminated (18)	
	m. shot up to
_____ 10. deprivation (19)	n. requested, sometimes in writing
_____ 11. prevalence (25)	o. the degree to which something is accepted or common
_____ 12. acculturate (35)	
_____ 13. naturalized (37)	
_____ 14. unwarranted (37)	
_____ 15. deportation (37)	

Hearts of Sorrow

James M. Freeman

Leaving your homeland is almost always sad and difficult, even if you eventually find a better life. The narrator of this selection, a Vietnamese teacher, tells his story to the author, James Freeman. The teacher was driven from his home; after a long and painful war he left for America.

Prereading

Make a list of problems that you think a family might have if they came from Vietnam to live in America. **[1a(1)]**

> **Word Highlights**
> **inadequate** not enough
> **intention** plan
> **status** position within a group

My family arrived in America in October 1976. At that time I spoke a little English; my wife spoke none. I had not had any intention of coming to America, but since I had a relative here, the International Rescue Committee contacted the American Embassy, and we were brought into this country.

2 I remember our first misunderstanding. We saw lots of people waving to each other in greeting. My wife said, "Oh, how do they know us like a friend, that they're calling us to go over to them?" For us, the gesture signified "Come here."

3 We were sent to a place in the South where the people were quite friendly, but the climate was too cold for us in the winter, and much too hot in the summer. There were mosquitoes and flies all over. It was not pleasant.

4 Although white people were friendly with us, we saw discrimination against blacks. I asked a black friend to go with me while I visited a friend. When he saw that I was about to enter the house of a white man, he said, "I'll stay outside and wait."

5 "Why not go inside?" I asked.

6   He replied, "My mother told me not to go to white people."

7   I tried one more time. I took a white man to a black man's house. The white man wouldn't go in. "Why?" I asked.

8   "My mother told me not to visit black people."

9   One day I went to the store and selected lots of oranges, apples, and vegetables. I had only ten dollars in my pocket. The girl at the checkout counter added up the cost of the items and said, "You owe fifteen dollars."

10   I replied, "I've only got ten, so I'll put back some oranges. Give me ten dollars' worth. Tomorrow I'll buy more."

11   A black woman standing behind me said, "Let him get everything; I'll pay the rest for him."

12   That was the first time something like that happened; I'll never forget it.

13   On another occasion, when I had moved to another state, an old man saw me buy a hamburger but nothing else at a hamburger stand. He asked, "Why did you buy only a hamburger, and nothing to drink?"

14   I replied, "I don't have enough money, only a little over a dollar."

15   The old man said, "I'll buy another hamburger for you."

16   "No, no," I said. "It's too much for me."

17   He bought me another hamburger and some orange juice. We sat down and ate together.

18   Some people are good, but others are not friendly. Where we live now, we cannot ride a bicycle, for young people shout loudly as they drive by in cars. I don't care what they say, but they startle me when they drive right behind me, pass me close by, on the narrow road, and then shout in my ear.

19   Sometimes my wife and I walk along the sidewalk. Even that we cannot do, for the young people shout out at us as they drive by. My wife feels bad when she hears this; she does not want to go out. I care about that. I say to her, "Let's drive to the park; then we can walk there." But walking nearby is better because we do not need a car.

20   My wife often feels so lonely here in America because she cannot walk near her home, for she is afraid that people will shout at her. She has friends around here, but if she wishes to visit them, she asks me to accompany her. So her behavior in America is quite different from how she lived in Vietnam, where she'd leave the house alone two, three, or four times a day, visiting the market, her parents, and her friends. She used to walk

a lot and enjoyed it very much; now she fears to do it. I don't know, the old people in America are very nice, but young people are rude and destructive. At the rear of my apartment stands a large, wheeled garbage bin. It is real dirty and has a bad smell that attracts lots of flies. Many people also go there to drink beer and smoke cigarettes. The manager of the apartment put up a sign to keep out of private property; still, two to three carloads of dirty young people with long hair gather around the garbage bin; they make so much noise, even at night. Often they are drunk. They throw cans and empty bottles on the roof; the clatter is terrible. Even though the manager calls the police, these people often return. And they end the evening by urinating on the fence.

21   Although some other Vietnamese people live near here, we do not see them often. They work all day, eat, sleep, watch television, but don't go out much except to work. Like my wife, they have stopped walking in the neighborhood because the youths shout at them. In Vietnam, the old people used to walk a lot, stopping along the way at restaurants, where they would meet friends, talk, and drink coffee. Sometimes they would go fishing or swimming, and at other times they would visit friends. All of that is gone for them in America, and it is no longer possible in Vietnam either.

22   My wife says, "I feel so lonely when you and the children are away from the house." She stays home and cooks and does housework. The children too are lonely. I tell them to take the car and visit friends, but they say, "That's a waste of gas and money." They understand our situation, that with my low-paying job, which may stop at any moment, we do not have enough money to support us. A couple of my children attend one of the colleges nearby; I drive them there before going to work, and I pick them up after work. But my wife remains alone all day. For companionship, I bought her two birds in a large cage. From time to time, one of the birds sings. Because she has poor eyesight, my wife cannot watch television. Her days are long. I work five days a week. On those days, I am tired. All I want to do is relax, eat, drink, and go to sleep. On the weekends, I take her to the market, and we go to the laundromat. Sometimes we write letters to our relatives and friends. But our life is a lonely one in America. That's why lots of old people want to return to Vietnam. Religion here won't help them; that's only for a few hours on Sunday. People still remain lonely. They

dream of fighting the Communists, throwing them out, and returning to live out their days peacefully in their homeland. But
this is only a dream.

23   Sometimes my friends call me on the telephone. We talk
about our lives here and what other people are doing. We sometimes invite one another to come by and take some food. This
is different from Vietnam, where we used to just arrive at the
door of our friend, and they'd invite us in. We'd say, "We've
got some food ready; why don't you stay and have some." We'd
travel around a lot and visit friends, more than here in America.
We'd help our friends get jobs, and we'd share room, clothes,
food. A friend might stay with us for months; we don't care
about that. During holidays, maybe four or five people will come
by and stay. That's how we do it.

24   For my wife, adjustment in America is very hard. For me
and my children, adjustment is not that difficult. I had some experience in dealing with Westerners before I left Vietnam. My
children are young enough to adapt to new customs. Within
three days of our arrival in America, I had enrolled them in
school; within four months, they were speaking English.

25   Somewhat difficult for us was learning to cope with American food, which contains too much salt and sugar, and very peculiar seasoning. We dislike it, and I still eat mostly Vietnamese-
style food. At my place of work, I eat food that I have taken from
home. My daughters have learned to tolerate American food,
but prefer Vietnamese.

26   Also hard for us is the speaking of English. Often we can
read well, but because of our pronunciation people think we are
not well educated. We find it quite difficult to ask for information over the telephone, so we may drive 20 or 30 miles to get
the information. Yesterday, I tried to call a pet shop where I had
bought two finches. I said to the man, "The mother bird has laid
five eggs, but after they hatched, she kicked them out of her nest
area, and they died. What should I do to prevent that?"

27   The man at the pet shop said, "Sorry, I cannot understand
what you said."

28   I asked an American friend to call for me. He received the
information and relayed it to me.

29   That's not the only language problem. One morning I was
cleaning our floor with a vacuum cleaner that made a lot of
noise. The people who live below us pounded on the ceiling with
something. They were angry, I guess. I went next door to an

American lady and asked her to explain to the people below that I was cleaning with a vacuum cleaner. She did that, and the people said it was okay.

30   In 1979, I enrolled in a technical training institute where I received nine months of instruction. I started out in one field, but a friend persuaded me to try another. It turned out I had quite a bit of skill for it, so my counselor at the institute let me switch. After completing my training, I went out to look for work. My friend, who was younger, was hired immediately; I had more difficulty, for when people saw that I was in my fifties, they were not anxious to hire me. After two months, one company offered me a job. The man who hired me said, "Take five dollars an hour."

31   I replied, "No, six."

32   "Okay," the man said. "I'll hire you."

33   In Vietnam, a man of my age would have retired. I would have been able to support my family to the end of my life. But not in America. I tell my children to work hard, because I will not be able to help them forever; one day they will be on their own. I have no security of any kind here; I must keep working as long as I have a job, and it might end at any moment.

34   I liked my job in Vietnam much more. I talked with people of a higher class, and people treated me with respect. I had three months of paid summer vacation every year. The status of my job in Vietnam was much higher than the factory labor I do here. That is very difficult, not only for me, but for many other Vietnamese men. We have lost our country. We are making a new life in another country. We don't care about our second life in a new country, that we are lower in status. Even though it is difficult, many of us are happy because our children have a chance here. I'm at the end of my life; I'm happy simply to sacrifice for my children. I'll take any job to help them. I do know some Vietnamese people who are unable to adjust to the loss of their status.

35   I am happy that I was able to change my life and start a new job in America. At least I showed I could make the adjustment. But if you ask me what life is like for me here in America, I have to tell you: Terrible! I say that because all the money I get from my new job is gone. Almost all of it goes for rent, which is increased too much. We have no money for heating. In the winter, we keep warm by wrapping blankets around ourselves, and we cover the windows with sheets. We can buy a blanket for seven

dollars and use it for a year. We have no need for heat. We never use our big oven, but boil all of our food to keep down the costs. For food, we don't pay too much. If food increases in price, we decrease how much we eat. If rent increases, there is no way to decrease. Rent is a major problem for us. I have some health coverage at my place of work, but it is so inadequate that when I am ill, I try to avoid doctors and hospitals because they are so expensive. I use home remedies; my wife uses herbal medicines. That's why we are able to survive on so much less than other Americans.

36   I often wonder what will happen to my family. The future of my children is bright, for they work hard and have talent. They know they must work hard, for I will not be able to help them much longer. The work I do requires good hand-and-eye coordination. One day I will lose that. What will happen to me then? Sometimes I worry about my future; at other times I don't care. ❏

EXERCISES

Comprehension

_____ 1. The main idea of the selection is **(5)**
         a. Black people treated a Vietnamese immigrant family with great kindness.
         b. Adjusting to a new life in a new country is very difficult.
         c. Immigrants require more help than just relocation to a new land.
         d. Loneliness is a major challenge for Vietnamese families.

_____ 2. The narrator came to America because **(6a)**
         a. he could speak English.
         b. his wife convinced him to contact the American embassy.
         c. all Vietnamese refugees are sent to the United States.
         d. the International Rescue Committee sent him to a country where he had a relative.

_____ 3. The narrator's wife speaks **(6a)**
         a. no English.
         b. a little English.

c. fluent English.

d. better English than her husband because she watches TV all day while he is at work.

_____ 4. The narrator came to America in **(6a)**

a. 1967.

b. 1976.

c. 1982.

d. 1991.

_____ 5. The wife is lonely because **(6a)**

a. she has no friends.

b. young people are rude.

c. she is afraid to leave the apartment.

d. her behavior in America is different.

_____ 6. The group of Americans who disturb the narrator most are **(6a)**

a. young people.

b. old people.

c. white people.

d. black people.

_____ 7. The author was forced to leave his country because **(6a)**

a. it was taken over by Communists.

b. his house was destroyed in the war.

c. he wanted a better life for his children.

d. he wanted a higher standard of living.

_____ 8. To help his wife feel less lonely, the narrator bought her **(6a)**

a. a television.

b. a telephone.

c. an automobile.

d. two birds.

_____ 9. Although he was a teacher in his native country, in America the narrator works in a **(6a)**

a. technical training institute.

b. factory.

c. pet shop.

d. bookstore.

_____ 10.   The narrator boils his food, uses blankets instead of heat,
              and makes home remedies for illness because **(6a)**
              a. these are the customs of his country.
              b. he is cheap.
              c. he is saving money for his retirement.
              d. he doesn't make much money.

Reading and Critical Thinking

_____ 1.   We can infer that the narrator's feelings about black people
             are **(8)**
             a. positive because black people have been kind to him.
             b. negative because black people have been mean to him.
             c. neutral because he rarely interacts with Americans.
             d. both positive and negative.

_____ 2.   The narrator did not like the South because the climate in
             his native country was **(8)**
             a. hotter in the winter.
             b. cooler in the summer.
             c. more moderate.
             d. tropical.

_____ 3.   We can infer that people shout at the narrator when he rides
             his bicycle because **(8)**
             a. he is a menace on the road.
             b. they are trying to be friendly.
             c. they have never seen Asians on bicycles before.
             d. they enjoy being mean to strangers.

_____ 4.   We can predict that in Vietnam if you wanted someone to
             come to you, you would **(10)**
             a. say "Come here."
             b. shout.
             c. wave.
             d. smile.

_____ 5.   We can infer that the narrator and his wife are bothered by
             shouting because **(8)**
             a. it is alien behavior to them.
             b. they have very sensitive hearing.
             c. Vietnamese people never shout.
             d. they find it distracting.

6. Based on information in the article, put a checkmark next to the behavior traits and customs you could predict that Vietnamese people value. **(10)**

_____   a. privacy

_____   b. rudeness

_____   c. courtesy

_____   d. socializing

_____   e. solitude

_____   f. respect

_____   g. watching television

_____   h. drinking beer

_____   i. getting rowdy

_____   j. sacrificing for the family

_____   k. education

_____ 7. We can conclude that the narrator and his wife will be **(10)**
   a. happy when they adjust to American customs.
   b. happy when Vietnam throws out the Communists and they can return home.
   c. unhappy until they die because adjustment to a new way is difficult for many older people.
   d. unhappy because Americans will continue to harass them.

_____ 8. "Life is terrible," says the narrator, because he is **(10, 11)**
   a. alienated.
   b. alienated and hungry.
   c. alienated and hungry and cannot buy medicine.
   d. alienated, unable to earn enough money, and forced to pay high rent.

_____ 9. The author believes that the future is bright for his children because **(10)**
a. someday they will be able to return to Vietnam.
b. they work hard and have talent.
c. they are smarter than their parents and will not get stuck in factory jobs.
d. they can marry Americans and become part of the mainstream.

_____ 10. A good guess about how the narrator's children feel about life in America is **(8)**
a. the same as their parents.
b. better than their parents.
c. worse than their parents.
d. they have no opinion.

_____ 11. From the article we can generalize that immigrants **(11)**
a. are amazed at how clean and modern America is.
b. are happy to live in a land of freedom.
c. face problems adjusting to things that Americans take for granted.
d. who do not appreciate America should go back to their native countries.

Connecting Ideas

1. Read the article "My Unsentimental Tutee" (pages 372–374). In that selection, the immigrant described also has mixed feelings about her and her husband's experience in this country. Compare their experience to that of the people described in this selection, and then compare the attitude they take toward that experience.
2. Many people who have lived in this country their whole lives, as well as many immigrants, find life here very difficult. Write several paragraphs describing what you find to be most difficult about life in this country.

Critical Thinking in Writing

1. Imagine that you are leaving your home forever to live in a strange country. You cannot take anything you enjoy with you. What are the things in your home you would miss the

most? What about your town, or about America as a culture, would you miss the most?

2. Over the last few years, in the wake of the Vietnam War, the Vietnamese government has tried to normalize relations with America. One of its goals has been to encourage Americans to visit Vietnam as tourists. Should we be friends with the Vietnamese or not? Write an essay in favor of forging a new friendship with this country or opposed to embracing a former enemy. You may want to check in your library for background information on the Vietnam War.

Vocabulary

Each of the following phrases comes from the selection. Using context clues or a dictionary, choose the correct definition for the words in italics. **(3a)**

_____ 1. a friend *persuaded* me
    a. intimidated
    b. convinced
    c. talked to
    d. tricked

_____ 2. my wife uses *herbal* medicines
    a. superstitious
    b. from natural roots and plants
    c. oriental
    d. synthetic

_____ 3. health coverage . . . is . . . *inadequate*
    a. excellent
    b. not enough
    c. barely enough
    d. more than enough

_____ 4. the gesture *signified* "Come here"
    a. suggested
    b. eliminated
    c. spoke
    d. meant

_____ 5. On another *occasion*
    a. event
    b. holiday
    c. fancy party
    d. day

_____ 6. they *startle* me
    a. shout at
    b. sneak up on
    c. frighten
    d. awaken

_____ 7. she asks me to *accompany* her
    a. go with
    b. go instead of
    c. stay away from
    d. ignore

_____ 8. the *clatter* is terrible
    a. large serving dish
    b. noise
    c. talking
    d. mess

_____ 9. They understand our *situation*
    a. place
    b. life
    c. position
    d. culture

_____ 10. For *companionship*, I bought her two birds
    a. company
    b. friendship
    c. distraction
    d. help

Immigrants

Aurora Levins Morales

This selection traces the author's life from her childhood in Puerto Rico to her adulthood in California. It compares and contrasts life before and after her family immigrates to the States. Read to understand how different environments shape our experiences, our attitudes, and our views of life.

Prereading

Make a list of questions that you would like to have answered in this selection. What questions does the title ("Immigrants") bring to mind? **[1a(4)]**

Word Highlights

bounteous generous
cadence rhythm
displacement being moved around
hubbub noise and confusion
phonetic sounding like
redolent smellingly pleasant
vulnerable able to be hurt

For years after we left Puerto Rico for the last time, I would wake from a dream of something unbearably precious melting away from my memory as I struggled desperately to hold on, or at least to remember that I had forgotten. I am an immigrant, and I forget to feel what it means to have left. What it means to have arrived.

2   There was hail the day we got to Chicago and we joked that the city was hailing our arrival. The brown brick buildings simmered in the smelly summer, clenched tight all winter against the cold and the sooty sky. It was a place without silence or darkness, huddled against a lake full of dying fish whose corpses floated against the slime-covered rocks of the south shore.

3   Chicago is the place where the slack ended. Suddenly there was no give. In Indiera there was the farm: the flamboyan tree,

the pine woods, the rainforest hillsides covered with alegría, the wild joyweed that in English is called impatiens. On the farm there were hideouts, groves of bamboo with the tiny brown hairs that stuck in your skin if you weren't careful. Beds of sweet-smelling fern, drowsymaking under the sun's heat, where the new leaves uncurled from fiddleheads and tendrils climbed and tangled in a spongy mass six feet deep. There were still hillsides, out of range of the house, where I could watch lizards hunt and reinitas court, and stalk the wild cuckoos, trying to get up close. There were mysteries and consolations. There was space.

4   Chicago was a wasteland. Nowhere to walk that was safe. Killers and rapists everywhere. Police sirens. Ugly, angry looks. Bristling hostility. Worst of all, nowhere to walk. Nowhere to go if it was early morning and I had to get out. Nowhere to go in the late afternoon or in the gathering dusk that meant fireflies and moths at home. Nowhere to watch animal life waking into a new day. The animal life was rats and dogs, and they were always awake because it never got dark here: always that sickly purple and orange glow they call sky in this place. No forest to run wild in. Only the lot across 55th Street with huge piles of barren earth, outlines of old cellars, and a few besieged trees in a scraggly row. I named one of them Ceres, after the goddess of earth and plenty who appeared in my high school production of *The Tempest*: bounteous Ceres, queen of the wasteland. There were no hills to race down, tumbling into heaps of fern, to slide down, on a slippery banana leaf; no place to get muddy. Chicago had grime, but no mud. Slush, but no slippery places of the heart, no genuine moistness. Only damp alleyways, dank brick, and two little humps in the middle of 55th Street over which grass had been made to grow. But no real sliding. No slack.

5   *There are generations of this desolation behind me, desolation, excitement, grief, and longing all mixed in with the dirty air, the noise, seasickness, and the strangeness of wearing a winter coat.*

6   My grandmother Lola was nineteen the day she married my grandfather and sailed away to Nueva York in 1929. She had loved someone else, but his family disapproved and he obeyed their orders to leave for the States. So her family married her to a son of a neighboring family because the family store was doing poorly and they could no longer support so many children. Two months after her first love left, she found herself married and on the boat. She says: "I was a good Catholic girl. I thought it was my duty to marry him, that it was for the good of my fam-

ily." I have pictures of her, her vibrant beauty wrapped up but not smothered in the winter coats and scarves, in my grandfather's violent possessiveness and jealousy. She is standing in Central Park with her daughters, or with her arms around a friend or cousin. Loving the excitement. Loving the neighbors and the hubbub. In spite of racist landlords. In spite of the girdle factory. In spite of Manolin's temper and the poverty and hunger. Now, retired to Manolin's dream of a little house in Puerto Rico with a yard and many plants to tend, she longs for New York or some other U.S. city where a woman can go out and about on her own, live among many voices speaking different languages, out of the stifling air of that house, that community, that family.

7   *My mother, the child in that Central Park photo, grew up an immigrant child among immigrants. She went to school speaking not a word of English, a small Puerto Rican girl scared out of her wits, and learned fast: learned accentless English in record time, the sweet cadence of her mother's open-voweled words ironed out of her vocabulary, the edges flattened down, made crisp, the curls and flourishes removed. First generation.*

8   The strangeness. The way time worked differently. The way being on time mattered. Four second bells. Four minutes of passing time between classes. A note from home if you were ten minutes late, which you took to the office and traded for a late pass. In Indiera the classroom emptied during coffee season, and they didn't bother to send the inspector up unless we were out for longer than four or five weeks. No one had a clock with a second hand. We had half days of school because there were only four rooms for six grades. Our room was next to the bakery, and the smell of the warm pan de agua filled our lungs and stomachs and mouths. Things happened when they were ready, or "cuando Dios quiere." The público to town, don Paco's bread, the coffee ripening, the rain coming, growing up.

9   The stiffness. The way clothing mattered with an entirely different kind of intensity. In Indiera, I wore the same wine-colored jumper to school each day with the same white blouse, and only details of the buttons or the quality of the cloth or the presence or absence of earrings, only the shoes gave information about the homes we left at dawn each day, and I was grateful to be able to hide my relative wealth. In Chicago, there were rituals I had never heard of. Knee socks and plaid skirts and sweaters matching each other according to a secret code I didn't under-

stand. Going steady and wearing name tags. First date, second date, third date, score. The right songs to be listening to. The right dances. The coolness.

10   In the middle of coolness, of stiffness, of strangeness, my joyful rushing up to say, "I come from Puerto Rico, a nest of beauty on the top of a mountain range." Singing "beauty, beauty, beauty." Trying to get them to see in their minds' eyes the perfect edge of a banana leaf against a tropical blue sky, just wanting to speak of what I longed for. Seeing embarrassed faces turning away, getting the jeering voices, singing "Puerto Riiiico, my heart's devotion . . . let it sink into the ocean!" Learning fast not to talk about it, learning excruciatingly slowly how to dress, how to act, what to say, where to hide. The exuberance, the country-born freshness going quietly stale. Made flat. Made palatable. Made unthreatening. Not different, really. Merely "exotic."

11   *I can remember the feelings, but I forget to give them names. In high school we read novels about immigrant families. In college we discussed the problems of other first generations, talked about displacement, talked about families confused and divided, pride and shame. I never once remembered that I was an immigrant, or that both my parents are the first U.S.-born generations of their families.*

12   My father is the First American Boy. His mother, Ruth, was born in Russia. Took the boat with her mother, aunt, and uncle when she was two. My grandfather Reuben was the second son of Lev Levinsky, the first one born in the new country, but born into the ghetto. Lev and the first son, Samuel, were orthodox, old-country Jews, but Reuben and his younger brother, Ben, went for the new. They worked three or four jobs at once. They ran a deli in shifts and went to law school in their free hours. So Rube grew up and out of the immigrant poverty, still weak and bent from childhood hungers, still small and vulnerable. The sicker he got, the harder he worked to safeguard his wife and sons, adding on yet another job, yet another project until he worked himself to death at the age of forty-six.

13   My father was the First American Boy: the young genius, the honors student, the Ph.D. scientist. Each milestone recorded in home movies. His letters and report cards hoarded through the decades, still exhibited to strangers. The one who knew what was what. The expert. The one who carried the family spark, the one to boast about. The one with the weight of the family's hope on his shoulders. First generation.

14   *And what am I?*

15   The immigrant child of returned immigrants who repeated the journey in the second generation. Born on the island with first-hand love and the stories of my parents' Old Country — New York; and behind those, the secondhand stories of my mother's father, of the hill town of his long-ago childhood, told through my mother's barrio childhood. Layer upon layer of travel and leaving behind, an overlay of landscapes, so that I dream of all the beloved and hated places, and endlessly of trains and paths and roads and ships docking and leaving port and a multitude of borders and officials waiting for my little piece of paper.

16   I have the passport with which my great-grandmother Leah, traveling as Elisavieta, and her sister Betty (Rivieka) and her brother Samuel and her mother Henke and my grandmother Riva, a round two-year-old to be known all her life as Ruth, and a neighbor who traveled with them as a relative, all came together into New York. I touch the seal of Russia, the brown ink in which their gentile names were recorded, the furriness of the old paper, the place where the date is stamped: June 1906. My great-grandfather Abe had come alone, fleeing the draft, by way of England and Canada, two years earlier.

17   I don't know what it looked like, the Old Country they left, the little farm in the Ukraine. I will never know. The town of Yaza was utterly destroyed in two gory days in 1942, eight thousand shot and buried in long trenches. My aunt Betty was unable to speak by the time I wanted to ask her: What was it like, a girl of fifteen, to come from that countryside to New York, to suddenly be working ten hours a day in a factory? I have the tiniest fragments, only the dust clinging to their shoes. The dreamy look on my great-grandmother's face one morning when I was ten, watching me play jacks. "There was a game we used to play on the farm, just like that, but with round little stones from the river, tossed from the fronts to the backs of our hands: how many times before they fall?" Pop's, my great-grandfather's painting of the farm he grew up on, and a dozen pages he left in phonetic yiddishy English about the place he grew up in, the horses, the pumpkins, the potatoes, the family decision for him to marry, to flee to New York, where you had to use *tsikolodzi* (psychology) to stay on top.

18   My grandmother Ruth unexpectedly answering my questions about her earliest memories with a real story, one whole, shining piece of her life: "*Dancing. We were on the boat from Russia.*

The sun was shining. The place we slept was smelly, stuffy, dark, so all the people were out on the deck as much as possible, sharing food, talking, laughing, playing music. Some of the other passengers were playing accordions and fiddles and I began to dance in the middle of the deck. I danced and danced and all the people around me were laughing and clapping and watching me as I spun round and round in my short skirts. It was the happiest moment of my life!"

19   My children will be born in California. It's not strange anymore, in this part of the world, in this time, to be born a thousand miles from the birthplace of your mother. My children will hear stories about the coquís and coffee flowers, about hurricanes and roosters crowing in the night, and will dig among old photographs to understand the homesick sadness that sometimes swallows me. Living among these dry golden hills, they will hear about rain falling for months, every afternoon at two o'clock, and someday I'll take them there, to the farm on the top of Indiera, redolent of my childhood, where they can play, irreverent, in the ruins of my house. Perhaps they will lie in bed among the sounds of the rainforest, and it will be the smell of eucalyptus that calls to them in their dreams.   ❑

EXERCISES

Comprehension

_____ 1. Which item from the selection best states the main idea? **(5a)**
   a. "Chicago was a wasteland."
   b. "On the farm there were hideouts, groves of bamboo with the tiny brown hairs that stuck in your skin if you weren't careful."
   c. "My father was the First American Boy: the young genius, the honors student, the Ph.D. scientist."
   d. "I am an immigrant, and I forget to feel what it means to have left. What it means to have arrived."

_____ 2. In paragraph 3 we learn that the author emigrated from **(6a)**
   a. Atlanta to San Juan.
   b. Chicago to Indiera.
   c. Chicago to California.
   d. Indiera to Chicago.

_____ 3. The last paragraph of the piece relates to the first paragraph because the writer **(6a)**
a. cannot forget her own childhood.
b. plans to teach her children about what it means to be an immigrant.
c. has no memories of her pre-immigrant life.
d. does not want to have children.

_____ 4. The main idea of paragraph 3 is that **(5b)**
a. the weather in Chicago is bad.
b. every place is different.
c. Chicago is very different from Indiera.
d. city life is better than country life.

5. Put a checkmark beside the two facts that the writer tells us about her grandmother Lola. **(6a)**

_____ a. She sailed to New York in 1929.

_____ b. She married the man she loved.

_____ c. She dislikes New York.

_____ d. She now lives in Puerto Rico.

6. Put an X beside each detail about the farm in Indiera. **(6b)**

_____ a. pine woods

_____ b. lizards and wild cuckoos

_____ c. slush

_____ d. bamboo groves

_____ e. dank brick

_____ f. horses

_____ g. hills

_____ 7. The writer compares Chicago to Indiera by describing the
             (7d)
             a. people.
             b. physical environment.
             c. language.
             d. weather.

_____ 8. The writer compares her Puerto Rican family and her Jew-
             ish family to show that **(7d)**
             a. they were very different.
             b. every family has unique experiences.
             c. immigrants share common experiences.
             d. Jews and Puerto Ricans do not get along.

_____ 9. Grandfather Reuben died because **(7e)**
             a. the family could not afford a doctor.
             b. he wouldn't go to the hospital.
             c. he didn't take care of himself.
             d. he worked hard to provide for his family.

_____ 10. According to the writer, immigration is a difficult experi-
              ence because you **(7e)**
              a. have to learn a new language.
              b. have to get used to a different way of life.
              c. never can earn a good living.
              d. are always a stranger in your new land.

Reading and Critical Thinking

_____ 1. We can infer from the selection that the author **(8)**
             a. liked Indiera more than she liked Chicago.
             b. felt more at home in Chicago than in Indiera.
             c. wants to raise her children in Indiera.
             d. likes her Jewish relatives better than her Puerto Rican rel-
                 atives.

_____ 2. From this piece we can infer that the author **(8)**
             a. feels that everyone should experience immigration.
             b. believes in the value of education.
             c. thinks family ties are very important.
             d. wants other Puerto Ricans to come to the United States.

_____ 3. In which of the phrases below does the author use figurative
             language? **(9)**

---

a. "Nowhere to watch animal life waking into a new day"
b. "buildings simmered in the smelly summer, clenched tight all winter"
c. "Loving the excitement."
d. "wine-colored jumper"

_____ 4. According to the writer, we can conclude that an immigrant experience **(10)**
a. is always difficult.
b. can be forgotten if one adjusts to a new life.
c. is not so special.
d. cannot be understood by people who are not immigrants.

_____ 5. From the selection we can generalize that the author believes **(11)**
a. Jewish people are smarter than Puerto Rican people.
b. life for immigrants is harder in Chicago than in New York.
c. life is more relaxed in Puerto Rico than in the United States.
d. growing up is easier in the United States than in Puerto Rico.

6. Indicate with an *F* or an *O* whether the following statements are facts or opinions. **(12a)**

_____ a. The author's grandmother Ruth was born in Russia.

_____ b. The author's father was a genius.

_____ c. The author's mother was in Central Park when she was a child.

_____ d. The author's mother was scared of school.

_____ 7. For which of the statements below does the author present supporting evidence? **(12b)**
a. Learning English is difficult for immigrants.
b. The farm in Indiera was poor.
c. School in Puerto Rico was more informal than school in Chicago.
d. Immigrants have difficulty finding work in a new country.

_____ 8. We can characterize the author's feeling for her childhood
in Puerto Rico as **(12c)**
a. sad and resigned.
b. hopeful and optimistic.
c. depressed and bitter.
d. happy and romantic.

Connecting Ideas

1. Compare the immigrant experiences in this selection with
those in "Hearts of Sorrow" (pages 347–352). How are the
people's attitudes similar? How are they different?
2. Have you lived in two different places? Do your parents or
other relatives come from different parts of the country or
world? Have you visited relatives that live elsewhere? Compare the ways of life in the two different places and discuss
how that affects the feelings of people who live there.

Critical Thinking in Writing

1. Pretend that you are a newly arrived immigrant to the United
States and describe the place where you live. What about your
current living situation surprises you? pleases you? frightens
you? Write a few paragraphs to answer these questions.
2. Write a brief outline of the selection. **(2c)**

Vocabulary

1. Match the words in Column A with their correct meanings in
Column B. Use context clues as much as possible. (Paragraph
numbers from the selection are in parentheses.) **(3a)**

	A	B
_____	1. unbearably (1)	a. easily swallowed
		b. looseness
_____	2. slack (3)	c. under attack
		d. extreme happiness
_____	3. consolations (3)	e. suffocating
		f. painfully
_____	4. bristling (4)	g. comforts in time of pain
_____	5. besieged (4)	h. damp and chilly
		i. not to be tolerated
_____	6. dank (4)	j. angry

_____ 7. stifling (6)

_____ 8. excruciatingly (10)

_____ 9. exuberance (10)

_____ 10. palatable (10)

2. Match each numbered definition below with the word from the word list and then write the word in the blank spaces. When you finish, unscramble the letters in the circles to spell a key word in the selection. **(3)**

WORDS

barren	milestone
barrio	multitude
desolation	scraggly
intensity	tendrils
irreverent	vibrant

Ⓞ_ _ _ _ _ _ _ _   1. important achievement

_ _ _ _ Ⓞ _ _   2. lively; colorful

_ _ _ _ _ Ⓞ   3. without vegetation

_ _ _ _ _ _ _ Ⓞ   4. slender extensions of a plant stem

_ _ _ _ Ⓞ _   5. neighborhood of Spanish-speaking people

_ _ _ _ _ _ Ⓞ _ _ _   6. ruin; wasteland

Ⓞ_ _ _ _ _ _ _ _   7. great force or power

_ _ _ _ Ⓞ _ _ _   8. dirty

_ Ⓞ _ _ _ _ _ _ _   9. disrespectful

Ⓞ_ _ _ _ _ _ _ _   10. large number

Unscrambled word: _____

Putting Thoughts Together

1. The selections in this unit discuss different reasons for people immigrating to the U.S.; these reasons relate to the hopes and fears people had as they arrived. Describe and compare the motivations and feelings about immigration of the people in these selections.

2. The people in these selections had different experiences of immigration to the U.S. Describe and compare what they experienced and how they felt about it.

3. In the selections in this unit, the experience of family is very much tied to the experience of immigration — both the families left behind and the families they experience in this country. Describe and compare the role families take in these stories of immigration.

4. Based on their experiences, the people described in the selections in this unit have different attitudes toward the U.S. Compare the feelings of the different people about this country.

5. Tell the story of the arrival of some part of your family (or ancestors) in the U.S., how they came, what their hopes and fears were, what they experienced, how they wound up viewing this country. Evaluate the experience of your family in this country over the years.

Education
and Learning ——

My Unsentimental Tutee   *Laura Billings*

Letting in Light   *Patricia Raybon*

**They Treat Girls Differently,
Don't They?**   *Timothy Harper*

Model Minority   *Felicia R. Lee*

My Unsentimental Tutee

Laura Billings

The writer shares her experiences as a tutor for a Chinese woman who has an unusual perspective about her new country.

Prereading

Make a list of typical attitudes, feelings, and reactions that you associate with new immigrants. **(1a)**

Word Highlights

epidural   an anesthetic injected into the spine, often used to ease pain during childbirth

episiotomy   a surgical procedure to ease childbirth

Miracle Worker   a play about how Helen Keller, who was deaf, blind, and dumb, learned to speak and read with the help of a gifted teacher

Pollyanna   an overly optimistic person who helps solve everyone's problems by a positive and hopeful attitude

Tiananmen Square   a large, central square in Beijing, China, where gatherings are often held. In 1989 students gathered here to demand greater freedoms. After the students refused to leave, government troops cleared the square, killing many.

unsentimental   not overly emotional or guided by strong emotion over reason

---

A literacy tutor is taught to connect with adult students by pointing out common beliefs. So when I first met Renzhen, a 30-something Chinese woman, I told her, hand on heart, how stirred I was by the spirit of the 1989 Tiananmen Square uprising. She cocked her head at me and blurted: "Why? That guy who fight the tank — he total crazy!" She then twirled an index finger around her temple, her way of saying

"Duh." Hardly a "Miracle Worker" moment. But it was typical of my experiences with Renzhen, a former university math instructor who came to the United States in 1991 believing (wrongly) that she would find a better teaching job. My reasons for becoming a tutor combined Pollyanna-ish social activism with too much free time. Her motivation was a more prosaic desire to pass the English-proficiency exam and a nagging suspicion that she was getting shortchanged in stores. After two years, our sessions have cured her of calling men "she," and I have been cured of something as well — my sometimes sentimental notions about what this country means to newcomers.

2   As a literacy volunteer, I'm often asked to interpret America for immigrant adults, to explain our confounding idioms, politics, bland customs, and television talk shows. Usually they're reverent about the United States and the salvation it can offer, but Renzhen remains unconvinced, an attitude I find as appealing as it is irritating.

3   "Who you want to win?" she asked just before the last Presidential election. I told her I was voting for Clinton. "You can vote?" she shrieked, astonished. I started to explain that, yes, every adult citizen enjoys this right, but she interrupted. "Choices aren't that different."

4   "Sure but ——."

5   "Sound like China," she said, dismissing democracy with a wave and a laugh.

6   In China, Renzhen and her husband held advanced degrees and lived in a comfortable apartment. Now they and their two children live in a one-bedroom with orange shag carpet and thin walls. Every day until her second child arrived, Renzhen put on a threadbare wool coat and shuffled off to her waitress job wearing a badge that said, "Hi, my name is JENNY." Once, I asked her a question from a lesson book: "How would a stranger describe you?"

7   "In China, as quality person," she answered. "If you look at me here, you think I'm poor."

8   Renzhen doesn't quite work as a victim, though. She's too prickly for that. She rails against Americans' materialism and then spends $25 for lipstick to secure the "bonus" mirrored compact. She's delighted to learn that her daughter's education is free and then outraged that American fifth graders don't study calculus. Recently I brought her a newspaper article about foreign-born professionals who are making the difficult adjustment

to life here. Instead of empathizing, she smiled sweetly and said: "Seem like there is too many Mexicans here. This I believe so."

9   Whether she will remain here is an open question. Her husband says it would be a loss of face to return to China. When Renzhen gets letters from friends and family back home, she lets them sit for months before she finally throws them out. "What do I say?" she asks me. "They say we are foolish leaving China. They are right."

10   She makes such comments with great cheer, shrugging lightly, but her thoughts sometimes weigh her down. Once, I spotted her struggling down the street with two heavy shopping bags, her permed black hair — an unfortunate result of her husband's suggestion that she try to look "Western" — kinking in the Portland mist. I shouted and ran after her for two full blocks before I got her attention.

11   "Oh, I am so far away," she said, startled. "Long ways."

12   Before Renzhen gave birth to her second child, we put aside the grammar books to focus on Basic American Patient with a vocabulary list that included "episiotomy" and "gimme the epidural!" We laughed over those lessons, Renzhen aping the hysterics of a delivering mother. We also had more serious discussions, about what she could expect for her child in this country, and what was expected of her — a Chinese woman about to be the mother of an American.

13   "Seems like I can't go back," she said one day. "Now I must be living an American." Was she scared? She whirled a finger by her temple. I didn't have to ask what that meant.   ❑

EXERCISES

Comprehension

_____ 1. The main idea of this selection is that **(5b)**
   a. literacy tutors have a special insight into the people they work with.
   b. Renzhen has learned much about America and the English language.
   c. Renzhen has an ironic view of her new life in America.
   d. Renzhen regrets moving to America.

_____ 2. This main idea is most directly stated in the **(5b)**
   a. title of the selection.
   b. first sentence of the selection.
   c. last sentence of the first paragraph.
   d. last paragraph of the selection.

3. Put a checkmark before each of the contrasts or comparisons that the selection makes. In the space after each item you have checked, write the number of the paragraph (or paragraphs) in which the comparison or contrast appears. **(7d)**

_____   a. shopping in China and shopping in the U.S. _____

_____   b. Renzhen's attitudes and her behavior _____.

_____   c. government in China and elections in the U.S. _____

_____   d. Renzhen's houses in China and in the U.S. _____

_____   e. tutors in America and tutors in China _____

_____   f. the motives of the tutor and the tutee _____

_____   g. the writer's notions about immigrant attitudes and the reality of Renzhen's ideas _____

_____   h. Renzhen's status in China and in the U.S. _____

_____   i. Mexicans in the U.S. and Chinese in the U.S. _____

4. Write *maj* before major details, *min* before minor details, or a minus sign (−) if it does not appear in the selection. **(6b)**

_____   a. Renzhen wore a badge with her name.

_____   b. Renzhen was a university math instructor in China.

_____   c. Renzhen's family now lives in a one-bedroom apartment.

_____   d. Renzhen's husband had an advanced degree from China.

_____   e. The tutor explains bland customs.

_____   f. American fifth graders don't study calculus.

_____   g. Renzhen buys products to get free gifts.

_____   h. Renzhen's daughter does well in math.

_____   i. Renzhen and the tutor live in Portland.

_____   j. Friends and family in China write that she was foolish to leave.

Reading and Critical Thinking

_____ 1. Comparing Renzhen's reports about her life in China and her life in the U.S., one can conclude that **(10)**
   a. life was better in China for everyone.
   b. her life was better in China than in the U.S.
   c. overall moving to the U.S. was the best thing for her children.
   d. she is a victim of a bad choice.

_____ 2. From the opening incident describing the tutor's and Renzhen's response to the Tiananmen Square uprising, we can infer that **(8)**
   a. Renzhen and her tutor communicated well.
   b. Renzhen is happy with the Chinese government.
   c. the tutor was totally unrealistic.
   d. Renzhen and her tutor have very different attitudes toward events.

_____ 3. From Renzhen's comments on Mexican immigrants, we can infer that **(8)**
   a. she has developed sympathy for others in a situation similar to hers.
   b. she sometimes does not connect her own experiences with the attitudes she expresses.
   c. she is not sympathetic to any other people.
   d. she thinks immigration is a bad idea and should be stopped before others make a mistake.

_____ 4. We can infer from Renzhen's hair style that she **(8)**
   a. has no sense of style.
   b. and her husband are trying to fit in the U.S.
   c. and her husband have no desire to fit in the U.S.
   d. and her husband are frustrated about their inability to fit in.

_____ 5. We can conclude from the joking about childbirth that Renzhen **(10)**
   a. doesn't take being a parent seriously.
   b. is terrified by giving birth.
   c. finds learning English funny.
   d. takes a realistic attitude toward life's pains.

_____ 6. We can generalize from the last paragraph that **(11)**
   a. children can influence parents' decisions about where to live.
   b. children have difficulty obtaining Chinese passports.
   c. China prevents people from returning once they leave.
   d. one can regret leaving a homeland.

_____ 7. We can infer from the last three sentences that **(8)**
   a. Renzhen was excited by her new commitment to America.
   b. Renzhen was fearful and anxious about her future in America.
   c. the U.S. was a wild and wacky place.
   d. children will make you a bit crazy.

       8. Put a checkmark before all the statements one can reasonably predict that Renzhen would support. **(10)**

_____   a. People should be given a realistic view of job opportunities before they immigrate.

_____   b. One should have the courage to stand up against unfair governments.

_____   c. Freedoms are more important than a comfortable life.

_____   d. A comfortable life is more important than freedoms.

_____   e. The United States offers more freedoms than other countries.

_____   f. America offers a high-quality education to its children.

_____   g. People should suffer the consequences of their choices.

_____   h. Children are an important commitment.

_____   i. Immigrants should be granted more support so that the U.S. can make best use of their talents.

_____   j. Life is hard and people must learn to take care of themselves.

9. Match each phrase in Column A to the writing technique listed in Column B. **(12c)**

A

_____ 1. "Hardly a 'Miracle Worker' moment."
_____ 2. "Pollyanna-ish social activism"
_____ 3. "Sound like China."
_____ 4. "Gimme the epidural!"
_____ 5. "She whirled a finger by her temple."

B

a. irony expressed by Renzhen
b. irony expressed by the writer
c. irony shared by the writer and Renzhen
d. self-ironic comment by the writer
e. self-irony by Renzhen

_____ 10. We can conclude that the tutor **(10)**
   a. has learned from Renzhen's realistic attitudes.
   b. finds Renzhen totally unrealistic.
   c. prefers to maintain idealism and avoid Renzhen's distrustful attitudes.
   d. has no sympathy for Renzhen's contradictory attitudes.

Connecting Ideas

1. This selection seems to present a very different role for a teacher or mentor from that presented in Patricia Raybon's essay, "Letting in Light" (pages 381–384). Compare how the selections characterize what the teacher teaches and what the teacher learns.
2. How would you characterize Renzhen's opinions? As a recent immigrant to this country, does she appreciate what it has to offer? Compare Renzhen's opinions about her former homeland and her new country to the opinions of an immigrant you know.

Critical Thinking in Writing

1. Write a paragraph commenting on and evaluating the opinions and attitudes expressed by the tutee described in this selection. How would you characterize Renzhen's attitude? What kind of reasoning and experiences do you think led her to the attitudes she expresses? How justified do you think she was in her thinking?
2. Following the model of this selection, describe a person you know who has unusual or complex attitudes and opinions that may have opened you up to a new point of view.

Vocabulary

For each word in Column A, write the letter of the best definition from Column B. (The number after each word refers to the paragraph in which it appears.) **(3)**

A

_____ 1. literacy (1)

_____ 2. cocked (1)

_____ 3. index (1)

_____ 4. motivation (1)

_____ 5. English-proficiency (1)

_____ 6. idioms (2)

_____ 7. reverent (2)

_____ 8. salvation (2)

_____ 9. prickly (8)

_____ 10. empathizing (8)

_____ 11. permed (10)

_____ 12. Basic American Patient (11)

B

a. worshipful
b. goal, what pushes a
   person to do something
c. adequate language skill
d. pointing; finger next to
   the thumb
e. set in a permanent wave
f. tilted
g. reading and writing
h. the language skills one
   needs to survive as a
   patient
i. phrases with special
   meanings
j. rescue
k. filled with sharp reactions
l. sensing someone else's
   feelings

Letting in Light

Patricia Raybon

This selection draws on the simple activity of window washing to explore family and racial values. Read this essay to understand the writer's feelings about her upbringing and the way she is raising her daughter. Can you think of an event in your life that symbolizes how you were raised and how you behave toward others?

Prereading

Try to remember an important incident that involved yourself and your mother, your father, or some other relative. Then free-write about how that incident makes you feel about yourself, your family, and your life. **[1a(3)]**

Word Highlights

disdain   disgust
glazed   covered with a shiny surface
resolute   refusing to yield
T-square   carpenter's tool

The windows were a gift or maybe a bribe — or maybe a bonus — for falling in love with such a dotty old house. The place was a wreck. A showoff, too. So it tried real hard to be more. But it lacked so much — good heat, stable floors, solid walls, enough space. A low interest rate.

2   But it had windows. More glass and bays and bows than people on a budget had a right to expect. And in unlikely places — like the window inside a bedroom closet, its only view a strawberry patch planted by the children next door.

3   None of it made sense. So we bought the place. We saved up and put some money down, then toasted the original builder — no doubt some brave and gentle carpenter, blessed with a flair for the grand gesture. A romantic with a T-square.

4   We were young then and struggling. Also, we are black. We

381

ILLUSTRATION BY VIVIENNE FLESHER/© 1993 *THE NEW YORK TIMES.*

looked with irony and awe at the task now before us. But we did not faint.

5   The time had come to wash windows.

6   Yes, I do windows. Like an amateur and a dabbler, perhaps, but the old-fashioned way — one pane at a time. It is the best way to pay back something so plain for its clear and silent gifts — the light of day, the glow of moon, hard rain, soft snow, dawn's early light.

7   The Romans called them *specularia.* They glazed their windows with translucent marble and shells. And thus the ancients let some light into their world.

8   In my own family, my maternal grandmother washed win-

dows — and floors and laundry and dishes and a lot of other things that needed cleaning — while doing day work for a rich, stylish redhead in her Southern hometown.

9   To feed her five children and keep them clothed and happy, to help them walk proudly and go to church and sing hymns and have some change in their pockets — and to warm and furnish the house her dead husband had built and added onto with his own hands — my grandmother went to work.

10   She and her third daughter, my mother, put on maids' uniforms and cooked and sewed and served a family that employed my grandmother until she was nearly 80. She called them Mister and Missus — yes, ma'am and yes, sir — although she was by many years their elder. They called her Laura. Her surname never crossed their lips.

11   But her daughter, my mother, took her earnings from the cooking and serving and window washing and clothes ironing and went to college, forging a life with a young husband — my father — that granted me, their daughter, a lifetime of relative comfort.

12   I owe these women everything.

13   They taught me hope and kindness and how to say thank you.

14   They taught me how to brew tea and pour it. They taught me how to iron creases and whiten linen and cut hair ribbon on the bias so it doesn't unravel. They taught me to carve fowl, make butter molds and cook a good cream sauce. They taught me "women's work" — secrets of home, they said, that now are looked on mostly with disdain: how to sweep, dust, polish and wax. How to mow, prune, scrub, scour and purify.

15   They taught me how to wash windows.

16   Not many women do anymore, of course. There's no time. Life has us all on the run. It's easier to call a "window man," quicker to pay and, in the bargain, forget about the secret that my mother and her mother learned many years before they finally taught it to me:

17   Washing windows clears the cobwebs from the corners. It's plain people's therapy, good for troubles and muddles and other consternations. It's real work, I venture — honest work — and it's a sound thing to pass on. Mother to daughter. Daughter to child. Woman to woman.

18   This is heresy, of course. Teaching a girl to wash windows

is now an act of bravery — or else defiance. If she's black, it's an act of denial, a gesture that dares history and heritage to make something of it.

19   But when my youngest was 5 or 6, I tempted fate and ancestry and I handed her a wooden bucket. Together we would wash the outdoor panes. The moment sits in my mind:

20   She works a low row. I work the top. Silently we toil, soaping and polishing, each at her own pace — the only sounds the squeak of glass, some noisy birds, our own breathing.

21   Then, quietly at first, this little girl begins to hum. It's a nonsense melody, created for the moment. Soft at first, soon it gets louder. And louder. Then a recognizable tune emerges. Then she is really singing. With every swish of the towel, she croons louder and higher in her little-girl voice with her little-girl song. "This little light of mine — I'm gonna let it shine! Oh, this little light of mine — I'm gonna let it shine!" So, of course, I join in. And the two of us serenade the glass and the sparrows and mostly each other. And too soon our work is done.

22   "That was fun," she says. She is innocent, of course, and does this work by choice, not by necessity. But she's not too young to look at truth and understand it. And her heart, if not her arm, is resolute and strong.

23   Those years have passed. And other houses and newer windows — and other "women's jobs" — have moved through my life. I have chopped and puréed and polished and glazed. Bleached and folded and stirred. I have sung lullabies.

24   I have also marched and fought and prayed and taught and testified. Women's work covers many bases.

25   But the tradition of one simple chore remains. I do it without apology.

26   Last week, I dipped the sponge into the pail and began the gentle bath — easing off the trace of wintry snows, of dust storms and dead, brown leaves, of too much sticky tape used to steady paper pumpkins and Christmas lights and crepe-paper bows from holidays now past. While I worked, the little girl — now 12 — found her way to the bucket, proving that her will and her voice are still up to the task, but mostly, I believe, to have some fun.

27   We are out of step, the two of us. She may not even know it. But we can carry a tune. The work is never done. The song is two-part harmony.   ❑

EXERCISES

Comprehension

_____ 1. The main idea in this selection is expressed in **(5b)**
   a. the first paragraph.
   b. the last paragraph.
   c. paragraph 2.
   d. many paragraphs.

2. Write the main idea of the selection in your own words. **(5b)**

_____

_____

_____

_____ 3. The writer's grandmother worked as a maid until **(6a)**
   a. she was nearly eighty.
   b. she couldn't work any longer.
   c. she was fired.
   d. all her children had grown up.

_____ 4. The writer was taught "women's work" by her **(6a)**
   a. grandmother.
   b. mother.
   c. grandmother and her mother.
   d. sister.

_____ 5. All of the following are reasons the writer gives for washing windows *except* **(6a)**
   a. it is therapy for troubles and muddles.
   b. it is real work.
   c. earning money for college.
   d. cleaning cobwebs out of the corners.

6. Write *maj* beside the major details and *min* beside the minor details. **(6b)**

_____   a. The house had a window inside a closet.

_____   b. The author's daughter started washing windows when she was five or six.

_____   c. The author showed her daughter how to wash windows because it was a way to teach her important values.

_____   d. "Women's work" has changed because women's roles have changed.

7. The essay mentions four people who washed windows. List them numerically in the order in which they are mentioned. **(7a)**

_____   a. the author's daughter

_____   b. the author's mother

_____   c. the author

_____   d. the author's grandmother

_____ 8. The writer has had a life of relative comfort because **(7e)**
a. she earned money washing windows.
b. her mother went to college.
c. her grandmother worked as a maid.
d. her father was wealthy.

Reading and Critical Thinking

_____ 1. We can infer that the writer **(8)**
a. is not aware of women's rights.
b. is not concerned about women's rights.
c. strongly favors women's rights.
d. strongly opposes women's rights.

_____ 2. We can infer that the writer is **(8)**
a. puzzled about racial stereotypes.
b. not concerned about racial stereotypes.
c. not involved with racial stereotypes.
d. teaching her daughter to ignore racial stereotypes.

_____ 3. Teaching a black girl to wash windows may be shocking to many people. Why? **(8)**
a. Young children should not have to do menial work.
b. Washing windows is a symbol of the menial jobs that black women have performed throughout history.

   c. Washing windows is poor preparation for the difficult housework a black woman has to do throughout her life.

   d. Young boys, not just young girls, should learn to wash windows so that they can help keep their homes clean.

_____ 4. In general the essay asserts that **(11)**

   a. writers should always wash windows.

   b. what people teach their children in turn will be taught to their children's children.

   c. parents should not teach their children simple chores.

   d. traditions are important.

_____ 5. The title of the selection, "Letting in Light," could refer to **(9, 11)**

   a. the fact that light comes into a house through the windows.

   b. the light of happiness that washing windows brings to the writer and her daughter.

   c. the writer's shedding new light on the complex issue of black identity.

   d. all of the above.

_____ 6. We can predict that the next time the writer asks her daughter to wash windows with her, her daughter will **(10)**

   a. join in willingly.

   b. insist that her brother join in as well.

   c. refuse to do the work because it is beneath her.

   d. ask for some spending money in return for doing the chore.

7. Place a checkmark beside the general statements with which the writer probably would agree. **(11)**

_____   a. Children learn to love their parents by working with them.

_____   b. Teaching values is as important as teaching good manners.

_____   c. Working together can be fun.

_____   d. Women should learn to do men's work.

8. Indicate with *F* or *O* which of the following statements are facts or opinions. **(12a)**

_____   a. The Romans called their windows *specularia.*

_____   b. The author's daughter enjoyed working with her mother.

_____   c. The author has lived in many houses.

_____   d. Washing windows is effective therapy.

9. For each of the following statements, write *E* if the statement is backed up by evidence or *N* if there is no supporting evidence. **(12b)**

_____   a. Working as a maid was a typical job for black women in the South.

_____   b. The writer owed her mother everything.

_____   c. Washing windows is good therapy.

_____   d. The writer and her family were young and struggling when they bought the house.

_____   e. The writer has had many "women's" jobs.

_____ 10. The tone of this selection is both philosophical and **(12c)**
       a. bitter.
       b. sentimental.
       c. angry.
       d. funny.

Connecting Ideas

1. This essay, like Timothy Harper's, "They Treat Girls Differently, Don't They?" (pages 391–396), discusses the role of parents in watching over and influencing the development of their children. Discuss the kinds of role these two selections present for parents in helping their children develop.
2. This essay presents as a matter of pride and value something

that many people look down on. Is there something that you have learned to take pride in that others may not appreciate? Describe what it is that you have learned to take pride in, what value you attach to it, and how you came to learn that value.

Critical Thinking in Writing

1. Write a paragraph about an incident in which your parents or some other relative taught you important values.
2. Write a paragraph or two to explain the meaning of these sentences from the selection: "Teaching a girl to wash windows is now an act of bravery — or else defiance. If she's black, it's an act of denial, a gesture that dares history and heritage to make something of it."

Vocabulary

Match the words in Column A with their correct meanings in Column B. **(3)**

A	B
_____ 1. consternations	a. denial of what is accepted as truth
_____ 2. defiance	b. solid
	c. allowing light in
_____ 3. forging	d. problems
	e. creating
_____ 4. heresy	f. rebellion
	g. confusions
_____ 5. stable	h. treatment
	i. diagonal cut on fabric
_____ 6. translucent	j. eccentric
_____ 7. dotty	
_____ 8. bias	
_____ 9. therapy	
_____ 10. muddles	

They Treat Girls Differently, Don't They?

Timothy Harper

Some research shows that even though girls are advancing further in education than they did previously, some teachers still favor boys in the classroom. This gender bias reflects life in society, but it also may prevent girls from gaining confidence and competence. The writer believes, however, that parents can help their daughters in and out of the classroom.

Prereading

Skim the selection to find the following facts. (1b)

1. What did a study by the American Association of University Women find?

2. According to Ellen Silber, are teachers aware they call on boys more?

3. What percentage of current law and medical students are women? How does that compare to the situation in 1970?

4. How many suggestions of how many types are offered for parents?

5. For whom else does the writer provide suggestions?

Word Highlights

attention-deficit learning disorders   difficulties in maintaining concentration that interfere with schooling

calculus   a form of advanced mathematics

hierarchies   organized levels of people with different power

mentors   people who act as guides or counselors

ream   a very large amount

Boys get more attention in the classroom than girls. There's no doubt about it. Reams of studies show that teachers, from preschool to grad school, interact more with males than with females. Especially in grade school, boys are called on more often. They get more constructive criticism, and they're asked more challenging questions.

2   A landmark study by the American Association of University Women found that when science teachers need help with demonstrations in front of their classes, four out of five times they call on a boy rather than a girl.

3   Those are the facts. What those facts mean, however, is not so clear. Some parents and teachers believe studies on classroom gender bias are misleading. Others believe they show that girls are being shortchanged by American education.

4   An important point to keep in mind from the outset is that gender bias does not start in school. What happens in classrooms, good or bad, is a reflection of society at large. All of us — parents, teachers, administrators, and students — have our baggage. Indeed, one of the remarkable aspects of the debate over classroom gender bias is the reluctance to blame anyone, especially teachers. Even the most vocal critics say teachers typically are not aware of the ways they show their own bias against girls; when it is pointed out, teachers are surprised and consciously try to treat boys and girls more equally.

5   While it is not within the scope of this article to suggest how to remedy a centuries-old cultural bias that generally favors males over females — in school, in the family, and on the job — there are some things that educators, students, and parents can do to counteract gender bias in the classroom.

6   Critics warn that classroom gender bias hurts girls in very real ways. They argue that when girls enter kindergarten they are just as outgoing as boys, and almost as interested in math and science. By the end of high school, according to studies, girls are more likely to suffer from low self-esteem and less likely to be taking courses in chemistry, calculus, computers, and other science and technology fields that hold such great growth potential in the 21st century. Boys gain confidence and competence; girls lose it. Boys learn that school is a place of opportunity. Girls are taught that it is a place of constraints.

7   "I don't think teachers mean for it to happen — they don't realize there's gender bias in their own classrooms," observes Ellen Silber, director of the Institute for the Education of Women and Girls at Marymount College in Tarrytown, New York. Silber, whose research and consulting include teacher training and parent awareness programs, says teachers who are videotaped are surprised to see that they call on boys more often. "But blame is not the point," she notes. "Girls are being conditioned to think that boys are smarter, or that boys need more attention because they're pains in the neck."

8   Indeed, blame is not the issue for those of us who have young children. We don't want to raise boys who think they are automatically in charge, whether in the classroom today or in the boardroom tomorrow. And we don't want to raise daughters who think they must wait to speak until all the boys are finished, or who might have been great scientists if only physics and chemistry hadn't been "boy subjects."

9   David Sadker, a professor of education at American University, did a number of studies with his late wife, Myra, showing gender bias to be deep-rooted in American classrooms. Their studies show that from grade school through graduate school, boys are more likely to shout out answers or otherwise make comments without being called on. Typically, teachers answered the boys who called out, but chastised the girls who called out with comments such as "Please raise your hand if you want to speak." Today, Sadker frets that a cure for cancer might be "locked in the mind" of a girl who never pursued the kind of science education that would unlock it.

10   Not everyone, of course, agrees that classroom gender bias is such a big problem. Diane Ravitch, the former assistant secretary of the U.S. Department of Education and now a research

scholar at New York University, says we should instead be celebrating "the successful conquest of American education by girls and women." In 1970, she says, women accounted for barely 40 percent of the college students in the United States; today it's 55 percent. Women earned less than 10 percent of the law and medical degrees awarded in 1970; today, they make up nearly 50 percent of the enrollment in U.S. law schools and colleges of medicine.

11   Yes, boys get more attention than girls, but some say that doesn't mean teachers are biased against girls. David Murray, director of research for the Washington-based Statistical Assessment Service, a private, nonprofit think tank that tries to debunk science myths, says, "The reality is that boys are far more disruptive, and what they get is more negative attention."

12   He says boys are more often found at the extremes of all types of performance, good and bad. Boys score higher on the Scholastic Aptitude Test and win more National Merit honors but also are more likely to have learning disabilities, drug or alcohol problems, and trouble with the law. Girls get better grades, are less likely to drop out of high school, and are more likely to go to college and get a degree.

13   Pat O'Reilly, professor of education in the field of developmental psychology and head of educational studies at the University of Cincinnati, agrees that many teachers call on boys more — because they have shorter attention spans, and the teachers are trying to keep them involved and interested. (Boys are also three times as likely to receive a diagnosis of attention-deficit learning disorders.) "How does this affect girls? They feel less involved and sometimes feel left out," says O'Reilly. "One of the ways we plan to deal with this issue is to encourage teachers to stop calling on the first person who raises a hand, because boys are more apt to raise their hands — even if it means the embarrassment and risk of the wrong answer.

14   "Maybe boys are more confident than girls . . . we're not quite sure. Girls tend to think about an answer before they respond. We are training teachers to be more patient and to wait a minute before they call on a student. We need to make sure that girls become more confident and we need to teach boys to think before they speak."

15   For whatever reason, boys and girls seem to learn differently. Boys are more individualistic and competitive. They create hier-

archies and function well in them. Girls are less competitive and more willing to cooperate. Instead of creating hierarchies, they find ways to collaborate. For some educators and parents, the answer is to segregate boys and girls, though single-sex schools or classes may not be constitutional under recent court rulings.

16   Legal or not, I wouldn't want my daughter to attend special single-sex science classes. What message will that send her about boys? And I wouldn't want my son to be left in a classroom of boys. Is that going to teach him to empathize with girls? I want my daughter to be able to compete with the boys, and my son to be able to collaborate with the girls. The easy answer, of course, is for us to make education better for everybody. But how?

17   From assorted experts and studies, here is a list of recommendations for parents and teachers concerned about gender bias in the classroom.

Parents, at Home:

18   • Ask your daughter (and son) to draw a picture of a scientist. If she (or he) draws a man — most do — talk about how more and more girls are doing well in science studies and growing up to become scientists, too.

19   • Listen to your daughter. Girls' voices are naturally softer and girls are often less aggressive about speaking up, so you may have to draw her out. Don't criticize. She should know that her thoughts, feelings, opinions, and experiences are valuable both to you and to herself.

20   • Encourage your daughter not to limit herself academically. Find mentors — older girls or women within or outside your family — whose academic and career achievements can serve as role models, and who are willing to talk to your daughter about their experiences and views.

21   • Play sports and engage in other physical activities, such as hiking or cycling, with your daughter. Encourage her to participate in sports — organized community or school teams and neighborhood pickup or playground games. If you put up a hoop for her in the driveway, she'll probably go out and shoot baskets.

22   • Encourage your daughter to keep a journal or diary, and to write and talk about her experiences and reactions to events large and small. Ask her for her opinion and for an explanation or defense of her point of view.

23   • If your daughter thinks a teacher is being unfair, in terms of calling on boys or anything else, encourage her to speak to the teacher. Many kids are too uneasy to do this, but many teachers are too busy to notice slights — real or imagined — unless a student speaks up.

24   • Criticize the media. Talk about the way women are portrayed on television and radio and in movies, magazines, newspapers, and elsewhere. Why did that character do or say that? Is anyone really that silly? What would you have done?

Parents, at School:

25   • Talk to teachers. Let them know you're concerned about the issue of gender bias. Ask whether your daughter speaks up in class. How does she respond to teachers' questions? Does she initiate discussions and talk about what she thinks?

26   • Ask teachers what they think of your daughter. If they tend to use words such as "kind," "nice," "quiet," and "conscientious," let teachers know you're just as interested in your daughter's acquiring skills and developing talents as you are in her being a "good girl."

27   • Visit the classroom for an hour or two. Keep track of examples of competitive and collaborative learning and combinations of the two. Count the times teachers address boys vs. girls: responding to them when they call out, answering questions, calling on them, asking them easy or tough questions.

28   • Grade the teachers' comments: How much of what they say is disciplinary? Is the criticism constructive? Are the questions complex and challenging? Is the praise for girls more about being nice and getting work in on time? Is praise for boys more about initiative and ideas? Are boys rewarded for calling out while girls are reprimanded?

29   • Talk to other parents. Compare notes, share concerns. Groups of parents are more likely to get a positive reaction, whether it's a teacher's promise to be more aware of gender bias or a principal's agreement to call a meeting or have a program on gender bias.

Teachers:

30   • Visit each other's classrooms, and talk about gender bias. Keep track of how other teachers relate to boys and girls, respectively. Record each other, either on audio- or videotape, and then go back and analyze the tapes.

31   • Don't always call on the first student to call out or raise a hand.

32   • Make sure to call on the quiet people, boys or girls, even if they don't raise their hands.

33   • Recruit role models from the community, both men and women, willing to come to the classroom and talk about their school and work experiences.

34   • Mix lectures and ask-and-answer reviews with exercises where students work in teams, collaborating instead of competing. Make sure different kids are appointed as the leaders for different team exercises and take turns speaking for the group.

35   • Give students a chance to speak to you privately about concerns they may not want to raise in front of the whole class.   ❏

EXERCISES

Comprehension

_____ 1. Which of the following sentences from the selection best expresses the main idea? **(5)**
   a. "Boys get more attention in the classroom than girls."
   b. "An important point to keep in mind from the outset is that gender bias does not start in school."
   c. "Critics warn that classroom gender bias hurts girls in very real ways."
   d. "I want my daughter to be able to compete with the boys, and my son to be able to collaborate with the girls."

_____ 2. How often do science teachers call on girls to assist with class demonstrations? **(6a)**
   a. four times out of five
   b. hardly ever
   c. half the time
   d. one time out of five

_____ 3. Boys are no more outgoing than girls **(6a)**
   a. when they aren't called on.
   b. in high school.
   c. at the beginning of kindergarten.
   d. in math and science classes.

_____ 4. In high school, girls take fewer courses than boys in **(6a)**
   a. chemistry, calculus, and computers.
   b. English and history.
   c. self esteem.
   d. test-taking and study schools.

5. Put *maj* next to major details and *min* next to minor details. Put a minus sign (−) next to statements that do not appear in the selection. **(6b)**

_____ a. David Sadker collaborated with his late wife, Myra, on their research.

_____ b. Boys in high school take more classes than girls in science, math, and technology.

_____ c. Marymount College in Tarrytown, New York, has an Institute for the Education of Women and Girls.

_____ d. Teachers interact more with males than with females.

_____ e. Videotaped teachers are surprised to see that they call on boys more than girls.

_____ f. Boys are more likely to go to college and get a degree.

_____ g. Girls are praised more often than boys for their neatness.

_____ h. Teachers are aware that they rely on boys more than girls for demonstrations.

_____ i. Girls are one-third as likely as boys to be diagnosed with attention-deficit learning disorders.

_____ j. Diane Ravitch is former assistant secretary of the U.S. Department of Education.

_____ k. Girls do better in single-sex math classes.

_____ l. Boys are found at the extremes of all types of behavior.

_____ 6. The main idea of the suggestions listed under the heading "Parents, at School" is that **(5b)**
   a. teachers may have limited views of students and may not bring out the most in young girls.
   b. parents should gain and share information about how the classroom works for their children.
   c. parents need to work together to get a positive response from teachers and principals.
   d. girls are often rewarded for being quiet, hard-working, good girls rather than for their initiative and creativity.

_____ 7. The main idea of the suggestions for teachers may be summed up as **(5b)**
   a. keep students active and thinking.
   b. use collaborative techniques wherever possible.
   c. reflect on what you do and find new techniques to help students speak out and participate.
   d. criticize your colleagues to make sure they do not engage in gender bias and reward overcompetitive masculine behavior.

_____ 8. The writer organizes the first part of the selection (through paragraph 17) according to **(7)**
   a. a series of claims backed by experts and studies.
   b. a time-order series of incidents that present cause and effect.
   c. a series of questions that are answered in order of importance.
   d. a series of proposals for changing the way children are treated in the classroom.

_____ 9. The writer organizes the latter part of the selection according to **(7)**
   a. lists of questions that parents should ask teachers and children.
   b. a series of claims about the best way to improve education for girls.
   c. lists of activities for girls to improve their self-esteem.
   d. lists of suggestions for parents and teachers.

_____ 10. Throughout the selection, what two issues does the writer regularly compare and contrast? **(7d)**
   a. the intelligence of boys versus the intelligence of girls
   b. the nature of girls versus the nature of boys
   c. the experience of girls in school versus the experience of boys
   d. the attitude of parents toward girls versus the attitude of teachers toward boys

Reading and Critical Thinking

1. Put a checkmark in front of each generalization we can appropriately make from the lists of suggestions at the end of the selection. **(11)**

_____ a. Girls will gain from having mentors and role models.

_____ b. Single-sex classrooms will help girls gain confidence.

_____ c. Competitive activities tend to favor boys.

_____ d. Girls could use encouragement to speak up and express their opinions.

_____ e. Students, especially girls, need opportunities to express their concerns to teachers in private.

_____ f. Parents should trust teachers' words about what goes on in class.

_____ g. Boys need help in learning how to collaborate.

_____ h. Teachers should encourage girls to call out in class.

_____ i. Sports and other activities can help build confidence.

_____ j. Quiet students need to be made more competitive and aggressive.

_____ k. Parents should work with teachers and other parents.

_____ l. Girls will gain by learning to be critical of what happens in class and in the media.

2. Match each opinion listed in Column A with the person ex-
    pressing the opinion listed in Column B. You can use names
    in Column B more than once. **(12a)**

A   *B*

_____ 1. A single-sex class will not help boys   a. Pat O'Reilly
               learn to empathize with girls.   b. critics
_____ 2. A cure for cancer may be "locked in   c. Ellen Silber
               the mind" of a girl.   d. David Murray
_____ 3. Females have successfully conquered   e. Tim Harper
               American education.   f. Diane Ravitch
_____ 4. Teachers call on boys more often be-   g. David Sadker
               cause boys have shorter attention
               spans.
_____ 5. Boys function well in hierarchies.

_____ 6. Boys gain confidence and competence.

_____ 7. Girls are conditioned to think boys
               are smarter.
_____ 8. Girls tend to think before answering a
               question.
_____ 9. Gender bias is a reflection of society
               at large.
_____ 10. Boys get more negative attention.

_____ 11. Girls learn that school is a place of
               constraints.
_____ 12. Teachers don't intend their classes to
               favor boys.
_____ 13. We don't want our daughters to learn
               they must wait to speak until the
               boys are finished.

_____ 3. The writer includes the opinions of Diane Ravitch and David
               Murray to show that **(12)**
               a. all experts agree with him.
               b. girls really do not have such a difficult time in school.
               c. boys have their troubles, too.
               d. not all experts agree that schools favor boys.

_____ 4. From the comments of Pat O'Reilly (paragraphs 13 and 14), we can infer that the reason teachers call on boys more often than girls is related to **(8)**
   a. the fact that boys are more frequently diagnosed with attention-deficit learning disorders.
   b. the girls' feelings of being not involved and left out.
   c. teachers' patience.
   d. embarrassment that occurs when the wrong answer is given.

_____ 5. From the comments of Pat O'Reilly, we can conclude that boys being called on more often causes **(10)**
   a. boys to be more frequently diagnosed with attention-deficit learning disorders.
   b. the girls' feelings of being not involved and left out.
   c. teachers' patience.
   d. embarrassment that occurs when the wrong answer is given.

_____ 6. We can conclude that David Murray (in paragraphs 11 and 12) and Pat O'Reilly **(10, 12a)**
   a. agree on all points.
   b. agree that boys are called on more, but disagree on the causes and the consequences.
   c. agree that boys are called on more and on some of the causes, but disagree on other causes and on the consequences.
   d. disagree on all points.

7. Put a plus sign (+) in front of the experts with whom we can conclude that the writer largely agrees and a minus sign (−) in front of those with whom he largely disagrees. **(10)**

_____   a. Ellen Silber

_____   b. David Sadker

_____   c. Diane Ravitch

_____   d. David Murray

_____   e. Pat O'Reilly

_____ 8. The writer addresses the essay to **(12c)**
  a. boys and girls in school.
  b. teachers only.
  c. parents only.
  d. parents and teachers.

_____ 9. The writer includes advice at the end of the article in order to **(12c)**
  a. present scientific results of studies.
  b. get readers upset at the current situation.
  c. develop readers' critical awareness of gender bias.
  d. provide practical ideas for action by readers.

Connecting Ideas

1. Compare how this selection and Felicia Lee's "Model Minority" (pages 405–410) present the effect of people's expectations on how students respond to schools and learning.
2. How does the writer's views of the different experiences of boys and girls in school compare with your own observations and experiences? Discuss whether you think girls are treated differently in class and, if so, what the consequences are.

Critical Thinking in Writing

1. The writer of this selection assumes that parents have a responsibility for education and should involve themselves in their children's learning, in what happens in the classroom, and in how teachers relate to their children. Do you agree? Or, do you think parents should let their children cope with school in their own way? What do you base your opinion on? Write a paragraph presenting your view of the role parents should take in their children's schooling.
2. This selection presents Diane Ravitch's view that women have succeeded in schools and the battle for women's equality in school is essentially over. However, the writer of the selection seems to hold the opposite opinion and argues for further change. Who do you think is correct? Write a paragraph or two arguing for the view you support.

Vocabulary

Using word part clues and context clues from the selection, determine the meanings of the words in italics. **(3a, b)**

_____ 1. "teachers *interact* more with males than with females"
a. interpret
b. listen to
c. talk and listen to
d. question

_____ 2. "more *constructive* criticism"
a. creating buildings
b. helpful
c. collaborative
d. truthful

_____ 3. "the *debate* over classroom gender bias"
a. agreement
b. argument
c. policy
d. question

_____ 4. "the debate over classroom *gender* bias"
a. sex-related roles
b. consistent
c. kind or type
d. discrimination

_____ 5. "the debate over classroom gender *bias*"
a. choice
b. favoritism
c. ideas
d. learning

_____ 6. "a place of *constraints*"
a. limitations
b. stress
c. delays
d. confusion

_____ 7. "*chastised* the girls who called out"
a. ran after
b. severely punished
c. criticized
d. talked to

_____ 8. "find ways to *collaborate*"
   a. talk
   b. struggle
   c. agree
   d. work together

_____ 9. "teach him to *empathize* with girls"
   a. cooperate
   b. compete
   c. understand the feelings
   d. tolerate

_____ 10. "words such as 'kind,' 'nice,' 'quiet,' and *'conscientious'*"
   a. happy
   b. hard-working
   c. pleasing
   d. aware

_____ 11. "How much of what they say is *disciplinary*?"
   a. supporting learning
   b. keeping order
   c. raising difficult questions
   d. unoriginal and boring

_____ 12. "Is praise for boys more about *initiative* and ideas?"
   a. winning in difficult circumstances
   b. a habit of questioning authority
   c. ability to carry out projects
   d. finding ways to please people

_____ 13. "Are boys rewarded for calling out while girls are *repri-manded*?"
   a. praised
   b. asked again
   c. not called on
   d. disapproved of

Model Minority

Felicia R. Lee

This reading examines the commonly held view that Asian schoolchildren are super students who effortlessly excel in all their classes, especially math and science. It shows how even positive stereotyping sometimes puts pressure on people to live up to false expectations.

Prereading

Freewrite about what you think typical Asian students are like. [1a(3)]

Word Highlights

advocacy   arguing in favor of something
cliques   small ingroups
docile   peaceful; tame
émigrés   people who have left their homeland permanently
harassment   continual annoyance
quotas   fixed numbers of people or things
schizophrenic   someone suffering from a mental illness
stoicism   a philosophy in which the ideal is to rise above
           both pleasure and pain and to accept all
           situations calmly

Z he Zeng, an 18-year-old junior at Seward Park High School in lower Manhattan, translates the term "model minority" to mean that Asian-Americans are terrific in math and science. Mr. Zeng is terrific in math and science, but he insists that his life is no model for anyone.

2   "My parents give a lot of pressure on me," said Mr. Zeng, who recently came to New York from Canton with his parents and older brother. He has found it hard to learn English and make friends at the large, fast-paced school. And since he is the only family member who speaks English, he is responsible for paying bills and handling the family's interactions with the English-speaking world.

3   "They work hard for me," he said, "so I have to work hard for them."

4   As New York's Asian population swells, and with many of the new immigrants coming from poorer, less-educated families, more and more Asian students are stumbling under the burden of earlier émigrés' success — the myth of the model minority, the docile whiz kid with one foot already in the Ivy League. Even as they face the cultural dislocations shared by all immigrants, they must struggle with the inflated expectations of teachers and parents and resentment from some non-Asian classmates.

5   Some students, like Mr. Zeng, do seem to fit the academic stereotype. Many others are simply average students with average problems. But, in the view of educators and a recent Board of Education report, all are more or less victims of myth.

6   "We have a significant population of Chinese kids who are not doing well," said Archer W. Dong, principal of Dr. Sun Yat Sen Junior High School near Chinatown, which is 83 percent Chinese. "But I still deal with educators who tell me how great the Asian kids are. It puts an extra burden on the kid who just wants to be a normal kid."

7   **The Dropout Rate Rises**   Perhaps the starkest evidence of the pressures these students face is the dropout rate among Asian-American students, which has risen to 15.2 percent, from 12.6 percent, in just one year, though it remains well below the 30 percent rate for the entire school system. In all, there are about 68,000 Asians in the city's schools, a little more than 7 percent of the student population.

8   Behind these figures, the Board of Education panel said, lies a contrary mechanism of assumed success and frequent failure. While teachers expect talent in math and science, they often overlook quiet Asian-American students who are in trouble academically.

9   The report also said that Asian students frequently face hostility from non-Asians who resent their perceived success. And though New York's Asian population is overwhelmingly Chinese, this resentment is fed by a feeling in society that the Japanese are usurping America's position as a world economic power. Some educators said that because they are often smaller and quieter, Asian students seem to be easy targets for harassment.

10   Teresa Ying Hsu, executive director of an advocacy group

called Asian-American Communications and a member of the board panel, described what she called a typical exchange at a New York City school. One student might say, "You think you're so smart," she said, then "someone would hit a kid from behind and they would turn around and everyone would laugh."

11   Since Asian cultures dictate stoicism, she explained, students in many cases do not openly fight back against harassment or complain about academic pressures. But though they tend to keep their pain hidden, she said, it often is expressed in ailments like headaches or stomach troubles.

12   **"Acutely Sensitive"**   "We have a group of youngsters who are immigrants who are acutely sensitive to things other students take in stride, like a door slamming in their face," said John Rodgers, principal of Norman Thomas High School in Manhattan.

13   Norman Thomas, whose student body is about 3 percent Asian, had two recent incidents in which Chinese students were attacked by non-Asian students. The attackers were suspended.

14   But tensions escalated after a group of 30 Chinese parents demanded that the principal, John Rodgers, increase security, and rumors spread that "gangs of blacks" were attacking Chinese. Both incidents, however, were one-on-one conflicts and neither attacker was black. In some cases, Mr. Rodgers said, Chinese students say they are attacked by blacks but that they cannot identify their attackers because all blacks look alike to them.

15   In response to the parents' concerns, Mr. Rodgers said, he increased security and brought in a speaker on cross-cultural conflict.

16   Traditionally, Asian parents have not been that outspoken, educators say. While they often place enormous pressures on their children to do well, most Asian parents tend not to get involved with the schools.

17   Lisa Chang, a 17-year-old senior at Seward Park — which is 48 percent Asian — recalled being one of six Asians at a predominantly black intermediate school.

18   "Inside the school was no big deal," she said. "I was in special classes and everyone was smart. Then I remember one day being outside in the snow and this big black boy pushed me. He called me Chink.

19   "Then, at home, my parents didn't want me to dress a certain way, to listen to heavy metal music," Ms. Chang said. When she

told her dermatologist that she liked rock and roll, the doctor accused her of "acting like a Caucasian."

20   Ms. Chang and other students say there are two routes some Asian students take: they form cliques with other Asians or they play down their culture and even their intelligence in hopes of fitting in.

21   **Wedged Between Two Cultures**   Most Asian students are acutely aware of being wedged between two cultures. They say their parents want them to compete successfully with Americans but not become too American — they frown on dating and hard-rock music. There is also peer pressure not to completely assimilate. A traitor is a "banana" — yellow on the outside, white on the inside.

22   There is anger, too, over the perception that they are nerdy bookworms and easy targets for bullies.

23   "A lot of kids are average; they are not what the myth says," said Doris Liang, 17, a junior at Seward Park. "In math, I'm only an average student and I have to work really hard."

24   Ms. Liang said she sometimes envies the school's Hispanic students.

25   **"Not Make Any Mistakes"**   "The Hispanic kids, in a way they are more open," she said. "They're not afraid to bring their dates home. If you're Chinese and you bring your date home they ask a lot of questions. My parents only went to junior high school in China, so when we got here they wanted us to do well in school."

26   Nicole Tran, a 15-year-old senior who spent the early part of her life in Oregon, said she believes her generation will be far more assertive.

27   "We are the minority minority," said Ms. Tran. "We are moving too fast for them," she said of the dominant white culture.

28   Dr. Jerry Chin-Li Huang, a Seward Park guidance counselor, said he believes that Asians in New York are in part experiencing the cultural transformations common to all immigrants.

29   He notes that more of the new Asian immigrants — whose numbers in New York have swelled 35 to 50 percent in the past five years to about 400,000 — are coming from smaller towns and poorer, less educated families.

30   It was the early waves of educated, middle-class Asian immi-

"A lot of kids are average, they are not what the myth says," Doris Liang, second from the front, said of Asian students. She is shown in her American Studies class at Seward Park High School in Manhattan.   © 1990 EDDIE HAUSNER/*The New York Times*

grants whose children became the model minority, Dr. Huang said. Many of the students he sees have problems.

31   For one thing, Dr. Huang said many Asian parents are reluctant to admit that their children need help, even in severe cases. He said he had a schizophrenic Chinese student who began constantly wearing a coat, even on the hottest summer days. The parents were of little help.

32   "I have other children who run away from home because of the pressures," said Dr. Huang. "I had two sisters who had to go to school, then work in the factories, sewing. Their parents could not speak English so they were helping them with the bills. The girls said they barely had time to sleep."

33   Dr. Huang said many non-Asian teachers come to him for his insights because they have few Asian co-workers. Asians are

1.4 percent of all school counselors; 0.8 percent of all principals, and 1.4 percent of all teachers in New York City.

34   Among its recommendations, the task force called for more Asian counselors and teachers.

35   People like Ms. Hsu, of Asian-American Communications, are optimistic that the situation for Asian students will improve as students and educators talk openly about it.

36   "I gave a workshop and I talked about the quotas, the Chinese exclusion act," said Ms. Hsu. "Two black girls came up to me. One said: 'You know, I always thought the Chinese kids were snooty. Now after hearing what you went through I feel you're my brothers and sisters.'" ❏

EXERCISES

Comprehension

_____ 1. The main idea of this selection is that **(5b)**
   a. all Asian-American students are whiz kids.
   b. Asian-American students may excel in math, but they get stomach aches as a result.
   c. despite the stereotype, Asian-American students face the same problems every student faces.
   d. newer groups of Asian-American students just aren't as smart as earlier immigrants, and they are having trouble living up to the myth.

_____ 2. The Asian-American students quoted in this article all live in **(6a)**
   a. California.
   b. Florida.
   c. Texas.
   d. New York.

_____ 3. The article says that in New York City, the proportion of Asian-American teachers is **(6a)**
   a. 14 percent.
   b. 1.4 percent.
   c. 0.14 percent.
   d. 0.014 percent.

_____ 4. The current dropout rate among Asian-American students is **(6a)**
   a. 11.4 percent.
   b. 12.6 percent.
   c. 15.2 percent.
   d. 30 percent.

_____ 5. What is the title of the report referred to in paragraphs 5, 8, and 9? **(6a)**
   a. "Report on Asian-American Students"
   b. "Board of Education Study on the Model Minority"
   c. "Asian-American Performance Report"
   d. No title is given.

_____ 6. Which of the following is *not* a finding of the report? **(6a)**
   a. All Asian-American students are more or less victims of the "model minority" myth.
   b. The number of Asian-American dropouts had risen dramatically in one year.
   c. Asian-Americans are docile whiz kids.
   d. Troubled Asian-American students often are overlooked.

_____ 7. New York's Asian-American population is overwhelmingly **(6a)**
   a. Japanese.
   b. Chinese.
   c. Korean.
   d. Vietnamese.

_____ 8. Asian-American students who listen to rock and roll, dress in Western styles, date, and downplay their culture are known as **(6a)**
   a. apples.
   b. bananas.
   c. cliques.
   d. dermatologists.

_____ 9. In the five years before this article was written, the number of Asians who immigrated to New York was **(6a)**
   a. about 400,000.
   b. more than 400,000.
   c. exactly 400,000.
   d. 35 to 50 percent.

_____ 10. The main idea of paragraph 5 is that **(5b)**
   a. all Asian-American students are victims of a myth.
   b. although some Asian-American students are only aver-
      age, Mr. Zeng is a genius.
   c. educators are trying to understand why Asian-American
      students are so much smarter than other people.
   d. most Asian-American students do fit the stereotype.

Reading and Critical Thinking

_____ 1. We can infer that for Asian-American students, the stereo-
       type "model minority" is **(8)**
   a. an unfair burden.
   b. an unrealistic goal.
   c. an unfulfilled dream.
   d. a myth.

_____ 2. The change in the dropout rate among Asian-American stu-
       dents suggests that **(8)**
   a. fewer Asian-American students drop out than Hispanic
      students.
   b. fewer Asian-Americans drop out now than in the past.
   c. more Asian-Americans drop out now than in the past.
   d. Asian-American students are trying hard to be average
      students.

_____ 3. The article suggests that Asian-Americans are resented by
       other groups because they **(8)**
   a. are smaller and quieter than other groups.
   b. are a small segment of the total population.
   c. do not fight back.
   d. are perceived to be successful.

    4. Put a *T* next to true statements reported in the article and
        an *F* next to false ones. **(12a)**

_____   a. Chinese students at Norman Thomas High School were
              beaten by gangs of blacks.

_____   b. Some Chinese parents object to their children listening
              to hard rock.

_____   c. All Chinese students excel in math.

_____ d. Most Chinese students are nerdy bookworms.

_____ e. Few teachers or guidance counselors in New York City schools are Asian-Americans.

_____ 5. We can infer that Asian-American Communications encourages activities that **(8)**
a. benefit Asian-Americans only.
b. stimulate dialogue between groups.
c. protect Asian-Americans from gangs.
d. benefit Japanese companies.

_____ 6. A good generalization about New York City high schools based on the information in this article would be that they are **(11)**
a. tough and dangerous.
b. full of students from many different ethnic backgrounds.
c. not really concerned about Asian-American students.
d. out of touch with their students' problems.

_____ 7. We can infer that one reason Asian-American parents are not more outspoken about school affairs is that **(8)**
a. they do not love their children as much as other parents.
b. they are not familiar with American customs and language.
c. there really isn't a serious need for them to do anything.
d. American educators discourage them from becoming involved.

_____ 8. From Teresa Ying Hsu's statement that Asian-American students do not like to complain or fight back we can conclude that if those students did complain, **(10)**
a. they would get beaten up.
b. fewer Caucasians would like them.
c. they would have fewer stomach problems.
d. they would be too much like American students.

_____ 9. We can infer that one reason why Asian-American students envy Hispanic students is that **(8)**
a. most Chinese parents have only gone to junior high school.
b. many Chinese parents are not as tolerant about dating as are many Hispanic parents.

    c. Hispanic parents encourage their children to listen to hard rock more than Chinese parents do.

    d. Hispanic parents let their children do pretty much whatever they want outside of school.

_____ 10. Based on paragraph 30, which conclusion may we draw about the early waves of Asian immigrants? **(10)**

    a. They were better in every way.

    b. They were the model minority.

    c. As a group, their children performed better academically than more recent arrivals.

    d. Many of them were average.

11. Put an *F* next to each statement that is a fact according to the text and an *O* next to each opinion. **(12a)**

_____ a. Asian-American students are moving too fast for the Caucasian majority.

_____ b. Asians are experiencing the same cultural transformations as other groups.

_____ c. New Asian immigrants come from less affluent backgrounds.

_____ d. Today's Asian-American students will grow up to be more assertive.

_____ e. Asian-American parents are less likely to seek outside help for their children's problems.

_____ f. Few New York City school principals are Asian-Americans.

_____ g. Talking openly about problems will improve the Asian-American situation.

_____ h. The task force called for more Asian-American counselors and teachers.

_____ i. Many Asian-American students excel in school.

Connecting Ideas

Read "Wilshire Bus" on pages 479–483. What similarities and differences can you see among the Asian-American people described in these selections? Discuss your responses in groups and then present your findings to the class. **(13b, 13c)**

Critical Thinking in Writing

1. Analyze the issue of stereotyping as it relates to the Asian-American students portrayed in this selection.
2. Have you ever been the victim of unrealistic expectations and perceptions? Write approximately a page discussing an experience you had in which people expected too much of you.

Vocabulary

All of the following phrases are in this selection. Use context clues or a dictionary, if necessary, and write a definition of the words in italics in the spaces provided. **(3a)**

1. handling the family's *interactions*

    _____

2. face the cultural *dislocations*

    _____

3. *inflated* expectations of teachers

    _____

4. fit the academic *stereotype*

    _____

5. the *starkest* evidence

    _____

6. resent their *perceived* success

    _____

7. the Japanese are *usurping* America's position

   _____

8. Asian cultures *dictate* stoicism

   _____

9. tensions *escalated*

   _____

10. a *predominantly* black intermediate school

   _____

11. peer pressure not to completely *assimilate*

   _____

12. they are *nerdy bookworms*

   _____

   _____

13. her generation will be far more *assertive*

   _____

14. experiencing the cultural *transformations*

   _____

Putting Thoughts Together

1. In each of the selections in this unit, the attitudes of the learners are important to how they learn, who they become, and how they express themselves. Write a short essay about the importance of attitude in learning, using examples from these essays as well as from your own experience.
2. The writers in these selections identify what they consider important to learn. In a short essay compare what the writers see as these important lessons.
3. In these selections, learning is presented as being influenced by other people. Write several paragraphs describing how these selections show people influencing the learning of others.
4. In these selections, learning occurs both in schools and out. Compare the different kinds of learning, and then present your own views comparing school learning to out-of-school learning.
5. Write several paragraphs describing one thing that you considered worth learning, how you learned it, and how other people were (or were not) involved in helping you learn this.

Making Connections

My Father's
Black Pride   *Marcus Bleecker*

A Cafe Reopens: Lunch Returns
to the Prairie   *William E. Schmidt*

Say Something. They're Only
Children   *Lucie Prinz*

Like Mother,
Like Daughter   *Lloyd Gite*

My Father's Black Pride

Marcus Bleecker

We often think a father's influence shows best when a son grows up like his father. Here the son says his father influenced him most by encouraging him to grow up to be different. Yet underneath the two may be very much the same.

Prereading

Make a word map about the phrase "parent's influence." **(1a)**

Word Highlights

Afrocentric   considering history and culture from an African, rather than a European, point of view
epitomize   represent the essence
genre   a kind or type
panacea   an easily accomplished total cure

I am black. My mother is black. My father is white. This wouldn't necessarily be important, but we live in a country where conflict runs deep between blacks and whites. We live in a country where white male slaveholders casually disavowed the black children they had sired. We live in a country where the worst of human traits — laziness, violence, and irrationality — are seen as defining characteristics of those of African descent. This makes my being a mixed-race person whose ethnic identity is black somewhat complicated. There is a dissonance between who I say I am — a proud black man trying to do something positive with his life — and who society says I am. Yet I feel strong, and I embrace my black heritage. I've often reflected on how I learned to keep my positive self-image. The answer is, my white father.

2   With my olive-colored skin, hazel eyes, and curly hair, I've been taken for Hispanic or Middle Eastern. In fact, in addition to being black, I am Jewish. And my father taught me to be proud of that heritage as well. When bullies at school demanded,

"Are you black or white?" there was no confusion. When I ran home and asked my father, he said, "Tell them you are African-American." That was in the early 1970s and it was a term I wouldn't hear until the Afrocentric movement of the 1990s made if fashionable again.

3   It wasn't that my father wanted me to deny my Jewish roots, it's just that he knew we live in a society where my African heritage would define me socially. He didn't want me to seem ashamed of my black roots. My father knew that love and hopes for an ideal world in the distant future would be no panacea for the bigotry and small-mindedness I would encounter in my lifetime. He didn't want me, my brother, or my sister to be unprepared for racism.

4   And so, my father, a writer and avid reader, lined my shelves with books about black American culture, African culture, and Jewish culture. He encouraged me to think, to come up with my own ideas. A simple question posed to him was sure to be followed by his search for a book on the subject, with articles and additional materials to follow. In this way he gave me not only his opinion, but also the keys to how he arrived at that opinion. Knowing that I had those keys, too, he thought that I could evaluate his opinion and come up with my own. He encouraged me to determine what being black meant to me.

5   In the predominantly white suburb near Princeton, N.J., where I grew up, my father knew that I needed to know black men. So when I started playing drums at age 14, my father took me to jazz clubs. He encouraged me to talk to the musicians and get their autographs. This introduction led to my decision to become a professional musician, and also filled my home with a black male presence. Jazz was more than a genre of music; it instructed me in the cool posture of black men — Max Roach's shades, Miles Davis's scowl and his always stylish threads. It also instructed me in a kind of heroism. These men were geniuses who created America's only enduring art form despite its best efforts to stifle and ignore them.

6   My father also hired James, a black 16-year-old, who became my favorite baby sitter. My father gave me book knowledge and taught me to have an open mind; James showed me how to deal with people on a practical level. My father was gentle, but James taught me that as a black man, you have to be ungentle sometimes. You have to speak up for yourself. James

never let me walk away from a confrontation without speaking my mind.

7   During the summers, my parents sent me to my mother's family in Virginia. My cousins — especially Jeffrey, who is seven years older than I — helped me become a mature black man. Jeffrey taught me to treat women with respect, through his example as well as through his words. These are lessons my father had taught me also, but he hoped that my summer visits down South would reinforce those values by being transmitted by black men of my generation.

8   In college, I counseled children from mixed backgrounds. I could see the emptiness in some of the kids either who didn't have a black parent around — usually the father — or whose parents weren't in agreement about how much emphasis should be put on black culture. Often these children would grow up in a predominantly white environment with a negative view of their black fathers or of black culture in general. I realized how fortunate I was to have both parents and to have a father who encouraged me to develop as a black person while never making me feel that I was any less his son because of my blackness.

9   In many ways what my father taught me about manhood was not related to color. He taught me that, ultimately, I determined through my behavior what a black man is. My father taught me to be a gentle man, to use my mind and not my fists. He taught me the value of education and encouraged me to ask questions. My father exposed me to black men who lived up to these universal ideals of manhood, and thereby emphasized that blacks shared in that tradition. All these things have made me the man, the black man, I am today.

10   My father and I are now the closest we have ever been. Of course, there are race-related topics, things I feel, that he will never be able to understand. I know that there are probably people who meet my father and see just another white man. But I know that there are things he has learned from me and my brother that have given him an insight into black masculinity that most white men will never experience. In this way, we have taught each other. Our relationship epitomizes a reality that is so rarely seen — a black man and a white man who are not adversaries. Who are more than father and son. They are men who love each other very deeply. ❏

EXERCISES

Comprehension

_____ 1. The opening three sentences of the selection identify the writer as being of **(5a)**
   a. the same ethnicity as both his parents.
   b. mixed ethnicity.
   c. the same ethnicity of his father, but not his mother.
   d. the same ethnicity of his mother, but not his father.

_____ 2. In the opening paragraph, what does the writer state about the mix of ethnicity in his family? **(6a)**
   a. It is not a problem in any way.
   b. It is a problem because it causes conflict among members of the family.
   c. It is a problem because of the way society treats his ethnicity.
   d. It is a problem because his father feels cut off from his son's identity.

_____ 3. For the writer, the way this country has treated blacks means that **(6b)**
   a. he personally suffered discrimination.
   b. his father has mixed feelings about him.
   c. he has had to struggle with his own bad traits so as to avoid ethnic stereotypes.
   d. to maintain his pride he had to struggle against social beliefs about his ethnicity.

_____ 4. The main idea of the first paragraph is that **(5b)**
   a. the writer's father helped him solve the problems raised by his black ethnic identity.
   b. the father caused confusion in the son's ethnic identity.
   c. choosing a black ethnic identity is difficult because it creates problems for the individual.
   d. this country has a history of making people ashamed of being black.

_____ 5. The main idea of paragraph 2 is that **(5b)**
   a. the writer's appearance allowed him to adopt any one of several ethnic identities.

b. the writer's father always directed the son to an African-American identity.

c. the writer was first confused by the question of ethnic identity.

d. the writer is proud of his Jewish heritage.

_____ 6. The father's main reason for wanting his children to identify themselves as black is that he **(6a)**
   a. wanted them to have strength to confront racism.
   b. had mixed feelings about his own background.
   c. had hopes for an ideal world in the future.
   d. thought some identities were better than others.

_____ 7. Paragraphs 5 through 8 are organized according to **(7)**
   a. time order of the writer's growing up.
   b. comparison of the writer's experience to that of people who grew up with black fathers.
   c. a listing of the ways the writer learned about black culture.
   d. order of importance of the experience recounted.

8. Match the individual in Column A with the lesson the writer gained from each person listed in Column B. **(6a)**

A

_____ 1. Miles Davis

_____ 2. James

_____ 3. the father

_____ 4. Jeffrey

_____ 5. children he counseled

B

a. how to treat women with respect
b. a cool posture
c. how to speak up for yourself
d. the value of having parents who encouraged black pride
e. gentleness and an open mind

_____ 9. Of the following details, which is most important for this selection? **(6b)**
   a. The father read many books.
   b. The father took the son to jazz clubs when the boy started playing drums.
   c. The son became a jazz musician.
   d. Miles Davis had stylish threads.

Reading and Critical Thinking

After each of the following passages in paragraphs 1–5 from the selection is a series of possible inferences, predictions, conclusions, or generalizations that can draw from the sentence. Put a checkmark in front of those that can be appropriately supported by the quoted passage. **(8, 10, 11)**

1. "This makes my being a mixed-race person whose ethnic identity is black somewhat complicated." (paragraph 1)

   _____   a. Race and ethnic identity are not the same.

   _____   b. Race is an important aspect of identity.

   _____   c. Race is more important for how people treat you than how you feel about yourself.

   _____   d. Ethnic identity is to some extent a matter of personal choice.

   _____   e. People who have a black parent or grandparent ought to identify strongly with their blackness.

2. "When I ran home and asked my father, he said, 'Tell them you are African-American.' That was in the early 1970s and it was a term I wouldn't hear until the Afrocentric movement of the 1990s made it fashionable again." (paragraph 2)

   _____   a. The father didn't want his son to be aware of other parts of his heritage.

   _____   b. The father wanted his son to develop a strong identity to counter other people's prejudices.

   _____   c. The father's thinking was ahead of his time.

   _____   d. The father helped his son overcome uncertainties.

   _____   e. The writer would support students being taught an Afrocentric school curriculum.

3. "He encouraged me to determine what being black meant to me." (paragraph 4)

_____   a. The father did not understand what being black meant.

_____   b. The father would have been disappointed if the son did not show much interest in his black heritage.

_____   c. The writer rejected his father's view of his black heritage.

_____   d. The writer believes that it was good for him to explore his black identity.

_____   e. The writer always followed his father's advice and encouragement.

4. "These men were geniuses who created America's only enduring art form despite its best efforts to stifle and ignore them." (paragraph 5)

_____   a. Jazz grew from the efforts of artistic geniuses.

_____   b. Anyone who now enters jazz as a profession will be ignored and stifled.

_____   c. Musicians entered jazz because other forms of expression were not open to them.

_____   d. America does not always appreciate its artists.

_____   e. Some jazz musicians showed courage and conviction in pursuing their careers.

_____   f. The cool style of jazz musicians was a reaction to the difficulties they met.

5. "Of course, there are race-related topics, things I feel, that he will never be able to understand. I know that there are probably people who meet my father and see just another white man. But I know that there are things he has learned from me and my brother that have given him an insight into black masculinity that most white men will never experience." (paragraph 10)

_____   a. The writer is disappointed in his father's limitations of understanding of the writer's experience.

_____ b. The writer respects his father's understanding of the black
male experience.

_____ c. Few white men have a good understanding of what it
means to be a black man.

_____ d. The brother feels the same way as the writer about their
father.

_____ e. If you haven't experienced the difficulties caused by racial
attitudes, it is hard to understand race-related topics fully.

_____ f. People make judgments about others' probable racial attitudes.

6. Match each of the following opinions reported in this article
to the person who holds or expresses that opinion, by placing
the number of the appropriate person in Column B in front
of the statement in Column A. You may use individuals from
Column B more than once in your answers, and you need
not use all of them. **(12a)**

A   B

_____ 1. Black children need   a. the writer
        not be acknowledged.   b. the writer's father
_____ 2. Having the keys to   c. the writer's mother
        arriving at an opinion was as   d. white male slaveholders
        important as the opinion.   e. James
_____ 3. You sometimes have to be   f. children the writer
        ungentle.   counseled
_____ 4. In this country people of   g. Jeffrey
        African descent are defined
        as having the worst of
        human traits.
_____ 5. Hopes for an ideal world are
        not adequate for dealing
        with the world.
_____ 6. Black fathers are somehow
        lacking.
_____ 7. Black and white men often
        see each other as adversaries.

_____ 7. What can you conclude from the fact that the writer barely
        mentions his mother after the second sentence? **(8)**
        a. His mother had little influence on him.
        b. He is focusing on his father's influence.
        c. He does not relate well to women.
        d. He feels we need to emphasize the importance of fathers,
           since we all know how important mothers are.

8. Define each of the following figurative terms in your own
    words and explain the relation between the literal and the
    figurative meaning. **(9)**

    a. small-mindedness _____

    _____

    b. shades _____

    c. threads _____

    d. insight _____

Connecting Ideas

1. Compare and contrast the father-son relation described in
    this essay with the mother-daughter business relations de-
    scribed in "Like Mother, Like Daughter" (pages 452–457).
    Do you find either preferable? Why? How much growth and
    of what kind does each relation make possible for both par-
    ent and child? What forms of closeness and distance occur
    in each? What are the difficulties and rewards in each?
2. The views in this selection relate to some of the views of
    various "black pride" movements that have occurred over
    the last two centuries. With your classmates find out about
    one or more of these movements and compare the beliefs
    expressed in the movements with the beliefs expressed in the
    selection.

Critical Thinking in Writing

1. The writer makes at least two strong and controversial points
    in this selection — that it is more important for him to iden-
    tify with his black heritage than his Jewish heritage, and that

there is hostility and little mutual understanding between white and black males. Do you agree or disagree with either of these points (or any other related ones you might identify in the selection)? How would you evaluate the writer's stand and how would you argue for or against it? Write a paragraph or two to explain your position.

2. The writer identifies how his own character and identity were formed through contact with many individuals. Write an essay describing how individuals in your life influenced you to become the person you have become.

Vocabulary

Each of the following phrases comes from the text. Using context clues or the dictionary, choose the correct definition for the word in italics. **(3)**

_____ 1. "white male slaveholders casually *disavowed* the black children they had sired"
   a. abused and mistreated
   b. sold
   c. refused to raise with a proper education
   d. denied responsibility for

_____ 2. "a *dissonance* between who I say I am . . . and who society says I am"
   a. conflict
   b. intensity
   c. bridge
   d. question

_____ 3. "I've often *reflected* on how I learned"
   a. turned around
   b. thought about
   c. mirrored
   d. warned by lights

_____ 4. "for the *bigotry* and small-mindedness I would encounter"
   a. prejudice
   b. cheating
   c. difficulties
   d. thoughtlessness

_____ 5. "In the *predominantly* white suburb"
a. totally
b. partly
c. mostly
d. unthinkingly

_____ 6. "these *universal* ideals of manhood"
a. admirable
b. arguable
c. supported by many different people
d. shared by everyone

A Cafe Reopens: Lunch Returns to the Prairie

William E. Schmidt

This selection tells about the reopening of a cafe in a small farming town, but it tells even more about the changing way of life in rural America. Read to understand how the reopening of the cafe means much more to the people than just a place to buy lunch.

Prereading

List any words or phrases that come to your mind when you think of the prairie. **(1a)**

Word Highlights

circuit box   a metal box in which the main electrical line for a house or building is split into separate circuits; often contains fuses or circuit-breakers

concentrated   brought together in one spot

facade   front exterior of a building

horizon   where sky and earth appear to meet

plight   unhappy fate

polka   a lively dance done by a couple

progeny   offspring; children; descendants

refuge   safe place, away from difficulties

urban   relating to the city

W hen Louisburg's last cafe closed its doors in 1988, Keith Hansen and John Lund and the other men who farm the rich, rolling prairies of western Minnesota found themselves confronting a new and lonely challenge: lunch.

2 Not only had they lost their midday refuge in town, a place to gather over coffee and talk prices and politics, but they had no one back at the house to cook for them either.

3 "My wife's got a job now," Mr. Lund said. "So does Keith

Hansen's and Spence's and Elmo's. You want to keep your farm these days, you need two incomes."

4   **$4,500 to Reopen the Doors**   So a few months ago, Mr. Lund and his neighbors near Louisburg did what seemed natural. Nearly 50 of them got together, raised about $4,500 in contributions and reopened the little cafe that has served this remote town of 60 residents since the turn of the century.

5   For the farmers in Louisburg and other small towns across America, the cafe represents more than just a yearning for hearty home-cooked meals at noon, which the men say they do not have the time or the skills to make for themselves.

6   The campaign to reopen the cafe is a measure of the way in which the rhythms of rural life have changed.

7   More and more farm women now have jobs off the farm, forcing their husbands and their children to adapt to life in families in which both parents are wage-earners just as their counterparts have in the cities.

8   **Creation of the Railroad**   What has happened in Louisburg also reflects the concerns that are shared by residents of many small towns who have watched their communities wither away, bled by declining populations and failing businesses along Main Street.

9   "There is not much left here in Louisburg, but we're not ready just yet to let go of it," said Mr. Hansen, surveying the afternoon crowd in the cafe, where Emily Hansen, who is no relation, and her husband, Harold, were busy filling coffee cups and chatting up the customers. "At least we managed to bring a little bit of action back to town."

10   Like most places in the far reaches of western Minnesota and the Dakotas and Montana, Louisburg was a creation of the railroad, one of hundreds of small towns built at regular intervals along rail lines during the late 19th century so that nearby farmers could deliver a horse-drawn wagon of grain to the rail siding and be back home again by nightfall.

11   The grain elevator is still the town's biggest enterprise, and its most imposing structure. Its tin-sided towers dominate the long, low prairie horizon, and it is easily seen from several miles away.

12   But Louisburg, almost straight west from Minneapolis and close to the South Dakota border, is not on the railroad's main

Louisburg, like many prairie towns, was a railroad creation.
© THE NEW YORK TIMES

line. It is not even on some highway maps, since it is several miles from the nearest state road. Although the population nearly reached 100 in the 1950s, mostly the progeny of the Scandinavian and German farmers who first settled the area, it began slipping in the 1960s.

13   In the mid-1970s the farm implement dealership closed, and the town's only gasoline station shut its doors a decade later, along with the last grocery store. Except for two soda machines on the sidewalk in front of empty storefronts, the only retail commerce conducted along the main street these days is at the cafe.

14   Steve Padgitt, a sociologist at Iowa State University who specializes in rural areas, said residents of Louisburg were confronting a plight common to farm people throughout the region: as small communities and their populations have shrunk, services have been concentrated in fewer and more distant places.

15   "From the house where I was raised, I could always see the smoke from two or three other chimneys," Mr. Padgitt said. "Now the countryside has thinned out so that people have to drive 10 miles to get their mail, or 30 miles to find a restaurant."

16   When the old cafe closed in 1988, Mr. Lund said, it meant that he was traveling 10 miles to Madison, the closest town, to buy lunch. It was either that or make do alone at home. "You can only eat Campbell's soup for so long," said Mr. Lund, whose wife, Nancy, works as a bank teller in Appleton, about 12 miles to the east.

17   As farm profits have declined in recent years, particularly among the operators of small family farms, both husbands

and wives have been forced to seek work off the farm. A 1988 Agriculture Department survey estimated that 50 percent of all farm households had someone in the family who was working off the farm. As often as not it is the wife, as most farms are operated by men. In farm communities closest to urban areas, Mr. Padgitt said, some studies suggest that more than half the farm wives now hold jobs off the farm. In any case, sociologists say the number has been growing slowly but steadily over the years.

18 **Offer from Former Resident** The idea of reopening Louisburg's cafe took root last December, when Catherine Wiese, who grew up in Louisburg but now lives in California, came home to visit her father. Since the cafe had closed her father, Arnold, an elderly widower, had lost a place to go for meals and companionship. She said she would help buy the cafe if others in the town could help fix it up and find someone to run it.

19 Mr. Lund and the men down at the elevator started taking up a collection, asking for donations of $50 or $100. "The names on the list just kept coming and coming," Mr. Lund said. Some nearby banks and businesses contributed, too, and the local power company offered three months of free electricity.

20 Most of the work was done by Harlan Wiese, who is Ms. Wiese's cousin. Along with helpers, he tore out the interior of the old cafe, a one-story storefront, and put up plywood paneling and installed floor tiles and new kitchen equipment. Dining tables were ordered and a new menu board was mounted on the wall for notice of the dinner special, which costs $3.50 and changes daily. Today it was roast beef with mashed potatoes.

21 Then they painted the facade and put out an American flag and a sign that reads: "Louisburg Cafe: Service with a Friendly Smile." At least that is what it was supposed to say: on one side the painter misspelled service as "sevrice."

22 The restaurant had its formal opening in mid-April. Toby Haug and His Playmores, a polka band from Madison, performed on the street out front, and most of the town turned out to dance and drink a little beer. Radio station KQLP from Madison broadcast live from the scene. So many people showed up to sample Mrs. Hansen's swiss steak that they had to wait in line for tables.

23 Since then, there have been some problems. The roof started leaking and the farmers had to go $4,000 into debt to replace it.

Copyright © Houghton Mifflin Company. All rights reserved.

Then the electrical system blew. Now they say they are going to have to install a new circuit box.

24   But Emily Hansen, who was managing a convenience store in Madison when she was asked to take on the cafe, says she and her husband, who had been laid off from his job, will stay on as long as they can. They work every day as it is, including Sunday, when the church crowd comes in for coffee.

25   "Even if we don't get rich, it's such a great feeling just to be here," said Mrs. Hansen, who had just finished baking a fresh batch of homemade doughnuts. "Whatever else, we feel like we're helping to hold this little community together." ❏

EXERCISES

Comprehension

_____ 1. The main point of the selection is to **(5b)**
   a. give credit to Catherine Wiese for helping to buy the cafe.
   b. discuss the crops grown by farmers on the prairie.
   c. discuss some of the ways in which rural life in America is changing.
   d. demonstrate how important trains are to the prairie states.

_____ 2. The first four paragraphs of the article tell the story of **(5b)**
   a. why the previous cafe closed.
   b. how and why people decided to reopen the cafe.
   c. how the cafe was rebuilt.
   d. how the town got into economic difficulties.

_____ 3. The first four paragraphs are arranged according to **(7)**
   a. order of importance.
   b. comparison and contrast.
   c. classification.
   d. time order.

4. Put a checkmark in front of each change or difficulty the farmers of Louisburg are facing, according to the selection. **(6a)**

_____   a. falling corn prices

_____   b. shrinking towns

_____   c. failing businesses

_____   d. finding lunch

_____   e. prairie fires

_____   f. decreasing railroad service

_____   g. working wives

_____ 5. The ethnic background of the farmers who first settled
             Louisburg, Minnesota, was **(6a)**
             a. very different from that of the current population.
             b. Scandinavian and German.
             c. Dutch and Hungarian.
             d. English and French.

      6. Put a _T_ before the statements that are true according to the
         selection and an _F_ before those that are false. **(6a)**

_____   a. The population of Louisburg began dropping in the
               1960s.

_____   b. The grain elevator is the town's biggest enterprise.

_____   c. there are many restaurants in Madison, within a very
               short drive of Louisburg.

_____   d. Farm profits have skyrocketed lately and farmers are
               prospering.

_____   e. In the mid-1970s the farm implement dealership in
               Louisburg closed.

_____   f. In the mid-1980s the only gas station in Louisburg
               closed.

_____   g. Fifty percent of farm households have someone working
               outside the farm.

_____   h. The population of Louisburg now is 60.

_____   i. The railroad tracks go right through the middle of Louis-
               burg.

_____   j. In the mid-1980s the last grocery store closed.

_____ 8. The selection generally follows time order **(7a)**
   a. from paragraph 6 to paragraph 9.
   b. only occasionally.
   c. from paragraph 10 to the end.
   d. in every paragraph.

_____ 9. The middle section of the selection, entitled "Creation of the Railroad," is about **(5b)**
   a. the federal government's farm subsidies and their effect on grain prices.
   b. the history of Louisburg and trends for small towns across the country.
   c. the problems faced by the Louisburg businesspeople in getting loans to reopen the cafe.
   d. Mr. Wiese's life and why his daughter wanted to reopen the cafe.

_____ 10. The last section of the selection, entitled "Offer from Former Resident," describes **(5b)**
   a. the details of the reopening of the cafe.
   b. the history of Minnesota and the founding of Louisburg.
   c. the financial woes of farmers.
   d. how Louisburg businesses have closed in the last two decades.

_____ 11. According to the selection, rural life is becoming similar to city life because **(6a)**
   a. every family has a computer.
   b. traffic is terrible.
   c. fast food chains are everywhere.
   d. both parents in many families are working.

Reading and Critical Thinking

_____ 1. We can infer that the people of Louisburg reacted to the reopening of the cafe with **(8)**
   a. anxiety.
   b. indifference.
   c. puzzlement.
   d. happiness.

_____ 2. We can infer that the cafe **(8)**
    a. represents a center in the life of the community.
    b. has had few problems.
    c. is quite profitable for the new owners.
    d. has caused wives to worry about where their husbands are.

   3. On the basis of information in the selection, predict whether
       you think each of the following events is likely to occur. Put
       a *Y* in front of those events that you would predict and an
       N in front of those you would not. **(10)**

_____   a. Few people will use the cafe.

_____   b. The population of Louisburg will increase substantially
               in the next few years.

_____   c. The cafe will give townspeople a chance to meet.

_____   d. The cafe will not raise its prices by much.

_____   e. The cafe will develop a number of regular customers.

_____   f. The cafe will go bankrupt soon.

_____   g. The cafe will draw enough people to bring back a number
               of other businesses to town.

_____ 4. You can infer that the farmers want to eat in the cafe not just
       because they can't cook but also because **(8)**
    a. they can do errands at the nearby shopping center.
    b. they want an excuse not to work.
    c. it is too cold to plow the fields.
    d. they want to socialize with other townspeople.

_____ 5. The sentence from the article that reads "What has happened
       in Louisburg also reflects the concerns that are shared by res-
       idents of many small towns who have watched their commu-
       nities wither away, bled by declining populations and failing
       businesses along Main Street" is a good example of **(8, 11)**
    a. dry, unfeeling prose.
    b. generalization on the part of the author.
    c. the use of figurative language.
    d. both b and c.

_____ 6. The author supports the claims made about changes in rural life in America with information from **(12b)**
a. census records and stock market reports.
b. quotes from a sociologist who studies rural areas.
c. a recent *Newsweek* magazine article.
d. the president of the bank near Louisburg.

_____ 7. The tone of the selection is **(12c)**
a. personal.
b. distant.
c. impersonal.
d. silly.

_____ 8. The author achieves the tone identified in the previous question by **(12c)**
a. telling in detail about several individuals involved with the cafe.
b. never mentioning people's names but referring to them as residents.
c. excluding direct quotes from the townspeople.
d. using a lot of statistics to back up his points.

Connecting Ideas

1. Discuss with your classmates where it is that people gather in your home town or on your campus, what people do at that gathering place, and how the place is important to their lives. Then, consider whether the gathering place is associated with eating or some other activity. Think about how basic activities help bring people together. **(13a, c)**

2. In this selection, William E. Schmidt describes how some people take responsibility for holding together the life of the community. Lucie Prinz, in "Say Something. They're Only Children" (pages 442–444), also argues that people need to take responsibility for the life of the community. In what ways are the actions described in this selection similar to those proposed by Prinz? In what ways are they different? Do you think Prinz would be pleased by what happened in Louisburg? Would the people of Louisburg agree with Prinz's recommendations? Would they be likely to respond to the children of the town in a way that Prinz would criticize or approve of?

Critical Thinking in Writing

1. Summarize in a few sentences some of the changes that the residents of Louisburg, Minnesota, have experienced in the last twenty-five years.
2. Write a paragraph describing the changes in your town, neighborhood, or city in recent years and how those changes have affected your life.

Vocabulary

Look at the numbered definitions below. Each of these definitions matches a word from the selection in the list on the right.

As you match each word with its definition, write in the word on the puzzle. **(3a)**

When you finish filling in the puzzle, unscramble the ten circled letters to complete the sentence below the puzzle.

1. (down) strong desire	remote
2. (across) things given	sociologist
2. (down) coordinated operations, like an army's maneuvers	grain elevator
	contributions
3. (down) make fit, get used to	
	campaign
4–5. (across) storehouse for grain	
	wither
5. (down) project	
	yearning
6. (across) rule over, take up a large part	
	adapt
7. (across) far off	enterprise
8. (across) dry up, lose liveliness	dominate
9. (across) one who studies society and the ways in which people interact with one another in groups	

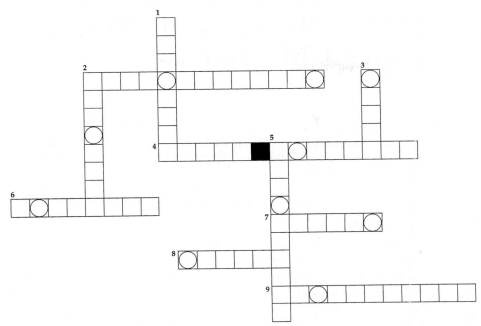

The stereotype of towns such as Louisburg is that they have a

s _ _ _ _ _   _ _ _ _   of life.

Say Something. They're Only Children

Lucie Prinz

What happens when adults are afraid of children? How does this fear hurt them both? How does it hurt society as a whole? Here the writer shares her ideas on overcoming the fear so that we can help children become part of a community and grow up safely.

Prereading

Freewrite about what responsibility adults should have for younger people around them, both relatives and others. Would you try to stop children doing something dangerous, reckless, or possibly harmful to others? Would you explain to children why what they are doing is wrong? **(1a)**

Word Highlights

ebullient   high-spirited
imperative   necessary course of action; demand
rambunctious   hard to control
telethon   around-the-clock television fund-raising show
testosterone   male hormone

I was sitting on the subway a few weeks ago when I looked up and saw a baby, just a little less than a year old, swinging from the overhead bar. She was flanked by two young teenage girls who thought this was a great way to entertain their little sister. As the train began to move, I could visualize the baby flying across the car. Without really thinking, I said to the girls, "Hey, that's not a good idea. That baby is going to get hurt. You better sit down with her on the seat." The kids gave me one of those "Who do you think you are?" looks they reserve for meddling adults, but they took the baby off the bar and sat down.

2 I was suddenly struck by the silence in the subway car. The normal hum of conversation had vanished. My fellow passen-

gers, who had witnessed my encounter with the kids, were now engrossed in their newspapers and books or staring at something fascinating on the subway-tunnel wall. The car was not very crowded, and everyone had seen that endangered baby just as clearly as I had, but they had chosen not to get involved. Although most of them now avoided eye contact with me, a few treated me to the kind of disdain reserved for troublemakers. Could it be that my fellow passengers didn't care about that baby? Or were they just afraid to interfere?

3   We've all heard the old African saying "It takes a whole village to raise a child." Americans have adopted it, and I understand why. It expresses some things that we can all easily accept: family values, shared responsibility, community spirit. But do we really believe in it as a guiding principle for our lives? When we repeat it, are we pledging ourselves to carry out its imperative? I don't think so.

4   Americans are known for generosity. We're ready to rescue the suffering children of the world. We send food to Ethiopia after our television screens show us little kids with huge eyes and distended bellies. We help the victims of floods, and we fund agencies to take care of refugees and abandoned children. We are the nation that invented the poster child and the telethon. These nameless suffering children touch our hearts — but they do not touch our lives.

5   The same adults who are profoundly moved by the plight of children they will never know seem to be willing to ignore the children they encounter every day, even if it is obvious that these children are in trouble or that they need a little adult guidance. I've watched adults actually move away from children they see approaching. I'm not talking about hostile, swaggering gangs of teenage boys — although even some of them are just exhibiting the high that comes with that first surge of testosterone. I'm talking about the ordinary, harmless children we all come in contact with every day on the streets of our cities, towns, and, yes, villages.

6   I'm keeping score, counting the number of times I find myself the only person in a crowd who dares to interact with a child she doesn't know.

7   A few days after the swinging-baby incident I was waiting on a crowded subway platform when someone pushed me from behind. I turned to see three teenage girls, giggling, ebullient, and so eager to get on the train just pulling into the station that

they were shoving. Again I reacted without thinking. "Stop pushing — we'll all get on," I said. After a few murmured remarks along the lines of "Get lost, lady," they stopped. So did the conversation around me. Eyes swiveled away. I felt a collective intake of breath. Disapproval hung in the air, but mainly I sensed fear.

8   Seconds later the train doors opened, and we all stepped in. The woman who dropped into the seat next to me said, "Wow, that was a brave thing to do." When I suggested that it was no such thing, she said, "Well, you can't be too careful these days." That's just it, I thought. You *can* be too careful.

9   In both these encounters I treated harmless children as if they were indeed harmless. They may have been foolish, thoughtless, rambunctious, rude, or annoying. But the only one in any danger was that baby swinging on the bar.

10   I live in a big city. I know that there are violent armed children, hopeless and desperate kids out there. There is no way that I can attack the serious urban problems we all hear about on the evening news. But I am convinced that I can contribute to the larger solutions by refusing to recoil from kids just because they are acting like kids. A lost child who encounters fear instead of concern is twice lost. By responding to these children we may begin to build a village where they will flourish and adults can live without fear. ❏

EXERCISES

Comprehension

_____ 1. The main idea of the first paragraph is that **(5b)**
   a. a baby girl was swinging from an overhead bar in the subway.
   b. teenage girls were playing with their sister.
   c. the writer told the girls to stop.
   d. the writer's intervention got the girls to stop.

_____ 2. The main idea of the second paragraph is that **(5b)**
   a. the other passengers stopped talking.
   b. the other passengers supported the writer's actions.
   c. the other passengers did not support the writer's actions out of fear.
   d. some people treated the writer as a troublemaker.

_____ 3. The main idea of the entire selection is that **(5)**
   a. we need to start interacting with children rather than fearing them.
   b. fear leads people to not interact with children.
   c. children will always be playful and high-spirited.
   d. Americans are generous.

_____ 4. The main idea of the selection is most directly stated in **(5)**
   a. the first paragraph.
   b. paragraph 2.
   c. paragraph 5.
   d. the last paragraph.

_____ 5. Which two paragraphs set up a contrast? On the line after the question, write in your own words what the contrast is. **(7d)**
   a. paragraphs 1 and 2
   b. paragraphs 4 and 5
   c. paragraphs 9 and 10
   d. the first and the last paragraphs

   _____

   _____

_____ 6. Which two paragraphs are told in time order? **(7a)**
   a. paragraphs 2 and 3
   b. paragraphs 4 and 5
   c. paragraphs 7 and 8
   d. paragraphs 9 and 10

     7. Paragraph 9 refers to previous paragraphs by opening with the phrase "In both these encounters . . ." To what paragraphs does the phrase refer? Put a checkmark in front of the correct answer. **(5)**

_____   a. paragraph 1

_____   b. paragraph 2

_____   c. paragraph 3

_____   d. paragraph 4

_____   e. paragraph 5

_____   f. paragraph 6

_____   g. paragraph 7

_____   h. paragraph 8

_____ 8. In the subway incident, who was in actual danger? **(6a)**
       a. the teenage girls
       b. the baby
       c. the writer
       d. the passengers

      9. Put a plus sign (+) next to details that indicate Americans'
          generosity; put a minus sign (−) next to details that indicate
          how Americans react to children around them; and put a
          checkmark next to details that indicate the writer's behavior
          to children. **(6a)**

_____   a. inventing the poster child

_____   b. staring at the subway wall

_____   c. adopting an African saying

_____   d. visualizing a baby flying

_____   e. helping abandoned children

_____   f. moving away from children

_____   g. refusing to recoil from children

_____   h. stopping girls from shoving

_____   i. sending food to Ethiopia

_____   j. being careful around children

_____   k. telling teenagers something is a bad idea

Reading and Critical Thinking

_____ 1. The relation of the main idea of the entire selection to the main ideas of the first two paragraphs is one of **(8, 10, 11, 12)**
a. inference.
b. generalization.
c. prediction.
d. evaluation.

_____ 2. In the subway incident, who, can you infer, felt the most fear? **(8)**
a. the teenage girls
b. the baby
c. the writer
d. the passengers

_____ 3. From the incident in the subway we can conclude that stopping teenagers from doing something dangerous **(10)**
a. can put one at risk.
b. sometimes works.
c. sometimes doesn't work.
d. is a moral responsibility.

_____ 4. We can generalize from the behavior of the various teenagers described in this selection that teenagers in America **(11)**
a. happily accept the advice of adults.
b. are insolent and stubborn.
c. present a danger to everyone around them.
d. will usually stop doing dangerous things if asked.

_____ 5. From the behavior of the various adults described in this selection the writer makes the generalization that adults **(11)**
a. fear youth far too much.
b. are not generous.
c. do not like children.
d. have a sharp eye for dangerous situations.

6. Put a checkmark in front of traditional sayings that are directly or indirectly referred to in the selection. **(12c)**

_____ a. A stitch in time saves nine.

_____ b. Kids will be kids.

_____ c. The love you take is equal to the love you make.

_____ d. Respect your elders.

_____ e. Boys will be boys.

_____ f. It takes a whole village to raise a child.

_____ g. You can never be too careful.

_____ h. A lost child who encounters fear instead of concern is twice lost.

7. Identify whether each statement below from the selection is a fact or an opinion by placing an *F* or an *O* in front of it. In the space after each *opinion,* identify the person or group that holds that opinion. **(12a)**

_____ a. A baby was swinging from an overhead bar in a subway.

_____

_____ b. Swinging from a bar is a great entertainment for a baby.

_____

_____ c. Swinging from a bar is dangerous for a baby.

_____

_____ d. The writer was meddling by telling the teenagers on the subway what to do.

_____

_____ e. Americans fund agencies to take care of refugees.

_____

_____ f. "Suffering children touch our hearts — but they do not touch our lives."

_____

_____   g. Some teenage boys appear hostile and swaggering.

_____

_____   h. "That was a brave thing to do."

_____

_____   i. The writer was not especially brave.

_____

_____   j. "You can't be too careful these days."

_____

_____   k. "You can be too careful."

_____

_____   l. Some children are armed.

_____

_____   m. Most children are harmless.

_____

_____ 8. We can infer from the writer's comments that she was keeping score about who interacts with children that she is **(8)**
a. doing a scientific study.
b. evaluating the behavior of people.
c. seeking an award for public-spirited behavior.
d. compulsive about keeping records.

Connecting Ideas

1. Both this selection and Marcus Bleecker's "My Father's Black
Pride" (pages 420–422) discuss the connection between generations. How do the two pieces agree and how do they differ on what those relations are like and the effects of having
good relations between younger and older people?

2. Where else have you heard the phrase "It takes a whole village to raise a child"? Who has used it, in what circum-

stances, and for which purposes? How do those uses affect your reaction to the phrase? How much truth do you now find in the phrase? How does that compare with the first time you heard the phrase? Discuss your thoughts in small groups with your classmates.

Critical Thinking in Writing

1. What is Lucie Prinz's overall view of youth? Do you think her view is an accurate characterization of teenagers? How does it contrast with the stereotype of youth as potentially dangerous, which Prinz says other adults have? Is there any truth in that stereotype? Do other adults really hold that view? Write several paragraphs discussing the views of youth described in this selection and then presenting your own views on how widespread and accurate these and other views are.

2. When you were younger, were you ever in a group of youth doing something that surrounding adults might have thought improper or dangerous? How did they react to you? How did you react to their reaction? On the basis of your experience, write several paragraphs evaluating Lucie Prinz's advice in this selection.

Vocabulary

Using context clues, choose the correct definition for the word in italics. **(3a)**

_____ 1. "I could *visualize* the baby flying across the car."
   a. actually see
   b. see in imagination
   c. draw a picture of
   d. be afraid of

_____ 2. "looks they reserve for *meddling* adults"
   a. interfering
   b. confused
   c. hostile
   d. arrogant

_____ 3. "now *engrossed* in their newspapers and books"
   a. writing
   b. looking at
   c. intensely involved with
   d. fiddling with

_____ 4. "the kind of *disdain* reserved for troublemakers"
   a. looking up to
   b. fear
   c. careful evaluation
   d. looking down on

_____ 5. "the kind of disdain *reserved* for troublemakers"
   a. bought in advance
   b. especially saved
   c. never given
   d. encountered

_____ 6. "we *fund* agencies to take care of refugees"
   a. desire
   b. think about
   c. work at
   d. pay for

_____ 7. "we fund *agencies* to take care of refugees"
   a. apartment houses
   b. schools
   c. organizations
   d. hospitals

_____ 8. "in both these *encounters*"
   a. fights
   b. meetings
   c. agreements
   d. comparisons

_____ 9. "refusing to *recoil* from kids"
   a. talk to
   b. hate and fear
   c. move away to avoid
   d. consider the opinions of

Like Mother, Like Daughter

Lloyd Gite

The writer points to a trend in the old tradition of family businesses, as women bring their daughters into the family firm. With this new development come new challenges. How would you define them?

Prereading

Identify an experience you had in working on a project with your family. Freewrite about that experience. Did you work well with your parents or brothers and sisters? What difficulties did you have? What problems did you solve? How did it affect your relations with them? What did you manage to accomplish and how did you feel about it? Overall would you rather have worked with family members or people outside of the family? Why? **(1a)**

Word Highlights

architecture   the profession of building design
entrepreneurial   willing to undertake the risks of a
                      business venture
sole proprietorship   owned by a single person

A ndrea, Cheryl, and Deryl McKissack were barely out of diapers when their father started teaching them the family business. William McKissack, the late owner and president of McKissack & McKissack, the nation's oldest black-owned architectural and engineering firm, used to bring his daughters to the company's job sites every Saturday, giving them an "inside look" into how the architecture business works. Moses McKissack II, William's father and the man who founded McKissack & McKissack in 1905, used to give his son that same up-close-and-personal look into the company.

2   Andrea McKissack, now 40, still remembers those Saturdays spent at various job sites. "The three of us started at the architec-

tural drawing board early on," she admits. "I remember going to my father's office when I was 6 years old, and I remember drawing architectural plans for my father when I was 13. By the time I got to high school, all of us were designing our own structures."

3   Today, these "designing women" are doing more than just blueprinting structures in their spare time. In 1983, when a stroke forced William into retirement, his wife, Leatrice, a former high-school math teacher with a master's degree in psychology, took over the Nashville, Tennessee–based firm and became its chairman and CEO. Five years later, when her husband passed away, she asked her daughters to join the company. "I didn't have any fears about bringing my daughters into the firm," recalls the 60-year-old Leatrice, whose company has designed more than 4,000 structures over the past 86 years, including facilities at Howard University and Tennessee State University. "I just decided that this was family. It was a legacy."

4   Cheryl, who at the time was a consultant for Weidlinger Associates, a New York–based engineering consulting firm, vividly remembers how her mother made the offer. "She said, 'I have all this work and I don't know what to do. I need some help.'"

5   Cheryl immediately came to her mother's rescue. For nearly two years, she commuted from New York to Nashville, where she served as the company's vice president of marketing. Cheryl, 30, also opened McKissack & McKissack branch offices in Memphis and New York. (She manages the latter.) In November 1989, Deryl McKissack-Cappell followed in Cheryl's footsteps. The 30-year-old twin sister joined the firm and opened a Washington, D.C., office. Andrea, who has a degree in architectural engineering from Tennessee State University, recently came on board at the New York office where she handles marketing, contract negotiations, and consulting.

6   So far, bringing her daughters into the family business has paid off handsomely for Leatrice — and McKissack & McKissack. When Leatrice took over, McKissack & McKissack was designing projects totaling $30 million. Last year, the 28-employee company handled $75 million worth of projects, 10 percent of which the company received as fees.

7   Since taking over, Leatrice has won over a multitude of fans. "I like the low-key, highly professional way in which Leatrice goes about business," says Benjamin F. Payton, president of Tuskegee University. (McKissack & McKissack has designed

several of the school's buildings.) "Her husband was a real professional — someone who cared deeply about the work he did. Leatrice is the same. She has demonstrated to us that she can carry out major architectural work."

8   **All in the Family**   According to the Small Business Administration (SBA), the number of family-owned companies — many of which are run by mothers and daughters — is on the rise. In 1988, of the nearly 19 million companies in the United States, more than 13 million were sole proprietorships. Most of those were described as family-owned businesses with two or more related individuals who were working together. While there are no hard numbers of how many mother-daughter companies exist, experts agree that more mothers and daughters are going into business together.

9   "About 90 percent of American businesses are family-owned and/or controlled," says Marta Vago, Ph.D., a Los Angeles family business consultant. "People still prefer, whenever possible, to work with people they know."

10   Experts say that during the go-go 1980s, many children of business owners shied away from working in their parents' companies. Instead, many elected to get their advanced degrees and to cut their teeth in corporate America. But now with the problems in the economy and the realization of the proverbial "glass ceiling," many women are returning to the entrepreneurial fold.

11   "Family members are going into business together because of their disenchantment with the corporate world," says Dennis T. Jaffe, Ph.D., author of *Working with the Ones You Love: Conflict Resolution & Problem Solving Strategies for a Successful Family Business* (Conari Press: Berkeley, CA), and co-owner with his wife, Cynthia, of The Heartwork Group, a San Francisco consulting firm specializing in family business. "Many women who want to get to the top think, 'Why don't I just join the family business or form a company with my mother?'"

12   Daughters who become partners with their mothers in business will face many challenges that traditional father-son or father-daughter companies won't. For starters, it's more difficult for women-owned firms to get start-up capital to launch their businesses. And for black women, the chase is even tougher.

13   Sexism often poses another major hurdle. Says Deryl McKissack: "We only deal with men. Most of the presentations I go to, I'm the only woman in the room and I'll get wisecracks like,

'Deryl, all you have to do is show your legs.' I usually just smile and continue the presentation. It goes with the territory."

14   Renee Ferrell, president of sales and operations for Bennie Ferrell Catering Co., says that many of the men in her company used to give her, her sister, and her mother a hard time. "Initially, the men in our company — especially some of the white men who worked for us — didn't want to listen to anything that we had to say because we were women," says Renee, who runs the 32-year-old Houston catering company with her mother, Norma, and her sister, Cynthia. "They figured that we didn't know what we were doing. But we had no problems getting rid of those men."

15   And the Ferrells didn't have any problems deciding that Bennie Ferrell Catering would have to be more aggressive in the 1990s if it was going to remain competitive. In May, the Ferrells opened a new retail outlet in River Oaks, a fashionable upper-middle-class neighborhood in Houston.

16   "We were dying in the area where we were," says Renee of the company's other location in West Houston, a heavily industrialized area of the city. The move marked a new beginning for the $1.2 million business that was launched in 1959 by the late Bennie Ferrell and his wife, Norma.

17   During the downturn in Houston's oil-based economy in the mid-1980s, Bennie Ferrell Catering, which has 12 full-time employees and 150 part-time workers, took a severe financial beating. In 1982, the company posted sales of $800,000. Three years later, revenues plummeted to $400,000.

18   In an effort to boost sagging sales, the Ferrells opened Catering Supplies, a company that sells such items as tablecloths, linens, silverware, and serving trays. They also teach gourmet cooking classes and sell cooking accessories. The Ferrells believe that diversification will help lift the company's sales to $5 million — an ambitious projection — by 1994. Says Renee of the new thrust, "We needed to breathe new life into our company."

19   **Making It Work**   Breathing life into a mother-daughter business venture won't be easy. Marta Vago says that if the mother and daughter have had a dysfunctional relationship throughout the years, that kind of relationship will also be taken into the business. She advises that if you're thinking about going into business with your mother, ask yourself the following questions:

- How uncomfortable am I with disagreeing with my mother openly?
- Are we able to respect each other's differences of opinion?
- Can we find common ground even if we don't agree on everything?
- How do we solve problems?
- Will I have a tendency to go along with my mother so I won't hurt her feelings, or am I going to be more outspoken about what I really think and feel?

20   Author Dennis Jaffe suggests that mothers and daughters work together in some informal setting before forming a business partnership. And that's just what Sharon Pryor did before she joined Cluttered Corners, her mother's 16-year-old, Detroit-based antique store. "As a child, I always worked with my mother on projects," says Sharon, the company's 36-year-old marketing and public relations manager. "We've always had a good working relationship."

21   **What Are the Drawbacks?**   That old saying, "Mothers will always be mothers," certainly applies here. Many daughters say that one of the major drawbacks to successfully running a mother-daughter company can be the inability of the mother to respect the daughter's professional skills. Some mothers still treat their daughters as "mommy's little girl" — despite the fact that they're adult business owners. That thinking can cripple a mother-daughter operation.

22   "Did I have reservations about working with my mother? Sure I did," says Cheryl McKissack. "Mom still likes to exert a certain amount of control over me. That's the biggest issue. My most difficult challenge is weaning myself from my mother. Her challenge is to look at her children more as trained professionals."

23   As in any company, it's also important to clearly define the roles and responsibilities of each employee. Cheryl McKissack remembers getting upset while she and her mother were making a presentation. "Mom answered a question that I should have answered because it was of a technical nature. Did that bother me? Yes. But, she has the savvy in dealing with people, and nobody seemed concerned about it but me," she says.

24   Objective job performance standards should also be adopted

to apply to all employees, including family members. "Everyone in the company, including the daughters, should go through a period of evaluation and performance review," says Vago. "The more objective those standards are, the more objective the judgments can be. Either you performed or you didn't perform. The less objective these job performances are, the greater the likelihood that the mother will either play favorites or will treat the daughter uncommonly harsh."

25   If it's difficult for mothers and daughters to deal with problems, Jaffe recommends using a mediator. "They might need somebody who can help them talk," he says. "It could be another family member involved in the company. But I think the best mediators are people outside the company — somebody they both trust."

26   Mother-daughter businesses can be very rewarding ventures. Just ask the McKissacks, the Ferrells, and the Pryors. "There are many advantages to working with my mother and sisters," says Deryl McKissack. "There are fewer restrictions placed on my professional growth. And we have strong relationships that make things work." □

EXERCISES

Comprehension

_____ 1. The main idea of this selection is that **(5b)**
   a. the mother-daughter firm of McKissack & McKissack has been a great success.
   b. mother-daughter business partnerships are on the increase, but they require special planning.
   c. mother-daughter businesses are filled with many potential problems.
   d. sexism in the workplace is forcing women into family partnerships.

_____ 2. The main idea of the selection appears most clearly in **(5b)**
   a. paragraph 7.
   b. paragraph 8.
   c. paragraph 19.
   d. no one place.

_____ 3. In the blank space to the left write the letter that identifies the person who started the architectural business of McKissack & McKissack. In the space after each name below, write the person's relation in the family (for example: *father*, *mother*, and so on). **(6a)**

a. Leatrice McKissack _____

b. Moses McKissack _____

c. William McKissack _____

d. Andrea McKissack _____

4. In the space *before* each woman named in Column A place a number to indicate the order in which she joined the firm. Use 1 for the first person, 2 for the second, and so on. In the space *after* each, select the reason she joined from Column B and write the appropriate letter in the blank. **(6a)**

A

_____ 1. Cheryl McKissack _____

_____ 2. Deryl McKissack-Cappell _____

_____ 3. Andrea McKissack _____

_____ 4. Leatrice McKissack _____

B

a. to open a branch office in Washington, D.C.

b. because her husband had a stroke and retired

c. because her mother needed help

d. to join her sisters and mother in the family legacy

_____ 5. Which sentence most clearly expresses the main idea of paragraph 8? **(5a)**
   a. the first sentence
   b. the second sentence
   c. the third sentence
   d. the last sentence

_____ 6. Families own and/or control **(6a)**
   a. around 13 million businesses.
   b. around 90% of American businesses.
   c. the same number of businesses that employ mothers and daughters.
   d. only sole proprietorships.

_____ 7. The main idea of paragraphs 12 through 14 is that mothers and daughters running companies face **(5)**
   a. the same kinds of challenges as male-run companies.
   b. special difficulties in raising capital.
   c. problems with sexism.
   d. all of the above.

_____ 8. Details in paragraphs 15 through 18 appear primarily **(7)**
   a. in time order.
   b. in order of importance.
   c. as a comparison and contrast.
   d. as a classification.

_____ 9. The saying "Mothers will always be mothers" **(6a)**
   a. applies to all mother-daughter work situations.
   b. is irrelevant to work situations.
   c. shows the concern and support mothers give to their daughters in the workplace.
   d. reflects a problem that comes up in many mother-daughter businesses.

_____ 10. Paragraphs 19 through 25 present **(6a)**
   a. the problems that occur when mothers and daughters work together.
   b. ways to overcome all difficulties that may arise in business.
   c. ways to foresee difficulties and techniques to address the difficulties when mothers and daughters work together.
   d. the ideas people have about mothers and daughters working together.

Reading and Critical Thinking

_____ 1. We can infer from Leatrice McKissack's comment "I just decided that this was family. It was a legacy" that **(8)**
   a. she considered daughters as capable of carrying on a family tradition as sons.
   b. she wanted the daughters to have the chance they were
   not getting in the outside world.
   c. she did not think her children were interested in architecture but they would feel obligated to stick together because of family.
   d. she believed that carrying on traditions is more important
   than creating your own successes.

_____ 2. We can infer from Benjamin F. Payton's comments in paragraph 7 that he thinks Leatrice McKissack **(8)**
   a. learned everything she knows about the business from
   her husband.
   b. has been an adequate substitute for her husband but cannot match his high standards.
   c. has provided a model of professionalism for the daughters.
   d. runs the business professionally and as well as her husband did.

_____ 3. We can infer from the advice in paragraph 24 that family
members **(8)**
   a. should hold each other to professional standards.
   b. should be especially forgiving of each others' mistakes.
   c. know each others' strengths and weaknesses better than
   anyone else.
   d. are often too critical of each other.

_____ 4. We can conclude that **(10)**
   a. most Americans work with their families.
   b. most large companies are controlled by a single family.
   c. most companies are owned and run by mothers and
   daughters.
   d. small businesses usually are family-run and employ more
   than one family member.

_____ 5. Based on the opening paragraphs, we can conclude that the McKissack sisters **(10)**
   a. received no training in architecture.
   b. learned architecture totally from their father as they grew up hanging around the office.
   c. did not learn as much of the business as they would have if they had been boys.
   d. learned the basics of architecture from their father, just as he learned from his father.

_____ 6. In paragraph 10 the term "glass ceiling" refers to **(9)**
   a. an ancient proverb that says those who challenge the heavens will never see the stars clearly.
   b. the skylights in the offices in the top floor of office buildings, given to the chief officers of the company.
   c. the name given to a clause in employment contracts.
   d. an invisible limit women and minorities experience that does not allow them to rise to the top positions.

_____ 7. We can generalize from the questions in paragraph 19 that family members planning to work together **(11)**
   a. are in for conflict and will inevitably put family relations under stress.
   b. will not respect each other the way they will respect strangers.
   c. need to learn how to be considerate of each others' feelings and should keep family unity ahead of business interests.
   d. need to make sure they can work together without letting family issues get in the way of professional work.

_____ 8. A safe generalization to draw from the selection is that **(11)**
   a. daughters will earn the respect of their mothers by working together in the family business.
   b. mothers will never let their daughters stand on their own.
   c. daughters are sometimes more sensitive about how they are treated by their mothers than they need be.
   d. mothers still need to take over from their daughters, no matter how much they respect their daughters when the best interests of the business are at stake.

9. Put a checkmark in front of each of the statements that you can conclude, predict, or generalize on the basis of this selection. **(10, 11)**

———   a. The number of businesses owned by women is increasing.

———   b. Families will increasingly bring their daughters into the family business.

———   c. Mother-daughter businesses will soon be as common as father-son businesses.

———   d. Family businesses are more successful than businesses made up of strangers.

———   e. People often prefer to work with family members.

———   f. Family businesses are better off if they have a parent working together with brothers and sisters.

———   g. Mother-daughter businesses have more obstacles to overcome than father-son businesses.

———   h. Mother-daughter business combinations do not work as well as father-son combinations.

———   i. Family businesses inevitably lead to family squabbles.

———   j. Family members working together should be aware of the potential problems so they can avoid difficulties.

———   k. Family members almost always have a hard time treating each other as professionals.

———   l. Family members working together do best to treat each other fairly and objectively.

———   m. Family businesses can offer family members greater opportunities than they may have outside.

———   n. Women still face obstacles to their career advancement in the job market.

Connecting Ideas

1. Americans often view career success as personal, separate from one's family. Children, accordingly, often feel the need to move away from their parents as they grow up, earn their own money, and become responsible for their own success. How do you think working in a family-owned business affects a child's sense of individual success? Will children's independence be limited? Can children find ways to prove their own worth even within a family business? Or, is this idea of independence perhaps not as important as people make it out to be? Discuss these ideas with your class. **(13b)**

2. This selection, like the selection "Creating Unique Names for Children" by Cindy Roberts (see pages 500–502), considers how children can gain opportunities and identity within family traditions and legacies. (Compare and contrast the kinds of identities offered to children in these two selections.) **(13b)**

Critical Thinking in Writing

1. In a few paragraphs, describe instances in which you have observed how sexism can limit the success of women.

2. From what you know of relations between mothers and daughters, fathers and sons, brothers and sisters, or any other family combination, explain in a few paragraphs the advantages and disadvantages of family partnerships. You may want to explain which kind of combination might succeed best.

3. Choose one activity that you have successfully carried out with a family member. Write one page of advice about how to get along and work well with family members in this activity and what difficulties to watch out for.

Vocabulary

In front of each of the definitions in Column A, write the matching word from the selection listed in Column B. The numbers after each word indicate the paragraph the word appears in so that you can use context clues. **(3a)**

	A		B

A

_____ 1. someone who gives professional advice

_____ 2. able to stay equal with other companies

_____ 3. well-known

_____ 4. inheritance

_____ 5. evaluation of how one is doing on the job

_____ 6. someone to help negotiate between people

_____ 7. an object from an earlier period

_____ 8. not working well

_____ 9. drawing plans for buildings

_____ 10. challenging

_____ 11. no longer pleased

_____ 12. relating to the design of buildings

_____ 13. including more kinds of business

_____ 14. having many factories

B

a. architectural (1)
b. blueprinting (3)
c. legacy (3)
d. consultant (4)
e. proverbial (10)
f. disenchantment (11)
g. competitive (15)
h. industrialized (16)
i. diversification (18)
j. ambitious (18)
k. dysfunctional (19)
l. antique (20)
m. performance review (24)
n. mediator (25)

Putting Thoughts Together

1. Write a short essay analyzing the title of this section, "Making Connections," in regard to at least two selections here.
2. Several of the writers explore the relations between adults and children and efforts of the two generations to coexist in harmony. Write a few paragraphs examining the relations between parents and adults.
3. Some of the selections in this section deal with the way parents and their children face life's challenges. What responsibilities do parents and children have to and for each other?
4. Some of the selections deal with our changing society and how values of the past do not always remain in the present. What is your view of changing society? Should we fight to preserve the values we hold dear now or should we be open to changes that may challenge our fundamental principles? Write a few paragraphs to explore your response.
5. In what way can people today "make connections" with others in different generations or different racial and ethnic groups? Write a brief essay explaining your views.

Identities
and Struggles

**Love Me, Love My
(Brown) Mother**   *Charity Plata*

Wilshire Bus   *Hisaye Yamamoto*

Zoot Suit Riots   *Albert Camarillo*

**Creating Unique Names
for Children**   *Cindy Roberts*

Love Me, Love My (Brown) Mother

Charity Plata

The writer, a college student in California, finds disturbing evidence of people who despise their own culture. When skin color and ethnicity challenge each other, tension and anger are the outcomes, she believes.

Prereading

Do freewriting on the title of this selection. What do you think the writer is trying to accomplish? Why does she place the word *brown* in parentheses? **(1a)**

Word Highlights

siblings   children of the same family; brothers and sisters

O ur neighbor, let's call her Debbie, looked at my mother with such disdain that it shocked me. She had never seen my mother before, but she had gone out of her way to be friendly to my father. I could not understand why she was so openly rude to my mom.

2   A friendlier neighbor later told my mother, "She tried to come into my house and tell me not to associate with you. She tried to say that I shouldn't let a Mexican into my house."

3   The worst part of it was that Debbie was also Mexican. Her given name had been Delores, but she changed it because Delores sounded "too Mexican."

4   Debbie had thought my father was a white man, so she respected him. When Debbie saw me with my dad, she figured we were one of the many white families in the neighborhood. Debbie only associated with white-skinned people. Talking to my tawny brown mother was out of the question. She would allow her children to bring home friends only if they were white.

5   The situation with Debbie was one of the first incidents I

remember where people who shared my family's ethnicity openly despised their own culture. To this day, why someone chooses to deny their own culture still puzzles me. And angers me.

6   I have been plagued for years by the fact that I am the whitest member of my family, except for the few *hueros* (light-skinned people) who married in. In elementary school, I fought with a girl because she hated the fact that I was Mexican but had light skin and sort of blond hair.

7   "You think you're all better because you're a *rubia* (blond)," the girl said, "You think you're so better."

8   The truth was, I never thought I was any better because I did not think I was any different. I figured I was of the same culture, just a different blend. But as I got older, I noticed how differently some people would deal with my mother and me. Once when we went shopping, the salesman followed my mother through the store. She kept telling him that she was browsing, but he stayed on her tail. He ignored me when I rushed past him.

9   At the perfume counter, I heard him whisper to the saleswoman who was helping me that he "didn't trust those Mexicans because they'll pocket anything they can carry."

10   Stunned, I called for my mother to come to the counter. I glared at the salesman, who was sporting a deer-in-headlights look, and loudly said, "Mom, our business is not appreciated here because this salesman says that we Mexicans can't be trusted."

11   His last name — at least on the name tag — was Garcia. Did he look into the mirror every day and see the same light brown face I saw when I looked at him? Did he have to deny his ethnicity to keep his job?

12   The worst memory I have of this ethnic denial is of my family friend and honorary cousin, whom we'll call Anita. She was a popular cheerleader at our high school. I knew she only hung out with the rich, white crowd, but she always was pleasant to me.

13   Anita could not deny her heritage since she was the same dark cocoa-brown color as her uncle. Unlike her mother and some of her siblings, she had dark hair, skin, and eyes. I thought she knew where she came from.

14   I was shopping with my mother when Anita introduced me to a friend and the friend's mother, who were both white. "This

is my cousin, Charity," Anita said with a smile. We were not really cousins, but Anita's father and my father were longtime close friends, so we grew up calling each other "cousin."

15   Steering her shopping cart in our direction, my mother smiled. She had not seen Anita for a long time and had always thought she was sweet.

16   I looked at Anita. She had that same panicked look I had seen on the salesman. As my mom approached, Anita turned and walked away without saying a word.

17   My mother was confused. I was furious. Later, I was told that Anita had said her relatives were white and was using me to prove it by telling people I was her cousin. She was embarrassed by my mother.

18   I was sick about her behavior then, and I am still disgusted by it. I cannot shrug off people like Debbie and Anita. I want to challenge them and ask, "Why?" But I do not expect to be satisfied with their answers. ◻

EXERCISES

Comprehension

_____ 1. The main idea of this selection is most directly stated in **(5b)**
a. paragraph 1.
b. paragraph 18.
c. paragraph 5.
d. paragraph 12.

_____ 2. How did Debbie relate to the writer's parents? **(6)**
a. She was friendly to them both.
b. She was rude to them both.
c. She was rude to the father and friendly to the mother.
d. She was rude to the mother and friendly to the father.

_____ 3. Debbie **(6a)**
a. liked being called Delores when she was in Mexico.
b. changed her name from Delores.
c. refused to talk to anyone with a Mexican name.
d. did not know what it was like to be Mexican.

_____ 4. Debbie was unfriendly to the writer's mother because **(6a)**
    a. she wanted to associate only with white-skinned people.
    b. she avoided being "Mexican."
    c. she denied her own culture.
    d. all of the above.

_____ 5. The writer's skin color led her to **(6a)**
    a. not being identified as a Mexican.
    b. being disliked by another Mexican girl.
    c. being trusted by a sales clerk when her mother was not.
    d. all of the above.

_____ 6. Debbie, the girl in elementary school, the salesman Garcia, and cousin Anita were all **(6a)**
    a. dark-skinned.
    b. light-skinned.
    c. Mexican.
    d. denying they were Mexican.

_____ 7. The incident in the store is told **(7)**
    a. in time order.
    b. in space order.
    c. as comparison and contrast.
    d. as cause and effect.

_____ 8. The four main incidents in this selection — involving Debbie, the girl in elementary school, the salesman Garcia, and cousin Anita — are told **(7)**
    a. in time order.
    b. in order of importance.
    c. as classification.
    d. as comparison and contrast.

9. Of the following details from the incident involving Anita, write *maj* in front of major and write *min* in front of minor details. **(6b)**

_____ a. Anita was a cheerleader.

_____ b. Anita hung out with the rich, white crowd.

_____ c. Anita was dark cocoa brown.

_____   d. Anita's mother and some of her siblings were lighter.

_____   e. Anita introduced the writer as a cousin.

_____   f. Anita's father and the writer's father were longtime close friends.

_____   g. Anita turned her back on the mother and walked away.

_____   h. Anita was using the writer to prove she had white relatives.

Reading and Critical Thinking

1. Put a checkmark before all the inferences one can appropriately make from statements in this selection. In the space after each inference that you select, place the number of the paragraph that provides information allowing the inference. **(8)**

_____   a. Debbie was light-skinned. _____

_____   b. Debbie was born in Mexico. _____

_____   c. Debbie had never visited Mexico. _____

_____   d. Debbie thought changing her name from Delores would make people less likely to think her Mexican. _____

_____   e. The writer's mother was hurt by Debbie's behavior. _____

_____   f. Debbie wanted her children to grow up associating only with whites. _____

_____   g. The salesman was worried that the mother might steal something. _____

_____ h. The salesman was under orders from his boss to watch

out for Mexicans. _____

_____ i. The writer intended to embarrass the salesman to expose

his attitudes. _____

2. Put a plus sign (+) before those beliefs and opinions that both the writer and the girl in elementary school shared or would be likely to share. Put a minus sign (−) before those they would disagree about. **(12a)**

_____ a. Each identified as Mexican.

_____ b. The writer was lighter-skinned than the other girl.

_____ c. The writer was lighter-skinned than most Mexicans.

_____ d. The writer had sort of blond hair.

_____ e. People treated light-skinned people better than dark-skinned (based on the writer's opinion as a child).

_____ f. People treated light-skinned people better than dark-skinned (based on the writer's opinion as she grew up).

_____ g. The lighter skin led the writer to think she was better (based on the writer's opinion as a child).

_____ h. The lighter skin led the writer to think she was better (based on the writer's opinion as she grew up).

3. Put a checkmark before each reason that might have led the writer to conclude that the incident with Anita was the worst. **(10)**

_____ a. Anita tried to pass for white even though she was dark-skinned.

_____ b. Anita was a popular cheerleader.

_____   c. Anita hung out with the rich, white crowd.

_____   d. Anita at first appeared to be fair-minded.

_____   e. Anita took advantage of family friendships.

_____   f. Anita tried to "borrow" the white-skin advantage from the writer.

_____   g. Anita was embarrassed by and snubbed the writer's mother.

_____   h. Anita reminded the writer that some people treat her skin color as an advantage.

_____   i. Anita was a false friend.

_____ 4. From this selection we can conclude that the writer **(10)**
   a. has complex feelings about being Mexican.
   b. denies that people treat her differently from darker members of her family.
   c. has never been treated with prejudice.
   d. is troubled by how people react to her lighter complexion.

_____ 5. From this selection we can also conclude that the writer **(10)**
   a. wishes people would not discriminate against her mother.
   b. wishes her mother were lighter so she would not be discriminated against.
   c. is upset that her mother feels so distressed by prejudice.
   d. feels that she and her mother are better than other people.

6. Put a checkmark before those generalizations we can appropriately make based on this selection. **(11)**

_____   a. People may be prejudiced against people of their own ethnic background.

_____   b. Neighbors and sales clerks always make harsh judgments about the people around them.

_____   c. Skin color more often than not makes a difference in how people judge you.

_____   d. Prejudiced individuals may treat people of the same family differently.

_____   e. Sometimes people may try to hide their own ethnicity by discriminating against people of the same background.

_____   f. Discrimination against one's parents can be as outrageous as discrimination against oneself.

_____   g. People should be forgiven for discrimination if it results from their own confusion about themselves.

_____   h. People may try to raise their own status by playing on social beliefs about whiteness.

_____   i. People may treat you as having a privilege even if you think that privilege is unfair and you don't want to take advantage of it.

_____   j. You can be troubled by how people treat you, even if they seem to be treating you well.

Connecting Ideas

1. In both this selection and Hisaye Yamamoto's "Wilshire Bus" (pages 479–483), we see divisions within groups that outsiders might perceive as unified. Describe and compare the internal divisions and where they came from, as presented in these two selections.
2. Have you ever witnessed a situation in which people treated a member of your family or a friend poorly or with prejudice? Describe the incident, how you felt about it, and why you think the other people acted as they did.

Critical Thinking in Writing

1. The four prejudiced people in this selection all have different motivations for their behavior. Write a paragraph or two comparing and contrasting their motives and describing the ways in which they were similar and different.
2. People often have complex feelings about their own backgrounds, and these complex feelings can lead them to act in troublesome ways. Have your own complicated feelings about your family or your background ever led you to be-

have in ways that you later regretted? Write a paragraph exploring such an incident in your life or the life of someone you know.
3. Have people ever treated you favorably in ways that you felt were unfair, inappropriate, or undeserved? Write a few paragraphs examining such an experience.

Vocabulary

Based on context clues, choose the best definition for each word. Then in the space following each item identify the context clue that helped you choose the correct definition. (3a)

_____ 1. tawny
    a. medium light
    b. shady
    c. medium dark
    d. cheerful

    _____

_____ 2. *hueros*
    a. dark-skinned people
    b. light-skinned people
    c. blond haired
    d. red haired

    _____

_____ 3. *rubia*
    a. dark-skinned people
    b. light-skinned people
    c. blond haired
    d. red haired

    _____

_____ 4. browsing
    a. buying
    b. looking for goods to steal
    c. just looking
    d. getting exercise

    _____

_____ 5. deer-in-headlights
     a. defiant
     b. friendly
     c. panicked
     d. trying to hide

_____ 6. heritage
     a. background
     b. friends
     c. ambitions
     d. attitude

Wilshire Bus

Hisaye Yamamoto

In this short story, a Japanese-American woman riding on a bus witnesses a racist incident. In thinking about her reactions, she realizes something disturbing about herself and society as a whole. Read to find out how she arrives at her realization by making sometimes painful admissions about her automatic responses to the incident.

Prereading

Have you ever been in a situation in which a racist comment was directed not to you but to someone else — either someone you knew or someone you didn't know? Freewrite about the experience — what happened, how you felt, what you thought or said. [1a(3)]

Sometimes the date when a story was written or first published appears at the end of the story. When was this story

written? _____

Word Highlights

bobbled   moved up and down
coolies   unskilled, poorly paid Chinese laborers
craw   stomach
desolate   deserted; joyless
diatribe   abusive speech
elegance   grace; dignity
eloquence   artfulness of speech
emphatic   forceful
exclusion   forced out; intentionally left out
gloating   delighting in someone else's misfortune
immune   protected; not affected
metaphor   word or phrase that compares two things
omission   something left out
somatotonic   aggressive, physical personality type
                  associated with a muscular body

W ilshire Boulevard begins somewhere near the heart of downtown Los Angeles and, except for a few digressions scarcely worth mentioning, goes straight out to the edge of the Pacific Ocean. It is a wide boulevard and traffic on it is fairly fast. For the most part, it is bordered on either side with examples of the recent stark architecture which favors a great deal of glass. As the boulevard approaches the sea, however, the landscape becomes a bit more pastoral, so that the university and the soldiers' home there give the appearance of being huge country estates.

2   Esther Kuroiwa got to know this stretch of territory quite well while her husband, Buro, was in one of the hospitals at the soldiers' home. They had been married less than a year when his back, injured in the war, began troubling him again, and he was forced to take three months of treatments at Sawtelle before he was able to go back to work. During this time, Esther was permitted to visit him twice a week and she usually took the yellow bus out on Wednesdays because she did not know the first thing about driving and because her friends were not able to take her except on Sundays. She always enjoyed the long bus ride very much because her seat companions usually turned out to be amiable, and if they did not, she took vicarious pleasure in gazing out at the almost unmitigated elegance along the fabulous street.

3   It was on one of these Wednesday trips that Esther committed a grave sin of omission which caused her later to burst into tears and which caused her acute discomfort for a long time afterwards whenever something reminded her of it.

4   The man came on the bus quite early and Esther noticed him briefly as he entered because he said gaily to the driver, "You robber. All you guys do is take money from me every day, just for giving me a short lift!"

5   Handsome in a red-faced way, greying, medium of height, and dressed in a dark grey sport suit with a yellow-and-black flowered shirt, he said this in a nice, resonant, carrying voice which got the response of a scattering of titters from the bus. Esther, somewhat amused and classifying him as a somatotonic, promptly forgot about him. And since she was sitting alone in the first regular seat, facing the back of the driver and the two front benches facing each other, she returned to looking out the window.

6   At the next stop, a considerable mass of people piled on and the last two climbing up were an elderly Oriental man and his

wife. Both were neatly and somberly clothed and the woman, who wore her hair in a bun and carried a bunch of yellow and dark red chrysanthemums, came to sit with Esther. Esther turned her head to smile a greeting (well, here we are, Orientals together on a bus), but the woman was watching, with some concern, her husband who was asking directions of the driver.

7   His faint English was inflected in such a way as to make Esther decide he was probably Chinese, and she noted that he had to repeat his question several times before the driver could answer it. Then he came to sit in the seat across the aisle from his wife. It was about then that a man's voice, which Esther recognized soon as belonging to the somatotonic, began a loud monologue in the seat just behind her. It was not really a monologue, since he seemed to be addressing his seat companion, but this person was not heard to give a single answer. The man's subject was a figure in the local sporting world who had a nice fortune invested in several of the shining buildings the bus was just passing.

8   "He's as tight-fisted as they make them, as tight-fisted as they come," the man said. "Why, he wouldn't give you the sweat of his . . ." He paused here to rephrase his metaphor, ". . . wouldn't give you the sweat off his palm!"

9   And he continued in this vein, discussing the private life of the famous man so frankly that Esther knew he must be quite drunk. But she listened with interest, wondering how much of this diatribe was true, because the public legend about the famous man was emphatic about his charity. Suddenly, the woman with the chrysanthemums jerked around to get a look at the speaker and Esther felt her giving him a quick but thorough examination before she turned back around.

10   "So you don't like it?" the man inquired, and it was a moment before Esther realized that he was now directing his attention to her seat neighbor.

11   "Well, if you don't like it," he continued, "why don't you get off this bus, why don't you go back where you came from? Why don't you go back to China?"

12   Then, his voice growing jovial, as though he were certain of the support of the bus in this at least, he embroidered on this theme with a new eloquence, "Why don't you go back to China, where you can be coolies working in your bare feet out in the rice fields? You can let your pigtails grow and grow in China. Alla samee, mama, no tickee no shirtee. Ha, pretty good, no tickee no shirtee!"

13   He chortled with delight and seemed to be looking around

the bus for approval. Then some memory caused him to launch on a new idea. "Or why don't you go back to Trinidad? They got Chinks running the whole she-bang in Trinidad. Every place you go in Trinidad . . ."

14   As he talked on, Esther, pretending to look out the window, felt the tenseness in the body of the woman beside her. The only movement from her was the trembling of the chrysanthemums with the motion of the bus. Without turning her head, Esther was also aware that a man, a mild-looking man with thinning hair and glasses, on one of the front benches, was smiling at the woman and shaking his head mournfully in sympathy, but she doubted whether the woman saw.

15   Esther herself, while believing herself properly annoyed with the speaker and sorry for the old couple, felt quite detached. She found herself wondering whether the man meant her in his exclusion order or whether she was identifiably Japanese. Of course, he was not sober enough to be interested in such fine distinctions, but it did matter, she decided, because she was Japanese, not Chinese, and therefore in the present case immune. Then she was startled to realize that what she was actually doing was gloating over the fact that the drunken man had specified the Chinese as the unwanted.

16   Briefly, there bobbled on her memory the face of an elderly Oriental man whom she had once seen from a streetcar on her way home from work. (This was not long after she had returned to Los Angeles from the concentration camp in Arkansas and been lucky enough to get a clerical job with the Community Chest.) The old man was on a concrete island at Seventh and Broadway, waiting for his streetcar. She had looked down on him benignly as a fellow Oriental, from her seat by the window, then been suddenly thrown for a loop by the legend on a large lapel button on his jacket. I AM KOREAN, said the button.

17   Heat suddenly rising to her throat, she had felt angry, then desolate and betrayed. True, reason had returned to ask whether she might not, under the circumstances, have worn such a button herself. She had heard rumors of I AM CHINESE buttons. So it was true then; why not I AM KOREAN buttons, too? Wryly, she wished for an I AM JAPANESE button, just to be able to call the man's attention to it, "Look at me!" But perhaps the man didn't even read English, perhaps he had been actually threatened, perhaps it was not his doing — his solicitous children perhaps had urged him to wear the badge.

18   Trying now to make up for her moral shabbiness, she turned

towards the little woman and smiled at her across the chrysanthemums, shaking her head a little to get across her message (don't pay any attention to that stupid old drunk, he doesn't know what he's saying, let's take things like this in our stride). But the woman, in turn looking at her, presented a face so impassive yet cold, and eyes so expressionless yet hostile, that Esther's overture fell quite flat.

19   Okay, okay, if that's the way you feel about it, she thought to herself. Then the bus made another stop and she heard the man proclaim ringingly, "So clear out, all of you, and remember to take every last one of your slant-eyed pickaninnies with you!" This was his final advice as he stepped down from the middle door. The bus remained at the stop long enough for Esther to watch the man cross the street with a slightly exploring step. Then, as it started up again, the bespectacled man in front stood up to go and made a clumsy speech to the Chinese couple and possibly to Esther. "I want you to know," he said, "that we aren't all like that man. We don't all feel the way he does. We believe in an America that is a melting pot of all sorts of people. I'm originally Scotch and French myself." With that, he came over and shook the hand of the Chinese man.

20   "And you, young lady," he said to the girl behind Esther, "you deserve a Purple Heart or something for having to put up with that sitting beside you."

21   Then he, too, got off.

22   The rest of the ride was uneventful and Esther stared out the window with eyes that did not see. Getting off at last at the soldiers' home, she was aware of the Chinese couple getting off after her, but she avoided looking at them. Then, while she was walking towards Buro's hospital very quickly, there arose in her mind some words she had once read and let stick in her craw: People say, do not regard what he says, now he is in liquor. Perhaps it is the only time he ought to be regarded.

23   These words repeated themselves until her saving detachment was gone every bit and she was filled once again in her life with the infuriatingly helpless, insidiously sickening sensation of there being in the world nothing solid she could put her finger on, nothing solid she could come to grips with, nothing solid she could sink her teeth into, nothing solid.

24   When she reached Buro's room and caught sight of his welcoming face, she ran to his bed and broke into sobs that she could not control. Buro was amazed because it was hardly her first

visit and she had never shown such weakness before, but solving the mystery handily, he patted her head, looked around smugly at his roommates, and asked tenderly, "What's the matter? You've been missing me a whole lot, huh?" And she, finally drying her eyes, sniffed and nodded and bravely smiled and answered him with the question, yes, weren't women silly?

1950 ❏

EXERCISES

Comprehension

_____ 1. The main idea of the short story is that **(5b)**
   a. Esther realizes that she has tried to protect herself by detaching herself from Asian Americans of different backgrounds.
   b. riding on buses puts you in the company of people who are very different, some of whom are unpleasant and even racist.
   c. Los Angeles has a wide variety of architectural styles that create different moods in different parts of the city.
   d. Esther's husband was wounded in the war while his wife was being mistreated by the country for which he was fighting.

_____ 2. This main idea, although never fully stated, is suggested most directly in **(5b)**
   a. the first paragraph.
   b. paragraph 3.
   c. paragraph 22.
   d. the last paragraph.

_____ 3. The story is entitled "Wilshire Bus" because **(5b)**
   a. the main character drives the bus that goes down Wilshire Boulevard.
   b. the bus plays a crucial role in bringing the story to a climax.
   c. it reveals a lot about Wilshire Boulevard as the bus travels down the street.
   d. the story's main incident takes place on the Wilshire Boulevard bus.

_____ 4. Esther Kuroiwa is riding the Wilshire bus to **(6a)**
a. come into contact with different people in the city.
b. visit her husband at the soldiers' home.
c. go shopping at a mall across town.
d. look at the elegant buildings along the boulevard.

_____ 5. More than halfway through the story, we learn that Esther's
family background is **(6a)**
a. Irish.
b. Chinese.
c. Japanese.
d. Korean.

_____ 6. Esther first thinks about being Japanese when **(6a)**
a. she remembers her husband's war injury.
b. the drunken man starts insulting a Chinese couple.
c. the drunken man begins making racist comments about
Japanese people.
d. she sees a man wearing an I AM KOREAN button.

_____ 7. Many Japanese-Americans were taken from their homes during World War II and put into camps for "national security"
reasons because the United States was at war with Japan. In
the story, Esther briefly refers to being in a concentration
camp in **(6a)**
a. New Mexico.
b. Arkansas.
c. California.
d. Nevada.

8. Place the following events of the story in order by placing
numbers in the blanks. The earliest event in the story would
be *1.* **(7a)**

_____   The elderly Asian woman turns around and looks at the loud
man.

_____   A handsome red-faced man gets on the Wilshire bus and
jokes with the driver.

_____   Esther feels detached.

_____   Esther remembers an elderly man she once saw wearing an
I AM KOREAN button.

_____   Esther cries when she gets to her husband's room.

_____   Esther wonders if the loud man realizes she's Japanese.

_____   The loud man begins insulting the elderly Chinese woman.

_____   An elderly Chinese man and woman get on the bus.

_____   A man with glasses smiles at the Chinese woman and shakes his head in sympathy.

_____   The man with glasses tells the Chinese couple that not everyone is racist like the drunk man.

_____   Esther realizes she is gloating over the fact that the drunk is insulting Chinese people, not Japanese people.

_____   The "somatotonic" loudly begins to criticize a famous man.

_____   Esther and the Chinese couple get off at the soldiers' home stop.

Reading and Critical Thinking

_____ 1. The story is primarily from the point of view of [12c(5)]
    a. Buro.
    b. Esther.
    c. the Chinese woman.
    d. the drunk man.

_____ 2. Because you know the story was written in 1950, you can infer that the recent war mentioned is (8)
    a. the Civil War.
    b. World War I.
    c. World War II.
    d. the Vietnam War.

_____ 3. Because Buro is in a soldiers' home in Los Angeles, you can infer that he (8)
    a. fought for the United States in World War II.
    b. fought for Japan in World War II.
    c. was interned in a concentration camp in World War II.
    d. was a paratrooper in World War II.

———— 4. The contrast between Buro's World War II experience and his wife's is an example of **(12c)**
   a. figurative language.
   b. sarcasm.
   c. precision.
   d. irony.

———— 5. You can infer that the man wore the I AM KOREAN button because **(8)**
   a. it was a time of ethnic and racial pride and all people identified themselves with buttons.
   b. Korean people had special privileges.
   c. the government made him wear it.
   d. he didn't want to be mistaken for being Japanese right after World War II.

———— 6. You can conclude that Esther originally reacted to the I AM KOREAN button by wanting to wear an I AM JAPANESE button out of **(10)**
   a. ethnic pride.
   b. a desire to avoid prejudice.
   c. a desire to show the man how he was hurting her.
   d. guilt at her own moral failings.

———— 7. You can conclude that Esther now remembers the man with the I AM KOREAN button because **(10)**
   a. she realizes that she, too, is denying her link with other Asian Americans by detaching herself from the drunk man's comments.
   b. she noticed him at a time when she was being persecuted for being of Japanese descent.
   c. she associated him with another powerful incident that happened on a bus.
   d. all of the above.

———— 8. Toward the end of the story, Esther remembers a saying: "People say, do not regard what he says, now he is in liquor." She then thinks, "Perhaps it is the only time he ought to be regarded." We can infer that she thinks a drunk man should be regarded because he **(8)**

a. has more control of his mental faculties.
b. can't hide his true feelings.
c. is louder than anyone else.
d. is so much stronger under the influence of alcohol.

_____ 9. At this moment in the story, when she thinks the drunk man ought to be regarded, Esther feels helpless. You can infer that Esther feels this way because she **(8)**
a. feels that racism is within everyone.
b. is worried that she will never see her husband again.
c. wants to move away from Los Angeles.
d. has decided to file a police report on the drunk man.

_____ 10. We can conclude that Esther's grave sin of omission is that she **(10)**
a. doesn't tell the Chinese woman that she was once in a concentration camp in Arkansas.
b. doesn't identify with the Chinese couple being harassed on the bus.
c. doesn't demand that the bus be stopped and the drunk put off.
d. hasn't learned more about Chinese culture.

_____ 11. In paragraph 3 of the story, the words *grave, tears,* and *acute discomfort* give the story a tone of **(12c)**
a. painfulness.
b. irony.
c. thoughtfulness.
d. sarcasm.

_____ 12. One purpose of the story is to **(12c)**
a. reveal the complexities of racism.
b. show how lonely Esther's life is.
c. show how the U.S. government persecuted Japanese-Americans during the war.
d. describe the many kinds of people in Los Angeles.

_____ 13. At the end we can predict that Esther will **(10)**
a. tell her husband about the incident.
b. think about her own racism.
c. forgive the drunk man.
d. apologize to the Chinese couple.

Connecting Ideas

1. Reread the short passage from Mary Paik Lee's autobiography on page 143. Compare and contrast the two racist incidents, and explain how the two characters reacted to them. **(13b)**
2. In both this selection and Charity Plata's "Love Me, Love My (Brown) Mother" (pages 468–470), the writers portray some people as being ashamed of their identity. Compare how the people deal with their shame and the results on their attitude and behavior.

Critical Thinking in Writing

1. In one sentence, describe how Esther feels at the beginning of the story. In another, describe how she feels at the end. Then, in several more, describe what happened to change her feelings.
2. Have you ever had an experience that has made you want to change the way you feel about something? Write one paragraph about what happened and a second paragraph about how the incident influenced your thinking.

Vocabulary

The words below are used in the story to describe characters, places, objects, and ideas. These words give you additional information to help you form a picture of what is happening in the story. Match each word in Column A with its definition in Column B by placing the letter of the definition in the space before each word. If you need help, use the context of the sentence. The paragraph number is given in parentheses next to each word. **(3a)**

A

_____ 1. stark (1)

_____ 2. pastoral (1)

_____ 3. amiable (2)

_____ 4. vicarious (2)

B

a. happy
b. rich with sound
c. serious
d. concerned
e. kindly; gently
f. not experienced directly
g. plain; bare
h. sharp; pointed

_____ 5. unmitigated (2)

_____ 6. acute (3)

_____ 7. grave (3)

_____ 8. resonant (5)

_____ 9. jovial (12)

_____ 10. detached (15)

_____ 11. benignly (16)

_____ 12. solicitous (17)

_____ 13. infuriatingly (23)

_____ 14. insidiously (23)

i. countrylike; peaceful
j. in a way that provokes great anger
k. gradually; without your noticing
l. friendly
m. without relief
n. withdrawn; separated

Zoot Suit Riots

Albert Camarillo

In this selection the author describes a part of the history of Los Angeles during World War II that most Anglos either never knew or would prefer to forget.

Prereading

Freewrite about what you think Los Angeles was like in the 1940s. **[1a(3)]**

Word Highlights

bravado   boldness
deviants   people whose actions fall outside the codes of accepted behavior
disdain   contempt
improprieties   unacceptable actions
quelled   put an end to
rampant   present everywhere
savored   enjoyed for its taste and smell
stigmas   marks; signs of shame
xenophobic   afraid of foreigners

N othing has come to symbolize more dramatically the racial hostility encountered by Chicanos during the 1930s and 1940s than the Sleepy Lagoon case and the Zoot Suit Riots. Both involved Chicano youth in Los Angeles city and county, local police departments, and the judicial system.

2   At the heart of these conflicts was the growing attention paid to Chicano youth by the local media. The press focused on *pachucos*, members of local clubs or neighborhood gangs of teenagers (both male and female). They separated themselves from other barrio youth by their appearance — high-pompadoured ducktail haircuts, tattoos, and baggy zoot suits for boys; short skirts, bobby sox, and heavy make-up for girls — and by their use of *caló*, a mixture of Spanish and English. Their characteris-

tics, according to the press, included unflinching allegiance to neighborhood territories, clannishness, and bravado. Though other teenagers in cities such as Detroit, Chicago, and New York dressed like their counterparts in wartime Los Angeles, *pachuquismo* became popularly identified with Chicano youth who came of age during the 1930s and 1940s in the Los Angeles area. Predominantly children of immigrant parents, these youths matured in an environment in which they saw themselves as neither fully Mexican nor American. Raised in impoverished barrios and alienated from a society that discriminated against Mexicans, they identified only with others of their age and experience. Pachucos constituted a minority among Chicano youth, and they set themselves apart by their disdain of the public schools, skipping classes and drawing together into neighborhood gangs where they found companionship and camaraderie. To outsiders who relied on the local media for their information, pachucos were perceived not only as marijuana-smoking hoodlums and violence-prone deviants, but also as un-American. These stigmas during the early 1940s, particularly during the first two years of a frustrating war for Americans, helped create a climate of repression for pachucos and, by extension, to others in the Chicano community.

3   In the hot summer days of August 1942, most Los Angeles residents had wearied of newspaper reports of setbacks against the Japanese forces in the Pacific. Japanese Americans on the home front had already been relocated to internment camps, thereby temporarily silencing Californians embittered by Pearl Harbor. Many xenophobic citizens also did not like Mexicans, especially the "foreign, different-looking" pachucos arrested following an incident at Sleepy Lagoon.

4   Sleepy Lagoon, a swimming hole frequented by Chicano youth of east Los Angeles, soon became the symbol of both popular outrage and repression. At a home near the lagoon, where the night before two rival gangs had confronted one another, the body of a young Chicano was discovered. Though no evidence indicated murder, the Los Angeles Police Department summarily arrested members of the 38th Street Club, the teenage group that had crashed a party the prior evening and precipitated the fighting.

5   The grand jury indicted twenty-two members of the club for murder and, according to Carey McWilliams, "to fantastic orchestration of 'crime' and 'mystery' provided by the Los Angeles

press seventeen of the youngsters were convicted in what was, up to that time, the largest mass trial for murder ever held in the country." Reflecting on the treatment of the Sleepy Lagoon defendants, the aroused McWilliams stated:

> For years, Mexicans had been pushed around by the Los Angeles police and given a very rough time in the courts, but the Sleepy Lagoon prosecution capped the climax. It took place before a biased and prejudiced judge (found to be such by an appellate court); it was conducted by a prosecutor who pointed to the clothes and the style of haircut of the defendants as evidence of guilt; and was staged in an atmosphere of intense community-wide prejudice which had been whipped up and artfully sustained by the entire press of Los Angeles. . . . From the beginning the proceedings savored more of a ceremonial lynching than a trial in a court of justice.

Concerned Anglo and Chicano citizens, headed by McWilliams, sharply criticized violations of the defendants' constitutional and human rights (such as beatings by police while the youths were being held incommunicado and the courtroom improprieties indicated above by McWilliams). They organized the Sleepy Lagoon Defense Committee and, with the support of such groups as the Congreso and UCAPAWA, faced down intimidation by the media and accusations of being "reds" by state senator Jack Tenney and his Committee on Un-American Activities. In 1944 they succeeded in persuading the District Court of Appeals to reverse the convictions, declare a mistrial, and release the defendants from San Quentin prison.

6   The Sleepy Lagoon case served as a prelude to an even more discriminatory episode in wartime Los Angeles — the so-called Zoot Suit Riots of 1943. Racial tensions intensified after the Sleepy Lagoon case as police continued to arrest large numbers of Chicano youth on a variety of charges. Adding to the unrest were confrontations between military servicemen and Chicano zoot suiters on city streets. Then on June 3, 1943, rumors circulated that Chicanos had beaten sailors over an incident involving some young Mexican women. The newspapers seized on the rumor and soon sailors and marines from nearby bases converged on the downtown area and on Chicano neighborhoods. There they attacked Chicano youth, regardless of whether they wore zoot suits, beat them, stripped off their clothes, and left them to be arrested by the police who did nothing to interfere with the

"military operations." A virtual state of siege existed for Chicanos in Los Angeles as hundreds of servicemen in "taxicab brigades" looked for Mexicans on whom to vent their anger. "I never believed that I could see a thing like that," recalled Josephine Fierro de Bright.

> I went downtown and my husband and I were standing there and we saw all these policemen hanging around . . . and hundreds of taxis with sailors hanging on with clubs in their hands, bullies just beating Mexicans on Main Street. And we went up and asked a cop to stop it: he says, "You better shut up or I'll do the same to you." You can't do a thing when you see people and the ambulances coming to pick them up and nobody is stopping the slaughter. It's a nightmare. It's a terrible thing to see.

The local press continued to feed the hysteria with headlines announcing the sailors' "war" against zoot-suited pachucos. After five days of beatings, mass arrests, and rampant fear in Chicano communities, military authorities — ordered by federal officials at the request of the Mexican consulate — quelled the riots by declaring downtown Los Angeles off limits to all naval personnel.

7   In the wake of the riots, which also occurred in San Diego and several other communities but with much less violence than in Los Angeles, the Chicano community remained paralyzed with fear of another occurrence. The Mexican government and many local citizens protested the outrages, and Governor Earl Warren appointed a committee composed of clergy, public officials, and other well-known citizens to investigate the incident. Even so, Chicano relations with the police remained tense for many years. Jesse Saldana, a Los Angeles resident who witnessed the riots, articulated the sentiment of many Chicanos: "Justice is blind; she can't see the Mexicans."

8   The Zoot Suit Riots climaxed an era of overt hostility against Chicanos in California. Beginning with mass deportations during the early years of the depression and the violent suppression of unionization efforts, the 1930s and early 1940s witnessed much sadness and frustration for Chicanos who struggled to keep family and neighborhood from moral and physical deterioration. The irony was that tens of thousands of Mexican fathers and sons were fighting overseas with the U.S. armed forces as their families on the home front were experiencing bigotry

and persecution. But this period of depression and repression also aroused in Chicanos a desire to gain the equality that eluded them. The post–World War II decades witnessed a new upsurge of activity and a sense of hope within the Mexican community. ◻

EXERCISES

Comprehension

_____ 1. The main idea of this selection is that **(5b)**
    a. the pachucos were delinquents and hoodlums.
    b. Mexicans and sailors just don't get along.
    c. the pachucos became a target of Anglo prejudice.
    d. Los Angeles has changed a lot since World War II.

_____ 2. The article refers to events that took place in the **(6a)**
    a. late 1940s.
    b. early 1940s.
    c. 1930s and 1940s.
    d. 1940s and 1950s.

_____ 3. The pachucos separated themselves from other young people in the barrio by **(6a)**
    a. getting tattoos.
    b. the way they looked and talked.
    c. using and selling drugs.
    d. dressing like their counterparts in other cities.

_____ 4. Sleepy Lagoon was **(6a)**
    a. an amusement park.
    b. a swimming hole in East Los Angeles.
    c. a popular spot for sailors.
    d. used only by the pachucos.

_____ 5. The 38th Street Club was **(6a)**
    a. a group of mass murderers.
    b. a Chicano citizens' group.
    c. a pachuco gang.
    d. the civic group that owned Sleepy Lagoon.

_____ 6. Seventeen of the youths accused of murder in the Sleepy Lagoon case were **(6a)**
   a. convicted and executed.
   b. found innocent and released.
   c. convicted but released two years later.
   d. found innocent but later confessed.

_____ 7. The Zoot Suit Riots were caused by **(6a)**
   a. Mexican women.
   b. rumors spread in the newspapers.
   c. the police.
   d. Chicano youths.

_____ 8. The Zoot Suit Riots lasted for **(6a)**
   a. five years.
   b. five days.
   c. two days.
   d. two weeks.

_____ 9. The outcome of the riots was **(6a)**
   a. mass deportations.
   b. an upsurge of political activity in the Mexican community.
   c. violent suppression and repression of Mexican Americans for decades.
   d. the U.S. victory in World War II.

_____ 10. One irony of the conflict between Anglos and Chicanos was that **(6a)**
   a. both groups were fighting a common enemy overseas.
   b. both groups lived in California.
   c. both groups were opposed to rioting.
   d. the conflict was instigated by "reds" and Japanese spies.

Reading and Critical Thinking

_____ 1. The tone of the selection is **[12c(2)]**
   a. angry and defiant.
   b. sad but hopeful.
   c. depressed and hopeless.
   d. very optimistic.

_____ 2. The selection suggests that teenagers became pachucos **(8)**
   a. in response to a society that was prejudiced against them.
   b. because they were unpatriotic and prone to violence.
   c. because all Mexicans automatically became pachucos.
   d. in response to fears about the war against Japan.

_____ 3. From the selection we can conclude that the media **(10)**
   a. were fair and reported both good things and bad things about the pachucos.
   b. at first were suspicious of but later helped the pachucos.
   c. made things more difficult but essentially were right about the pachucos.
   d. were prejudiced and made the situation worse.

_____ 4. We can infer that the Anglo community in Los Angeles **(8)**
   a. was more threatened by Mexican Americans than by Japanese Americans.
   b. had more reason to fear Japanese Americans than Mexican Americans.
   c. generally felt embittered about and threatened by foreign-born Americans.
   d. was proud of any Mexican American who supported the war effort.

_____ 5. We can infer that Carey McWilliams was a **(8)**
   a. member of the 38th Street Club.
   b. concerned citizen.
   c. member of the press.
   d. lawyer hired by the pachucos.

_____ 6. The author concludes that the Zoot Suit Riots **(10)**
   a. were even more discriminatory than the events of the Sleepy Lagoon case.
   b. were a criminal act caused solely by the pachucos.
   c. were a direct result of the Sleepy Lagoon case.
   d. marked the end of Anglo-Chicano tension.

_____ 7. The phrase *taxicab brigade* probably was **(8)**
   a. invented by the press.
   b. invented by the author.

c. a description of a World War II vehicle.

d. derived from a new type of weapon invented by the pachucos.

_____ 8. We can conclude that as a result of her experiences, Josephine Fierro de Bright **(10)**

a. developed great respect for the Los Angeles police department.

b. joined the rioting.

c. became disillusioned and mistrustful.

d. became an active member of a civic organization.

_____ 9. We can infer that the author **(8)**

a. was a serviceman in World War II.

b. is a newspaper reporter.

c. was a pachuco.

d. is sympathetic to Mexican Americans.

10. Put an *F* beside any statement that is a fact and an *O* next to any statement that is an opinion or judgment. **(12a)**

_____ a. Mexican Americans faced the future with hope.

_____ b. The riots were caused by rumors of pachucos beating servicemen.

_____ c. The police did not try to stop the rioting.

_____ d. Servicemen attacked people at random.

_____ e. The Mexican consulate helped stop the rioting.

_____ f. All Mexican Americans distrusted the police.

_____ g. There was no other incident as important after the riots.

_____ h. Conditions in Chicano neighborhoods improved rapidly after the riots.

_____ i. Governor Warren appointed a committee to investigate the riots.

Connecting Ideas

1. In both this selection and Hisaye Yamamoto's "Wilshire Bus" (pages 479–483), treatment by others set up the problem of self-definition and identity for the people described. Compare the effect of others' attempts to stigmatize these individuals in creating the identity struggles described.

2. Although the author mentions Japanese Americans in the selection, he does not dwell on their plight during World War II. Look up the internment of Japanese Americans in a history book or encyclopedia. How does the discrimination experienced by Japanese Americans compare with the Mexican-American experience?

Critical Thinking in Writing

1. Write a summary of the events leading up to the Zoot Suit Riots that puts the events into chronological order. How would the order of details change if you were to put the events into a list by order of importance?

2. Based on the details provided in this article, write a description of the way a typical Zoot Suit boy and girl looked.

Vocabulary

1. The following words are of Spanish origin. Look them up in the text or use a Spanish-English dictionary to write their definitions in the spaces provided. (3a)

   a. pachuco _____

   b. caló _____

   c. barrio _____

   d. incommunicado _____

   e. marijuana _____

2. Use an English dictionary to look up the meanings of the following words and the language that each word comes from. (Appendix)

a. camaraderie _____

b. lagoon _____

c. consulate _____

d. tattoo _____

e. zoot suit _____

f. pompadour _____

3. Each of the following phrases contains a poetic use of the word in italics. Write the literal meaning and then, below, write the figurative meaning the author is trying to convey. **(9, 3a)**

a. Sleepy Lagoon was a *prelude*

   literal meaning: _____

   figurative meaning: _____

b. local press *fed* the hysteria

   literal meaning: _____

   figurative meaning: _____

c. *ceremonial* lynching

   literal meaning: _____

   figurative meaning: _____

d. *climate* of repression

   literal meaning: _____

   figurative meaning: _____

Creating Unique Names for Children

Cindy Roberts

This selection describes the current trend, especially among African-American parents, of giving children original names. Read about why parents are choosing the unique over the ordinary.

Prereading

Write a journal entry about your first name. Is it a familiar or an unusual name? Does your name have a special meaning or history? Did your parents tell you how or why they picked your name? What does your name mean to you? How do other people react to your name? Is it the name you would have picked for yourself, knowing who you are now?

Word Highlights

Alex Haley   African-American author of *Roots*, a major novel of the 1980s
appellations   names
forename   first or personal name
surname   last or family name
Swahili   official language of East Africa and the Congo
turbulent   troubled, chaotic, confused
WASP   *White Anglo-Saxon Protestant*
Yoruba   African language used in East Guinea and the lower Niger

---

2   Long before YaMaya Cimone Pugh was born, her mother already had picked her name.

"I had known a young lady several years ago named YaMaya, and I always said if I had a daughter I would name her YaMaya. I just named her that because it was different," said LaRhonda Gilstrap, a 22-year-old computer science student.

3   She's not alone. Among those sharing the nursery with YaMaya recently at Crawford Long Hospital: Tria Armania

500

Holloway, Jamecia Thermutus Hawkins and Ja-Min O'Haad Newson.

4   The explosion of originality in naming children has touched nearly every class, race and region, but experts say it is most pronounced among black Americans.

5   "Blacks are refusing to take white people's names," said Leonard Ashley, author of *What's in a Name?* and an English professor at Brooklyn College in New York. "They are saying, 'We are different. We are going to have our own Christmas holiday, we are going to have our own names.'"

6   At the turn of the century, the 10 most popular names in each gender category sufficed for half of all boys and girls, Mr. Ashley said.

7   Today, the top 10 account for an estimated 25 percent of all American names, he said. The other 75 percent, he said, are largely names rarely seen in this country until recent years, if at all.

8   The quest for originality and individuality began in the politically turbulent 1960s and '70s. For black parents, the search has meant going outside the WASP mainstream to invent names or dust off ancestral ones, Mr. Ashley said.

9   "Basically, the majority of African-Americans are now naming outside the tradition," said Jerrilyn McGregory, a professor of African-American studies and English at the University of Georgia.

10   "It's a statement of cultural identity," she said. "Some people predicted it to be a fad, but it seems to be going beyond one generation."

11   No one has had more influence than the late Alex Haley, whose book *Roots* inspired many black Americans to trace their African origins.

12   Kinte, the surname of the book's hero Kunta, began popping up across the country, as did Kizzie, the character's daughter, Ms. McGregory said.

13   Nia Damali, owner of Atlanta's Medu Bookstore, was Pat before she changed her name to reflect her African roots in 1986, when she published her book *Golden Names for an African People.*

14   Her 6-month-old son, Sekou Ebun Malika, has an African forename.

15   "People said, 'Where did you get that name? Is his father African?' I said, 'Well he's African-American,'" said Ms. Damali.

16   Funmilayo Nonye-John, a native of Nigeria who has been a maternity ward nurse at Crawford Long for the past five years, said black parents frequently ask her to help them choose an African name.

17   "I try to educate people how to give a name," she said. "People make up names. There's a lot of 'sha' names that are not really African names."

18   Some don't care whether a name is African as long as it has a nice ring to it and isn't Anglo-Saxon. The result is a treasure trove of appellations pieced together from various sources — Swahili, Yoruba, Spanish, French — and a lot of imagination.

19   "Blacks are creating names out of bits and pieces of names," Mr. Ashley said. "The main thing they sound is African-American. They're fake African names, but they are genuine African-American names."

20   "Da," "La," "Sha" and "Ja" have emerged as among the most popular ingredients. Hence Lavar, LaKeisha, LaTonya, Jabar, Sheshandra, and Daquisha.

21   For her master's thesis, Ms. McGregory analyzed black birth records from Gary, Ind., from 1945 to 1980. Over the years, there were more and more unconventional names. Of 274 girls born in 1980, 213 had different names. Some names differed only in spelling; she found 40 versions of Tamika, for example.

22   The names symbolize the degree to which black Americans have felt excluded from American life, she said.

23   "It's like a gift," Ms. McGregory said. "It's like saying, 'I can't give you much, but I can give you a name no one else will bear.'"   ❏

EXERCISES

Comprehension

_____ 1. The main idea of this selection is that (5)
   a. television influences which names are popular.
   b. original names come from a variety of sources.
   c. original names for black American children make a statement about identity.
   d. African Americans are more likely to give their children original names than are other Americans.

_____ 2. The overall idea that emerges from the first four paragraphs of the selection is that **(5b)**
   a. people want to be different.
   b. parents are giving their children original names.
   c. many children born at Crawford Long Hospital are given original names.
   d. LaRhonda Gilstrap gave her child an original name.

_____ 3. In 1900 the ten most popular names for boys and girls accounted for the names of **(6a)**
   a. 50 percent of the children born in the United States.
   b. 25 percent of the children born in the United States.
   c. 75 percent of the children born in the United States.
   d. black and white children equally.

_____ 4. The current trend of giving children original names began **(6a)**
   a. at the turn of the century.
   b. in the 1960s and 1970s.
   c. after the publication of *Roots*.
   d. in 1945.

5. Check all the sources mentioned in the selection of the original names that parents give their children. **(6a)**

_____ a. French

_____ b. Swahili

_____ c. Spanish

_____ d. Egyptian

_____ e. Yoruban

_____ f. African

_____ g. English

_____ h. the imagination

_____ i. books

_____ j. movies

_____ 6. According to the selection, many African-American parents choose original names for their children for all the following reasons *except* **(6a)**
   a. "refusing to take white people's names."
   b. helping children stand out from the "mainstream" culture.
   c. following a fad.
   d. reflecting their African roots.

   7. Write *maj* before major details and *min* before minor details. **(6b)**

_____   a. "Da," "La," "Sha," and "Ja" are the most popular "ingredients" of the original names that parents are giving their children.

_____   b. Although many original names are "fake African names," they are "genuine African-American names."

_____   c. Some examples of original names are "Ja-Min O'Haad Newson," "Tria Armania Holloway," and "Jamecia Thermutus Hawkins."

_____   d. Alex Haley's book *Roots* inspired many African Americans to trace their African origins.

_____   e. "Kinte" is the surname of the hero of *Roots*.

_____   f. The trend of giving children original names cuts across class, race, and region.

_____   g. Many African Americans invent new names or dust off ancestral ones.

_____   h. In 1980, 213 of 274 African-American females born in Gary, Ind., were given original names.

_____   i. The name "Tamika" can be spelled over 40 different ways.

_____   j. Nia Damali is the author of *Golden Names for an African People.*

_____   k. Nia Damali changed her name from "Pat."

_____   l. Nia Damali changed her name to reflect her cultural roots.

_____ 8. Jerrilyn McGregory's study of black birth records shows that **(6a)**
   a. African-American parents like to make up original spellings.
   b. the majority of African-American children are given original names.
   c. children in Gary, Ind., have more original names than other children.
   d. the trend of giving children original names has grown.

_____ 9. Overall this selection is organized by **(7)**
   a. time order.
   b. classification.
   c. cause and effect.
   d. comparison and contrast.

Reading and Critical Thinking

_____ 1. We can infer that LaRhonda Gilstrap **(8)**
   a. had parents who believed in traditional names.
   b. differs from other parents in her community.
   c. influenced the parents of Jamecia Thermutus Hawkins.
   d. is part of a trend in her community.

_____ 2. We can infer that "Kinte" and "Kizzie" **(8)**
   a. are names that have meaning for many African Americans.
   b. were ancestors of many African Americans.
   c. are the most popular names for African-American children.
   d. are names invented by Alex Haley.

_____ 3. We can infer from the selection that WASP parents are less likely than African-American parents to choose original names for their children because WASP parents **(8)**
   a. are part of the mainstream culture.
   b. do not want their children to develop unique identities.
   c. do not have a sense of their roots.
   d. do not know any African names.

_____ 4. From the trends reported here, we can predict that in the 21st century **(10)**
   a. most African-American parents will choose original names for their children.
   b. traditional American names will vanish entirely for black youngsters.
   c. other ethnic groups will start to copy African-American names.
   d. other ethnic groups will begin to use traditional American names again.

_____ 5. We can predict that African-American parents who feel a part of mainstream America would not choose the name **(10)**
   a. Thomas.
   b. Barbara.
   c. Raymond.
   d. LaTonya.

_____ 6. From the selection we can conclude that many African Americans **(10)**
   a. are in contact with African relatives.
   b. identify strongly with Africa.
   c. know a lot about the cultures and languages of Africa.
   d. have visited Africa.

7. Put a checkmark beside each generalization that we can make from the selection. **(11)**

_____ a. Many Americans believe names are an important indication of personal identity.

_____ b. Political change can stimulate cultural change.

_____ c. Many African-American parents feel a part of the American mainstream.

_____ d. African-American families reject most traditional American values.

_____ e. Most African-American parents today choose only African names for their children.

8. From the selection we can generalize that many African Americans put a strong value on certain characteristics. Put a checkmark beside those characteristics in the list below. **(11)**

_____ a. cultural roots

_____ b. originality

_____ c. historical authenticity

_____ d. conformity

_____ e. identity

_____ f. feeling included

9. In the space before each opinion in Column A, place the letter identifying the name of the person who holds it from Column B. You may need to use inference skills to determine who holds which opinion. **(8, 12a)** Some names may be used more than once.

A

_____ 1. People need to be educated how to give African names.

_____ 2. There are at least 40 spellings for "Tamika."

_____ 3. Giving original names is more than a fad.

_____ 4. African Americans can have African names.

_____ 5. "Da," "La," "Sha," and "Ja" are popular parts of African-American names.

_____ 6. It is not important that African Americans have African names, only that their names sound African-American.

_____ 7. Black Americans should learn about their African roots.

B

a. Leonard Ashley
b. Funmilayo Nonye-John
c. LaRhonda Gilstrap
d. Experts
e. Jerrilyn McGregory
f. Cindy Roberts
g. Nia Damali
h. Alex Haley

_____ 8. It is good for a name to be different.

_____ 9. Giving original names has touched nearly every class, race, and region in the United States.

_____ 10. Giving original names is most pronounced among black Americans.

_____ 10. Which of the following claims is not backed up by evidence? **(12b)**
   a. "Da," "La," "Sha," and "Ja" are popular "ingredients" in African-American names.
   b. Names symbolize the degree to which black Americans feel excluded from American life.
   c. Over the years the use of unconventional names has increased.
   d. YaMaya Cimone Pugh was not the only child with an original name in the nursery at Crawford Long Hospital.

_____ 11. Overall the tone of the selection is **(12c)**
   a. argumentative.
   b. informative.
   c. persuasive.
   d. ironic.

12. Explain the figurative comparison in the word _mainstream._ How is the word used in the phrase "going outside the WASP _mainstream_"? **(9, 3)**

_____

_____

_____

Connecting Ideas

1. In both this selection and Charity Plata's "Love Me, Love My (Brown) Mother" (pages 468–470), the importance of individuals recognizing and asserting their ethnic identities is stressed. Describe why both authors think identity is so important, and then give your thoughts on the subject.

2. Discuss with your classmates the ways in which different groups name their children and why. Compare naming practices with other ways of maintaining one's cultural or ethnic heritage such as language, religion, traditions, and clothing.

Critical Thinking in Writing

1. Write a paragraph or two to share your thoughts about the trend of giving children original names. Do you think that original naming is just a fad that will die out after the names become more common? Why or why not?
2. Write a paragraph in which you describe the names you might give your children and the reasons why.

Vocabulary

Each of the following comes from the selection. Using context clues, choose the correct definition for the words in italics. **(3a)**

_____ 1. experts say it is most *pronounced* among black Americans
   a. said
   b. noticeable
   c. concerned
   d. unclear

_____ 2. I can give you a name no one else will *bear*
   a. possess
   b. desire
   c. become
   d. fear

_____ 3. Some people predicted it to be a *fad*
   a. long-term trend
   b. tradition
   c. temporary craze
   d. disappearance

_____ 4. there were more and more *unconventional* names
   a. similar
   b. inconvenient
   c. unusual
   d. symbolic

_____ 5. The *quest* for originality and individuality began
        a. asking
        b. search
        c. testing
        d. achievement

_____ 6. the 10 most popular names in each gender category *sufficed*
        for half of all boys and girls
        a. was not certain
        b. considered
        c. demanded more
        d. was enough

_____ 7. dust off *ancestral* ones
        a. original
        b. related to family history
        c. covered with soot
        d. unknown

Putting Thoughts Together

1. Names and categories help assert people's identities, but they also are used by others to suggest that some people ought to be treated differently. Describe and compare how names and categories are both positive and negative forces in the selections in this unit.

2. In each of the four selections in this unit, writers describe the struggles they and others have had in discovering and asserting positive identities. Describe and compare the process by which people come to their identities in these selections.

3. In each of these selections, the writer pays attention to a different aspect of identity. Compare and describe the parts of identity that are considered in these four selections.

4. Identity sometimes is created by oneself, sometimes comes from one's relations with people around one, and sometimes is placed on oneself by hostile people. Describe and compare the sources of identity presented in these four selections.

5. Which identities are important to you? Where did they come from and how did you come to recognize and accept them? How have these identities affected your life, positively and negatively? Write several paragraphs describing the meaning of identity in your life.

Appendix: Using a Dictionary

A dictionary is an important tool to help build your reading skills. Here is what you can find in a dictionary:

- How to spell a word or its special plural form
- Whether a word is capitalized
- Whether a word is abbreviated
- How to break a word into syllables
- How to pronounce a word
- How a word fits into the English system of grammar (what part of speech it is: verb, noun, adjective, and so forth)
- Different meanings of a word, along with *synonyms* (words that have the same meaning) and *antonyms* (words that have opposite meanings)
- A sentence or an expression that uses a word correctly
- The meaning of important prefixes and suffixes
- The special uses of a word
- The history of a word
- Words made from a main word

Some dictionaries also have special sections for other information:

- Foreign words and phrases
- Abbreviations
- Addresses of colleges or government offices
- The population of cities and countries

Depending on how complete they are and on what their purposes are, dictionaries vary in length. *Unabridged dictionaries* — which try to include information on all the words in our language (about half a million!) — take up thousands of pages. For much of your work in class and at home, however, you can use a *pocket dictionary*, a small book that contains only the most common words. The example from the *American Heritage Dictionary* on page 514 and the following discussion will help you improve your dictionary skills.

Guide words ———— 481 ———— **marathon / markka**

Main entries

Pronunciation

Part of speech

Special forms and spellings

Meaning

History of the word

Pronunciation key

mar•a•thon (măr′ə-thŏn′) n. 1. A long-distance race, esp. one on foot. 2. A contest of endurance. —mar′a•thon′ adj.

ma•raud (mə-rôd′) v. To rove in search of booty; raid for plunder. [F marauder.] —ma•raud′er n.

mar•ble (mär′bəl) n. 1. A metamorphic rock, chiefly calcium carbonate, often irregularly colored by impurities. 2. a. A small ball used in children's games. b. marbles (takes sing. v.). A game played with such balls. —adj. Consisting of or resembling marble. [< Gk marmaros, marble, any hard stone.]

mar•bling (mär′bling) n. A mottling or streaking that resembles marble.

march¹ (märch) v. 1. To walk or cause to walk in a military manner with measured steps at a steady rate. 2. To advance or proceed with steady movement. 3. To traverse by marching. —n. 1. The act of marching. 2. Forward movement. 3. A regulated pace. 4. The distance covered by marching. 5. A musical composition in regularly accented meter, to accompany marching. [OF marcher, marchier, to walk, trample.]

march² (märch) n. A border region or frontier. [< OF marche, marc, borderland.]

March (märch) n. The 3rd month of the year. March has 31 days. [< L Mārtius (mēnsis), (month) of Mars.]

mar•chion•ess (mär′shən-ĭs, mär′shə-nĕs′) n. 1. The wife or widow of a marquis. 2. A peeress of the rank of marquis in her own right. [< ML marchiō, marquis.]

Mar•di gras (mär′dē grä′). The last day before Lent. [F, "fat Tuesday."]

mare¹ (mâr) n. A female horse, zebra, etc. [< OE mere, miere. See marko-.]

ma•re² (mä′rā) n., pl. -ria (-rē-ə). Astron. Any of the large dark areas on the moon or Mars. [< L, sea.]

mar•ga•rine (mär′jə-rĭn) n. A butter substitute made with vegetable oils. [F.]

mar•gin (mär′jən) n. 1. An edge and the area immediately adjacent to it; border. 2. The blank space bordering the printed area on a page. 3. A limit of a state or process: the margin of reality. 4. A surplus measure or amount: a margin of safety. 5. A measure or degree of difference: a margin of 500 votes. [< L margō (margin-).] —mar′gin•al adj.

mar•gi•na•li•a (mär′jə-nā′lē-ə) pl.n. Notes in a book margin.

Ma•rie An•toi•nette (mə-rē′ ăn′twə-nĕt′) 1755–1793. Queen of France; wife (1770) of Louis XVI; guillotined.

mar•i•gold (măr′ə-gōld′, mâr′-) n. A widely cultivated plant with showy yellow, orange, or reddish flowers. [ME marygould.]

mar•i•jua•na, mar•i•hua•na (măr′ə-wä′nə) n. 1. The hemp plant. 2. The dried flowers and leaves of this plant, esp. when smoked to induce euphoria. [Mex Span mariguana, marihuana.]

ma•rim•ba (mə-rĭm′bə) n. A large xylophone with resonators.

ma•ri•na (mə-rē′nə) n. A boat basin for small pleasure boats. [< L marinus, MARINE.]

mar•i•nade (măr′ə-nād′) n. A liquid, as vinegar or wine, in which food is soaked before cooking. [< Span marino, "briny," marine.]

mar•i•nate (măr′ə-nāt′) v. -nated, -nating. To soak (meat or fish) in a marinade. [Var of MARINADE.]

ma•rine (mə-rēn′) adj. 1. a. Of or pertaining to the sea: marine exploration. b. Native to the sea: marine life. 2. Pertaining to shipping or maritime affairs. 3. Pertaining to sea navigation: marine chart. —n. 1. Shipping in general; maritime interests as represented by ships: merchant marine. 2. a. A soldier serving on a ship. b. Marine. A member of the U.S. Marine Corps. [< L marinus < mare, sea.]

Marine Corps. A branch of the U.S. Armed Forces composed chiefly of amphibious troops.

mar•i•ner (măr′ə-nər) n. A sailor or seaman.

mar•i•o•nette (măr′ē-ə-nĕt′) n. A jointed puppet manipulated by strings.

mar•i•tal (măr′ə-təl) adj. Of or pertaining to marriage. [< L maritus, married, husband.]

mar•i•time (măr′ə-tīm′) adj. 1. Located on or near the sea. 2. Of or concerned with shipping or navigation. [< L mare, sea.]

mar•jo•ram (mär′jər-əm) n. An aromatic plant with leaves used as seasoning. [< ML majorāna.]

mark¹ (märk) n. 1. A visible trace or impression on something, as a spot, dent, or line. 2. A written or printed symbol: a punctuation mark. 3. A grade, as in school. 4. A name, stamp, etc., placed on an article to signify ownership, quality, etc. 5. A visible indication of some quality, property, etc. 6. A standard or criterion of quality. 7. Quality; note; importance. 8. A target. 9. That which one wishes to achieve; a goal. 10. An object or point that serves as a guide. —v. 1. To make a visible impression (on). 2. To form, distinguish, or separate by making a visible impression on. 3. To pay attention to. 4. To characterize; set off. 5. To grade (school papers). [< OE mearc, boundary, landmark, sign. See merg-.] —mark′er n.

mark² (märk) n. See Deutsche mark, ostmark.

Mark (märk) Saint. Christian apostle; reputed author of the 2nd Gospel of the New Testament.

marked (märkt) adj. 1. Having a mark or marks. 2. Having a noticeable trait. —mark′ed•ly (mär′kĭd-lē) adv.

mar•ket (mär′kĭt) n. 1. An open place or building where merchandise is offered for sale. 2. A store that sells a particular type of merchandise: a meat market. 3. a. A region in which goods can be bought and sold: the European market. b. A type of buyer or demand: the college market. 4. Demand for goods. —v. 1. To offer for sale. 2. To sell. 3. To buy household supplies. [< L mercāri, to trade.] —mar′ket•er, mar′ke•teer′ n.

mar•ket•place (mär′kĭt-plās′) n. 1. A public square in which a market is set up. 2. The world of trade.

mark•ka (mär′kä′) n., pl. -kaa (-kä′). The basic monetary unit of Finland.

ă pat/ā ate/âr care/ä bar/b bib/ch chew/d deed/ĕ pet/ē be/f fit/g gag/h hat/nw what/ ĭ pit/ī pie/îr pier/j judge/k kick/l lid, fatal/m mum/n no, sudden/ng sing/ŏ pot/ō go/ ô paw, for/oi boy/ou out/ŏŏ took/ōō coo/p pop/r run/s sauce/sh shy/t to/th thin/th the/ ŭ cut/ûr fur/v van/w wag/y yes/z size/zh vision/ə ago, item, edible, gallop, circus/

A1 The Guide Words

If you want to look up the word *margin*, for example, the left-hand guide word *marathon* is a hint that the word is on the page because *marg* comes after *mara* in alphabetical order. The right-hand guide word is *markka*. *Marg* comes before *mark*, so you know *margin* must appear between these two guide words.

A2 The Main Entry

Main entries are printed in bold (heavy black) letters. Centered dots mark each syllable. The main entry tells you the preferred spelling of a word and may be followed by a *variant*, the same word spelled correctly but in another way.

A3 The Pronunciation Key

The groups of letters right after the main entry tell you how to say the word. (You know from words like *cough, bough,* and *through* that spelling sometimes does not help you pronounce words.) The letters that appear in parentheses, or between slanted lines in some dictionaries, stand for special sounds. To find out what sound a letter stands for in the word you are looking up, check the pronunciation key at the bottom of the page or in the special section at the front of the dictionary. Checking the pronunciation spelling that follows the main entry against the pronunciation key at the bottom of the page, you can see that the *a* in *mare* (meaning "a female horse") has the same sound as the *a* in *care*. Notice that the *a* in the next entry, *mare* (meaning a "dark area on the moon or Mars"), has the same *a* as the word *bar*, giving *mare*, the astronomical term, a very different pronunciation.

A4 The Parts of Speech

The parts of speech tell you how the word fits into the system of English grammar. The *n.* after the pronunciation spelling for *marinade* means "noun." The *v.* after *marinate* means "verb." The *adj.* after *marine* means "adjective." The *adv.* after *markedly* means "adverb." Sometimes a word has different meanings based on what part of speech it is. The word *march* may be a verb meaning "to walk or cause to walk in a military manner." Used as a noun, *march* means "a border region or frontier." Another meaning for *March* (written with a capital *M*) is "the 3rd month of the year."

A5   Special Forms and Spellings

Marauder is made from the word *maraud,* so it is included as part of the entry for *maraud* instead of as another main entry. Notice too that in addition to singular forms, the dictionary gives unusual plural forms, especially for foreign words or words that do not simply add an *s*. The plural of *markka* is formed by adding an *a* as the final letter.

A6   The Meanings of the Word

Next the word is defined. The meanings of words that can be used in more than one sense are separated and numbered in bold print. Usually the most important definitions come first. An example sometimes appears to show how the main word is used. *Syn.* is an abbreviation for *synonym.* Words that come after *syn.* have the same meaning as the main word.

A7   The History of the Word

The information that appears in brackets tells the way the word has developed in our language. Many words have origins in foreign languages like Latin (L) or Greek (Gk). In fact a good dictionary can be your best first source for a word's *etymology* — a summary of its origin and historical development. For example, *market* comes from the Latin word *mercari,* meaning "to trade." The place where goods are traded became known as a *market.*

Some Dictionary Pointers

- Review your skill with alphabetical order. Can you arrange words correctly?
- Use the guide words. They save you time.
- Check all abbreviations and symbols in the special section.
- If you look up a word and it's not where you expect it to be, don't think it's not in your dictionary! Check under several possible spellings. If you couldn't spell the word *crime*, for example, the sound of the word might suggest these spellings:

cryme	krime
kryme	krhyme
criem	crhyme

If you couldn't spell the word correctly, you might have to check them all before you found *crime*.

- Test the meaning you find for the word in the sentence in which you found the word. You may not have picked a definition that works for the word as it is used.
- Try to say the word aloud after you look at the pronunciation key.

ANSWERS
to Chapter Tests

CHAPTER 1

1. thinking in advance about the subject of a reading before you read the selection   **2.a.** making a list   **b.** drawing a word map   **c.** doing free-writing   **d.** raising questions   **3.** writing nonstop about a topic without editing   **4.** rapid reading for facts   **5.** looking ahead to the contents of a reading before actually reading it   **6.a.** introductory material or headnote   **b.** title   **c.** headings   **d.** pictures, charts, and drawings   **e.** first paragraph   **f.** first sentence of each paragraph   **g.** questions after the reading   **h.** key words in different print   **i.** summaries **7.a.** copyright page   **b.** table of contents   **c.** preface   **d.** index **e.** special features (glossary, appendix)   **f.** introduction   **g.** bibliography or references   **h.** parts books include or exclude

CHAPTER 2

1. a. Underline only in books you own.
    b. Mark main ideas and major details differently.
    c. Underline sentences that state main ideas; invent sentences for implied main ideas.
    d. Circle key words; use other symbols to mark important words or phrases.
    e. Make comments of your own in the margins.
2. a. Write down main ideas of a selection.
    b. Identify major details and connect them to notes on main ideas.
    c. Use clear abbreviations to help you shorten words and sentences.
    d. Add your own comments and thoughts.
    e. Apply similar strategies in taking notes for class lectures.
3. Any three of these: list only main ideas as main headings; relate subheadings to main headings they follow; make sure all headings in a series logically fit together; make sure headings are clearly different and do not overlap; when you break down a heading, you must have at least two subheadings; use sentences or phrases or single words, but use them consistently at all heading and subheading points; indent correctly; use a period after all letters and numbers on the outline format
4.
I. SQ3R is a study system that stands for *survey, question, read, recite, and review.*
    A. Survey your reading for an overview.
        1. Look at chapter outlines.
        2. Skim materials.
        3. Note headings.
        4. Read summaries or introductory material.

    B. Ask questions about what you should be learning as you read.
    C. Read the selection.
    D. After reading, talk about what you've read.
       1. Speak aloud.
       2. Take notes at this point.
       3. Reread if necessary.
    E. Review what you have read.
       1. See how the parts connect with each other.
       2. Determine what the overall message is.

CHAPTER 3

A. 1. b prevented; turned away   2. b total disorder   3. c descriptions
that produce mental pictures   4. c festive and merry   5. a rise above
B. 1. c   2. c   3. a   4. d   5. b
C. 1. c   2. b   3. b   4. a   5. c
D. 1. c   2. e   3. a   4. b   5. d

CHAPTER 4

1. a   2. b   3. b   4. c   5. c

CHAPTER 5

A. 1. c   2. b   3. b   4. a   5. c
B. 1. d   2. a   3. c   4. b   5. a
C. 1. a   2. b   3. d   4. c   5. a
D. 1. b   2. c   3. d   4. a   5. d

CHAPTER 6

A. 1. b   2. −   3. +   4. −   5. +   6. −   7. +   8. +
9. −   10. −
B. 1. c   2. a. maj   b. min   c. maj   d. min   e. min   f. maj
g. min   h. maj

CHAPTER 7

A. 1. a. 2   b. 3   c. 1   d. 4   2. a
B. 1. a   2. b   3. a. +   b. −   c. +   d. +
C. 1. d   2. c   3. a. N   b. S   c. S   d. N
D. 1. c   2. b   3. d   4. c
E. 1. c   2. a   3. d   4. c   5. a

CHAPTER 8

A. 1. d   2. b   3. a   4. d   5. c
B. 1. The American periodical press has had a technological and social impact on the rest of the world.   2. b   3. c   4. d   5. b

CHAPTER 9
1. a   2. d   3. c   4. d   5. d

CHAPTER 10
A. 1. c   2. a   3. a   4. d   5. c
B. 1. c   2. b   3. d   4. a   5. a

CHAPTER 11
A. 1. +   2. +   3. −   4. −   5. +   6. −   7. +   8. +
9. −   10. +

CHAPTER 12
A. 1. b   2. c   3. d   4. d   5. c
B. 1. I   2. N   3. E   4. E   5. I
C. 1. f   2. a   3. c   4. e   5. h   6. b   7. d   8. g   9. c
10. h
D. 1. S   2. S   3. T   4. S   5. S   6. S   7. S   8. T   9. S
10. S

CHAPTER 13
1. a. independent views of what they read
   b. able to show how own views compare with what's read
   c. able to provide reasons or evidence for points of view
   d. able to relate ideas read in one piece to ideas read in other pieces
   e. able to express ideas to others
2. a. Ask the question, "Where did I read or see or hear about something like this before?"
   b. Use skill at identifying topic to make reading connections.
   c. Use skill at stating main idea to make connections between readings.
   d. Test generalizations from one reading against generalizations in other areas.
   e. Write down relations among different presentations of ideas.

Acknowledgments

Pp. 11–13   Biehler, Robert F. and Jack Snowman, "Stages of Psychosocial Development," *Psychology Applied to Teaching, 7/e*. Houghton Mifflin, 1993, pp. 43–44.

Pp. 17–22, 69   Getchell, Bud, excerpts from *Houghton Mifflin Health*, pp. 378–381. Copyright © 1989 by D.C. Heath and Company. Reprinted by permission of D.C. Heath.

Pp. 25–26, 29, 40–41, 43, 112   Blackford and Kerr, Table of Contents, excerpts, and Index from *Business Enterprise in American History*, 1986, pp. v–viii, 373–376, and 446. Reprinted by permission of Houghton Mifflin.

Pp. 31–34   Paredes and Paredes, excerpts from *Mexican-American Authors*, pp. 1–4, edited by Americo Paredes and Raymond Paredes. Copyright © 1976, 1972 by Houghton Mifflin Company. Reprinted by permission of Houghton Mifflin Company.

Pp. 44–45, 156   DeFleur and Dennis, excerpts from *Understanding Mass Communications*. Copyright © 1996 by Houghton Mifflin Company. Reprinted by permission.

Pp. 69, 115   Brown, Betty and John E. Clow, excerpt from *Our Business and Economic World*. Copyright © 1987 by Glencoe Publishers. Reprinted by permission of the publisher.

Pp. 71–72, 80–81, 183   Schaefer, Richard T., excerpts from *Sociology, 6/e*. Copyright © 1995 by McGraw-Hill, Inc. Reprinted by permission of McGraw-Hill, Inc.

Pp. 75, 126, 175–176   Biehler, Robert F. and Lynne M. Hudson, excerpts from *Developmental Psychology: An Introduction, 3/e*. Copyright © 1986 by Houghton Mifflin Company. Used with permission.

Pp. 89–91   Bernstein, Douglas A., et al., excerpt from *Psychology, 3/e*. Copyright © 1994 by Houghton Mifflin Company. Reprinted by permission.

Pp. 100–105   Boyes and Melvin, excerpt from *Economics, 3/e*. Copyright © 1997 by Houghton Mifflin Company. Reprinted by permission.

P. 109   Perry et al., map, "Middle East Trouble Spots," from *A History of the World*, p. 810. Copyright © 1988 by Houghton Mifflin Company. Reprinted by permission of McDougal Littell, Inc.

P. 120   Resnick, Seth, excerpt from, "Jorge Zamora," *Newsweek*, June 28, 1993, p. 51. © 1993, Newsweek, Inc. All rights reserved. Reprinted by permission.

Pp. 125, 257   Gelman, David, excerpt from "I'm Not a Role Model," from *Newsweek*, June 28, 1993, pp. 56–57. Copyright © 1993, Newsweek, Inc. All rights reserved. Reprinted by permission.

Pp. 127, 251–252   Ying, Yu-Lan (Mary), "Five New Words At a Time," *New York Times*, Op-ed. Copyright © 1993 by The New York Times Company. Reprinted by permission.

P. 128   Engelberg, Isa N. and Diana R. Winn, excerpt from *Working Groups*. Copyright © 1997 by Houghton Mifflin Company. Reprinted by permission.

Pp. 129, 172   Hardy, Richard, excerpts from *Government in America*, pp. 153, 364, 366, 398. Copyright © 1988 by Houghton Mifflin Company. Reprinted by permission of Houghton Mifflin Company.

Pp. 130–131   Johnson, Tim, excerpt from, "Big Dreams in 'Little Havana'," *MacLean's*, April 30, 1990, p. 33. Reprinted by permission of the publisher.

Pp. 130, 135, 166–171   Shertzer, Bruce, excerpts from *Career Planning, 3/e*, pp. 119, 157, 325–329. Copyright © 1985 by Houghton Mifflin Company. Used with permission.

P. 143   Paik Lee, Mary, excerpt from *Quiet Odyssey*. Copyright © 1990 by Mary Paik Lee. Reprinted by permission of the University of Washington Press.

P. 147   "Alice Harris: A Dream Maker." Reprinted with permission of Amway Corporation and Johnson Publishing Company, Inc.

Pp. 148–149   Pride, William M. and O. C. Ferrell, excerpt from *Marketing, 6/e*, pp. 16, 36–37, 521–522, and 592. Copyright © 1989 by Houghton Mifflin Comapny. Used with permission.

Pp. 149–150   Mulligan, Tom, excerpt from, "Hey, What's That Guy Doing Here?," *Los Angeles Times*, Monday, May 17, 1993. Copyright © 1993, Los Angeles Times. Reprinted by permission.

Pp. 151, 198–200   Ornstein & Levine, excerpt from *Foundations of Education, 6/e*. Copyright © 1997 by Houghton Mifflin Company. Reprinted by permission.

Pp. 176–177   Richardson, Cecilia, "Different Roommates," from Harvey S. Wiener, *Creating Compositions, 5/e*, pp. 133–134. Copyright © 1987. Reprinted by permission of McGraw-Hill, Inc.

Pp. 184–185   Smith, Richard, from Harvey S. Wiener, *The Writing Lab, 2/e*. Copyright © 1974, 1980 by Harvey S. Wiener. Reprinted by permission.

Pp. 185–189   Rodriguez, Richard, excerpt from, "None of this is Fair." Copyright © 1977 by Richard Rodriguez. Reprinted by permission of Georges Borchardt, Inc. for the author.

Pp. 216–217   Burns, Diane, "Sure You Can Ask Me a Personal Question."

Pp. 219–221   Navarrette, Ruben, Jr., excerpt from "Who's Afraid of Political Correctness?" *Hispanic*, March 1992, p. 68. Copyright © 1992 by *Hispanic Magazine*.

P. 231   Hughes, Langston, *Dream Deferred (Harlem)* from *The Panther and the Lash*. Copyright © 1951 by Langston Hughes. From *Collected Poems*. Copyright © 1994 by the Estate of Langston Hughes. Reprinted by permission of Alfred A. Knopf, Inc.

P. 233   Advertisement, courtesy of Amtrak and the Garrett A. Morgan, St. Foundation.

Pp. 242–243   Hayes, Patty, "Creating the Barrier-Free Environment," *Habitat World*, June 1989.

P. 254   Altman, Lawrence K., "For Some 'No Beards' Is a Painful Rule," *New York Times*, July 19, 1990. Copyright © 1990 by The New York Times Company. Reprinted by permission.

P. 263   Ad, "Teachers: Our best and last defense." Reprinted by permission of Mobil.

P. 272   Garcia, Robert, Letter To The Editor, "Bilingual Education Means Equal Opportunity," *New York Times*, August 18, 1989. Reprinted by permission of the author.

Pp. 274–276   Rosmann, Ronald L., "This Land is Your Land," by Ronald L. Rosmann. *Newsweek*, May 4, 1992, p. 17. Reprinted by permission of the author.

Pp. 279, 280   Janda, Kenneth, et al., excerpts from *The Challenge of Democracy, 3/e*, Houghton Mifflin Company, 1992, pp. 26–27, 151, 593–595. Copyright © 1992 by Houghton Mifflin Company. Reprinted by permission of the publisher.

P. 303   Feinblatt, John, "Teach Kids to 'Talk It Out'," *New York Times*, January 4, 1991. Copyright © 1991 by The New York Times Company. Reprinted by permission.

Pp. 303–304   Fyfe, James J., "Use a Gun, Do Federal Time," *New York Times*, January 4, 1991. Copyright © 1991 by The New York Times Company. Reprinted by permission.

Pp. 304–305   Zimring, Franklin E., "Trace Illegal Firearms," *New York Times*, January 4, 1991. Copyright © 1991 by The New York Times Company. Reprinted by permission.

Pp. 309–312   Israeloff, Roberta, "Role Reversal," from *Woman's Day*, September 13, 1988. Copyright © 1988 by Roberta Israeloff. Reprinted by permission.

Pp. 318–322   Moses, Sam, *A New Dawn*. Reprinted courtesy of *Sports Illustrated*, April 23, 1990. Copyright © 1990, Time, Inc. All rights reserved.

Pp. 330–338   Villapando, Venny, "The Business of Selling Mail-Order Brides," from *Making Waves* by Asian Women United of California. © 1989 by Asian Women United of California. Reprinted by permission of Beacon Press, Boston.

Pp. 347–352   Freeman, James M., *Hearts of Sorrow: Vietnamese-American Lives*. Reprinted from *Hearts of Sorrow: Vietnamese-American Lives* with the permission of the publishers, Stanford University Press. © 1989 by the Board of Trustees of the Leland Stanford Junior University.

Pp. 359–364   Levins Morales, Aurora, "Immigrants," from *Getting Home Alive* by Aurora Levins Morales and Rosario Morales. Firebrand Books, Ithaca, New York. Copyright © 1986 by Aurora Levins Morales.

Pp. 372–374   Billings, Laura, "My Unsentimental Tutee," from *The New York Times Magazine*, January 26, 1997, p. 80.

Pp. 381–384   Raybon, Patricia, *Letting in Light*. Copyright © 1993 by The New York Times Co. Reprinted by permission.

Pp. 391–396   Harper, Timothy, "They Treat Girls Differently, Don't They?" from the December, 1996 edition of *Sky Magazine*. Reprinted by permission of the author.

Pp. 405–410   Lee, Felicia R., "Model Minority Label Taxes Asian Youths." Copyright © 1990 by The New York Times Co. Reprinted by permission.

Pp. 420–422   Bleecker, Marcus, "My Father's Black Pride," appeared in the August 15, 1995 issue of *The New York Times Magazine*. Copyright © 1995 by The New York Times Co. Reprinted by permission.

Pp. 431–435   Schmidt, William E., "A Cafe Reopens: Lunch Returns to the Prairie," *New York Times*, June 10, 1990. Copyright © 1990 by The New York Times Co. Reprinted by permission.

Pp. 442–444   Prinz, Lucie, "Say Something," from the October, 1996 edition of *The Atlantic*, p. 44. Lucie Prinz is a Staff Editor at *The Atlantic Monthly*.

Pp. 452–457   Gite, Lloyd, "Like Mother, Like Daughter," from *Black Enterprise*, August 1991, pp. 93–96. Reprinted by permission.

Pp. 468–470   Plata, Charity, "Love Me, Love My (Brown) Mother," appeared in the December 16, 1995 issue of *Los Angeles Times*, p. B7. Copyright © 1995 Los Angeles Times. Reprinted by permission.

Pp. 479–483   Yamamoto, Hisaye, *Wilshire Bus*. Copyright © 1988 by Hisaye Yamamoto. Used by permission of Kitchen Table: Women of Color Press, P.O. Box 908, Latham, NY 12110, and the author.

Pp. 490–494   Camarillo, Albert, "Zoot Suit Riots," from *Chicanos in California: A History of Mexican Americans in California*. Copyright 1984 by Boyd & Fraser Publishing Company, San Francisco, CA 94118.

Pp. 500–502   Roberts, Cindy, "Parents Creating Unique Names." Reprinted by permission of the Associated Press.

Subject Index

Advertisements
  figurative language in, 232–233
  generalizing from public service,
    262–264
  persuasive techniques in, 293
Aids in reading. *See* Reading aids
Alternating method of comparison and
  contrast, 176
Antonyms, 513
Appendix, 24, 34–35
Asking questions, for prereading, 9–
  10
Authors, techniques of. *See* Writing techniques

Biased writing, 290
Bibliography, 24
Block method of comparison and contrast, 175
Books
  appendix, 24, 34–35
  bibliography, 24
  copyright page, 23
  index, 23, 28, 29
  introduction, 24, 28, 30–34
  parts of, 22–35
  preface, 23
  table of contents, 23, 24–28
  See also Textbooks

Cartoons, inferences from, 213–214
Cause and effect, in paragraph patterns,
  182–191
Chronology, in paragraphs, 158, 159,
  161
Classification, as paragraph pattern,
  172–175

Clues to meanings. *See* Word meanings
Collaborative learning, 305–307
Comparison
  and contrast, 158, 175–182
  in figurative language, 228–229
Comprehension
  of details, 165–172
  drawing conclusions, 236–253
  of facts, 141–147
  of figurative language, 227–235
  generalizing from, 254–266
  of main ideas, 110–132
  of paragraphs, 158–191
  predicting outcomes, 236–253
  prereading for, 5–10
  previewing for, 5, 15–35
  reading aids, 5–35, 97–107
  of sequence of ideas, 159–164
  visual aids for, 97–107
  of word meanings, 51–83
  See also Reading
Conclusions, drawing, from reading,
  236–253
Connections in reading, 298–307
  collaborative techniques, 305–307
  idea connections, 301–305
  personalizing, 298–301
Connotation, 62–65
Contents, table of, 23, 24–28
Context clues to word meanings, 52–
  57
Contrast and comparison, 158, 175–
  182
Copyright page, 23
Critical thinking in reading, 207–307
  drawing conclusions, 236–253
  evaluating ideas, 267–293
  figurative language, 227–235
  generalizing, 254–266

Critical thinking in reading (*cont.*)
  making connections, 298–307
  making inferences, 207–226
  predicting outcomes, 236–253

Denotation, 62–65
Details
  listing of, 165–172
  major, 39, 148–153
  minor, 148–153
  in paragraphs, 165–172
Diagrams, 98
Dictionaries, 513–517
  guide words in, 515
  main entry in, 515
  parts of speech in, 515–516
  pocket, 513
  pointers on use of, 517
  pronunciation key in, 515
  special forms and spellings in, 516
  unabridged, 513
  word history in, 516
  word meanings in, 516
Drawing conclusions, from reading,
  236–253

Effect and cause, in paragraph patterns,
  182–191
Essays, fact and opinion in, 274–276
Etymology, of word, 516
Evaluating ideas, 267–293
  evidence, 277–282
  fact and opinion, 267–276
  truth-twisting techniques, 290–293
  writer's techniques, 282–284
  See also Critical thinking in reading
Evidence, evaluation of, 277–282
Extended metaphors, 229

Fact-finding, 141–147
Facts, 267–276
  defined, 268
  distinguishing from opinions, 269–270
  evaluation of evidence, 277–282
  how to locate, 141–143
  and opinions, 267–276

Figurative expressions, 230
Figurative language, 227–235
  in advertisement, 232–233
  common expressions, 230
  comparisons, 228–229
  defined, 227
  original, 227–228
  in poetry, 231–232
  in speech, 232
  understanding, 229–232
Foreword, 23
Freewriting, 7–9

Generalizing, 254–266
  defined, 254
  how to generalize, 256
  from textbooks, 260–262
Glossary, 23–24
Graph, 99
Guide words, in dictionary, 515

Headings, for previewing, 15
Helping words, 52
Hyperbole, 229

Ideas
  connecting, 301–305
  evaluation of, 267–293
  main (key), 39, 110–132
  ordering (sequence) of, in paragraphs,
    159–164
  See also Main (key) ideas
Implied main ideas, 122–126
Importance order, in paragraphs, 160,
  161
Index, 23, 28, 29
Inferences, 207–226
  building skills, 213
  from cartoons, 213–214
  definition of, 207
  from longer selections, 219–
    222
  from poetry, 216–219
Information, reading for, 141–147
Introduction of book, 24, 28, 30–
  34

Key ideas. *See* Main (key) ideas
Key words, for previewing, 16

Language, figurative. *See* Figurative language
Learning, collaborative, 305–307
Listing of details, 165–172
List making, for prereading, 6–7
Long material. *See* Books; Textbooks

Main (key) ideas, 39, 110–132
    implied, 122–126
    in paragraph, 113–132
    in sentences, 110–112
    stated, 116–122
    in textbooks, 112–113
Main idea sentence, 116–119
Major details, 39, 148–153
Making connections. *See* Connections in reading
Maps, word, 7
Meanings of words. *See* Word meanings
Metaphors, 228
Minor details, 148–153
Mood, of writer, 283

Note taking, 41–43, 298–299

Opinions, 113, 267–276
    defined, 268
    distinguishing from facts, 269–270
    and evidence, 278–282
    and facts, 267–276
Order of ideas, in paragraphs, 159–164
Order of importance, in paragraphs, 160, 161
Outcomes, predicting, from reading, 236–253
Outlining, 45–47

Paragraph patterns, 158–191
    cause and effect, 182–191
    classification, 172–175

combined, 185
comparison and contrast, 158, 175–182
listing details of, 165–172
order of ideas, 159–164
order of importance, 160, 161
place order, 159–160, 161
time order (chronology), 158, 159, 161
Paragraphs
    classification in, 172–175
    definition of, 113
    first, 15
    listing details of, 165–172
    main ideas in, 113–132
    ordering ideas in, 159–164
    patterns of, 158–191
    topics in, 113–116
Parts of speech, in dictionary, 515–516
Personalizing, in reading, 298–301
Personification, 228
Photograph, 98
Place order, in paragraphs, 159–160, 161
Pocket dictionaries, 513
Poetry
    figurative language in, 231–232
    inferences from, 216–219
Point-by-point method of comparison and contrast, 176
Point of view, of writer, 284
Predicting outcomes, from reading, 236–253
Preface, 23
Prefixes
    as clues to word meanings, 58–59
    definition of, 58
    no or not, 58
    of number, 59
    of place, 59
    of time, 59
Prejudiced writing, 290
Prereading, 5–10
    freewriting, 7–9
    list making, 6–7
    question asking, 9–10
    word mapping, 7
Previewing, 5, 15–35
    appendix, 24, 34–35
    index, 23, 28, 29
    introduction, 24, 28, 30–34

Previewing (*cont.*)
   parts of book, 22–35
   table of contents, 23, 24–28
Prior knowledge, 5
Pronunciation key, in dictionary, 515
Propaganda, 290–293
Purpose, of writer, 284, 288–290

Question asking, for prereading, 9–10
Questions, in previewing, 15–16

Rapid reading (skimming), 5, 11–14
Reading
   between the lines (inferences),
      207–226
   collaborative, 305–307
   critical, 207–307
   drawing conclusions from, 236–253
   evaluating ideas in, 267–293
   for facts, 141–147
   for information, 141–147
   for main (key) idea, 110–132
   making connections in, 298–307
   personalizing in, 298–301
   predicting outcomes from, 236–253
   prereading, 5–10
   previewing, 5, 15–35
   rapid (skimming), 5, 11–14
   See also Comprehension
Reading aids, 5–35
   prereading, 5–10
   previewing, 5, 15–35
   skimming, 5, 11–14
   visual, 97–107
Reading journal, 299–300
Reading selections
   "Business of Selling Mail-Order
      Brides, The" (Villapando), 330–346
   "Cafe Reopens, A: Lunch Returns to
      the Prairie" (Schmidt), 431–441
   "Creating Unique Names for Chil-
      dren" (Roberts), 500–510
   "Hearts of Sorrow" (Freeman),
      347–358
   "Immigrants" (Morales), 359–370
   "Letting in Light" (Raybon), 381–389
   "Like Mother, Like Daughter" (Gite),
      452–464

   "Love Me, Love My (Brown) Mother"
      (Plata), 468–477
   "Model Minority" (Lee), 405–416
   "My Father's Black Pride" (Bleecker),
      420–430
   "My Unsentimental Tutee" (Billings),
      372–380
   "New Dawn, A" (Moses), 318–329
   "Say Something. They're Only Chil-
      dren" (Prinz), 442–451
   "They Treat Girls Differently, Don't
      They?" (Harper), 390–404
   "Wilshire Bus" (Yamamoto), 478–
      489
   "Zoot Suit Riots" (Camarillo),
      490–499
References, 24
Roots
   defined, 58
   important, 59–60

Sentence hints for word meanings,
   52–53
Sentences
   first, in previewing, 15
   main ideas in, 110–112
   predicting outcomes of, 239–240
   topic, 116–119
Sequence of ideas, in paragraphs,
   159–164
Simile, 228
Skimming, 5, 11–14
Slanted writing, 284, 290–292
Speech, figurative language in, 232
Spellings, in dictionary, 516
Stated main ideas, 116–122
Stems. *See* Roots
Stereotyping, 293
Style, of writer, 282–283, 287–288
Suffixes
   defined, 58
   important, 60
Summaries, in previewing, 16
Synonyms, 513

Table of contents, 23, 24–28
Tables, statistical, 98
Taking notes, 41–43

Techniques of writer. *See* Writing techniques
Textbooks
    drawing conclusions from, 244–249
    generalizing from, 260–262
    main ideas in, 112–113
    opinion and evidence in, 278–282
    visual aids in, 100–107
    word meanings in, 68–76, 80–83
Thinking while reading. *See* Critical thinking in reading
Time order, in paragraphs, 158, 159, 161
Title, previewing use, 15
Tone, of writer, 283, 288–290
Topics, of paragraphs, 113–116, 130–132
Topic sentence, 116–119
Topic statement, 116–119
Truth-twisting techniques, 290–293

Unabridged dictionaries, 513
Underlining, 39–41

Visual aids, 97–107
    chart showing types of, 98–99
    diagrams, 98
    graph, 99
    photograph, 98
    statistical table, 98
    in textbooks, 100–107
    word charts, 98, 99
Vocabulary building, 51–83
    connotation, 62–65
    context clues, 52–57
    denotation, 62–65
    shades of meaning, 65–83
    See also Word meanings; Words, key, for previewing

Word charts, 98, 99
Word history, in dictionary, 516
Word maps, 7
Word meanings, 51–83
    connotations, 62–65
    context clues to, 52–57
    denotations, 62–65
    in dictionary, 516
    how to find, 51
    recognizing, 77–80
    sentence hints for, 52–53
    shades of, 65–83
    in textbooks, 68–76, 80–83
    word part clues to, 57–62
    See also Vocabulary building; Words, key, for previewing
Word parts as meaning clues, 57–62
Words, key, for previewing, 16
    See also Word meanings
Works Cited, 24
Writing
    freewriting, 7–9
    mood of, 283
    point of view in, 284
    purpose of, 284, 288–290
    slanted, 284, 290–292
    techniques of, 282–293
    tone of, 283, 288–290
Writing techniques, 282–293
    mood, 283
    point of view, 284
    purpose, 284, 288–290
    style, 282–283, 287–288
    tone, 283, 288–290
    truth-twisting, 290–293

Name Index

Abramson, Leonard, 111
Allen, Woody, 286
Altman, Lawrence K., 254
Amway Corporation, 147
Anderson, Ronald E., 121
Aristotle, 288
Asimov, Isaac, 140

Bazerman, Charles, 249
Bennett, Gwendolyn, 230
Berliner, David C., 113
Bernstein, Douglas A., 90
Berry, Jeffrey M., 248, 280
Bettelheim, Bruno, 241
Biehler, Robert F., 13, 75, 126, 176
Billings, Laura, 372
Black Elk, 160
Blackford, Mansel G., 29, 112
Bleecker, Marcus, 420
Boyes, William, 105
Broad, William J., 230
Brown, Betty J., 69, 115
Brown, Dee, 268
Burns, Diane, 217, 219

Cabeza deBaca, Fabiola, 111
Camarillo, Albert, 490
Churchill, Winston, 283
Clark, Kenneth B., 117
Cleaver, Eldridge, 139
Clow, John E., 69, 115
Culhane, John, 150

Dahl, Robert A., 118
Davis, P. W., 193

DeFleur, Melvin L., 45, 156
Dennis, Everette E., 45, 156
Diehl, William, 116
Donnelson, Kenneth L., 115
Dorman, Michael, 122
Duke, Lynne, 174

Ebony, 232, 233
Ekman, Paul, 137
Ellis, David B., 126
Engelberg, Isa N., 128
Evitt, Marie Faust, 119

Feinblatt, John, 303
Ferrell, O. C., 149
Food and Wine, 194
Fraiberg, Selma H., 259
Freeman, James M., 347
Fulbright, J. William, 180
Fyfe, James J., 304

Gage, N. L., 113
Garcia, Robert, 272
Gelman, David, 125, 257
Getchell, Bud, 22, 69
Gewertz, Catherine, 127
Gite, Lloyd, 452
Givens, Charles J., 196
Goldman, Jerry, 248, 280
Graff, Henry F., 112
Greer, Germaine, 154

Hahn, Harlan, 181
Hardy, Richard J., 129, 172

Harper, Timothy, 390
Hayakawa, S. I., 112
Hayes, Patty, 243
Hazleton, Lesley, 124
Holt, John, 301
Howe, Irving, 160
Hsu, Kai-yu, 130, 133
Hudson, Lynne M., 75, 126, 176
Hughes, Langston, 230, 231–232
Hull, Gloria T., 230

Israeloff, Roberta, 312
Italiatour!Inc, 286

Janda, Kenneth, 248, 280
Jet, 153, 299
Jimenez, Francisco, 127
Johnson, Tim, 131
Johnson Publishing Company,
    147

Kazin, Alfred, 164
Keogh, Richard N., 70, 112
Kerr, Kathel Austin, 29, 112
King, Martin Luther, Jr., 232, 288
King, Richard A., 112
Koch, Joanne B., 260
Koch, Lewis Z., 260
Kurosawa, Akira, 159
Kwitny, Jonathan, 285

Laird, James D., 49
Larson, Milton E., 123
Lee, Felicia R., 405
Lee, Mary Paik, 143, 144
Lenburg, Grey, 285
Lenburg, Jeff, 285
Levande, Diane I., 260
Levine, Daniel V., 151, 200
Lin, Cho-Liang, 111, 238

Maclean's Magazine, 140
Mead, Margaret, 246

Melvin, Michael, 105
Meyers, Jeff, 118
Mobil Oil Company, 262–264
Morales, Aurora Levins, 359
Morgan, Clifford T., 112
Moses, Sam, 318
Mulligan, Tom, 150

Naverrette, Ruben, Jr., 221
Nilsen, Aileen Pace, 115
Nist, Sherrie L., 116
Norton, Mary Beth, 245
Nyerges, Christopher, 165

Ornstein, Allan C., 151, 200
Orwell, George, 122, 228
Otero, Niña, 215

Palubinskas, Helen, 130, 133
Pauk, Walter, 125
Peplau, Letitia Anne, 114, 116
Perry, Marvin, 121, 145
Pike, Arthur, 195
Plata, Charity, 468
Poe, Edgar Allan, 285
Popkin, Gary, 195
Pride, William M., 149
Prinz, Lucie, 442

Raybon, Patricia, 381
Resnick, Seth, 120
Richardson, Cecilia, 177
Roberts, Cindy, 500
Robinson, Nancy H., 112
Rodriguez, Richard, 189, 191
Rorabacher, Louise E., 117
Rosmann, Ronald L., 273
Rubin, Zick, 114, 116

Salovey, Peter, 114, 116
Scarry, Richard, 286
Schaefer, Richard T., 72, 81, 183
Schiffer, Michael Brian, 137

Schmidt, William E., 431
Schulberg, Budd, 265
Sherman, A., 192
Shertzer, Bruce, 130, 135, 171, 172
Skretvedt, Randy, 285
Smith, Griffin, Jr., 114
Smith, Richard S., 185
Snowman, Jack, 13
Solomon, E. P., 193
Suárez, Mario, 223
Sullivan, David R., 121
Sweeney, Amin, 285

Thompson, Nicholas S., 49
Thompson, Pamela Kleibrink, 129
Time, 111
Tobin, Daniel, 230
Twain, Mark, 284

Villapando, Venny, 330

Weisz, Paul B., 70, 112
Wellness Encyclopedia, The, 134
White, Jack E., 120
Wiener, Harvey S., 249
Wilde, Oscar, 283
Wilder, Ludlum, and Brown, 138
Winn, Dianna R., 128
Wolseley, Roland E., 225

Yamamoto, Hisaye, 478
Ying, Yu-Lan (Mary), 127, 151–153

Zelan, Karen, 241
Zimring, Franklin E., 305